KIERKEGAARD'S *THE SICKNESS UNTO DEATH*

The Sickness unto Death (1849) is commonly regarded as one of Kierkegaard's most important works – but also as one of his most difficult texts to understand. It is a meditation on Christian existentialist themes including sin, despair, religious faith and its redemptive power, and the relation and difference between physical and spiritual death. This volume of new essays guides readers through the philosophical and theological significance of the work, while clarifying the complicated ideas that Kierkegaard develops. Some of the essays focus closely on particular themes, others attempt to elucidate the text as a whole, and yet others examine it in relation to other philosophical views. Bringing together these diverse approaches, the volume offers a comprehensive understanding of this pivotal work. It will be of interest to those studying Kierkegaard as well as existentialism, religious philosophy, and moral psychology.

JEFFREY HANSON is Senior Philosopher in the Human Flourishing Program at Harvard University. He is the author of *Kierkegaard and the Life of Faith: The Aesthetic, the Ethical, and the Religious in* Fear and Trembling (2017) and the editor of *Kierkegaard as Phenomenologist: An Experiment* (2010).

SHARON KRISHEK is Lecturer in Philosophy at the Hebrew University of Jerusalem. She is the author of *Kierkegaard on Faith and Love* (Cambridge, 2009), *Kierkegaard's Philosophy of Love* (in Hebrew, 2011) and *Lovers in Essence: A Kierkegaardian Defense of Romantic Love* (2022).

T0384615

CAMBRIDGE CRITICAL GUIDES

Titles published in this series:

(*Continued after the Index*)

KIERKEGAARD'S
THE SICKNESS UNTO DEATH
A Critical Guide

EDITED BY

JEFFREY HANSON
Harvard University

SHARON KRISHEK
The Hebrew University of Jerusalem

CAMBRIDGE
UNIVERSITY PRESS

Shaftesbury Road, Cambridge CB2 8EA, United Kingdom

One Liberty Plaza, 20th Floor, New York, NY 10006, USA

477 Williamstown Road, Port Melbourne, VIC 3207, Australia

314–321, 3rd Floor, Plot 3, Splendor Forum, Jasola District Centre, New Delhi – 110025, India

103 Penang Road, #05–06/07, Visioncrest Commercial, Singapore 238467

Cambridge University Press is part of Cambridge University Press & Assessment,
a department of the University of Cambridge.

We share the University's mission to contribute to society through the pursuit of
education, learning and research at the highest international levels of excellence.

www.cambridge.org
Information on this title: www.cambridge.org/9781108793308

DOI: 10.1017/9781108883832

First published 2022
First paperback edition 2024

A catalogue record for this publication is available from the British Library

Library of Congress Cataloging-in-Publication data
NAMES: Hanson, Jeffrey, editor. | Krishek, Sharon, editor.
TITLE: Kierkegaard's The sickness unto death : a critical guide / edited by Jeffrey Hanson, Harvard
University, Massachusetts, Sharon Krishek, The Hebrew University of Jerusalem.
DESCRIPTION: Cambridge, United Kingdom ; New York, NY, USA : Cambridge University Press,
2022. | SERIES: Cambridge critical guides | Includes bibliographical references and index.
IDENTIFIERS: LCCN 2021063088 (print) | LCCN 2021063089 (ebook) | ISBN 9781108835374
(hardback) | ISBN 9781108793308 (paperback) | ISBN 9781108883832 (epub)
SUBJECTS: LCSH: Kierkegaard, Søren, 1813-1855. Sygdommen til døden. | Sin–Christianity. |
Despair–Religious aspects–Christianity. | BISAC: PHILOSOPHY / History & Surveys / Modern
CLASSIFICATION: LCC BT715.K533 K54 2022 (print) | LCC BT715.K533 (ebook) | DDC 233/.14–
dc23/eng/20220322
LC record available at https://lccn.loc.gov/2021063088
LC ebook record available at https://lccn.loc.gov/2021063089

ISBN   978-1-108-83537-4   Hardback
ISBN   978-1-108-79330-8   Paperback

Contents

Contributors

CLARE CARLISLE Professor of Philosophy, King's College London

C. STEPHEN EVANS University Professor of Philosophy and Humanities, Baylor University

ROE FREMSTEDAL Professor of Philosophy, Norwegian University of Science and Technology

RICK ANTHONY FURTAK Associate Professor of Philosophy, Colorado College

JEFFREY HANSON Senior Philosopher, Human Flourishing Program at Harvard University

ELEANOR HELMS Associate Professor of Philosophy, California Polytechnic State University

SHARON KRISHEK Senior Lecturer in Philosophy, The Hebrew University of Jerusalem

GEORGE PATTISON Retired Priest and Scholar, Scotland

ROBERT C. ROBERTS Distinguished Professor of Ethics Emeritus, Baylor University

ANTHONY RUDD Associate Professor of Philosophy, Saint Olaf College

PATRICK STOKES Associate Professor of Philosophy, Deakin University

SYLVIA WALSH Retired Teacher of Philosophy, Stetson University

MEROLD WESTPHAL Distinguished Professor of Philosophy Emeritus, Fordham University

Acknowledgments

We wish to thank each of our contributors for their hard work and efforts. Their cooperation, patience, and investment – particularly during the unusual time of a pandemic – are deeply appreciated. We are very grateful to Hilary Gaskin of Cambridge University Press for the initiation of this project and her support and encouragement all along the way. We would like to thank two anonymous readers for Cambridge University Press, for their detailed reports, good suggestions, and enthusiasm for the project. This work was begun during a period of collaboration at Harvard University's Human Flourishing Program, and we are grateful to the program for providing us with material support. Finally, we are grateful to the Israel Science Foundation for supporting this project.

Abbreviations

Standard abbreviations are employed throughout this volume for the following texts by Kierkegaard, all published by Princeton University Press. For other editions cited, and for works by other authors, see the Bibliography and footnotes to individual chapters.

BA   *The Book on Adler: The Religious Confusion of the Present Age Illustrated by Magister Adler as a Phenomenon*, edited and translated by Howard V. and Edna H. Hong (1998)

CA   *The Concept of Anxiety: A Simple Psychologically Orienting Deliberation on the Dogmatic Issue of Hereditary Sin*, edited and translated by Reidar Thomte in collaboration with Albert B. Anderson (1980)

CD   *Christian Discourses* and *The Crisis and a Crisis in the Life of an Actress*, edited and translated by Howard V. and Edna H. Hong (1997)

CI   *The Concept of Irony, with Continual Reference to Socrates*, together with *Notes of Schelling's Berlin Lectures*, edited and translated by Howard V. and Edna H. Hong (1989)

CUP   *Concluding Unscientific Postscript to* Philosophical Fragments, edited and translated by Howard V. and Edna H. Hong (1992)

E/O1 *Either/Or, Part I*, edited and translated by Howard V. and Edna H. Hong (1987)

E/O2 *Either/Or, Part II*, edited and translated by Howard V. and Edna H. Hong (1987)

EPW   *Early Polemical Writings: Articles from Student Days, From the Papers of One Still Living, The Battle between the Old and the New Soap-Cellars*, edited and translated by Julia Watkin (1990)

EUD   *Eighteen Upbuilding Discourses*, edited and translated by Howard V. and Edna H. Hong (1990)

FSE   *For Self-Examination* and *Judge for Yourself!*, edited and translated by Howard V. and Edna H. Hong (1990)

FT   *Fear and Trembling* and *Repetition*, edited and translated by Howard V. and Edna H. Hong (1983)

LD   *Kierkegaard: Letters and Documents*, edited and translated by Henrik Rosenmeier (1978)

MLW   *"The Moment" and Late Writings: Newspaper Articles 1854–1855, The Moment 1–10, This Must Be Said; So Let It Be Said, What Christ Judges of Official Christianity*, and *The Changelessness of God*, edited and translated by Howard V. and Edna H. Hong (1998)

PC   *Practice in Christianity*, edited and translated by Howard V. and Edna H. Hong (1991)

PF   *Philosophical Fragments, or A Fragment of Philosophy* and *Johannes Climacus, or De omnibus dubitandum est*, edited and translated by Howard V. and Edna H. Hong (1985)

PV   *The Point of View: On My Work as an Author, The Point of View for My Work as an Author*, and *Armed Neutrality*, edited and translated by Howard V. and Edna H. Hong (1998)

SUD   *The Sickness unto Death: A Christian Psychological Exposition for Upbuilding and Awakening*, edited and translated by Howard V. and Edna H. Hong (1980)

TDIO   *Three Discourses on Imagined Occasions*, edited and translated by Howard V. and Edna H. Hong (1993)

UDVS   *Upbuilding Discourses in Various Spirits*, edited and translated by Howard V. and Edna H. Hong (1993)

WA   *Without Authority: The Lily in the Field and the Bird of the Air, Two Ethical-Religious Essays, Three Discourses at the Communion on Fridays, An Upbuilding Discourse*, and *Two Discourses at the Communion on Fridays*, edited and translated by Howard V. and Edna H. Hong (1997)

WL   *Works of Love*, edited and translated by Howard V. and Edna H. Hong (1995)

References to Kierkegaard's journals and notebooks have been provided to available versions, including the following editions.

JP   *Søren Kierkegaard's Journals and Papers*, edited and translated by Howard V. and Edna H. Hong, assisted by Gregor Malantschuk. 2nd ed. Bloomington: Indiana University Press, 1990.

KJN   *Kierkegaard's Journals and Notebooks*, edited by Niels Jørgen Cappelørn et al., 11 vols. Princeton, NJ: Princeton University Press, 2007–2019.

Pap.   *Søren Kierkegaards Papirer*, edited by P. A. Heiberg et al., 16 vols. Copenhagen: Gyldendal, 1909–1978.

Whenever possible correlating references to the authoritative scholarly edition of Kierkegaard's works in Danish have been provided by volume and page number or in the case of the journals and notebooks by volume and entry number.

SKS   *Søren Kierkegaards Skrifter*, edited by Niels Jørgen Cappelørn et al., 55 vols. Copenhagen: Gads Forlag, 1997–2013.

Introduction

Jeffrey Hanson and Sharon Krishek

Søren Aabye Kierkegaard (1813–1855) was a prolific author who published his philosophical writings in various styles and often pseudonymously. In this diverse authorship, *The Sickness unto Death* stands as something of an exception. Although signed pseudonymously – a method that Kierkegaard often used to put distance between his own view and the one expressed in the text – Kierkegaard regarded this book as highly reflective of his own understanding of the religious life. Rapidly written in the spring of 1848 and published in 1849 after some agonizing, the motivation behind *The Sickness unto Death*, according to Kierkegaard's journal, was in part a conscientious conviction that the whole of his authorship needed to be curated in the direction of the religious. The appearance of the second edition of *Either/Or* in particular provoked him to accompany the reissue with a new and more religiously inflected text. "The second edition of *Either/Or* really can't be published without something accompanying it," he fretted in his journal. "Somehow the emphasis must be on the fact that I've made up my mind about being a religious author … If this opportunity passes, virtually everything I've written, viewed as a totality, will be dragged down into the aesthetic" (KJN 5, NB10:69/SKS 21, 293–294).

Even in the final publication, though, Kierkegaard felt compelled to defend the form of the book, which, given its argumentative elements, would seem to resemble his earlier "aesthetic" works, as opposed to his more explicitly religious edifying writings. In the voice of Anti-Climacus – the pseudonymous persona upon which he belatedly settled, keeping his own name as editor on the title page – the opening words of the Preface signal his recognition of the unusually hybridized style of the work, and read as follows: "Many may find the form of this 'exposition' strange; it may seem to them too rigorous to be upbuilding and too upbuilding to be rigorously scholarly. As far as the latter is concerned, I have no opinion. As to the former, I beg to differ" (SUD, 5/SKS 11, 117). Anti-Climacus pursues this objection by arguing that everything "from the Christian point of view" should be upbuilding (SUD, 5/SKS 11, 117), even the scholarly. Introducing for the first time a medical metaphor that will recur throughout the text, Anti-Climacus asserts that Christian communication must resemble the "way a physician speaks at the sickbed; even if only medical experts understand it, it must never be forgotten that the situation is the bedside of a sick person" (SUD, 5/SKS 11, 117). Aspects then of *The Sickness unto Death* are indeed highly technical, but the technical in this work is tempered by the theological conviction that all insight must serve the interests of edification. This blend of styles is anticipated by the book's subtitle – *A Christian Psychological Exposition for Upbuilding and Awakening* – and ultimately the Preface defends the book's methodological approach as both achieving the goals of upbuilding and awakening (which call to mind the aim of religious edification) and attaining the more "psychologically correct" effect (which satisfies the readers' expectation that they have in their hands a work of philosophy that attempts to explore the psyche of its readers) (SUD, 6/SKS 11, 118).[1]

The title itself is not invoked and explored until the Introduction, which Anti-Climacus opens with a citation of John 11:4, wherein Jesus declares of his dying friend Lazarus that his "sickness is not unto death," the irony of which, as Anti-Climacus notes right away, is that "and yet Lazarus did die" (SUD, 7/SKS 11, 123). Continuing with the medical metaphors, Anti-Climacus interprets Jesus to have meant that even fatal sickness is not "unto death" in the sense that even physical death is not the same as – or as dire as – spiritual death. Raising Lazarus from his grave, hence "nullifying" his physical death, signifies that the real death at issue is rather a spiritual one. This is the first indication in the text of the book's central topic: despair, which is a spiritual sickness, the true "sickness unto death."

The main body of the text opens with arguably the most notorious paragraph in Kierkegaard's oeuvre:

> A human being is spirit. But what is spirit? Spirit is the self. But what is the self? The self is a relation that relates itself to itself or is the relation's relating itself to itself in the relation; the self is not the relation but is the relation's relating itself to itself. A human being is a synthesis of the infinite and the finite, of the temporal and the eternal, of freedom and necessity, in short, a synthesis. A synthesis is a relation between two. Considered in this way, a human being is still not a self. (SUD, 13/SKS 11, 129)

---

[1] Contemporary readers should not be misled by Kierkegaard's terminology, which predates the rise of psychology as an empirical science. He designated a few of his works as "psychological," but he meant by this term something like the philosophical analysis of mental states.

So densely tangled is this opening that some commentators have contended that it is a deliberate satire on the tortured prose of Kierkegaard's frequent target, G. W. F. Hegel, but this verdict has not been seconded much in the literature. Nevertheless, echoes of Hegel's thought do resonate in the text. Much of Anti-Climacus's diagnostic follows a dialectical path: first through four forms of despair that are mutually defined without respect to whether or not the despairer is conscious of being in despair or of what despair even is, and then through a number of stages defined by increasing consciousness, from comparatively passive weakness to active defiance.[2] The dense core sections of Part One are littered with Hegelian vocabulary, and a celebrated passage from the opening of Part Two is unmistakably a reference to Hegel's dialectic of the master and servant:

> A cattleman who (if this were possible) is a self directly before his cattle is a very low self, and, similarly, a master who is a self directly before his slaves is actually no self – for in both cases a criterion is lacking. The child who previously has had only his parents as a criterion becomes a self as an adult by getting the state as a criterion, but what an infinite accent falls on the self by having God as the criterion! (SUD, 79/SKS 11, 191)

The theory of selfhood put forward in this text has been enormously influential on contemporary thinking about personal identity and related themes. To be a self, according to the account developed by Anti-Climacus, is to relate properly to the constitutive dimensions of the human being. The human being just is a synthesis of limiting and expansive aspects that are in dynamic relation with each other; to be a self is to be conscious of oneself as exercising this dynamic relation, this interplay of openness and limit.[3] The self though is not self-isolated; if it has not "established itself" but rather "been established by another" (SUD, 13/SKS 11, 130), then that means that the self sustains a further relation – to the other that established it. That this is so, Anti-Climacus argues, is attributable to the fact that there are two types of despair: It is possible for the self who is in a state of despair either "to will to be oneself" or "not to will to be oneself" (SUD, 14/SKS 11, 130). In the absence of a constitutive relation

---

[2] An analysis of the Hegelian form of dialectic in this text is provided by Jon Stewart in his "Kierkegaard's Phenomenology of Despair in *The Sickness unto Death*," *Kierkegaard Studies Year Book* (Berlin: DeGruyter, 1997), 117–143. See also Alastair Hannay, "Kierkegaard and the Variety of Despair," in *The Cambridge Companion to Kierkegaard*, ed. Alastair Hannay and Gordon D. Marino (New York: Cambridge University Press, 1998), 329–348.

[3] The complexity of Kierkegaard's conception of the self invites different understandings. Indeed, various interpretations of Kierkegaard's analysis, which do not necessarily concord in every respect, are presented in this collection.

4

to another, one could of course not will to be oneself, because one could always reject or resist being oneself. But because it is possible to affirm oneself – to will to be oneself – and yet still be in despair, this possibility entails that the self is in relation to another that has some decisive bearing on the self, a bearing that the self rejects or resists. For the sake of clarity, it might be more appropriate to say that such a self in despair wills to be its *own* self; it wills to be itself on its own terms or without relation to another.

The detailed analysis of these two forms of despair comprises much of the book, and the chapters that follow will exposit this material for the reader. For now let it be noted that Anti-Climacus claims that "all despair ultimately can be traced back to and be resolved in" this form – that is, the self's will to be its *own* self (SUD, 14/SKS 11, 130). All despair is a rejection of or resistance to relation with another; even when despair has the form of not willing to be oneself, this unwillingness is reducible to a will to be one's own self, on one's own terms, without relation. The critical consensus seems to be that the "another" to whom the self might be related is paradigmatically God, such that the highest pitch of despair, which Anti-Climacus will call demonic defiance, is defined by its willful refusal of relation to God, by open rebellion against not just *an*other but *the* Other. At the same time, it is plain that there are many "anothers" to whom the self can be related and generally is, namely, other human beings. All of us are who we are by way of relations with others: family, friends, lovers, people in our milieu and beyond it, and so on. The account of the self put forward by *The Sickness unto Death* alone of all of Kierkegaard's writings ought to suffice to put to bed once and for all the persistent criticism of his thought as endorsing anti-socialism and self-sufficiency. The antidote to despair according to Anti-Climacus is precisely the opposite of self-sufficiency: "The formula that describes the state of the self when despair is completely rooted out is this: in relating to itself and in willing to be itself, the self rests transparently in the power that established it" (SUD, 14/SKS 11, 140). To be free of despair is to be at peace with one's self, at peace with others, and at peace with the Other that is the divine. This situation of the self Anti-Climacus will later call "faith."

The exact relation between the seemingly more philosophical Part One and the apparently more theologically inflected Part Two is a matter of ongoing discussion. Some earlier engagements with the text seemed content to disregard Part Two entirely, but this evasiveness is not much countenanced today. It is natural to read the book as something of a companion to 1844's *The Concept of Anxiety*. Kierkegaard designated both

The Sickness unto Death and *The Concept of Anxiety* as "psychological" texts (in the sense noted earlier). Yet from the outset of the former it is evident that the subtitle of that work is not arbitrarily chosen but marks out a significant difference in methodology. Vigilius Haufniensis, the pseudonymous author of *The Concept of Anxiety*, is engaged in a strictly philosophical study of anxiety and how that phenomenon sheds light on the theological issue of hereditary sin. Haufniensis does not borrow from or depend upon theological presuppositions, and he sharply delimits the concerns and object of philosophical psychology and dogmatic theology. That a philosophical examination can serve dogmatic theology, however, is foreshadowed by Haufniensis from the very beginning of the work. While distinct sciences, the discipline that Kierkegaard called psychology can nevertheless hand over the results of its deliberation for theological reflection and use, a possibility signaled by Haufniensis again at the very end of the book. The final words of *The Concept of Anxiety* are: "Here this deliberation ends, where it began. As soon as psychology [i.e., philosophical psychology] has finished with anxiety, it is to be delivered to dogmatics" (CA, 162/SKS 4, 461). Haufniensis, though, does not himself submit a Christian psychology or deliver the results of his psychological-philosophical investigation to dogmatics. Anti-Climacus can be read as having done so, hence the reference in his subtitle to the text being both "Christian" and "psychological." *The Sickness unto Death* is thus a diagnostic, hence normative, and not merely descriptive, text. The goal is healing, which is why *The Sickness unto Death* is "for upbuilding and awakening."

CHAPTER I

Kierkegaard's Place of Rest

George Pattison

Introduction

Commentators have widely followed Kierkegaard himself in judging the pseudonym Anti-Climacus to be a Christian to an extraordinary degree, as much "above" Kierkegaard's own relation to Christianity as Johannes Climacus is "below" it (e.g., JP 6, 6433/KJN 6, NB11:209/SKS 22, 130). The "severity" of Anti-Climacus's writings seems to presage the "Attack on 'Christendom,'" an impression that is not entirely false but that does give a one-sided view of his work. The two books ascribed to Anti-Climacus are not to be read solely as exposing the universal despair rotting the foundations of Christendom (*The Sickness unto Death*) or as the refusal of discipleship by a soft and degenerate church (*Practice in Christianity*). As in the earlier "aesthetic" pseudonymous authorship, discussed in the Introduction, what we read in these works is also significantly complemented by accompanying upbuilding discourses, in this case three sets of discourses titled *The High Priest–The Tax Collector–The Woman Who Was a Sinner* (1849), *An Upbuilding Discourse* (1851), and *Two Discourses at the Communion on Fridays* (1851). These constitute a closely knit group: three have texts from Luke 7, two are on the woman who is at the center of the episode described in that chapter, and all have more or less explicit discussions of love. Also, they all have the form of communion discourses.

Both the Anti-Climacus works and these last discourses emerge from a ferment of literary-religious productivity running from 1848 through to 1851, overlapping with the closing stages of Kierkegaard's work on *Christian Discourses* (published 1848) and concluding with the *Two Discourses*. At various points in this period Kierkegaard considered publishing varying combinations of works in a single volume titled *The Works of Accomplishment* (see, e.g., JP 1, 493/KJN 5, NB8:15/SKS 21, 151). In an early stage of writing, he also toyed with the idea of publishing *The*

Sickness unto Death with parts of what became *Christian Discourses* and *Practice in Christianity* under the title "Thoughts That Give Fundamental Healing: Christian Medicine" (JP 5, 6110/KJN 4, NB4:76/SKS 20, 324).[1] Although neither of these projects at that point included the discourses before us, their relation to the two Anti-Climacus works is well evidenced in the journals (see, e.g., JP 6, 6515/KJN 6, NB13:57/SKS 22, 309). Kierkegaard vacillated extensively over whether to publish various combinations of these works pseudonymously or under his own name, so although the discourses are signed and *The Sickness unto Death* is pseudonymous, this is not an entirely impermeable distinction (and Kierkegaard did allow his name to appear on the title page as editor).

The aim of this chapter is to explore further the relationship between these late discourses and *The Sickness unto Death* and to see how they illustrate or add to our understanding of that work. I should straightaway emphasize that the relationship in question is not one in which the discourses "correct" what we find in the pseudonym, as might sometimes seem to be the case in the relationship between the earlier, aesthetic pseudonymous works and their accompanying discourses. Rather, I shall argue that these discourses are saying essentially the same thing as the pseudonymous work and for this reason provide us with a valuable heuristic tool for drawing out what may in some respects be only implicit or perhaps scarcely discernible in the latter. Thus, it is not the case that the devotional tone of the discourses is to be understood as softening the severity or rigor of the Anti-Climacan writings; on the contrary, they point us to what is already central in those writings themselves. With specific regard to *The Sickness unto Death*, this hermeneutic approach suggests that the pseudonymous text is not to be read in the first instance as a negative exposure of the sinful condition of contemporary humanity but as an approach to clarifying the possibility and meaning of forgiveness. Thus read, *The Sickness unto Death* too finds its resting place "at the foot of the altar" (see WA, 165/SKS 12, 281 and discussion later in this chapter). Among other implications of this reading is that *The Sickness unto Death* is not primarily about despair, or about the self, but about the (Christian) experience of forgiveness.[2] Does this, then, mean that the reader must accede to Christian dogmatic presuppositions, and, if so, what are the

---

[1] Translations throughout are my own, though I have supplied references to available English translations.

[2] See Emmanuel Hirsch's comment on *The Sickness unto Death* that "The accompaniment provided by the Friday discourses to the main works is essential to understanding them. And this [i.e., Christ's] grace is essentially understood in the same way as previously: as the entire forgiveness of the

consequences for a philosophical interpretation of the work? I shall return
to these questions in my conclusion, but first we need to examine the texts
themselves. I start, however, with the question of Kierkegaard's "method."

Kierkegaard's Method

One of the most discussed approaches to *The Sickness unto Death* in recent
years has been what Michael Theunissen called Kierkegaard's negativistic
method.[3] Theunissen's idea is that Kierkegaard approaches the constitution of the self and the self's fundamental orientation toward God in a
thoroughly philosophical manner that is guided solely by how human
beings become aware of deep-rooted "deficiencies" in their lives as soon
as they begin to reflect on themselves. This leads to a vision of the self as
fundamentally despairing and to the claim that this despair can be cured
only by appeal to God. Theunissen is, of course, aware that *The Sickness
unto Death* opens with the famous definition of the self that relates itself to
itself and strives to become transparent to the power by which it is
grounded. This would seem to presuppose the outcome of the enquiry,
but Theunissen argues that although this definition comes first in the order
of presentation, it does not do so with regard to the investigation itself. In
other words, Kierkegaard's method is properly negativistic but, like many
researchers, he sets a preliminary summary of the outcome at the beginning of the enquiry.[4]

Reading the discourses alongside *The Sickness unto Death* in the manner
I am proposing might seem to work against the negativistic approach,
especially if we think that all of the writings associated with Anti-Climacus
are parts of a single movement that present the "Accomplishment" or
"Completion" of Kierkegaard's literary career and are directed toward

---

sinner that is new in each moment, so that the one in despair surrenders himself in confessing God
and the desire for grace. In and with this forgiveness, [the believer] is transformatively enflamed by
the life-giving Spirit, and for the one who [thus] confesses and desires, there is a new movement in
faith, hope, and love." Emmanuel Hirsch, *Kierkegaard Studien*, vol. 2 (Gütersloh: Bertelsmann,
1933), 296/898.

[3] Michael Theunissen, "Kierkegaard's Negativistic Method," in *Kierkegaard's Truth: The Disclosure of
the Self*, ed. Joseph H. Smith (Princeton, NJ: Princeton University Press, 1981), 381–423. For
discussion see Arne Grøn, "Der Begriff Verzweiflung," *Kierkegaardiana* 17 (1994): 25–41.

[4] This reading can be contrasted with approaches that take the opening definition of the self as a
relation that relates itself to itself as the methodological starting point, from which the various forms
of despair are dialectically developed. See, e.g., John D. Glenn, Jr., "The Definition of the Self"
(5–22) and Alastair Hannay, "Spirit and the Idea of the Self as a Reflexive Relation" (23–38), both in
International Kierkegaard Commentary, vol. 19: *The Sickness unto Death*, ed. Robert L. Perkins
(Macon, GA: Mercer University Press, 1987).

"fundamental healing." For this procedure supposes that the negative analyses of the various deficient forms of selfhood encountered in *The Sickness unto Death* are a kind of diagnosis undertaken by someone – a doctor of the soul, let's say – who already understands what is required to bring healing and wants to share that knowledge with readers. Importantly, we should note that unlike most of the earlier sets of upbuilding discourses these have the form of actual talks given in the context of the communion service and some were delivered by Kierkegaard himself in that context. Consequently, they presuppose a commitment to Christian practice that some of the earlier discourses do not. In other words, they have profound and essential theological commitments.

Related to the negativistic approach is the view that *The Sickness unto Death* offers a kind of phenomenology of the self, and we see both approaches coming together in the book *Subjektivitet og Negativitet* (*Subjectivity and Negativity*) and a series of articles by Arne Grøn.[5] On this view, Kierkegaard's procedure is not determined by its Christian doctrinal outcome but follows the dynamics of the self along a strictly phenomenological path. The intuition that this is what Kierkegaard is attempting is enforced by the seemingly Hegelian structuring of the work, a feature that led one theological commentator to see it, despite Kierkegaard's intentions, as essentially atheistic.[6] Nor should we forget that at the outset of the *Phenomenology of Spirit*, Hegel describes his own work as tracking the journey of Spirit down a "highway of despair."[7]

Reading *The Sickness unto Death* as integrated with the communion discourses does not preclude seeing it as being also in some way "phenomenological." Certainly, it is highly plausible to see important passages across the range of Kierkegaard's writings as phenomenological, at least in a loose sense.[8] However, such a reading by no means requires a commitment to finding the defining center of Kierkegaard's view of the

[5] See Arne Grøn, *Subjektivitet og Negativitet: Kierkegaard* (Copenhagen: Gyldendal, 1997); Arne Grøn, "Kierkegaards Phänomenologie?" in *Kierkegaard Studies Year Book 1996*, ed. Niels Jørgen Cappelørn and Hermann Deuser (Berlin: De Gruyter, 1996), 91–116.
[6] S. U. Zuidema, *Kierkegaard* (Philadelphia: Presbyterian and Reformed Publishing, 1960).
[7] The "Hegelian" aspect of Kierkegaard's phenomenology is discussed by Grøn, and by Michael Theunissen in *Der Begriff Verzweiflung: Korrekturen an Kierkegaard* (Frankfurt am Main: Suhrkamp, 1993), 149–156. See also Jon Stewart, "Kierkegaard's Phenomenology of Despair in *The Sickness unto Death*," in *Kierkegaard Studies Year Book 1997*, ed. Niels Jørgen Cappelørn and Hermann Deuser (Berlin: De Gruyter, 1997), 117–143.
[8] On my reservations regarding this approach see George Pattison, "Kierkegaard and the Limits of Phenomenology," 188–207; the collection of which this article is a part (*Kierkegaard as Phenomenologist: An Experiment*, ed. Jeffrey Hanson (Evanston, IL: Northwestern University Press, 2010)) gives a good overall view of the relevant issues.

human condition in the "negativity" of the despairing self's self-experience. It can just as well serve to support the claim that this center is ultimately constituted by the "positivity" of the Christian experience of forgiveness and reconciliation with God. Nevertheless, to the extent that Kierkegaard's method was phenomenological it could only present this experience in a way that made it accessible to every well-intentioned reader who was prepared to follow where it led. As phenomenology, it seems unlikely that it could go further and compel the reader also to accept the metaphysical or doctrinal claims that, in Christian teaching, usually underwrite these experiences. Phenomenology does not take us beyond the human.

I leave open the question of phenomenology. Even if some aspects of the discourse material can be read phenomenologically, this does not apply to all aspects, and we need to take seriously that these discourses are thoroughly self-conscious rhetorical performances, speaking in and to particular situations as well as to a particular audience that the discourse itself also constructs in a manner comparable to the way in which a novel creates its ideal reader.[9] In these terms, the existential descriptions that Kierkegaard evokes in them may be better compared to the kinds of model used in scientific explanation than to the products of phenomenological investigations. Few physicists, I suppose, actually believed that atoms or molecules looked like the conglomerations of billiard balls that were standard visual aids in physics teaching in the mid-twentieth century, but they did believe that these could illustrate the kinds of relation and proportion that were most relevant to understanding atomic structures, at least for introductory purposes. Although Vigilius Haufniensis's comments about his own experimental method have been taken as supporting the phenomenological approach, they seem to fit more naturally with the model paradigm (see CA, 75–76/SKS 4, 378–379). To the extent that this analogy with the use of models in science is correct, it provides a way of reading the characters and situations in the discourses that does not require us to see them as the primitive data of phenomenological inter-pretation. Instead they appear as hypothetical exemplifications of particu-lar spiritual stages or attitudes that are not necessarily instantiated otherwise than when they are appropriated by the reader.[10] They are a call to existential appropriation, not a representation of how things are.

---

[9] See George Pattison, *Kierkegaard's Upbuilding Discourses: Philosophy, Literature, Theology* (London: Routledge, 2002), 69–85.

[10] In this respect, the role of the model is like that of the puppets described in Martin Thust, "Das Marionettentheater Sören Kierkegaards," *Zeitwende* 1 (1925): 18–38.

But if this is true of the discourses in question, then this call can be seen to be reflected back into the text of *The Sickness unto Death* itself, which then appears in a rather different light than when we insist on its "severity."

Sin, Forgiveness, Christ

Before proceeding to some of the concrete ways in which the discourses can inform our reading of *The Sickness unto Death*, I shall make one further preliminary move. Whether we are or are not living in a post-religious age, it is clear that many of the standard tropes of Christian doctrine are now unfamiliar to the majority of readers who are not theologically educated. This even includes many Christian believers, since the kind of focus on detailed doctrinal definition that was for many centuries characteristic of Western Christendom is no longer common even in the churches. Kierkegaard, however, was living at a time when such knowledge could be assumed among his readership and was himself well-instructed in these debates in the course of his theological studies.[11] I shall therefore very briefly comment on some of the doctrinal themes most relevant to this particular cluster of texts. These are the doctrines of forgiveness, of sin, and of the role of Christ.

These are, of course, not isolated topics. Christian doctrine at its best has an organic and holistic character, and as H. R. Mackintosh, a Scottish theologian of the first half of the twentieth century (who was also one of the earliest Kierkegaard commentators in Great Britain), put it, "Forgiveness clearly is one of the foci . . . from which it is at once possible and natural to survey the whole circumference of Christian truth, and to determine the relationship which obtains between one conviction and another. It implies a distinctive view of God, of man, of sin, of the universe as supernaturally constituted, of Jesus."[12] This claim applies quite particularly to the relationship between *The Sickness unto Death* and the accompanying discourses, as, read together, they bring into sharp focus the interconnected themes of sin, forgiveness, and the role of Christ.

The connection between forgiveness and sin is perhaps obvious. Forgiveness is needed because we are in a state of sin as a result of Adam and Eve's disobedience in the Garden of Eden, an act that theology has

---

[11] See, e.g., his notes on the lectures on dogmatics by H. N. Clausen in JP 1, 36; JP 5, 5058/KJN 3, Not1:2–Not1:9/SKS 19, 9–85.

[12] Hugh Ross Mackintosh, *The Christian Experience of Forgiveness* (London: Fontana, [1927] 1962), 11; for Mackintosh's view of Kierkegaard see Hugh Ross Mackintosh, *Types of Modern Theology: Schleiermacher to Barth* (London: James Nisbet & Co., 1937).

understood as the rejection of God's ordering of human existence in creation and in which subsequent generations are also complicit (a point to which I shall return). Consequently, the divine image in which we were created is diminished or, in some Christian traditions, utterly destroyed, leaving us abandoned to anxious egoism rather than enjoying the freedom in love that had been God's desire for us.

How is this to be made good? Following a trajectory leading from Paul through Luther, the Reformed churches have consistently emphasized our need to be forgiven before we become capable of practicing forgiveness and other works of love. This is because of the judgment that our fall is so total that we are unable to put ourselves right by our own efforts. We do not have the goodwill necessary to genuinely offer forgiveness to others or even to forgive ourselves (a phrase with which Kierkegaard pointedly takes issue at SUD, 110–112/SKS 11, 222–224).

This situation is often described in forensic or legal imagery, as when the human condition is compared to that of a criminal brought before the judge. In this context forgiveness is glossed as "justification," a Pauline term that became central to Reformation teaching. Sometimes this justi-fication is said to be "imputed" in the sense that although we are too corrupt ever to become righteous, God regards us as if we were – a kind of legal fiction. Although forgiveness and justification are often used inter-changeably in Christian teaching and worship, however, forgiveness sug-gests a context of personal relationships (in biblical terms relating to the figuring of Israel as God's beloved but unfaithful spouse and to other family relationships, as in the parable of the prodigal son) rather than the legal imagery of justification.

Just how bad is our condition, apart from forgiveness? In classical Reformation teaching, it was very bad indeed. To live in sin is to be odious to God and rightly damnable (a point of Reformation teaching that is covered in Kierkegaard's student notes). But how can God forgive us, when this would imply his accepting the permanent failure of his original plan for creation? Wouldn't God have to break his own laws to do so? And even supposing that God were minded to forgive us, how could he make that forgiveness known? In Eden, God spoke with Adam and Eve as a matter of course, but since the Fall he no longer does so, or, more precisely, we have lost the capacity for hearing and understanding his call.[13] God must now speak to us in a manner adapted to our fallen

---

[13] Setting the problem up as one of communication is at the heart of Kierkegaard's parable of the king in love with a poor girl – see PF, 25–29/SKS 4, 232–235.

condition, which (Christian doctrine maintains) means speaking to us in, with, and under the conditions of fallen existence, as one of us – in short, he must become human and assume our human flesh, which (some have supposed) means assuming sinful flesh. This, of course, is what Christianity claims we see in Jesus Christ, God Incarnate, effecting the forgiveness of sins that we cannot forgive ourselves.

Virtually every statement in the last two paragraphs was multiply contested in the polemical debates subsequent on the Protestant Reformation. We have neither space nor need to go deeply into those debates here, but we should note one important development. This concerns the theological revolution effected by F. D. E. Schleiermacher at the start of the nineteenth century. The book by Mackintosh quoted earlier has the title *The Christian Experience of Forgiveness*, which succinctly focuses on the issue of Schleiermacherian religion since, for Schleiermacher, Christian doctrines are the systematic articulation of what is primarily given in Christian experience. Doctrines are not deduced from biblical teaching or inferred from metaphysical views of God, nor are they merely imaginative aids to moral striving: Doctrines arise from the flow of lived Christian life, in which will and feeling are as fundamental as intellect.

Kierkegaard was deeply familiar with the doctrinal tradition, through both his upbringing and his theological training. His relation to it is, however, debatable. Some see him as offering a powerful restatement of Reformation teaching, others suggest a more nuanced picture. Again, these are discussions we need not go deeply into here, except for two points. The first is that while *The Concept of Anxiety* is presented as a treatise on the doctrine of original sin and *The Sickness unto Death* itself speaks of despair (sin) as universal, Kierkegaard does seem to qualify some versions of Reformation teaching on original sin by virtue of his emphasis on the abiding freedom of the human individual. As opposed to a strict interpretation of the Augsburg Confession, Kierkegaard holds that each individual's fall is a repetition of Adam's fall rather than a straightforward extension or consequence of it. We do not "inherit" sin: We each enact it, freely. Although we are entangled in what he calls a "quantitative" history of sin, the "qualitative" leap into sin is something we each do for ourselves. We still need help to get out of our predicament, but we are capable of knowing what we need since it is part of our own individual life history, and our contribution to a restored God-relationship is therefore both necessary and relevant.[14] The second point relates to the

---

[14] See George Pattison, *Kierkegaard and the Theology of the Nineteenth Century* (Cambridge: Cambridge University Press, 2012), 124–149.

Schleiermacherian revolution in theology. Clearly, Kierkegaard shares with Schleiermacher a deep commitment to a subjective approach to doctrine. However, where Schleiermacher emphasized the role of feeling, Kierkegaard supposed a more catastrophic and fractured ontology of the subject. He certainly never despised the immediacy of feeling, but – without reverting to a straightforward embrace of "original sin" – his "self" is a self that is constantly missing itself, a divided self that is not immediately transparent to the power that grounds it (to God, let's say), but that still has the freedom to choose how it is to relate to itself.

To sum up: Kierkegaard's approach to the interrelated issues of sin, forgiveness, and the relation to Christ in the texts we are to examine is only fully comprehensible against the background of Reformation doctrinal traditions. At the same time, partly following Schleiermacher, what he offers will prove a critical revision of those same traditions. In this revision, the role of human freedom proves the hinge on which the decisive differences turn – although, as we shall see, this is not for Kierkegaard the freedom of self-determination but the freedom to know oneself as a being-in-relationship.

Christ Is Near

The preface to the set of discourses titled *The High Priest–The Tax Collector–The Woman Who Was a Sinner* quotes extensively from the preface to the first two upbuilding discourses published in 1843 and subsequently presented by Kierkegaard as "accompanying" *Either/Or*. The pairing of pseudonymous and upbuilding works became a pattern that would be repeated throughout the first pseudonymous authorship, even if the connections are not always as neat as Kierkegaard suggested. So too in the case of the higher pseudonym Anti-Climacus. However, the discourses accompanying the Anti-Climacus works are not the simple meditations of the 1843–1844 discourses but are specifically discourses for the Friday Communion service held in Copenhagen's Vor Frue Church, a service that Kierkegaard regularly attended and at which he sometimes spoke.[15] This gives them a very specific imagined context. They are not addressed to the world in general but to those who have received the assurance of divine forgiveness and have now gathered at the altar to take communion – overseen by the imposing statue of Christ by Bertel

---

[15] "The High Priest" is based on a communion talk given by Kierkegaard in Vor Frue Church on September 1, 1848. His draft for this talk is at JP 4, 3928–3931/KJN 5, NB7:14/SKS 21, 83.

Thorvaldsen, arms opened to welcome the communicants and with the words "Come unto me" inscribed on the base. These discourses therefore presuppose that those to whom they are spoken have a dynamic and developing relation to Christ; they have confessed, received forgiveness, and now kneel before him, ready to receive his body and blood. This corresponds to the "potentiation" in *The Sickness unto Death* itself between "before God" and "before Christ."

Another small difference draws attention to the significance of this scenario. In the preface to the two 1843 discourses, Kierkegaard spoke of the discourse seeking out the individual whom he called "*my* reader." He ends the 1849 preface by invoking this quest once more but with a slight twist. Now it is not only a question of the discourse seeking the reader but, as he writes, "I saw and see that the little book is received by that individual whom it seeks *and who is seeking it*" (WA, 111/SKS 11, 247, emphasis mine). In other words, the discourse is firmly contextualized in a two-way relationship, just as the communicant comes to the altar both as a recipient and as a seeker. A relationship does not at this point have to be initiated but is presupposed.

As the discourse on the High Priest begins, it directly addresses the possibility of being in a relationship with Christ. Kierkegaard observes that it is typical of those who suffer to say that no one else can understand them, no one else can feel what they feel, no one else can put themselves in their place. It is to this situation that the appointed text speaks: "For we do not have a high priest who is unable to sympathize with our weaknesses, but we have one who in every respect has been tested as we are, yet without sin" (Heb. 4:15). Such a High Priest, Kierkegaard comments, not only can but must sympathize with us since it was from sympathy or compassion that he exposed himself to being tested by the trials and temptations of human life when he took human flesh, suffered, and died for us. He is one "who, as a result of his own free decision was tempted in all things in the same way [as we are], he, who is completely able to put himself in your, in my, in our place and does so completely" (WA, 116/SKS 11, 252).

Much of the discourse that follows is dedicated to setting out the temptations and sufferings that he endured, arguing that there is nothing by which we could be tempted and nothing we could suffer that he didn't know. This may not be entirely persuasive, at least not in the terms that Kierkegaard sets out here. The twentieth century seems to have expanded the repertoire of human malice in terrible ways, though Kierkegaard might have regarded this statement as a characteristic piece of modern self-flattery. For our purposes, however, this is not crucial. What is crucial is that Kierkegaard here rejects the view that the inner core of our being, the place of our deepest vulnerability and hurt, is knowable only in first-person self-experience. He imagines a sufferer who insists that no one else knows what it is like and that his pain is quite unique – but he also suggests that this very insistence betrays a doubt. Perhaps (and here I add to Kierkegaard's explicit argument) the mere fact that the one who says he is entirely alone *speaks* his complaint gives the lie to what he says, since the very fact of speech involves an appeal to others.

There are themes here that run through the entirety of Kierkegaard's authorship, pseudonymous and signed. Not least is the idea that the fundamental malaise of modernity is the attempt of the hyper-autonomous individual to create their own world, pursuing a myth of rational, emotional, and volitional self-sufficiency. The "Diapsalmata" of *Either/Or* Part 1 show the aesthete to be aware that this also involves the renunciation of happiness, but he is seemingly prepared to pay that price for the sake of being spared the complexity and frustration of disappointed relationships. *The Concept of Anxiety* speaks of the demonic temptation of "inclosing reserve" [*Indesluttethed*], which would be another extreme development of the same fundamental strategy. "The despair of defiance" of *The Sickness unto Death* itself would be another example. In these and many other passages Kierkegaard helps inaugurate a current of nineteenth- and twentieth-century *Zeitkritik*, according to which "modern man" is guilty of a kind of self-divinization that ultimately leaves "him" alone in a dreadful solitude from which there is "no exit." Yet this pursuit of autonomy and its accompanying myth of *homo deus* is based on a fundamental error. We do not create ourselves, and we cannot correct ourselves entirely on our own. For the Christian Kierkegaard there is always at least one other human being who is able to enter into all that we can be, do, and suffer and has in fact done so – Jesus Christ. At the same time, he also hints that the misunderstood sufferer might in the meantime help himself out by following Christ's example of trying to give others the comfort he thinks no one is capable of giving to him (WA, 119/SKS 11, 256).[16] We don't need to be alone in our suffering, and in fact we are not alone.

---

[16] Here I do not examine the further important question as to how the forgiveness the believer receives from God relates to the gospel injunction to forgive the neighbor. Grøn argues that for Kierkegaard these are inseparable (see Grøn, *Subjektivitet og Negativitet*, 347–348). The question concerns both the interpretation of Kierkegaard's Christian writings as a whole but also the psychological dynamics of love. As such it therefore requires a much fuller treatment than can be given here.

But We Must Dig Deeper

Sufferers who insist on their uniqueness seem at first to be defined by their attitudes to others, shutting them out by the same gesture with which they shut themselves in. But the self as it is defined in *The Sickness unto Death* is, famously, a thoroughly relational self, a relation that relates itself to itself. The ultimate (or, better, penultimate) "other" that is being excluded is not my neighbor Christopherson or Madame Petersen of Bathhouse St.; it is myself.

To illustrate what this means we turn to one of the most searing passages in these late discourses, in which Kierkegaard addresses himself directly to Christ. Although this is common practice in Christian preaching, it is rare in Kierkegaard's discourses, early and late, and therefore implies an exceptional emphasis. Usually, God or Christ is spoken of in the third person. Even the speaker's own "I" is avoided, often being substituted by circumlocutions such as "the discourse says." Here, however, without warning, quite out of the blue, the discourse switches to the vocativity of I–Thou discourse.

> And therefore, my Lord and Savior, You, whose love hides a multitude of sins, when I feel my sin and the multitude of my sins as I should and when heaven's righteousness is served only by the wrath that rests upon me and on my life, when there is only one person on earth I hate and despise, one person whom I would fly to the world's end to avoid, and that is myself – then I will not begin so as to begin in vain and in such a way as would only lead either deeper into despair or to madness, but I will flee at once to you, and you will not deny me the hiding-place you have lovingly offered to all. You will tear me from the inquisitorial eye of righteousness and save me from that person and from the memories with which he torments me. You will help me to dare remain in my hiding-place, forgotten by righteousness and by that person I despise, by my becoming a changed, another, a better person. (WA, 187/SKS 12, 301)

There are several points to note here. The first is that the primary effect of sin on a person is to produce a division in the self that is so extreme as to result in self-hatred. Second, love takes precedence over justice and its demand for righteousness, a theme that recurs in several of these discourses (see especially WA, 175/SKS 12, 291). Third, although the self's relation to others is not explicitly flagged in this passage, the discourse on the High Priest began by explaining how a readiness to cover others' sins, to turn a blind eye (as Kierkegaard puts it), is a feature of human love (WA, 181/SKS 12, 295). Such concealment gives the other person space to grow in love, rather than being made resentful by endless condemnation. Healing the internal division of the self and learning what we now call self-acceptance establishes a pattern of basic trust that is a precondition of open and trusting relations to others in which the whole self is committed and not just a part (a part that is perhaps being continuously undermined by the contrary efforts of the other part). Fourth, it is implicit in the passage quoted and explicit at many points in these late writings that the possibility of such self-acceptance is continuously available to all in Christ.

Kierkegaard follows a long line of Christian theologians (including, notably, Paul, Luther, and Augustine) who argue we are incapable of such inner healing without help. As an earlier upbuilding discourse put it, no one is stronger than themselves, and the attempt to take control of one's own life will always be frustrated by the equal and opposite force of one's other "self."[17] In that discourse, he argued that this situation brings about the annihilation of the self and that it is in that annihilation that we are made ready to be recreated by God. Now, however, this account is qualified by the focus on Christ, suggesting that we do not need to drive ourselves deeper and deeper into despair by following the way of self-annihilation but are free to turn to Christ at whatever point on the trajectory we may find ourselves. We do not need to go "all the way" since we can at any point accept that we are loved and allow ourselves to be hidden in Christ's love, even if we cannot explain why or how (a rather common experience even in erotic love, as Kierkegaard was certainly aware).

If only it were that easy, we might say! Even apart from the fact that those living in a religiously plural or straightforwardly secular society will not even be aware of turning to Christ as an existential option, it might seem as if a simple switch in the orientation of our will is not so simple. This is precisely the argument of those in the Pauline–Augustinian–Lutheran tradition who insist on human incapacity. We just cannot do it, and God must do it for us. Kierkegaard certainly accepts that we cannot invent ourselves as new and better selves alone, as self-isolating individuals. However, as we have seen, his argument is that we are, in fact, not alone. We are always in a relationship to Christ, whether or not we are aware of it, and the dynamics of this relationship mean that our contribution is not irrelevant. At one point in the 1849 discourse on the sinful woman he goes so far as to say that her great love ("if I dare say it") made her "indispensable" to the Savior: He gained and keeps open the possibility of

---

[17] See "To Need God Is a Human Being's Highest Perfection" in EUD, 297–326/SKS 5, 291–316.

forgiveness, but she "made it into truth" (WA, 143/SKS 11, 279). From a strict Reformed position this sounds very much like an unacceptable admission of human agency – a work of merit. Kierkegaard was aware of this potential criticism and in one of the two 1851 discourses affirms the Reformed view that forgiveness is not earned by "works," but in the same sentence he affirms that *it is earned* by love (WA, 175–176/SKS 12, 191). Since our being is always from the ground up a being-in-relationship, the nature of that relationship is itself shaped *at least in part* by the attitude we ourselves take to it. Where Reformed theology insists on the sole agency of God working in Christ to defeat sin and give forgiveness, Kierkegaard's model is closer to what Orthodox theology speaks of as "synergy."[18]

But even if we concede with Kierkegaard that human agency is involved in the effective realization of forgiveness in the divine–human relationship, we might still feel that we want more by way of knowing how, exactly, this works out for the human being concerned. If Christ's nearness to the self establishes the possibility of a productive two-way relationship, as argued in "The High Priest," how does this possibility take shape in human lives? To answer this question we turn to "The Tax Collector" and "The Woman Who Was a Sinner."

"The Tax Collector" and "The Woman Who Was a Sinner"

If "The High Priest" brought to the fore a possibility of reestablishing a synergistic relation to God that might seem veiled beneath the emphasis on the universality of sin in *The Sickness unto Death*, the two discourses on the tax collector and the sinful woman return us to an aspect of despair briefly flagged in *The Sickness unto Death*, namely, the difference between masculine and feminine despair.[19] This time, however, it is masculine and feminine ways of accepting forgiveness that take center stage. Although Kierkegaard does not explicitly set the discourses up in this way, it seems to accord well with his strategy in these works as well as with his more general assumptions about gender differences, and he will explicitly emphasize the female attributes that make the sinful woman a suitable "teacher" in the introductory section of the 1851 discourse dedicated to her.

---

[18] This point is also made by M. Jamie Ferreira, *Kierkegaard* (Chichester: Wiley-Blackwell, 2009), 158. Kierkegaard refers to human beings as "God's co-workers" at WL, 62–63/SKS 9, 69.

[19] For discussion see, e.g., Sylvia Walsh, "On 'Feminine' and 'Masculine' Forms of Despair," in *International Kierkegaard Commentary*, vol. 19: *The Sickness unto Death*, ed. Robert L. Perkins (Macon, GA: Mercer University Press, 1987), 121–134.

In *The Sickness unto Death* Kierkegaard described masculine despair as typically represented by the despair of defiance, the self-assertion of a maximalist autonomous ego. Feminine despair, he said, corresponded more to the despair of weakness, not being willing to be the self that one is. A similar duality appears in inverse form in these discourses: The tax collector is portrayed as isolated and alone, the woman as passionate and submissive, weeping at the feet of the Savior. Of course, the comments about masculine and feminine despair already acknowledge that this is only a general way of talking and does not apply to all men or all women. It may even prove to be the case that one is more properly basic than the other and therefore the universal basis of all despair in men and women. Here too, it is especially clear in the 1851 discourse that the woman is a teacher for all and that men must learn to be like her; similarly (we may infer) the experience of the tax collector is not gender-specific in any absolute sense. Whether we take all this to mean that Kierkegaard is doing some creative riffing on available gender stereotypes without necessarily endorsing them or, conversely, that he is giving them religious sanction is a whole other discussion. Here, the focus is simply on bringing to the fore the dynamics of the experience of forgiveness.

The tax collector appears in a parable told by Jesus in which two men go to the temple to pray, one a Pharisee, the other a tax collector (Lk. 18:9–14). The Pharisee thanks God that he is not like others (the tax collector, for example) since he has kept God's commandments. The tax collector stands apart, dares not look up to heaven, but beats himself on the chest, saying only, "God be merciful to me, a sinner." But, Jesus concludes, it is the latter who went home justified, while the Pharisee is condemned for trusting in his own righteousness (Lk. 18:9). Neither in the parable itself nor in Kierkegaard's interpretation do we learn anything about the emotional impact of justification on the tax collector or even whether he was aware of it. We have seen that one strand of Reformation teaching adopted the legal fiction that righteousness could be "imputed" to the sinner, which could be taken as implying that the psychological state of the one being justified is a secondary matter: All that matters is God's judgment, and the one who is justified only has to believe or have faith that it is so.

In Kierkegaard's version, the tax collector could well be someone who is discovering the fruits of masculine despair in that he is so absorbed in his self-consciousness as to have become isolated from others. In an image that we would not be surprised to find in the writings of the aesthete of *Either/Or*, he is like someone alone in a desert, more alone than on "the most abandoned byway" (WA, 131/SKS 11, 267). His feeling of isolation is broken only by the consciousness of sin driving him to plead for divine mercy. There is nothing forced or studied about this plea, it is entirely spontaneous, Kierkegaard says, like the cry of a solitary desert traveler who is suddenly surprised by robbers or some "ravenous beast" (WA, 130–131/SKS 11, 266–267). Awareness of sin forces it from him. This self-complaint, Kierkegaard suggests, is precisely "the possibility of justification" (WA, 132/SKS 11, 268), which, again, pushes against the limits of the Reformation teaching that human beings can contribute nothing to justification. Arguably opposed to – or at the very least in tension with – the teaching of *Philosophical Fragments*, it seems that "the condition" for the God-relationship does not come entirely from outside but the sinner makes some contribution, albeit a negative one.

In terms of the imaginary setting of the discourse, this self-confession of the tax collector is precisely what the communicant has experienced in the act of confession, while the plea for grace, spoken with downcast eyes, is the epitome of what it is to kneel at the altar in expectation of justification (WA, 133/SKS 11, 269).

Nevertheless, as I have said, there is no hint as to the emotional impact of this kind of justification and, rather curiously, Kierkegaard ends by providing an oblique segue to the discourse that follows on the sinful woman, saying that in choosing to kneel penitently and adoringly at the altar, the worshipper is like "that woman ... who chose the good part when she sat at the Savior's feet" (WA, 134/SKS 11, 269). This probably refers to the story of Martha and Mary, the latter having chosen to sit and listen to Christ's words while Martha was busy about the house. She is, of course, not the nameless woman who is the subject of the story of "the sinful woman" told in Luke 7, although the two have often been conflated in Christian tradition (and both identified with Mary Magdalene). This conflation is without textual foundation, but there is a clear typological parallel in terms of the motif of sitting at the Savior's feet – as we see in the story of the sinful woman that immediately follows.

This time it is not a parable but a reported incident in the life of Jesus that provides the subject matter. Jesus is the dinner party guest of a Pharisee when an unnamed woman, known to be a sinner (probably of a sexual kind) bursts in, falls at Jesus's feet, weeping, bathing his feet with her tears, drying them with her hair, and anointing them with ointment. The Pharisee and other guests are scandalized that Jesus lets her do this, to which he responds with the words that form Kierkegaard's text: "Therefore, I tell you, her sins, which were many, have been forgiven; for she has shown great love" (Lk. 7:47).

Pictorially, the two figures could not be more different. The tax collector
stands alone, absorbed in his solitary thoughts. There is no visible presence of
God in the story. Everything is concentrated in the inward orientation of the two
actors. In the case of the woman, by way of contrast, we have a scene of intense
physical intimacy in which her hands, her tears, and her hair are in contact with
the very skin of the Savior. If the tax collector shows the isolating force of
penitence, the woman shows that this is nevertheless directed toward union – or,
if we take the two figures not just as contrasting types but as representing a
progressive deepening of the God-relationship, the deeper motive of penitence is
now shown to be love. And, unlike the tax collector's almost abstract relation to
his justification, the woman is fully emotionally engaged in the forgiveness she
receives. If the tax collector is a figure of the communicant kneeling at the altar,
awaiting the grace of the sacrament, the woman becomes a figure of what it is to
find "rest" at the altar (WA, 144/SKS 11, 280). If the tax collector may be
presumed to have found faith, she finds peace in the synergistic work of
forgiveness effected by love. Interestingly, the ending of the discourse on the
sinful woman also provides a segue to the two discourses of 1851, in the preface
to which Kierkegaard speaks of his entire authorship as coming to a "decisive
resting-point" at the foot of the altar (WA, 165/SKS 12, 281) while the first
discourse takes up the relationship between love and forgiveness as set forth in
Luke 7, although the role of the woman is not specifically thematized.

In considering the Christian experience of forgiveness, I noted a potential distinction between the forensic imagery of justification and the more
personal implications of forgiveness. It seems that the tax collector and the
sinful woman illustrate just this distinction. But while they may represent
legitimate variations within the spectrum of the Christian experience, it is
also possible to see them, as I have suggested, as increasingly intense phases
of a single movement. This would reflect the idea that the divine
forgiveness manifested in Christ has established a perpetual possibility in
human existence and that this possibility is most completely realized not in
the isolating penitence of the tax collector but in the loving, affective, and
intimate penitence of the woman. Ultimately, the Christian dialectic is not
one of condemnation and justification but a movement within a relationship of love that is always already present as an existential possibility and
remains insistently present even in the midst of our refusals or ignorance.[20]

---

[20] I take this to be implicit in those of Kierkegaard's upbuilding discourses that focus on the theme of
the lilies and the birds and on the text "Every good and perfect gift comes from above" (James 1.17).
These typically emphasize that the mere fact of human existence reveals God's creative benevolence
toward us. This benevolence is further underwritten by the gracious advent of God in Christ, as we
see in "The Invitation" at the start of *Practice in Christianity*: "What love! It is already loving, when

Whether this throws retrospective light on the debate as to whether masculine or feminine despair, defiance or weakness, is more fundamental is unsure. One could imagine any application going either way (masculine despair as the fundamental form of despair countered by feminine forgiveness as its polar opposite, or feminine despair as the more fundamental form needing, precisely, a feminine response[21]). But what it does suggest is that it is not the negative consciousness of despair that drives us to faith but the possibility of a love that has already been shown and offered. This is why the ultimate forms of despair are those that refuse forgiveness, either because one despairs over one's own sin, believing it to be of such an exceptional nature that it cannot be forgiven; or because one believes more generally that forgiveness is impossible; or, finally, because one finds Christianity to be simply untrue. However, although I have indicated some points of difference between the *Philosophical Fragments* and *The Sickness unto Death*, we may here apply the claim of the *Philosophical Fragments* that unbelief is itself an "acoustic illusion," which is to say that it is not a primitive datum of consciousness but an offended response to divine grace (PF, 49–54/SKS 4, 253–257); here too, not to believe in the possibility of forgiveness is itself a response to that very possibility, made present in the figure of Christ. The negative is in the end only an empty reflex of the positive.

Conclusion

What if anything does an approach to *The Sickness unto Death* via these explicitly Christian devotional texts mean for a philosophical interpretation? Some will probably think it is injurious to any attempt to retrieve Kierkegaard for a secular age insofar as it makes the content of *The Sickness unto Death* dependent on teachings peculiar to Christianity. Some theologians might also concur in the view that a properly Christian Kierkegaard

---

one is able to help, to help the one who asks for help, but to offer the help oneself! And to offer it to all!" (PC, 11/SKS 12, 21). The message is confirmed by Kierkegaard's appeal to Thorvaldsen's statue of Christ, waiting at the altar with arms open in welcome (see, e.g., WA, 169/SKS 12, 285). The theme of God being a God of patience who bears with human beings' persistence in sin until they repent points in the same direction (e.g., WA, 31–32/SKS 11, 35–36).

[21] This may seem counterintuitive, but I would argue that the sinful woman offers a "correct" response also to the "feminine" despair of weakness and this response too is "feminine." In other words, despairing of finding forgiveness, she throws herself at the feet of the Savior, she implores his assistance – rather than self-isolating in an ever deepening pit of guilty self-accusation.

must be kept separate from philosophy. However, both these views involve oversimplification. Clearly, to the extent that the interpretation presented earlier is correct, *The Sickness unto Death* presupposes the "positive" assumption that our existence is rooted and grounded in the love of God as that is made manifest and present in Christ. But this should not be taken as implying that the truth of the human condition is ultimately knowable only by Christians. Since this claim also implies that whatever is to be said of God is congruent with the basic ontological structure of human existence, it must be intelligible to all those defined by this structure, i.e. to all human beings. In the New Testament, Paul states that his appeal is ultimately to the consciences of his listeners, implying that they have the moral capacity to test the truth of what he says (e.g., 2 Cor. 4:2). So too here, some God-relationship is assumed as prior to any awareness of ourselves as in despair and needing salvation. This is indeed the kind of view developed throughout his career in different contexts by Paul Tillich, basing himself on the dialectic of what he called mysticism and guilt-consciousness in Schelling.[22] Contra *Philosophical Fragments*, we are never entirely outside the truth. Indeed, we could not have knowledge of sin (despair) if we did not have some sense, however obscure, of the good that is lacking in despair. To see human beings as ontologically incapable of good would lock us into a situation of incurable despair – a position for which the early Sartre can be seen as a consistent representative.[23]

From the point of view of Christian apologetics, it is clear that this precedent good is to be identified with God acting in Christ. However, insofar as this claim is set up in relation to a universal human situation, it allows for debate as to whether the revelation of what Tillich called the "new being" in Christ is only one of many possible revelations. It might even be possible to argue that a basic orientation toward love and toward the hope that love engenders is feasible on purely nonreligious grounds. Reading *The Sickness unto Death* as in this sense a "positive" text does not therefore resolve the debate between a philosophical and a theological Kierkegaard in favor of the theological. Like the entire textual inheritance

---

[22] See Paul Tillich, *Mysticism and Guilt-Consciousness in Schelling's Philosophical Development* (Lewisburg, PA: Bucknell University Press, 1974).

[23] See Kate Kirkpatrick, *Sartre on Sin: Between Being and Nothingness* (Oxford: Oxford University Press, 2017).

of historical Christianity, the discourses are human documents that invite interpretation within the horizons of humanly meaningful interpretability. The debate between the theological and the philosophical does not stand outside this horizon but within it. The question is simply whether the defining topic of *The Sickness unto Death* is in fact despair or whether despair is an acoustic illusion generated by the real primacy of forgiveness and love.

CHAPTER 2

Publishing The Sickness unto Death
A Lesson in Double-Mindedness

Clare Carlisle

Søren Kierkegaard wrote *The Sickness unto Death* in the spring of 1848 and published it over a year later, on July 30, 1849. Those months between writing and publication were a period of personal crisis for Kierkegaard, and when the book finally appeared in Copenhagen bookshops it signaled a landmark in his authorship. At the time he thought this could be his last book – a "halt" in the literary production that had begun in earnest with the bestselling *Either/Or* in early 1843 – but it turned out to be a relaunch (or a resurrection) of his writing life. While other contributions to this collection explore the themes and arguments in *The Sickness unto Death*, this chapter takes a more biographical approach in focusing on Kierkegaard's relationship to the text.

After he had composed the work, Kierkegaard spent months deliberating over whether or not to publish it, shuttling back and forth between a series of provisional decisions one way or another. This process eventually produced an important new pseudonym, Anti-Climacus, to whom *The Sickness unto Death* and, later, *Practice in Christianity* were attributed. This chapter offers a fresh interpretation of the meaning of the pseudonym and shows that the process by which Anti-Climacus came into being discloses a pattern of psychological, literary, and religious double-mindedness. This pattern can be traced through Kierkegaard's writings, and it shows up in the theological anthropology presented in *The Sickness unto Death*. If we accept Anti-Climacus's description of a human self as "a relation that relates itself to itself," we can say that Kierkegaard's relation to himself as an author is characterized by deep ambivalence.

The Decision to Publish *The Sickness unto Death*

Kierkegaard, who loved writing, often struggled with the process of publication. The transition from the inwardness and freedom of creative work to the brutal or banal determinacy of public judgment caused him great anxiety – and perhaps this was never more acute than in the case of *The Sickness unto Death*. Kierkegaard vacillated for months over whether or not to publish this book. This was partly because he had doubts about its form. It has an analytical or, as Kierkegaard put it, "dialectical" structure – similar in this respect to his *Philosophical Fragments* (1844) and *Concluding Unscientific Postscript* (1846) – but he also intended it to be "upbuilding," like his more lyrical discourses on biblical texts. Its title, after all, came from John 11:4, the story of the raising of Lazarus. On May 13, 1848, Kierkegaard wrote a brief "Report on 'The Sickness unto Death'" in his journal: "There is one difficulty with this book: it is too dialectical and stringent for the proper use of the rhetorical, the soul-stirring, the gripping. The title itself seems to indicate that it should be discourses – the title is lyrical." In typical fashion, Kierkegaard debated with himself in this journal entry, eventually concluding – at least for the time being – that "the task is much too great for a rhetorical arrangement . . . The dialectical algebra works better" (SUD, xiv/SKS 20, 365).

At this time, Kierkegaard was preoccupied not only with the literary form of *The Sickness unto Death* but with the shape of his authorship as a whole. He had come to see his works from *Either/Or* onward as a single work of art, and this holistic view of his authorship posed the problem of how to complete it. He ruminated on this question throughout 1848 and in the autumn of that year composed *The Point of View for My Work as an Author* in an attempt to settle it. Yet this, of course, produced the further question of whether or not to publish *that* book. By 1849 Kierkegaard had a growing pile of unpublished manuscripts – including *The Sickness unto Death* and parts of *Practice in Christianity* – which he at one point planned to publish "in one volume, all under my name – and then to make a clean break" (SUD, xv–xvi/SKS 22, 321).

For Kierkegaard, these questions about his authorship were inseparable from questions about his life. He had become an author after breaking up with his fiancée, Regine Olsen, in 1841. This event – perhaps the original existential crisis – marked a fork in his path through life. Abandoning marriage and a career in the church or the university, Kierkegaard embraced his vocation as a writer, bachelor, and critic of ecclesial and academic life. By 1848, however, his inheritance from his father – which had lavishly sustained his life as an author – was running low. In late March 1848, when he was in the middle of writing *The Sickness unto Death*, he moved house to a rented apartment, having sold his childhood home at 2 Nytorv, where he had written many of his books. (This personal upheaval mirrored Denmark's revolution, which took place that spring and issued in major state and church reform.) By 1849, still concerned about his financial situation, Kierkegaard was seriously considering seeking an official appointment in the Danish State Church. This would, he felt, be incompatible with continuing his authorship, not least because his unpublished manuscripts enacted an increasingly explicit critique of Danish "Christendom," or official Christianity. As in 1841, Kierkegaard faced an either/or: seek a job in the church or continue to be an author. By the summer of 1849 he reached a tentative resolution in favor of the former course and visited Bishop Mynster, head of the church, to discuss a possible appointment in Copenhagen's Pastoral Seminary – but Mynster avoided discussing this topic and ushered him out. "He's frightened of getting too involved with me," wrote Kierkegaard in his journal: no doubt an accurate assessment of Mynster's view (KJN 6, NB11:193/SKS 22, 116).

This visit to the bishop pushed Kierkegaard back to the other horn of his dilemma, and three days later, on June 28, he wrote to Bianco Luno, the printer, asking him to print *The Sickness unto Death*. Luno agreed to receive the manuscript the following day and print it right away. That evening, however, Kierkegaard heard the news that Regine Olsen's father had died. To a casual observer unacquainted with Kierkegaard's journals, this event would seem to have little to do with publishing *The Sickness unto Death*: Nearly eight years had passed since their engagement, and in the meantime Regine had married someone else. However, she remained an enormously significant figure in Kierkegaard's inner life. His relation to her was inseparable from his relationship to himself – and to his authorship. In his inward psychic landscape, Regine was situated on that fork in the road that led away from being a writer and toward a career in the church. Choosing this professional path in 1849 was bound up with his hope of reconciling with Regine – not in any romantic sense but through renewed communication, forgiveness, and friendship after years of silence between them. Regine's father, an upstanding councilor of state who had been upset and angered by Kierkegaard's treatment of his daughter, had stood in the way of this possible reconciliation. On the eve of printing *The Sickness unto Death*, Kierkegaard wondered whether Councilor Olsen's death was a sign from God that he should relinquish the path of authorship and pursue the alternative course that led in the direction of Regine and a respectable position in Copenhagen society.

That night, Kierkegaard's months of deliberation and indecision culminated in an episode of intense anxiety that brought him to the brink of mental collapse. Unable to sleep, he spent the night in an internal dialogue about *The Sickness unto Death*. He found himself, quite literally, in two minds, which he later struggled to piece together:

> I remember the words: See, now he intends his own destruction. But I cannot say for sure whether it was because it was I who wanted to call off sending the manuscript to the printer and make an overture to her, or the reverse, that it was I who stood firm on sending the manuscript to the printer. I can also remember the words: After all, it is no concern of (but I cannot remember exactly whether the word was *yours* or *mine*) that Councilor Olsen is dead. I can remember the words but not the particular pronoun: You – or I – could, in fact, wait a week. I can remember the reply: Who does he think he is. (SUD, xix/SKS 24, 354–355)

This frightening experience issued in a renewed resolve. Kierkegaard reasoned that his anxiety need not be taken as a warning sign but, on the contrary, as an encouragement to press ahead "in fear and trembling." He sent *The Sickness unto Death* to the printer: "I desperately needed a decision; it had been a frightful strain to have these manuscripts lying there and every single day to think of publishing them, while correcting a word here and there" (SUD, xix/SKS 24, 356).

The next act of this inward drama was Kierkegaard's last-minute decision to publish the book under a pseudonym. On the title page he replaced "S. Kierkegaard" with "Anticlimacus" – which he then amended slightly to "Anti-Climacus" – and added his own name as editor (SUD, 136–139). Thus out of an intense artistic and existential crisis, a new pseudonym was born. As we shall see in the following section, the choice of the name "Anti-Climacus" is emblematic of Kierkegaard's double-minded relation to himself as an author.

Kierkegaard's Double-Mindedness

The story of the publication of *The Sickness unto Death* and the creation of its pseudonym reveals some significant features of Kierkegaard's relation to his "work as an author," as he put it in 1848. Of course, it demonstrates how much his authorship meant to him: He was invested in it to a remarkable degree, and his meticulous revisions and anguished struggles alike were a sign of intense passion. Moreover, it shows how his relationship to his writing was inextricably bound up with the other significant relationships of his life – to God, to the church (embodied in the person of Bishop Mynster), and to Regine – and that all these relationships were elements of his relation to himself.

This personal investment is an important feature of *The Sickness unto Death*. In a draft note relating to the text, Kierkegaard reflected on his own identity as an author: "The best thing about me is my author-existence . . . my existence . . . is still essentially a poet-existence" (SUD, 159/Pap. X⁵ B 18). Though this explicitly personal reflection did not make it into the final edition, Kierkegaard opens Part Two of the book, titled "Despair Is Sin," with a description of "a poet-existence verging on the religious," which is "the most dialectical frontier between despair and sin" (SUD, 77/SKS 11, 191). More specifically, this poet-existence involves "the sin of poeticizing instead of being" (SUD, 77/SKS 11, 191). Kierkegaard defines sin as a kind of despair that is "before God, or with the conception of God" (SUD, 77/SKS 11, 191). A "poet-existence" is sinful because it is before God; yet it is equivocally before God – and thus a "frontier" or borderline condition – because the religious poet may allow himself "to poetize God as somewhat different from what God is" (SUD, 78/SKS 11, 192). In other words, while the religious poet is situated "before God," there is a question over whether he is truly before *God* or before an image of God that he himself has created or "poeticized." This particular category of despair does not necessarily exhaust the complexities of Kierkegaard's inner life, but it captures a self-diagnosed tendency. Kierkegaard's internal debates about whether to stop or continue being an author could, then, be analyzed in terms of the taxonomy of despair set out in *The Sickness unto Death*. And no doubt he did analyze them in precisely this way during the period that stretched between beginning the book at 2 Nytorv and seeing it through the press about sixteen months later.

His decisions – and indecisions – concerning *The Sickness unto Death* also bring to light a distinctive feature of his relation to himself, to his authorship, and to the world: his double-mindedness. This encompasses his vacillation and, relatedly, his ambivalence toward precisely those things that mattered most to him, not least being an author. In his 1847 discourse "Purity of Heart Is to Will One Thing," which might be read as a precursor to *The Sickness unto Death*, he asks, "Is not despair actually double-mindedness; or what else is it to despair but to have two wills?" (UDVS, 30/SKS 8, 144). Indeed, this conception of despair is embedded in the Danish word *Fortvivlelse*.[1]

---

[1] See Roe Fremstedal, "Kierkegaard's Post-Kantian Approach to Anthropology and Selfhood," in *The Kierkegaardian Mind*, ed. Adam Buben, Eleanor Helms, and Patrick Stokes (London: Routledge, 2019), 319–330.

Kierkegaard's tortured night thoughts, which split his mind in two on the eve of sending the manuscript to the printer, is a particularly striking and intense manifestation of a deep structural duplicity discernible through his published writings and his journals. This double-mindedness, or ambivalence, is a distinctive feature of his view of the religious life. "Although Abraham arouses my admiration, he also appalls me," declares Johannes de silentio in *Fear and Trembling* – and then, looking from Abraham to the Virgin Mary, Johannes asks, "Is it not true here also that the one whom God blesses he curses in the same breath?" (FT, 60, 65/SKS 4, 153, 158). In an 1847 discourse, Kierkegaard applies this thought to Christ:

> Though [Jesus] possesses the blessing [he] was like a curse for everyone who came near him . . . like an affliction for those few who loved him, so that he had to wrench them out into the most terrible decisions, so that for his mother he had to be the sword that pierced her heart, for the disciples a crucified love. (UDVS, 254/SKS 8, 352)

Practice in Christianity develops the idea that Christian teaching – and, indeed, Christ himself – attracts and repels at the same time (PC, 147–262/SKS 12, 149–253). And in *The Sickness unto Death*, this logic of ambivalence finds expression in the claim that despair is at once a blessing and a curse: "Is despair an excellence or a defect? Purely dialectically, it is both" (SUD, 14/SKS 11, 130). Understood analytically, despair has two different aspects: It is an "excellence" insofar as it reflects our capacity for living in the right and a "defect" because it reflects the fact that a person is *not* living in the right. From the perspective of the suffering individual, however, these two aspects combine in a single experience of despair, and they produce double-mindedness in relation to both God and the self.

The religious ambivalence we find in these passages cannot be explained by the distinction between institutional religion and authentic spirituality – the distinction, in other words, between Christendom and Christianity. This distinction is fundamental to Kierkegaard's thought, as I have argued elsewhere.[2] The distinction between Christendom and Christianity structures Kierkegaardian irony: In his authorship, the "task of becoming a Christian" is predicated on the difference between a concrete, determinate,

---

[2] See Clare Carlisle, "How to Be a Human Being in the World: Kierkegaard's Question of Existence," in *Kierkegaard's Existential Approach*, ed. Arne Grøn, René Rosfort, and K. Brian Söderquist (Berlin: DeGruyter, 2017); and Clare Carlisle, *Philosopher of the Heart: The Restless Life of Søren Kierkegaard* (London: Allen Lane, 2019), 13–14, 40, 84, 130–132, 139–141, 207, 237, 245.

publicly recognizable form of Christian life and a less determinate, more open-ended Christian ideal, which takes the form of an aspiration that animates Christendom yet cannot be fully captured by it.[3] This logic shaped Kierkegaard's thinking about *The Sickness unto Death*. He explained in his journal that "a pseudonym had to be used" because "when the demands of ideality are to be presented at their maximum, then one must take extreme care not to be confused with them himself, as if he were the ideal." In an important late journal entry, Kierkegaard referred to this as "keeping the ideal free" – free, that is, from anything determinate, precisely to preserve its character as an aspiration (MLW, 341/SKS 13, 405). It would be simplistic to say that Kierkegaard has a negative attitude to Christendom and a positive attitude to "true" Christianity and that this explains away his apparent religious ambivalence.[4] Rather, he was ambivalent toward the Christian ideal itself. He was powerfully drawn to this ideal, indeed passionately committed to it; and yet at the same time he felt that its demands were too high: He shrank from the fear, the suffering, the anxiety he believed it must entail. (It is also true – though less significant in relation to *The Sickness unto Death* – that Kierkegaard was somewhat ambivalent toward Christendom as well: Though he made it the target of a sustained critique and polemic, he attended Copenhagen's Vor Frue Kirke for almost all his adult life, preached some sermons in that church, and, as we have seen, considered an official church appointment as late as 1849.)

Kierkegaard's ambivalence seems to have had roots in his early life. (This gives a new twist to his childhood nickname, "Gaflen" or "The Fork," coined after young Søren expressed his wish to spear anything on the dinner table – and to spear anyone who challenged him.[5]) During the summer of 1848 – shortly after leaving 2 Nytorv and completing *The Sickness unto Death* – he undertook intense reflection on his life as well as his authorship. In a journal entry from that period, he traces his complicated view of Christianity to his relationship with his father:

[3] See Jonathan Lear, *A Case for Irony* (Cambridge, MA: Harvard University Press, 2011); see also Carlisle, "How to Be a Human Being in the World."
[4] M. G. Piety makes this claim in "Alone for Dinner: Kierkegaard's Sombre Outlook," a review of my biography *Philosopher of the Heart: The Restless Life of Søren Kierkegaard. Times Literary Supplement*, October 10, 2019. Her suggestion that I conflate Christianity and Christendom in arguing that Kierkegaard was ambivalent toward Christianity fundamentally misunderstands (or misrepresents) my book, and – more important – Kierkegaard's thought.
[5] See Joakim Garff, *Søren Kierkegaard: A Biography*, trans. Bruce H. Kirmmse (Princeton, NJ: Princeton University Press, 2005), 7–9; Alastair Hannay, *Kierkegaard: A Biography* (Cambridge: Cambridge University Press, 2001), 60.

> He ... made my childhood an unparalleled torture, and made me, in my heart of hearts, not far from being offended by Christianity ... even if out of respect for it [I] resolved never to say a word about it to any person and, out of love to my father, to portray Christianity as truly as possible ... And yet my father was the most loving father. (KJN 4, NB5:68/SKS 20, 400–401)

Michael Pedersen Kierkegaard's love for his sons was, it seems, both emotionally confusing and closely associated with a certain form of Christian faith. This confusion deepened young Søren's religious ambivalence: "I acquired such anxiety about Christianity, and yet I felt myself strongly drawn toward it" (KJN 5, NB8:36/SKS 21, 160).[6]

It should be now be clear that, at least in Kierkegaard's case, ambivalence certainly does not imply indifference or a lack of commitment. On the contrary, he exhibited an ambivalent love toward those things and people about whom he felt most intensely. His relationships to Regine Olsen and to Bishop Mynster – perhaps the two most significant figures during his adult life – both showed this kind of ambivalence.[7] Indeed, the only important relationship that does not appear to have had this character is his relationship with his mother, Anne Sørensdatter Kierkegaard, who died in 1834. Kierkegaard, at that time twenty-one years old, was devastated by this loss, though since he never wrote about his mother we know very little about his relationship with her.[8]

It is not surprising, then, that Kierkegaard was ambivalent toward his authorship – perhaps the greatest love of his life, and certainly inseparable from his other great loves: God, Christianity, Regine. As his anxieties about publishing *The Sickness unto Death* attest, this ambivalence could be a source of intense suffering. In July 1849, looking back on his struggle with the question of publication, he described his indecision as a painful skewering "on the pinnacle of possibility": "What has strained me so much recently is that I have wanted to overexert myself and have wanted too much; and then, however, I myself have realized that it was too much;

---

[6] See also JP 6, 6327/KJN 5, NB9:78/SKS 21, 248–251 and JP 6, 6389/KJN 5, NB10:191/SKS 21, 356–359.

[7] "Let us pay tribute to Bishop Mynster. I have admired no one, no living person, except Bishop Mynster, and it is always a joy to me to be reminded of my father. His position is such that I see the irregularities very well, more clearly than anyone who has attacked him ... There is an ambivalence in his life that cannot be avoided, because the 'state Church' is an ambivalence" (JP 5, 6076/SKS 20, 253). On Kierkegaard's ambivalence toward Bishop Mynster, see Carlisle, *Philosopher of the Heart*, 89, 210; on his ambivalence toward Regine, see Carlisle, *Philosopher of the Heart*, 160–161, 182–183.

[8] See Bruce H. Kirmmse, *Encounters with Kierkegaard: A Life as Seen by His Contemporaries*, ed. Bruce H. Kirmmse, trans. Bruce H. Kirmmse and Virginia R. Laursen (Princeton, NJ: Princeton University Press, 1996), 196; See also Carlisle, *Philosopher of the Heart*, 103.

therefore did not do it, but again could not escape the possibility and, to my own torment, have kept myself on the pinnacle of this possibility" (KJN 6, NB12:7/SKS 22, 149). As this image vividly suggests, the question "To be, or not be ... an author?" constituted a protracted existential dilemma for Kierkegaard, a deep division in his desire – and his new pseudonym, Anti-Climacus, came into being as a solution to this dilemma. Anti-Climacus allowed him to go ahead and publish *The Sickness unto Death*, freeing him from the state of vacillation that had tormented him for months. Kierkegaard reflected in a note on the manuscript that a pseudonym, precisely because he is not an existing human being, has the great advantage of *not* suffering from double-mindedness: "a fictitious character has no other possibility than the one he has ... he has no identity that encompasses many possibilities" (SUD, 140/SKS 22, 135).

Having said this, the character of Anti-Climacus also gave a new expression to Kierkegaard's double-mindedness. His name clearly indicates that this pseudonym is twinned with – and opposed to – Johannes Climacus, pseudonymous author of *Philosophical Fragments* and *Concluding Unscientific Postscript*. Johannes Climacus is named after a seventh-century Greek Orthodox monk and author of the *Ladder of Paradise* (*Klimax tou Paradeisou*), a book on the contemplative life. This pseudonym could with some justification claim to be the one most closely (though by no means entirely) identified with Kierkegaard himself: He first came into being in a semi-autobiographical text about a philosophy student, written in 1842–1843 and left unfinished.[9] As we have seen, *Philosophical Fragments* and *Concluding Unscientific Postscript* have a literary form – an "algebraic," dialectical construction – that mirrors the structure of *The Sickness unto Death*.[10] Whereas the original Johannes Climacus's "ladder" was a contemplative ascent to God, nineteenth-century Climacus's ladder is "an ascending series of logical plateaus."[11] *Concluding Unscientific Postscript* was supposed to be, as its title suggests, the conclusion or "climax" of Kierkegaard's pseudonymous authorship – a

[9] See Lee C. Barrett, "Johannes Climacus: Humorist, Dialectician and Gadfly," in *Kierkegaard's Pseudonyms, Kierkegaard Research: Sources, Reception and Resources*, vol. 17, ed. Jon Stewart and Katalin Nun (Farnham: Ashgate, 2015), 141–166.
[10] See Jakub Marek, "Anti-Climacus: Kierkegaard's 'Servant of the Word,'" in *Kierkegaard's Pseudonyms, Kierkegaard Research: Sources, Reception and Resources*, vol. 17, ed. Jon Stewart and Katalin Nun (Farnham: Ashgate, 2015), 39–51.
[11] See D. Anthony Storm, "Johannes Climacus," *D. Anthony Storm's Commentary on Kierkegaard*, http://sorenkierkegaard.org/johannes-climacus.html.

climax that involved the witty gesture of revoking the authorship, kicking away the ladder – and in a sense the joke continues with the invention of Anti-Climacus, the anti-climax to this spectacular "conclusion" to the authorship.

Yet there is more to Anti-Climacus's relationship to Johannes Climacus than this humorous play on words. In a marginal note on the Preface to *The Sickness unto Death*, Kierkegaard spells out these pseudonyms' contrasting relationships to Christianity: "Climacus is lower, denies he is a Christian. Anti-Climacus is higher, a Christian on an extraordinarily high level" (SUD, 140/SKS 22, 136). This note is often quoted by commentators seeking to make sense of the relationship between the two pseudonyms – and their relation to Kierkegaard himself.[12] A draft preface to *The Sickness unto Death*, however, is more revealing on this question. Here Anti-Climacus explains that he and Johannes Climacus are brothers, exactly the same age, with everything in common and yet utterly different:

> We are not twins, we are opposites. Between us there is a deep, a fundamental relationship, but despite the most desperate efforts on both sides we never get any farther, any closer, than to a *repelling contact*. There is a point and an instant at which we touch, but at the same instant we fly from each other with the speed of infinity. Like two eagles plunging from a mountain top toward one point, or like one eagle plunging down from the top of a cliff and a predatory fish shooting from the ocean's depth to the surface with the same speed, we two both seek the same point; there is a contact, and at the same instant we rush from each other, each to his extremity. (JP 6, 6349)

This compelling image of a divided self, split between inseparable antagonists, echoes Kierkegaard's own double-mindedness, which he articulates in his journals from this period. This image is a miniature literary performance that seems to dramatize his relationship to himself and, more specifically, his attitude to being an author.

Indeed, this passage also echoes the preface to Kierkegaard's very first book, *From the Papers of One Still Living*, which discusses Hans Christian Andersen's novel *Only a Fiddler*. In his preface to this lengthy review, Kierkegaard stages an antagonistic literary dialogue between two minds. "One Still Living" is a kind of pseudonym, denoting a "friend" and "alter

---

[12] See Julia Watkin, *The A to Z of Kierkegaard's Philosophy* (Plymouth: Scarecrow Press, 2001), 401. Watkin suggests that "Anti" means "both 'contrast' or 'opposite' and 'ante' or 'before,'" and she emphasizes the latter sense: "Anti-Climacus comes before, or takes precedence over, Johannes Climacus because of the superiority of his ethical-religious life." My interpretation here places more emphasis on the oppositional sense of "Anti."

ego," and the book's title page indicated that "S. Kjerkegaard" had published his papers against their author's will. The preface, signed "The Publisher," expresses Kierkegaard's ambivalent relationship to himself as a writer:

> Our opinions nearly always differ and we are perpetually in conflict with each other, although under it all we are united by the deepest, most sacred, indissoluble ties. Yes, although often diverging in magnetic repulsion, we are still, in the strongest sense of the word, inseparable, even though our mutual friends have seldom, perhaps never, seen us together, albeit that someone or other may at times have been surprised that just as he has left one of us, he has, almost instantaneously, met the other. We are, therefore, so far from being able to rejoice as friends in the unity for which poets and orators in their repeated immortalizations have only a single expression – that it was as if one soul resided in two bodies – that with respect to us it must rather seem as if two souls resided in one body. (EPW, 55/SKS 1, 9)

Having sketched this striking image of double-mindedness, Kierkegaard stages an argument between his "two souls" about whether or not to publish the book. Characteristically, this duplicity blends humor with pathos. The author declares that "I consider writing books to be the most ridiculous thing a person can do," and expresses his anxiety about readers' judgments – then the Publisher overrides him: "I will not hear another word. The essay is now in my power; I have the command" (EPW, 55/ SKS 1, 12). Thus the author is silenced, and his will crushed, at the very moment his work is offered to the world.

Highlighting these expressions of authorial ambivalence need not, of course, suggest a purely biographical or psychological account of Kierkegaard's pseudonyms in general or of Anti-Climacus in particular. The decision to attribute *The Sickness unto Death* to this new pseudonym also had a literary and rhetorical significance. As we have seen, Kierkegaard debated with himself over the form of the text – whether it should be primarily a logical analysis of despair or a "stirring," upbuilding, lyrical work – just as he agonized over the question of publication. Since the pseudonym was introduced late in the process, when the text was largely complete, we cannot see Anti-Climacus as *essential* to its literary form. Nevertheless, Kierkegaard had literary reasons for choosing to make the book pseudonymous. He came to believe this was required in order to protect the ideal of faith from being contaminated by any actual, existing example – including himself; he sought to position himself, alongside his imagined readers, not as a source or exemplar of the Christian ideal, but as someone who was striving for that ideal. "It's quite true that a pseudonym had to be used," he wrote in his journal in July 1849, after the deed was done: "When the requirements of ideality are to be set forth at their maximum, one ought to do everything to guard against being confused with them, as though one were oneself the ideal. Assurances could of course be used to safeguard against this. But the only certain way is this reduplication. The difference from the earlier pseudonyms is merely this, but it is essential: that I do not retract the whole business humorously, but define myself as someone striving" (KJN 6, NB12:9/SKS 22, 151). Here, Kierkegaard sees the question of the author's relation to the work as inseparable from the effect – and, indeed, the meaning – of the work itself.

"I Came to Understand Myself by Writing"

As we have seen, Kierkegaard wrote *The Point of View on My Work as an Author* during the fraught, self-scrutinizing period between writing and publishing *The Sickness unto Death*. In this searching work, Kierkegaard reflected that writing was the means by which he had gained an understanding of his own life, from childhood to maturity: "Assigned from childhood to a life of torment that perhaps few can conceive of, plunged into the deepest despondency, and from this despondency again into despair, I came to understand myself by writing" (PV, 162/SKS 21, 45). The place of "despair" in this personal narrative suggests that the phenomenology of despair presented in *The Sickness unto Death* was part of the process of literary self-understanding described here. More than this, though, Kierkegaard came to regard his extensive (and intensive!) wrestling with the question of whether, when, and how to publish *The Sickness unto Death* as a crucial phase in his understanding of himself and of his authorship.

Notebook 12, written in July 1849 as Kierkegaard awaited the book's publication, reckons with the significance of his new pseudonym:

> *The Sickness unto Death* is now in print, pseudonymously, by Anti-Climacus.
>
> *Practice in Christianity* will also be pseudonymous. I now understand myself so completely.
>
> The point of the whole thing is that there is an ethically rigorous, highest point of Christianity that must at least be heard. But no more than that. It must be left to every individual's conscience to decide whether he is capable of building his tower so high.

But it must be heard. And the trouble is simply that the whole of Christendom, including the clergy, not only lives in worldly shrewdness, but that they do so in shameless defiance, and consequently they are compelled to declare Christ's life to be fantasy.

Therefore the alternative must be heard – heard, if possible, like a voice in the clouds, heard as a flight of wild birds over the heads of the tame ones.

No more than that. Therefore it must be pseudonymous, I am merely the editor.

Ah, but what haven't I suffered before reaching this point, which indeed was essentially clear to me early on, but which I was compelled to understand for a second time. (KJN 6, NB12:7/SKS 22, 149)

This journal entry lends support to the view that *The Sickness unto Death* effectively launches a "second" Kierkegaardian authorship, though Kierkegaard's sense that he had understood his role as an author "for a second time" also highlights continuity with the earlier works. While many scholars take seriously the idea that Kierkegaard's corpus can be divided into a first and second authorship, they do not entirely agree on the dividing date and the precise nature of the shift – no doubt because Kierkegaard himself made several attempts to halt his authorship between 1846 (following *The Corsair Affair*) and 1849, repeatedly revising his sense of its overall shape.[13] In the passage quoted above, we see Kierkegaard

[13] See John Elrod, *Kierkegaard and Christendom* (Princeton, NJ: Princeton University Press, 1981), xi–xii: "Kierkegaard's second literature reflects a spiritual turn from the aesthetic orientation of the earlier pseudonyms to a consistent preoccupation with exploring and developing that ethical-religious mode of existence that some of his earlier pseudonyms described and appreciated but did not existentially adopt. This spiritual turn, which Kierkegaard began slowly to make in 1846, involves a change in his conception of himself as an author ... The second literature is devoted to enabling his reader to understand that the essence of Christianity is to love one's neighbour as one loves oneself"; George Pattison and Steven Shakespeare (eds.), *Kierkegaard: The Self in Society* (Basingstoke: Macmillan, 1998), 5: "The latter part of Kierkegaard's writing career, from 1846 onwards, saw not only his final attack on contemporary culture and Church, but also the publication of works of social criticism and interpersonal ethics, as well as a renewed emphasis on the practical consequences of a life of discipleship"; David Lappano, *Kierkegaard's Theology of Encounter: An Edifying and Polemical Life* (Oxford: Oxford University Press, 2017), 8: "The year of 1846 to 1847 signals a turning point within Søren Kierkegaard's literary output, which sees a shift in emphasis towards a presentation of religious existence and its impact on modern life"; Justin Sands, *Reasoning from Faith: Fundamental Theology in Merold Westphal's Philosophy of Religion* (Bloomington: Indiana University Press, 2018), 139: "the term ['second authorship'] denotes a change in writing style shortly after the 'Corsair Affair' ... The works that are included in the second authorship are authored by Kierkegaard himself with no pseudonyms." Sands places *Two Ages, Works of Love, Upbuilding Discourses in Various Spirits*, "Phister as Captain Scipio," and *The Crisis and a Crisis in the Life of an Actress* in this category; Graeme Nicholson, "The Intense Communication of Kierkegaard's Discourses," in *International Kierkegaard Commentary: Upbuilding Discourses in Various Spirits*, ed. Robert L. Perkins (Macon, GA: Mercer University

gearing up for the more direct attack on Christendom that distinguishes his work from 1849 onward. *Practice in Christianity*, Anti-Climacus's next book, would take a decisive step in this direction, with its unmistakable critique of Bishop Mynster, leader of Denmark's State Church (now renamed, following the 1848 revolution, as the People's Church [*Folkekirke*]). The conclusions summarized in this journal entry gave Kierkegaard the clarity to resolve never to publish *The Point of View of My Work as An Author*: "And so not one word about myself in relation to the entire authorship, such a word changes everything and misrepresents me" (KJN 6, NB12:7/SKS 22, 149). Perhaps by now it will not be surprising to learn that our double-minded author did not entirely stick to this resolution: He published an essay titled "On My Work as an Author" in 1851.

It is not only Kierkegaard who learned something from his experience of publishing *The Sickness unto Death*. We, too, can draw from this episode a deeper understanding of Kierkegaard and his works. Kierkegaard's remark that he came to understand himself through writing suggests a parallel with psychoanalysis: He treated writing as a practice, a discipline, a site and a method of enquiry into the truth and meaning of his life. A psychoanalyst friend of mine describes the psychoanalytic relationship as "two people together occupying a space of unknowing," and this strikes me as an apt description of Kierkegaard's literary practice, which so often performs a division between two selves: author and publisher, editor and pseudonym, writer and reader, physician and patient.[14] Like a psychotherapeutic relationship, this literary practice created an intimate space – significantly separate from the rest of life, secluded from "the world" – in which to explore, deconstruct, and reconstruct the drama of his inner life. No wonder he was anxious about bringing his writing into public view.

I am not proposing to psychoanalyze Kierkegaard or his authorship: That is something I am not qualified to do, even if I wanted to. Treating the psychoanalytic relationship simply as an analogy for Kierkegaard's

---

Press, 2005), 349: "The 1847 publication *Upbuilding Discourses in Various Spirits* . . . was the opening of Kierkegaard's 'second authorship.'" In *The Point of View*, Kierkegaard writes: "The first division of books is esthetic writing; the last division of books is exclusively religious writing – between these lies *Concluding Unscientific Postscript* as the *turning point*. This work deals with and poses *the issue*, the issue of the entire work as an author: becoming a Christian . . . *Concluding Unscientific Postscript* is not esthetic writing, but, strictly speaking, neither is it religious" (PV, 31/ SKS 16, 17).

[14] A draft postscript to *The Sickness unto Death* reads: "This book seems to be written by a physician; I, the editor, am not the physician, I am one of the sick" (SUD, 162/SKS 22, 365; see also SUD, 160–161/Pap. X⁵ B 19).

relationship to writing, we can view his literary practice as a secluded space that discloses deep structures, certain patterns of relating, which are enacted within this space. Freud called this enactment and disclosure "transference."[15] For example, Kierkegaard's anxieties about publishing his work express his uncertainty about his relationship to the world: whether to be a recluse, a knight of resignation; or whether to seek success and recognition in the public sphere; or whether to make himself a figure of conspicuous protest against worldly values, like Simon Stylites or Jesus on the cross.

The deep pattern of ambivalence or double-mindedness enacted in Kierkegaard's relationship to writing seems to repeat a psychological pattern that was expressed in his relations with several significant people: his father, Regine, Bishop Mynster. The pattern also repeats his relation to Christianity, his relation to God, and it finds expression in the structure of his thinking – in his theology. In the works following *The Sickness unto Death*, Jesus became the focus of Kierkegaard's religious ambivalence. *Practice in Christianity* depicts Jesus as embodying two extremes: leniency and rigor. While Jesus offered his followers grace and love, promised to ease their burdens and give them rest (Matt. 11:28–30), Kierkegaard notes that they were first "rent asunder in terror and fear." "You became a sword through the heart of your mother, a scandal to your disciples," he wrote in his journal in 1850:

> Oh, why did you not cut the price ... When I have doubts about myself, and it seems to me as if I must first and foremost cut the price for my own sake, and when it seems to me as if I owe it to others to cut the price – now it can cause me anxiety to think of you, as if you would become angry, you, who never cut the price yet nonetheless were love. (KJN 7, NB18:27/SKS 23, 267–268)

The works attributed to Anti-Climacus sharpen Kierkegaard's sense that the human condition, in its spiritual relation to God, is at once a blessing and a curse. Anxiety and despair are the unavoidable price of being a self: "A relation that relates itself to itself and in relating itself to itself relates itself to another" – that is to say, to God (SUD, 13–14/SKS 11, 129). The ideal of faith described in *The Sickness unto Death* is based on this definition of the self: "In relating itself to itself and in willing to be itself, the self rests transparently in the power that established it" (SUD, 14, 131/SKS 11, 130, 242). The dialectical structure of the text enacts

---

[15] See Jonathan Lear, *Therapeutic Action: An Earnest Plea for Irony* (Abingdon: Routledge, 2018), which offers a Kierkegaardian reading of the psychoanalytic concept of transference.

Kierkegaard's claim that the path to faith must lead through despair, just as the path to rest leads through the spiritual labors of anxiety. Already in 1843 Kierkegaard insisted that "only the one who was in anxiety finds rest ... that only the one who draws the knife gets Isaac" (FT, 27/SKS 4, 123).

Anxiety and rest appear to be two more polar opposites structuring Kierkegaard's thought. Yet at the same time, rest means respite from the fluctuation between opposing poles that characterizes Kierkegaardian double-mindedness. In *The Sickness unto Death* Anti-Climacus argues that the human being can only find this rest in God. The pseudonym orients this thought in an explicitly Christian direction in *Practice in Christianity*, which begins with an extended discourse on Matthew 11:28: "Come here to me, all you who labor and are burdened, and I will give you rest" (PC, 5–68/SKS 12, 13–80).[16] For Kierkegaard, rest was the unambiguous element of the Christian ideal – precisely because it was the antidote to his multifaceted ambivalence and to the unrest this caused him personally. Two years after *The Sickness unto Death* was published, Kierkegaard preached a sermon in Copenhagen's Citadel Church on "The Changelessness of God" – another decisive occasion that provoked a short but intense psychological crisis, not dissimilar to the crisis over publishing *The Sickness unto Death*.[17] Here he reiterated Anti-Climacus's insight in a different literary register.

> It is almost as if it were far, far beyond human powers to have to be involved with a changelessness such as that; indeed, it seems as if this thought must plunge a person into anxiety and unrest to the point of despair.
>
> But then it is also the case *that there is reassurance and blessedness in this thought*. It is really so that when you, weary from all this human, all this temporal and earthly changefulness and alteration, weary of your own instability, could wish for a place where you could rest your weary head, your weary thoughts, your weary mind, in order to rest, to have a good rest – ah, in God's changelessness there is rest! (MLW, 278/SKS 13, 336–337)

---

[16] This New Testament text was crucial both for Kierkegaard's Christian formation and for his later authorship: "Kommer til mig" ("Come to me") is inscribed on Bertel Thorvaldsen's *Christus* statue in Copenhagen's Vor Frue Kirke, where Kierkegaard was confirmed, attended services, and preached Friday Communion discourses: see Carlisle, *Philosopher of the Heart*, 82–88.

[17] See Carlisle, *Philosopher of the Heart*, 225–228.

CHAPTER 3

Kierkegaard on the Self and the Modern Debate on Selfhood

Anthony Rudd

After a Preface and Introduction, the main text of *The Sickness unto Death* gets underway with a passage of notorious density and obscurity:

> A human being [*Mennesket*] is spirit [*Aand*]. But what is spirit? Spirit is the self [Selvet]. But what is the self? The self is a relation that relates itself to itself or is the relation's relating itself to itself in the relation; the self is not the relation, but is the relation relating itself to itself. A human being is a synthesis of the infinite and the finite, of the temporal and the eternal, of freedom and necessity; in short, a synthesis. A synthesis is a relation between two. Considered in this way, a human being is still not a self. (SUD, 13/SKS 11, 130)

This chapter will try to unpack this formidable definition of the self (while ranging more widely in the text of *The Sickness unto Death* in order to do so). As I proceed, I will consider some other philosophical accounts of the nature of the self (both early modern and recent). I don't have the space to do full justice to them here; I am, rather, using them to shed light by comparison and contrast on Kierkegaard's view and to help indicate where it stands in the modern philosophical debate on the nature of the self.

The Human Being and the Self

In this definition a "human being" is first identified as "spirit" and spirit as "self," but then we are told that a human being "is still not" (or, in Hannay's translation, "not yet"[1]) a self. This seems to be a problem: Logically, if A is B and B is C, then A must be C. But perhaps

---

[1] Søren Kierkegaard, *The Sickness unto Death*, trans. Alastair Hannay (London: Penguin, 1989), 43.

Kierkegaard (or Anti-Climacus)[2] can be saved from the charge of blatant self-contradiction, for he doesn't just say that a human being is not a self but is "not yet" a self. There are a couple of ways in which we might take this. First, we might take Kierkegaard to be saying that the relation between "human being" and spirit/self is a developmental one. After all, you don't say a caterpillar is "not yet" a carrot, but you might say that a caterpillar is not yet a butterfly. This implies that it is a butterfly in potential (while it is not even potentially a carrot). Similarly, we might take the initial claim that a human being is (spirit and therefore) a self to mean that a human being is *potentially* a self. But the biological analogy can only take us so far, for it becomes clear that the self is not, for Kierkegaard, something a human being automatically or naturally develops into; the concept is a *normative* one. The self is what a human being *should* become. So although it is true that a human being is potentially spirit, still, becoming spirit is not a natural developmental process. But neither is it just one possible option a human being might choose to actualize, among others. It is what a human being is *supposed* to become, is set up to become, and to fail to become spirit (self) is to fail to realize oneself as a human being. Despair, we soon learn, is this failure (ultimately this refusal) to become a self. And "if you have lived in despair, then, regardless of whatever else you won or lost, everything is lost for you" (SUD, 28/SKS 11, 144).

The second way in which we might take the "not yet" is to see it as a comment on the definition of a human being, as a synthesis of the infinite and the finite etc., given in the previous sentence. The point would then be that this definition, though correct as far as it goes, is not by itself enough to explain the sense in which a human being is not just a synthesis of contrasting factors but a self. I think Kierkegaard's language is rich enough to admit of both interpretations, and I don't think they need be taken as competing with one another. (The definition is of a human being as a potential self but does not get us to what it is for a human to actually be a self.) The second reading does however encourage us to move still further away from the implications of my earlier image of biological metamorphosis. For in becoming a self, I do not cease to be a human

---

[2] *The Sickness unto Death* is only a weakly pseudonymous work: It was not originally written with the intention of being pseudonymous, and its eventual pseudonymity does not indicate any disagreement on Kierkegaard's part with the content of the work. (See the Hongs' "Historical Introduction" in SUD, ix–xxiii, and Gregory Beabout, *Freedom and Its Misuses: Kierkegaard on Anxiety and Despair* (Milwaukee, WI: Marquette University Press, 1996), 77–80.) Accordingly, I will refer to the author as "Kierkegaard" rather than "Anti-Climacus."

being (as a butterfly does, plausibly, cease to be a caterpillar, while
remaining the organism that was once a caterpillar). So the distinction
between a human being and the self is not a straightforwardly ontological
one, like the Cartesian distinction between body and mind. It isn't even
like Descartes's distinction between the mind considered by itself and the
human being considered as a union of mind and body (a union so close
that "I and the body form a unit"[3]). But the Kierkegaardian self does not
relate to the "human being" as a part to a whole or as a sort of inner core.
This is why the self is said to be a "relation" – or, more precisely, "the
relation's relating itself to itself" – rather than a substance. (I will return to
this idea shortly.)

If we are looking for familiar philosophical analogies for Kierkegaard's
distinction, it might seem that a more plausible candidate than Descartes's
dualism would be Locke's distinction between the identity of a "man" –
i.e., a human being, considered as a biological organism[4] – and that of a
"person": "a thinking intelligent being that has reason and reflection and
can consider itself as itself, the same thinking thing in different times and
places."[5] Locke's definition of person, like Kierkegaard's of self, is essentially reflexive. And although, like Descartes's cogito argument, it makes
essential use of the notion of self-consciousness, and although it allows for
the identities of "person" and "man" to diverge, it still does not treat them
as distinct substances. But Locke's distinction isn't Kierkegaard's either.[6]
To be a person, for Locke, is to be a self-conscious subject, something that
any normal adult human being is. However, for Kierkegaard a normal,
adult human being is "not yet" a self and does not naturally develop into
one as an infant might be said to grow into being a Lockean person (see
SUD, 58–59/SKS 11, 174). Indeed, given that despair is the failure to be a
self and that despair is said to be (almost?) universal (SUD, 22–28/SKS 11,
138–144), it would seem that selfhood is a rare achievement and most
normal adult humans, although they are Lockean persons, are not
Kierkegaardian selves.[7]

[3] René Descartes, *Meditations on First Philosophy*, in *Selected Philosophical Writings*, trans. John
Cottingham, Robert Stoothoff, and Dugald Murdoch (Cambridge: Cambridge University Press,
1988), 116.
[4] See John Locke, *An Essay Concerning Human Understanding*, ed. John Yolton (London: Everyman
Books, 1993), Book II, chapter 27, §6.
[5] Locke, *Essay*, Book II, chapter 27, §9.
[6] For an interesting discussion of Locke in a Kierkegaardian context, see Patrick Stokes, *The Naked
Self: Kierkegaard and Personal Identity* (Oxford: Oxford University Press, 2015), chapter 1.
[7] It is worth noting that there could be creatures that are not of our species but that could still be
characterized in the way that Kierkegaard characterized a human being – as a synthesis of the finite

The conclusion that most human beings are "not yet" selves can be mitigated by noting that Kierkegaard does not actually think of selfhood as an all-or-nothing state; it comes in degrees: "Generally speaking, conscious- ness – that is, self-consciousness – is decisive with regard to the self. The more consciousness, the more self; the more consciousness, the more will; the more will, the more self. A person who has no will at all is not a self, but the more will he has, the more self-consciousness he has also" (SUD, 29/SKS 11, 145). So a human being may be more or less of a self in Kierkegaard's sense. And, as the quote just given makes clear, self-consciousness also comes in degrees for Kierkegaard. But it seems that a human being who ranks very low on Kierkegaard's scale should still be self-conscious enough to be able to pass Locke's test for being a person. Indeed, even "the man of immediacy" of whom Kierkegaard says "a self he was not and a self he did not become" (SUD, 52/SKS 11, 168) is presumably still able to consider himself as himself in different times and places, and thus count as a person for Locke.

Degrees of Selfhood and Types of Despair

Kierkegaard's concept of the "self," then, is not to be identified with Descartes's concept of the mind or soul or Locke's concept of the person. Even if a human being as such is "not yet" a self, still a self is a human being (one that has succeeded in becoming a self). So what is the relation between a self and a human being, and what indeed is a "human being" in Kierkegaard's sense? We need to be careful with the language here. As we have just seen, when Kierkegaard talks about a "human being" he is assuming it to be a conscious subject (not just a physical organism as a behaviorist might consider it); and much of the debate about "personal identity" or "selfhood" in recent analytical philosophy seems to concern the "human being" in this sense, rather than the (Kierkegaardian) self. So, although it is true that, as Patrick Stokes says, "Kierkegaard's articulations of the self are thoroughly non-substantialist,"[8] putting it that way could be misleading. Kierkegaard does not think of the "self" in his technical sense as a substance, but it doesn't follow that he would reject the idea that a

---

and the infinite, etc. – perhaps members of intelligent alien species. I will continue to use his term "human being" in this discussion but without intending to suggest that what he says could not in principle apply to beings other than those of our species. I will also continue to use the term without addressing the difficult question of whether there could be creatures that are biologically members of the human species but that cannot be characterized as Kierkegaard characterizes human beings – e.g., persons with severe brain damage. I'm not aware that Kierkegaard anywhere directly addresses this issue.

[8] Stokes, *The Naked Self*, 13; see also 145.

"self" or "person" in the sense that these terms mostly have in recent analytical debates about personal identity is a substance. He certainly was not interested in defending what is often presented as the main alternative to substantialist views – the reductionist or "bundle" theory of the self advocated by neo-Lockeans such as Derek Parfit.[9] Indeed, although Kierkegaard isn't directly engaging in that debate, his position seems to me compatible with a variety of substantialist views, including a non-straw-man version of dualism,[10] and a neo-Aristotelian hylomorphism, as well as the view of P. F. Strawson, who defined a person as a unitary substance to which both material and psychological predicates can properly be ascribed.[11] Strawson particularly insists that "person" is a "primitive concept," not one that can be analyzed into more basic components of mind and body, and also that persons, so understood, are categorically different kinds of entity from mere physical objects. I think Kierkegaard could be quite happy to accept that this describes (albeit not fully or adequately) what (in his terminology) "a human being" is. And so he could be quite happy to accept that you and I are, actually, substances.

What is inadequate about Strawson's definition was pointed out by Harry Frankfurt, who noted that Strawson referred only to "states of consciousness" rather than of self-consciousness as defining marks of persons, and thus failed to distinguish between human (and perhaps other, nonhuman) persons and subpersonal animals.[12] This isn't – and wasn't taken by Frankfurt to be – a critique of Strawson's substantive claims. Frankfurt was wanting to add something to Strawson's account that is, I think, perfectly compatible with it. However, by so doing Frankfurt shifts the debate about the nature of persons away from Strawson's metaphysical account to issues of moral psychology that are much closer to Kierkegaard's concerns. According to Frankfurt, the distinguishing mark of a person "is to be found in the structure of a person's will."[13]

[9] According to this approach, the self is simply a collection or "bundle" of particular mental states or events (thoughts, feelings, sensations, etc.) and not something over and above those states that "has" them. See, e.g., Derek Parfit, *Reasons and Persons* (Oxford: Oxford University Press, 1984), part 3.

[10] See, for example, Charles Taliaferro, "The Promise and Sensibility of Integrative Dualism," in *Contemporary Dualism: A Defense*, ed. Andrea Lavazza and Howard M. Robinson (London: Routledge, 2014).

[11] See P. F. Strawson, *Individuals: An Essay in Descriptive Metaphysics* (London: Methuen, 1959), 101–102. For his critique of what he calls the "no-ownership theory" – basically a reductionist bundle theory – see 94–103.

[12] Harry Frankfurt, "Freedom of the Will and the Concept of a Person," in *The Importance of What We Care About* (Cambridge: Cambridge University Press, 1988), 11.

[13] Frankfurt, "Freedom of the Will," 12.

A person is not only a conscious subject but a conscious subject that is able to have second-order desires, or, more to the point, second-order volitions. That is, a person has the ability to stand back from their potentially conflicting first-order desires and identify with some of them while repudiating others.[14] This seems close to Kierkegaard's concept of the self, especially as it not only adds self-consciousness to Strawson's picture but makes the will central to personhood. For Kierkegaard's account of self-hood is an active and dynamic one; I am not just passively aware of myself as a continuing subject through time but am constantly taking up an attitude toward myself, shaping myself through time.[15] This is why "the self is freedom" (SUD, 29/SKS 11, 145).[16]

Kierkegaard initially defined the self as a "relation" but then modified or expanded that claim to "the self is the relation's relating itself to itself" (SUD,13/SKS 11, 130). He wanted to emphasize that selfhood does not just consist in the fact of a relation (as perhaps one could say that water consists in a relation between hydrogen and oxygen) but in the activity of relating. Hence the self is not something that carries out an act of relating and can then sit back, as it were, once that activity has been completed and the relation established. To be a self is to be constantly working at synthesizing the polarities of one's being. It is a continuous task. What the self relates are the properties that it possesses as a human being. Again, one needs to emphasize that the self is not one thing and the human being another; a human being *is* a Kierkegaardian self to the extent that it properly relates to itself or continues in properly relating itself to itself. Being a self is a way in which a human being can be or – in despair – fail to be.

What then is a human being as such (whether or not it succeeds in becoming a Kierkegaardian self)? "A human being is a synthesis of the infinite and the finite, of the temporal and the eternal, of freedom and necessity" (SUD, 13/SKS 11, 130). So even when considered as "not yet" a self, a "human being" is a synthesis, not just an indifferent substratum in which properties inhere, as though they might simply sit indifferently

---

[14] Frankfurt, "Freedom of the Will," 16–19. The repudiated desires may still have a compulsive power over the person who repudiates them – hence Frankfurt's example of the unwilling addict (17–18).

[15] For an account of Kierkegaardian self-shaping, which distinguishes it from the more radical notion of self-constitution, see Anthony Rudd, *Self, Value, and Narrative: A Kierkegaardian Approach* (Oxford: Oxford University Press, 2012).

[16] For Frankfurt, one can be a person but (like his unwilling addict) not free, freedom for him being the ability to make one's will effective.

alongside one another (as a book might be red and oblong and heavy).[17] The properties of a human being with which Kierkegaard is concerned might indeed be thought contradictory (how can one be both infinite and finite?). In effect though what he gives us are three polarities. A human being is finite, limited, but (unlike a stone, say, which is also finite) it has a drive to transcend its limits. So a human being is not simply a "synthesis" in the way that water is a synthesis of hydrogen and oxygen but an inherently unstable synthesis, an (ideally creative) tension between forces pulling in opposite directions. Which is why, if a properly balanced synthesis is to be maintained, it must take charge of actively synthesizing itself. Selfhood, unlike natural processes of human maturation, is not something that just happens automatically. Note though that a human being that is not, or not much of, a self (like the "man of immediacy" mentioned earlier) is still a synthesis but an unbalanced one. A human being cannot simply slough off its finitude or its infinitude; if it exaggerates one and represses the other, it lives on as a synthesis of the two – though a distorted one. (Kierkegaard gives vivid descriptions of ways in which the polarities of infinitude and finitude and of freedom and necessity may become unbalanced in SUD, 29–42/SKS 11, 145–157.)

That a human being is finite is obvious enough. We are mortal; we occupy only limited amounts of space; we have certain capacities and not others. We are also "infinite" in that we can think and imagine beyond the boundaries of our finite nature. (For instance, we can only see so far, and in so much detail, but a theoretical physicist can think about the whole structure of space–time, the moment after the Big Bang, or the nature of elementary particles.) We are limited by necessity in that there are things about us that are simply set and fixed and that we cannot change; we are, however, also constituted by possibility in that we are not just fated to a predetermined path through life but always have options. These two polarities are very closely related; finitude and necessity are expressions of what I have elsewhere called our "immanence," our having definite natures with the limits and constraints those involve, while infinitude and possibility are expressions of what I have called "transcendence" – our ability to

---

[17] One does not need to think of a substance as a substratum in this sense; that a human being is not a characterless substratum does not imply that it can't be a substance. See Anthony Rudd, "Narrative, Expression, and Mental Substance," *Inquiry* 48, no. 5 (2007): 413–435. According to Merleau-Ponty, indeed, *no* substance should be thought of in this way. See Maurice Merleau-Ponty, *Phenomenology of Perception*, trans. Donald A. Landes (Abingdon: Routledge, 2013), part 2, chapter 3.

project ourselves beyond any definite limits.[18] We as human persons are defined by the tension between our finite given natures and our capacities to project beyond them. The basic idea is obviously not original to Kierkegaard (and it would hardly be plausible if it had been; if this is such a basic feature of the human condition it would surely have been noticed before the mid-nineteenth century). But Kierkegaard's formulation of it has a particular force and clarity and has certainly had its influence on many subsequent thinkers. For instance, Heidegger's account of Dasein (human existence) as "thrown projection" is very clearly indebted to Kierkegaard, especially as for Heidegger too this structure makes possible the "fall" into what he calls "inauthenticity" – literally not being oneself.[19]

There is less direct discussion in *The Sickness unto Death* of the third polarity – that of temporality and eternity. It does seem plausible enough to associate temporality with finitude and eternity with infinitude. It might seem though that temporality is best associated with possibility, that it is only in time that possibilities appear and are opened up. By contrast, "eternal truths" such as those of mathematics are *necessary* truths. However, the eternal truths or principles with which Kierkegaard is concerned are primarily ethical ones. Like Kant, he supposes that someone who is guided by (eternal) ethical principles is always aware that it is possible (because obligatory) to act in accordance with them, however much one may appear to be compelled by forces of natural necessity inside or outside oneself to act otherwise. In this sense, eternity correlates more to possibility and temporality to the necessities that limit the application of eternal principles in time (for instance, I cannot undo what is now past). Moreover, for Kierkegaard of course "the Eternal" is a religious as much as an ethical notion; indeed, it is inextricably both at once.[20] And the key to escaping from the kind of despair in which necessity overwhelms possibility is to have faith in the God for whom "everything is possible" (SUD, 38, 39/SKS 11, 154). Kierkegaard makes a point of distinguishing this God – eternal but ethical and interventionist – from the (Spinozistic) God of the fatalist whose "God is necessity" (SUD, 40/SKS 11, 157). (It is also true of course that eternal ethical principles are connected to necessity as well as

---

[18] See Rudd, *Self, Value, and Narrative*, 41–42. Kierkegaard doesn't define any of these terms, but his understanding of them emerges from the sections on the forms of despair generated by the imbalances in the two polarities. See SUD, 29–42/SKS 11, 145–57.

[19] See Martin Heidegger, *Being and Time*, trans. John Macquarrie and Edward Robinson (Oxford: Blackwell, 1962), division I, chapter V B.

[20] In *Purity of Heart* (UDVS, 3–154/SKS 8, 120–249) "God," "the Good," and "the Eternal" are used throughout essentially as synonyms.

possibility, since they are concerned with what should be done – with normative necessity.) On the other side of Kierkegaard from a Spinozistic determinist, who sees everything "under the aspect of eternity" and thus as necessary,[21] is Heidegger, for whom Dasein is indeed a synthesis of necessity and possibility but not a synthesis of temporality and eternity. Without eternal principles from which to take its bearing, Dasein just *is* temporality, and Heidegger interprets the structure of thrown projection itself as that of temporality, with the past representing the limiting, constraining factor of necessity and finitude, the future standing for openness and possibility and the present as the "moment" (also an important Kierkegaardian term) of decision.[22] But Dasein is constrained by no eternal principles (normative necessities), only the brute-fact constraints of the situation into which it has been "thrown." I will return later to the implications of this view and its contrast with Kierkegaard's.

A self is a human being that is actively taking responsibility for shaping or "synthesizing" itself; freedom (as we have seen) and thus responsibility are predicates only applicable to selves (so not to sub-personal animals).[23] But since one is responsible for whether or not one becomes a self, becoming a self cannot be something that happens either by chance or necessity; it is itself a free and responsible act. That means it must be the act of a self, and so only someone who already is a self can become a self. Kierkegaard is well aware of the apparent paradox here, which he had grappled with throughout the pseudonymous literature that preceded *The Sickness unto Death*. For instance, Judge William in *Either/Or* claims, in his account of ethical self-choice, that the ethical self "has not existed before, because it came into existence through the choice." But he is careful to immediately qualify this claim: "and yet it has existed, for it was indeed 'himself.'"[24] An aesthete who chooses to become ethical does not simply disappear, to be replaced by a new being, an ethical self. Rather, the same continuing person chooses to order and organize his or her desires and plans under the guidance of ethical principles. Similarly, it cannot be *literally* true that the "man of immediacy" mentioned above "has no self"; if that were true, he would simply be a piece of nature, not to be held

[21] Benedict de Spinoza, *Ethics*, in *A Spinoza Reader: The* Ethics *and Other Works*, ed. Edwin Curley (Princeton, NJ: Princeton University Press, 1994), book II, proposition 44, corollaries 143–144.
[22] See *Being and Time*, division II, chapters 3 and 4.
[23] It is important to distinguish *freedom* from *possibility*. Possibility is an aspect of the human being as such, but freedom involves more than simply following up possibilities as whim or desire may take one; it is the active taking up of possibilities (in a way that it is also cognizant of our necessities).
[24] E/O 2, 215/SKS 3, 206.

responsible. Kierkegaard sometimes uses terms in different senses according to the rhetorical needs of a particular passage. However, I think his considered view is that a "human being" is always a self in the minimal sense of having the *capacity* to be an active self-synthesizer but may or may not choose to activate that capacity, or to activate it fully, or make good use of it.

These failures constitute different forms of despair, which Kierkegaard devotes a good deal of attention to classifying and distinguishing. The lowest form of despair is "not to be conscious of oneself as spirit" (SUD, 44/SKS 11, 160). Yet not to be conscious of that, and therefore not conscious that one is in despair, is nevertheless despair; and to be unaware of oneself as spirit does not mean that one ceases to be spirit. Indeed, it is the awareness of oneself as spirit, and the fear of the demand for self-realization (for becoming a self in the sense of a complete or adequate synthesis) that this places on one, that motivates the repression of this knowledge; for the ignorance of one's nature as spirit is not just an innocent mistake or something that could simply be corrected by better information. Discussing the Socratic thesis that sin is ignorance, "that he who does not do what is right has not understood it," Kierkegaard agrees up to a point but then adds that the person hasn't understood what is right "because he is unwilling to understand it, and this again because he does not will what is right" (SUD, 95/SKS 11, 208). One might, however, think that this charge cannot apply to the "spiritless" person, since he or she does not really *will* at all but simply acts on the strongest desire of the moment. Such a character, who "is completely dominated by the sensate and the sensate-psychical [who] ... lives in sensate categories, the pleasant and the unpleasant" (SUD, 43/SKS 11, 158), might be compared to Frankfurt's "wanton," who has first-order desires but no second-order volitions. Hence the wanton "is not concerned with the desirability of his desires themselves ... Not only does he pursue whatever course of action he is most strongly inclined to pursue, but he does not care which of his inclinations is the strongest."[25] This seems to be a good description of at least a certain kind of Kierkegaardian aesthete. Frankfurt's wantons include sub-personal animals and young children, but he considers it possible that they could include some adult – and rational – humans as well.[26] Presumably the former kinds of wantons can't help being wantons. While Frankfurt seems unconcerned with the question of whether this may be true even of his possible rational adult wantons, Kierkegaard certainly holds that wantonness for such beings is always at some level a kind of

---

[25] Frankfurt, "Freedom of the Will," 17.   [26] Frankfurt, "Freedom of the Will," 16–17.

choice – minimally, a refusal to make the effort to exercise self-control that any normal adult person could have made. Although he talks of the despair of "spiritlessness" (SUD, 45/SKS 11, 159), the people who fall into this category are not literally spirit-less, but they try to pretend to themselves that they are.

Other forms of despair are marked by a greater degree of self-consciousness; that is, they involve some degree of awareness "of having a self in which there is something eternal." (That involves, as noted above, it having a recognition of its responsibility to nonrelativistic ethical principles and, ultimately, to God.) The first subset of these forms of despair is the despair of weakness, which recognizes the goal of living as spirit but does not find the strength to do so (SUD, 49–67/SKS 11, 165–180). The second kind of conscious despair is the despair of defiance, which self-consciously wills to be, not as God would have it be but as it itself wills to be. The despairer in this sense does have

> consciousness of an infinite self. This infinite self, however, is really only the most abstract form, the most abstract possibility of the self. And this is the self that a person in despair wills to be, severing the self from any relation to a power that has established it ... he himself wants to compose himself by means of being the infinite form. (SUD, 67–68/SKS 11, 182)

One can understand why Kierkegaard, with his strong theistic convictions, would deplore this quest to be the self one has chosen for oneself to be without reference to God, but it might seem strange to find this strong-willed character being classified as lacking in self. Surely he or she[27] is a (Kierkegaardian) self in four senses: she or he has the capacity for active self-formation; is aware of having that capacity (unlike the "spiritless"); has actualized that capacity (unlike the "weak"); and has by so doing created a self in the sense of a consistent self-formed personality. To see why Kierkegaard nevertheless considers such a person not so much as a bad self but as still not fully a self, we need to go back to a crucial aspect of his understanding of selfhood that we have not yet considered.

The Self in Relation to God

Having set out the basic ideas I have been unpacking so far in his initial definition, Kierkegaard continues: "Such a relation that relates itself to itself, a self, must either have established itself or have been established by another ... the human self is such a derived, established relation, a relation

---

[27] Although Kierkegaard does declare this kind of despair characteristically "masculine" at SUD, 49/SKS 11, 165.

that relates itself to itself and in relating itself to itself relates itself to another" (SUD, 13–14/SKS 11, 130). Its ideal state, "when despair is completely rooted out, is this: in relating itself to itself and in willing to be itself, the self rests transparently in the power that established it" (SUD, 14/SKS 11, 130). *The Sickness unto Death* is written throughout from an explicitly Christian point of view, and "the power that established" the self is clearly intended to be understood as God. It is true that specifically Christian theological themes are only brought in – at least in an explicit way – in Part Two of *The Sickness unto Death*. Still, even in Part One we can see that God is both origin and *telos*. We were made by God, for a relationship to God, and human fulfillment consists in that proper relation to God. In *The Sickness unto Death* Kierkegaard assumes his claim about the self as having been established by God rather than arguing for it. If there is an argument for it in his work, it is to be found in the whole rich phenomenology of the quest for selfhood that runs through the pseudonymous writings. The various forms of aesthetic existence and of nonreligious (or not decisively religious) ethical existence leave something deep in us unsatisfied, which only can be satisfied by an authentic Godrelationship. Thus the whole pseudonymous literature could be regarded as an extended illustration of Augustine's famous statement: "You have made us for yourself, and our hearts are restless till they rest in You."[28] (This is of course very close to Kierkegaard's own wording: the self resting transparently in the power that established it.) In *The Sickness unto Death* Kierkegaard is sketching this understanding of selfhood in summary form. The more or less clearly perceived need for God that drives one through the stages of life (or that one resists – it is not an automatic process) is a result of the self being essentially constituted by its relation to God. This is not an external relation that the self may or may not choose to enter into; it is an internal relation, that is, one that makes the self what it is. (Both in that, for Kierkegaard, the human being is created by, and always sustained in being by, God, but also because full selfhood involves the self relating to itself by self-consciously – "transparently" – relating to God.) And just as we remain syntheses of the finite and infinite etc. whether we synthesize them in a properly balanced way or not, so we remain essentially – constitutively – related to God, whether we recognize it or not and whether or not we live this God-relationship properly. It should be noted

---

[28] Augustine, *Confessions*, trans. Henry Chadwick (Oxford: Oxford University Press, 1991), 3. For an Augustinian reading of Kierkegaard's corpus, see Lee Barrett, *Eros and Self-Emptying: The Intersections of Augustine and Kierkegaard* (Grand Rapids, MI: William Eerdmans, 2013).

that, although Kierkegaard's is an essentially theological account of the self, it is still one that gives the self an essential freedom to make or fail to make itself fully a self. It must therefore be sharply distinguished from any kind of theological determinism that would take the self to be simply a given entity, made by God so that it must be, ineluctably, what God has made it to be. "God, who constituted man a relation, releases it from his hand as it were ... upon it [the self] rests the responsibility for all despair at every moment of its existence" (SUD, 16/SKS 11, 132).

The alternative to his account that Kierkegaard explicitly notes (the self establishing itself) was probably intended mainly as an allusion to Fichte's idealist theory of the self. For Fichte, the self is constituted by its awareness of itself, and, as pure activity rather than substance, has no nature apart from, or prior to, its self-awareness. Accordingly, he argues, the self cannot depend on anything other than itself, but "posits" itself through its own self-awareness (and then posits the non-self so as to have resistance to define itself against).[29] What, though, of more naturalistic or materialist theories, according to which the self isn't "established" by either itself or God but emerges naturally from more basic physical processes? Kierkegaard doesn't discuss philosophical materialism in *The Sickness unto Death*, but I think he would say that materialism cannot recognize the reality of the self at all (that is, in his sense, as a free, dynamic activity of self-synthesizing). For materialism there are just psycho-physical processes associated with (and ultimately determined by) the physical states of a particular organism. Materialism has no conception of self as "spirit" in the Kierkegaardian sense, and therefore whatever account it may give of the emergence of psychological processes is not an alternative to either the Kierkegaardian or the Fichtean accounts of the establishment of the self.[30]

Is this fair to materialism? I think it is true that the more radical forms of materialism are incompatible not only with Kierkegaard's idea of selfhood but even with much more modest and everyday notions of ourselves as (self-)conscious agents. (And some of them are indeed happy to present

---

[29] "*That whose whole being or essence consists simply in the fact that it posits itself as existing* is the self as absolute subject. As it *posits* itself, so it *is*." J. G. Fichte, *The Science of Knowledge*, trans. Peter Heath and John Lachs (Cambridge: Cambridge University Press, 1982), 98.

[30] Moreover, just to twist the knife a bit further, Kierkegaard would, I think, consider philosophical materialism – as a philosophy that denies the reality of spirit and freedom – to be the intellectual equivalent of the practical materialism of the "spiritless" "man of immediacy" discussed earlier (SUD, 43/SKS 11, 158) or an expression of the "philistine-bourgeois mentality," which is also defined as "spiritlessness" (SUD, 41, 157). (Fichte also interpreted theoretical materialism as an expression of the self's self-deceptive flight from its own freedom. See Fichte, "First Introduction," in *The Science of Knowledge*.)

themselves as such, as offering revolutionary alternatives to our everyday "folk psychology," which they seek not to reform but to abolish.[31]) However, many contemporary philosophers embrace some form of non-reductive naturalism, which tries to avoid those extremes while still seeing the mind as emerging in a smoothly "natural" way from more basic physical processes. Of course, "naturalism" is a notoriously vague term,[32] and there is a large range of views that claim to be both naturalistic and nonreductive.[33] Whether one can really retain our ordinary mentalistic self-understanding within an otherwise naturalistic framework is indeed one of the major philosophical issues of recent times. Whether or to what extent one could be a naturalist and still maintain a specifically Kierkegaardian conception of the self is a less explored issue. Some forms of naturalism are liberal enough to be compatible with theism;[34] they might in that case be compatible with a wholly Kierkegaardian understanding of the self. It is an interesting question whether other nontheistic versions of naturalism could consistently maintain an account of the self as an autonomous self-shaping agent that was robust enough to count as an alternative account of spirit to Kierkegaard's and Fichte's rather than simply as a denial of spirit. I suspect that, in order to do so, one would need to stretch the notion of naturalism so far that it would risk losing any significant content. But this is (unfortunately!) too large a question to explore further in this context.

The self is a (self-relating) relation that also relates as a whole to another (the power that established it). These two relations (the relation of the self to itself and its relation to God) cannot be understood independently of one another, and so neither can their misrelation: "The misrelation in that relation which is for itself also reflects itself infinitely in the relation to the power that established it" (SUD, 14/SKS 11, 130). One cannot relate properly to God if the elements in the synthesis are unbalanced. So, for instance, an exaggeration of infinitude results in a fantasized form of

---

[31] In particular, the "eliminative materialism" of Paul and Patricia Churchland and (with a few qualifications) Daniel Dennett. See, e.g., Paul Churchland, *Scientific Realism and the Plasticity of Mind* (Cambridge: Cambridge University Press, 1979); Patricia Churchland, *Neurophilosophy* (Cambridge, MA: MIT Press, 1988); D. Dennett, *Consciousness Explained* (Harmondsworth: Penguin, 1991)

[32] It is sometimes used more or less as a synonym for materialism, sometimes for something more expansive.

[33] See, for example, Mario De Caro and David Macarthur, eds., *Naturalism in Question* (Cambridge, MA: Harvard University Press, 2008); and Lynne Rudder Baker, *Naturalism and the First-Personal Perspective* (Oxford: Oxford University Press, 2013).

[34] See, for example, Fiona Ellis, *God, Value, and Nature* (Oxford: Oxford University Press, 2017).

religious existence "which can so sweep a man off his feet that his state is simply an intoxication" (SUD, 32/SKS 11, 148). On the other hand, an exaggeration of necessity over possibility results in the fatalism mentioned earlier, which is also incompatible with a proper relation to God: "The fatalist's worship of God is at most an interjection and essentially it is a muteness, a mute capitulation; he is unable to pray" (SUD, 40/SKS 11, 157). But one can also look at the problem the other way around; it is the failure to relate properly to God that throws the synthesis out of balance. It is as though the potentially centrifugal tensions within the self can only be held together in the creative tension that is ideal selfhood if the self as a whole is directed toward God. So we can see the fantasist's tendency to lose hold of concrete reality as due to his fantastical conception of God (regarded not just as an intellectual mistake in theology, of course, but as a practical notion of God that is yet so abstract that it cannot be lived in concrete circumstances). And it is because the fatalist cannot conceive of God or relate to God as other than "necessity" that he or she is unable to have a live sense of possibility or hope. It isn't a question of choosing between two rival accounts of causality here – does the misrelation in the self cause the misrelation with God, or does the misrelation with God cause the misrelation in the self? Both kinds of misrelation go together, as two sides of a coin.

Self-Constitution without a Telos?

Kierkegaard's theory is strongly teleological in a twofold sense. First, it posits the goal of becoming a self through synthesizing the potentially conflicting aspects of the personality and, second, it claims that this can only be done through the self as a whole directing itself to an external reality. And this is not just some external reality or other (perhaps a person, a community, a cause) but, quite specifically, God, and it is only through relating to God that the self can synthesize itself and thus find fulfillment and wholeness.[35] The account is basically and irreducibly normative; the self can only find its good by relating to The Good. Kierkegaard is certainly well aware that even a self that "rests transparently" in God will have other goals and other relationships and that they may be of great importance for one's sense of who one is. One does not relate to God *instead* of relating, for

---

[35] *Pace* Dreyfus, who claims that "Any such unconditional commitment to some specific individual, cause, or vocation, whereby a person gets an identity and a sense of reality, would do to make the point that Kierkegaard wants to make." Hubert L. Dreyfus, "Kierkegaard on the Self," in *Ethics, Love, and Faith in Kierkegaard: Philosophical Engagements*, ed. Edward F. Mooney (Bloomington: Indiana University Press, 2008), 16.

example, to other human beings, to communities, to causes, to vocations, etc. But the God-relationship provides the normative criterion for determining what other relationships to pursue, and how to do so (lovingly, not obsessively or selfishly). So we may have many *teloi* (goals) that may be of deep importance to us, but only God is our ultimate or unconditional *telos*.

Among those who agree with Kierkegaard that the self is an actively self-shaping being (so not just an epiphenomenon of, or reducible to, neuro-logical processes and also not just given by divine *fiat*) some have argued for a (rather more modest kind of) neo-Fichtean view of the self as established (or constituted) by itself. I have already noted that Heidegger gives a strikingly Kierkegaardian account of the self (Dasein) as "thrown projection." Dasein is not a given being with a determinate nature but a project of self-shaping (despite its own tendency to fall into inauthenticity and to pretend to itself that it has a substantial nature): "The 'essence' [Wesen] of this entity lies in its 'to-be' [Zu-sein]. Its being-what-it-is (*essentia*) must, in so far as we can talk of it at all, be conceived in terms of its Being (*existentia*)."[36] But I have also noted his insistence that Dasein is not a synthesis of the eternal and the temporal but pure temporality. In taking responsibility for directing itself it has no *telos*; no constituent other to which it needs to relate; and no "eternal" principles to which it can look for direction. These ideas were taken up by Sartre[37] and given a more explicitly and dramatically neo-Fichtean touch: "Existence precedes essence ... man first of all exists – and defines himself afterwards ... to begin with he is nothing, he will not be anything until later and then he will be what he makes of himself."[38] But this seems remarkably close to what Kierkegaard had diagnosed a century earlier as the despair of defiance: "Severing the self from any relation to a power that has estab-lished it ... the self in despair wants to be master of itself or to create itself, to make his self into the self he wants to be, to determine what he will have or not have in his concrete self" (SUD, 68/SKS 11, 182). Our "infinitude" may make this seem a possibility but only through neglecting our finitude. The "infinite form of the negative self" may step back from the "natural capacities, predispositions, etc." (SUD, 68/SKS 11, 182) that it has, but "no derived self can give itself more than it is in itself by paying attention to itself – it remains itself from first to last" (SUD, 69/SKS 11, 182). And

---

[36] Heidegger, *Being and Time*, 67. I should say that I am only concerned here with the "early" Heidegger of *Being and Time*; the later Heidegger moved away considerably from this decisionism.

[37] Although Sartre puts these ideas in a different context from Heidegger's, and his overall philosophical project is substantially different.

[38] Jean-Paul Sartre, *Existentialism and Humanism*, trans. Philip Mairet (London: Methuen, 1948), 28.

given the lack of any positive *telos* or principles that might give this
"negative self" criteria for what to make of itself, its projects in the
end become indistinguishable from whims and can be abrogated as soon
as the self-creative self decides to. As a result, "the self in despair is
always building only castles in the air, is only shadowboxing" (SUD,
69/SKS 11, 182).

This is why – to revert to the question I raised at the end of the second
section – the self-willed self, whatever its intensity and concentration, is,
for Kierkegaard, ultimately not (fully) a self. Because there is nothing it
takes itself to be responsible to, its projects of self-creation have in the end
a fantastical, unreal quality. Untethered to the eternal and identifying only
with its aspects of infinitude and possibility, the self remains merely
abstract, a capacity for negation that can never make itself anything
genuinely concrete.[39] Such notions of self-constitution are not confined
to the Continental tradition. Frankfurt, as we have seen, is concerned with
how our second-order volitions enable us to identify with some, but not
other, desires. However, he claimed that this is a capacity that doesn't only
define us as being persons but enables us to constitute ourselves: "The
decision [the second-order volition] determines what the person really
wants by making the desire on which he decides fully his own. To this
extent, the person in making a decision by which he identifies with a
desire, *constitutes himself* . . . These acts of ordering and rejection . . . create
a self out of the raw materials of inner life."[40]

Frankfurt rejects any kind of ethical or normative realism; for him as for
Sartre there are no normative constraints on which desires one should
identify with or, therefore, on what self one should (self-)create. But nor
then are there any criteria for when or whether one should change the self
one has made or in what direction. As a number of critics have pointed

---

[39] Sartre would not really disagree with this; for him, the human subject *is* essentially a negating force
("Nothingness") that is however haunted by the impossible desire to become something substantial,
hence a "useless passion" (Jean-Paul Sartre, *Being and Nothingness*, trans. Hazel Barnes (New York:
The Philosophical Library, 1956), 615). Heidegger, by contrast, seems to have tried to avoid
arbitrary decisionism by taking the authentic life to involve simply a conscious choosing of those
possibilities that one's culture and history have in fact made available to one. But this seems to
threaten us with social or cultural conformism – a lurch back from exaggerating infinitude to
exaggerating finitude. In any case, since those historical possibilities will typically be multiple, it's
not clear that this proposal does really avoid decisionism. See Lawrence Vogel, *The Fragile "We":
Ethical Implications of Heidegger's* Being and Time (Evanston, IL: Northwestern University Press,
1994), chapters 2 and 3.
[40] Harry Frankfurt, "Identification and Wholeheartedness," in *The Importance of What We Care
About*, 170.

out, Frankfurt's position seems to end up as emptily decisionistic as Sartre's.[41] However, Frankfurt has in his more recent work played down the decisionistic elements, arguing that "[a] person's will is real only if its character is not absolutely up to him ... It cannot be unconditionally in his power to determine what his will is to be ... Therefore, we cannot be authors of ourselves ... We can be only what nature and life make us, and that is not so readily up to us."[42] His final position seems to be that what desires we identify with depends on what we care about, and what we care about is shaped, beyond our control, by "nature and life" – by the evolutionary history of our species and by the accidents of our personal histories.[43] Yet now it seems that his initial distinction between persons and "wantons" has become relativized. A person does assess his or her first-order desire in the light of higher-order basic cares and commitments. But these are not themselves assessed in terms of any overriding normative principles; they are, in the last analysis, just accepted as brute facts. Is this really more than higher-level wantonness? From a Kierkegaardian perspective, Frankfurt has shifted from an unbalanced stress on infinitude and possibility to an unbalanced stress on finitude and necessity. The constant factor though is his rejection of the "eternal" normative principles, the orientation that Kierkegaard sees as necessary for the synthesis of these centrifugal tendencies. Without them, from a Kierkegaardian standpoint, the project of self-shaping collapses either into arbitrary decisionism or into a surrender to brute contingencies.[44]

The point of the last few paragraphs has not, of course, been to refute the complex thinkers I have skimmed over in them. (There are also, of

---

[41] See Gary Watson, "Free Agency," in *Free Will*, 2nd ed., ed. Gary Watson (Oxford: Oxford University Press, 2003); Charles Taylor, "Responsibility for Self," in *The Identities of Persons*, ed. Amélie Rorty (Berkeley: University of California Press, 1976); Susan Wolf, "Sanity and the Metaphysics of Responsibility," in *Free Will*; and Susan Wolf, "The True, the Good, and the Lovable: Frankfurt's Avoidance of Objectivity," in *Contours of Agency: Essays on Themes by Harry Frankfurt*, ed. Sarah Buss and Lee Overton (Cambridge, MA: Bradford Books/MIT Press, 2002).
[42] Harry Frankfurt, "The Faintest Passion," in *Necessity, Volition, and Love* (Cambridge: Cambridge University Press, 1999), 100–101.
[43] See Harry Frankfurt, *The Reasons of Love* (Princeton, NJ: Princeton University Press, 2004).
[44] For detailed Kierkegaardian critiques of Frankfurt see Rudd, *Self, Value, and Narrative*, chapters 4 and 5; John J. Davenport, *Narrative Identity, Autonomy, and Mortality: From Frankfurt and MacIntyre to Kierkegaard* (New York: Routledge, 2012), 100–114. Anthony Rudd and John J. Davenport's *Love, Reason, and Will* (London: Bloomsbury, 2015) collects a number of papers exploring both the commonalities and the differences between Kierkegaard's and Frankfurt's moral psychologies.

course, many other relevant thinkers I have not discussed.[45]) I have tried, however, by indicating briefly the problems with their theories that appear from a Kierkegaardian perspective, to bring out how their accounts both resemble and differ from Kierkegaard's own. And I do also hope to have at least indicated why I think Kierkegaard's unabashedly normative and metaphysical account of the self and its self-formation has real advantages over its rivals.

[45] For example, Christine Korsgaard (see her *The Sources of Normativity* (Cambridge: Cambridge University Press, 1996) and *Self-Constitution: Agency, Identity, and Integrity* (Oxford: Oxford University Press, 2009)), who ties her account of self-constitution to a supposedly Kantian ethics; and Jürgen Habermas who, in *The Future of Human Nature*, trans. Hella Beister and William Rehg (Cambridge: Polity Press/Blackwell, 2003), suggests replacing Kierkegaard's God with the human linguistic community. I discuss Korsgaard in *Self, Value, and Narrative*, chapter 5, and have some critical comments on Habermas in Anthony Rudd, "Kierkegaard and the Critique of Political Theology," in *Kierkegaard and Political Theology*, ed. Roberto Sirvent and Silas Morgan (Peabody, MA: Pickwick Publications, 2018).

CHAPTER 4

From Here to Eternity
Soteriological Selves and Time

Patrick Stokes

The Great Discoveries

Discussions of *The Sickness unto Death* tend to start from the infamous opening passage, with its forbidding ontology of the self. Instead, let's begin near the end of the book, where the pseudonymous author Anti-Climacus deploys one of Kierkegaard's characteristically striking analogies:

> The situation of the guilty person traveling through life to eternity is like that of the murderer who fled the scene of his act – and his crime – on the express train: alas, just beneath the coach in which he sat ran the telegraph wires carrying his description and orders for his arrest at the first station. When he arrived at the station and left the coach, he was arrested – in a way, he had personally brought his own denunciation along with him. (SUD, 124/SKS 11, 235)

Why start with this analogy? Because it is perfectly emblematic of two crucial aspects of *The Sickness unto Death* that are easily overlooked if we simply dive straight into the schematic account of how the self (*selv*) emerges from the synthetic structure of the person (*menneske*) and how this structure plays out in the diagnosis of despair (*fortvivlelse*). Uncovering and understanding these two aspects are, as we will see, enormously helpful in discerning just what Anti-Climacus is up to in this book.

The analogy brings together Kierkegaard's two examples of the "great discoveries" or "great inventions" (*store Opdagelser*) (JP 4, 4233/KJN 10, NB32:9/SKS 26, 123) of the age: the railway and the telegraph. For Kierkegaard's contemporaries, these references were not merely modern but cutting edge: Though the book would not appear in print until 1849, Kierkegaard wrote *The Sickness unto Death* in the politically tumultuous period of March to May 1848 (SUD, ix), less than a year after Denmark

61

proper's first railway line opened between Copenhagen and Roskilde[1] and only four years after Samuel Morse sent the message "What hath God wrought?" to demonstrate the Washington, DC–Baltimore telegraph line. Kierkegaard had used the word "telegraph" several times in his writings before this point but generally in reference to the optical telegraph (lamp signals).[2] A detail that gets lost in the Hong translation is that Anti-Climacus actually writes *elektromagnetiske Telegraph* – the technology is so new that he needs to specify which form of telegraphy he's talking about.

It's also worth noting in passing that *The Sickness unto Death* is somewhat neutral about the technology itself, whereas Kierkegaard's subsequent journal references to the telegraph will be particularly caustic.[3] The two "great discoveries" are also, spiritually speaking, great disasters – but if Kierkegaard has already formed this negative view of Morse's invention by the time he wrote *The Sickness unto Death*, he doesn't let on.[4]

One thing that's easy to overlook about this vignette, however, is that this is not actually how telegraphs work. That Kierkegaard apparently thought telegraph lines ran under train carriages may be a simple and excusable confusion (they did often run *alongside* train tracks) given how new the technology was, but there's something more going on in the strange image of the telegraph message *riding along with* the *already* condemned man in his railway carriage. Moreover, while the technology is new-fangled, the topic – eternal salvation – is one that by Kierkegaard's time had become "an old-fashioned turn of speech no longer used but retained only because it is so quaint" (EUD, 254/SKS 5, 251). This reference to new technology is deployed in the service of a vision of final judgment that a Hegel-inflected strand of European modernity had begun to jettison. Like the book as a whole, the analogy is, first, a dialectical interplay of modern and antimodern and, second, suffused with the

---

[1] Holstein, which was ruled by Denmark until lost in the Second Schleswig War of 1864, had opened a railway line between Kiel and Altona in 1844.
[2] For example, see FT, 39/SKS 4, 133; CD, 340/SKS 16, 139.
[3] For example: "Rejoice, O human race, that you have invented the telegraph; be proud of your discovery which is so appropriate to the times, calculated to lie on the greatest possible scale" (JP 6, 6911/SKS 26, 150). I discuss Kierkegaard's attitude to the telegraph and his wider attack on the media in Patrick Stokes, "Kierkegaard's Critique of the Internet," in *Kierkegaard and Contemporary Ethics*, ed. Mélissa Fox-Muraton (Berlin: De Gruyter, 2020).
[4] Kierkegaard uses a further railway metaphor elsewhere in *The Sickness unto Death*: To ignore the state of a sinner at the times between individual sinful acts is "just as superficial as supposing that a train moves only when the locomotive puffs. No, this puff and the subsequent propulsion are not what should be considered but rather the steady impetus with which the locomotive proceeds and which produces that puffing. And so it is with sin" (SUD, 106/SKS 11, 218).

distinctive dual temporality of soteriology, the temporality of the "moment" (*øjeblikket*), which we will describe later.

With that in mind, let's now loop right back to the start of the book and to that forbidding structure of selfhood. As we'll see, this interplay of modern and antimodern and of temporal and eternal is there right from the outset.

The Non-Substantialist Self

It's sometimes suggested that the infamous opening pages of Part One section A of *The Sickness unto Death* are intended as a parody of the impenetrable prose of Hegel or at least of the Danish Hegelians.[5] Yet Kierkegaard himself was perfectly capable of deploying his own dense, schematic text, as anyone who has read the unfinished *Pars Secunda* of *Johannes Climacus* or *De Omnibus Dubitandum Est* can attest. Even so, the language of *The Sickness unto Death*, at least at this point in the text, is unmistakably contemporary.

One thing that's strikingly modern about *The Sickness unto Death*'s account of selfhood is its nonsubstantialism. Like just about every other discussion of mind and self since the seventeenth century, Descartes's account of selfhood haunts *The Sickness unto Death*, at least in the references later in the book to the infamous *cogito ergo sum* formulation (SUD, 119–120/SKS 11, 231). That shouldn't surprise us: The from-the-inside character of Descartes's meditations, the way in which first-person experience leads to a perspectivally grounded problem about foundations ("how do I know any of this is real?"), is very much in keeping with the tenor of Kierkegaard's method. Descartes wants to find a transcendent ground for experience; Anti-Climacus is concerned to ground the self such that it "rests transparently" in its ontological source (*grunder Selvet gjennemsigtigt i den Magt, som satte det*) (SUD, 14/SKS 11, 130). Both, in other words, end up reasoning from the first-person perspective back to God, albeit a somewhat abstracted God.

Where Descartes and Anti-Climacus diverge, however, is partly methodological – Descartes uses a priori reasoning to secure the existence of the thinking subject, and then of a God who would not allow this subject to be systematically deceived by our senses, while Anti-Climacus sets up a structure of selfhood and then proceeds to explain various psychological

---

[5] On the relationship between Kierkegaard and Danish Hegelianism see, for example, Jon Stewart, *Kierkegaard's Relations to Hegel Reconsidered* (Cambridge: Cambridge University Press, 2003).

phenomena in terms of it – and partly in the metaphysics that emerges as a result. For Descartes, what I am turns out to be a "thing that thinks" (*res cogitans*). On the assumption that thought and matter are categorically different, this yields, through a chain of fairly straightforward deductions, a thinking subject that is immaterial and so nonextended and therefore indivisible – meaning it is also incorruptible and therefore immortal. A classically Greek (and specifically Platonic) answer to an early modern problem: We are immaterial souls.

Anti-Climacus, however, is having none of this; his self is no ghost in the machine. He does indeed use the word "soul" (*sjel*) but does *not* identify it with what we fundamentally *are* as Descartes does and does not freight it with metaphysically dualist assumptions either. *Sjel*, for Anti-Climacus, simply names the mental or psychical dimension of the human being.[6] From a Platonic-Cartesian perspective, that mental component is what we fundamentally *are*. That conclusion also serves to eternalize the self by making it indivisible and so immortal. For Anti-Climacus, no such escape into one dimension of what we are at the expense of the others is possible; to identify exclusively with one "pole" of the dyads that make up a person (finite–infinite, possible–necessary, etc.) to the exclusion of the other pole is precisely despair. (Just as, for Sartre a century later, this would be bad faith.) The Anti-Climacan self is not an unchanging immaterial entity locked inside a fleshy prison. Rather, *sjel* is one of the components of a human being (*menneske*), and it is this compound entity that can, by relating to itself in a particular way, *become* a self (*selv*). It cannot do this in isolation from the body or social context.

Hence while there are Platonic as well as Aristotelian elements in Anti-Climacus's account, he also goes beyond these, as both Merold Westphal[7] and John Davenport[8] have argued. It's precisely this idea of selfhood as a state to be achieved that marks this difference. You're a Platonic soul or Cartesian *res cogitans* or an Aristotelian synthesis of form and matter no matter what you do. No sooner do you apprehend that this is what you are

[6] The Hongs usually render *sjel* as "psychical" or similar. Alastair Hannay has argued for translating the term as "soul," but as "soulish" isn't available, he has sometimes had to use terms like "psychical" in his own translations. Alastair Hannay, "Spirit and the Idea of the Self as a Reflexive Relation," in *International Kierkegaard Commentary: The Sickness unto Death*, ed. Robert L. Perkins (Macon, GA: Mercer University Press, 1987), 23–38, at 23.
[7] Merold Westphal, "Kierkegaard's Psychology and Unconscious Despair," in *International Kierkegaard Commentary: The Sickness unto Death*, ed. Robert L. Perkins (Macon, GA: Mercer University Press, 1987), 39–66.
[8] John J. Davenport, "Selfhood and 'Spirit,'" in *The Oxford Handbook of Kierkegaard*, ed. John Lippitt and George Pattison (Oxford: Oxford University Press, 2013), 230–251.

than it becomes apparent that this is what you already were. A Kierkegaardian self, by contrast, is something you must try to become, may fail to be – and can apparently easily lose (SUD, 33/SKS 11, 148). Selfhood is an achievement of self-relation on the part of the human being.

Described in these terms, selfhood seems less like a Cartesian ghost or a reborn Platonic soul looking to shake off its temporary embodiment and rejoin the Forms, and more like an emergent property of the human animal. The idea that selfhood is an emergent property – a property of a system that emerges as the parts of that system interact, yet which the parts do not possess on their own – would seem to fit just as well with the predominant physicalist metaphysics of our own era as with nineteenth-century idealism. Just as consciousness can be viewed as an emergent property of matter, a property of brains that only comes into being as huge numbers of neurons interact with each other without each neuron being conscious in itself, so too selfhood/spirit could here be understood as an emergent property of the human animal, something that supervenes upon a distinctive kind of organism when it performs a distinctive kind of action or puts itself into a particular state, namely, self-relation. The physicality of the Kierkegaardian self would be important to any such interpretation: For all Anti-Climacus's talk of *sjel* in declaring the self to be a synthesis of the physical and the mental, we are a long way from the Platonic-Cartesian identification of the self with a nonphysical mind that can exist independently of the body after death.

But as Kierkegaard often reminds us: not so fast. While there is something deeply modern in *The Sickness unto Death*'s picture of selfhood, there is something pulling equally hard in the other direction too. While a tripartite, synthetic structure of selfhood immediately reminds us of Hegel (and his acolytes in Kierkegaard's Copenhagen), Anti-Climacus's anthro-pology also directly echoes Luther. Luther too holds that human beings are composed of spirit, soul, and body, corresponding to Anti-Climacus's categories of self, mind, and body. The soul in this picture was not to be understood as a bearer of full personhood that survives death as a conscious entity, as in Descartes. That idea, Luther insisted, was a Platonic – and thus pagan – interpolation into Christianity, and worse, one that gave license to the Catholic doctrine of purgatory and thus of the practice of indulgences. Rather than a *modern* rejection of the soul doctrine, Luther wanted to strip original Christianity of its non-Christian accretions. Just as self (which for Anti-Climacus is coterminous with "spirit" [*aand*]) is a higher category than body and mind in *The Sickness unto Death*, so too for

Luther it is through spirit that we are "enabled to lay hold on things incomprehensible, invisible, and eternal."[9]

It's easy to look at the structure of *The Sickness unto Death* and conclude, as many have, that the first part of the book is a work of philosophical anthropology while the second part is theological. On that reading, the first half furnishes us with a very modern and largely religiously neutral philosophical psychology, to which the second half adds a theological overlay of sin and judgment. In fact, as the Lutheran basis of the tripartite anthropology might indicate, the account of selfhood we get in the first part is far more deeply concerned with matters of salvation than we might think. The Anti-Climacan self is a soteriological self right from the outset.

Selfhood and Judgment

Questions of "selfhood" in contemporary philosophy tend to be understood as metaphysical questions that are conceptually prior to ethical ones. Personal identity (for the most part, philosophers working on these topics use "self" and "person" interchangeably) is of course central to ethical practices of blaming, praising, rewarding, and punishing,[10] and so questions about what selves are have obvious and pressing ethical implications. We can't punish someone unless we're sure they're the same person as the one who did the nefarious deed. But the assumption is that we need to get clear on what selves are first, *before* we can say what any particular self happens to be responsible for.

This has not always been the case. Problems of personal identity were, for most of the previous millennium, understood primarily as questions about personal salvation. The early church fathers scrambled to come up with a biology, a physics, and a metaphysics that would ensure that those living now would be identical to the bodies that would be resurrected to receive their doom on the Day of Judgment.[11] The metaphysics waited on the ethics, not the other way around. That motivation is still central as late as 1690, in John Locke's "Of Identity and Diversity" chapter in *An Essay*

---

[9] Martin Luther, *Works* XXI, ed. Jaroslav Pelikan and Hilton C. Oswald (St. Louis, MO: Concordia House, 1956), 303.

[10] Marya Schechtman notes that personal identity is essential to four features of our experience that we are practically concerned with: survival, moral responsibility, self-interested concern, and compensation. See her *The Constitution of Selves* (Ithaca, NY: Cornell University Press, 1996).

[11] On the origins and history of this discussion see, for example, Raymond Martin and John Barresi, *The Rise and Fall of Soul and Self* (New York: Columbia University Press, 2006).

Concerning Human Understanding. That chapter is justly viewed as instituting contemporary discussions of personal identity – but this is largely true insofar as the contemporary discussion took on board Locke's focus on psychological continuity across time as constitutive of personhood, while quietly setting aside his soteriological concern for "the Great Day, wherein the Secrets of all Hearts shall be laid open."[12] Questions that in early modernity were still recognizably about survival and final judgment came out the other side of the Enlightenment as questions about persistence and continuity across time. The moral questions were still there of course, but they sat downstream of a metaphysics that was assumed to be, in itself, normatively neutral. Moral facts, such as what you are answerable for (on the Great Day or any other day) were understood to supervene upon nonmoral facts about what you are.

By Kierkegaard's time, the concept of individual, personal salvation remained a tenet of everyday religious belief but was increasingly coming to be rejected in scholarship.[13] A Left-Hegelian position had emerged, with analogues in figures such as Feuerbach, that saw the afterlife not as a continuation of individual conscious existence but as a sort of sublation of the individual person into a higher or universal category. Kierkegaard's favorite teacher, Poul Martin Møller, had criticized both this religiously unorthodox view and the attempts of Right Hegelians to insist Hegel's view of the afterlife was a Christianly orthodox one. Johan Ludvig Heiberg, the leading Hegelian of Kierkegaard's Denmark, was telling lecture audiences as early as 1834, just three years after Hegel's death, to think of immortality not as something to befall us in the future but as something to be achieved here and now.[14] The situation among the

---

[12] John Locke, *An Essay Concerning Human Understanding*, ed. Peter H. Nidditch (Oxford: Clarendon Press, 1975), 344. For attempts to recover this aspect of Locke see Raymond Martin and John Barresi, *Naturalization of the Soul: Self and Personal Identity in the Eighteenth Century* (London: Routledge, 2000); Udo Theil, *The Early Modern Subject: Self-Consciousness and Personal Identity from Descartes to Hume* (Oxford: Oxford University Press, 2011); Galen Strawson, *Locke on Personal Identity: Consciousness and Concernment* (Princeton, NJ: Princeton University Press, 2011). I discuss Locke and Kierkegaard at length in Chapter 1 of Patrick Stokes, *The Naked Self: Kierkegaard and Personal Identity* (Oxford: Oxford University Press, 2015).

[13] Todd Weir, "The Secular Beyond: Free Religious Dissent and Debates over the Afterlife in Nineteenth-Century Germany," *Church History* 77, no. 3 (2008): 629–658. On the history of this debate in Kierkegaard's intellectual context and Kierkegaard's own reaction to it, see Tamara Monet Marks, "Kierkegaard's 'New Argument' for Immortality," *Journal of Religious Ethics* 31, no. 1 (2010): 143–186.

[14] Robert Leslie Horn, *Positivity and Dialectic: A Study of the Theological Method of Hans Lassen Martensen* (Copenhagen: C. A. Reitzel, 2007), 104. On this see Patrick Stokes, "The Science of the Dead: Proto-Spiritualism in Kierkegaard's Copenhagen," in *Kierkegaard and the Religious Crisis of the 19th Century*. Acta Kierkegaardiana IV, ed. Roman Králik, Peter Šajda, and Jamie Turnbull

Danish Hegelians is perhaps best summed up by an anecdote recorded in Johanne Louise Heiberg's memoirs about the horrified reaction of her mother-in-law – the writer Thomasine Gyllembourg:

> The two gentlemen [Heiberg and Martensen] had discussed Hegel's view that the immortality of individuals was dissolved in the entire great universe. At this Heiberg's mother was completely beside herself. Again and again she came back, in increasing stages of undress, as she attacked the doctrine. To this attack Heiberg only responded, "Go to bed, it's late." "Merge together!" she exclaimed, "Do you think I will merge together with the many loathsome drops?" – "Go to bed!"[15]

It should come as little surprise that the anonymous author whose work spurred Kierkegaard to write *Two Ages* shares Anti-Climacus's concern for individuation in the context of final judgment. As Vigilius Haufniensis, Kierkegaard had earlier taken a subtle dig at Heiberg's hit comedy "A Soul After Death" (perhaps unfairly) for taking ethical judgment out of his vision of immortality.[16] In both *The Sickness unto Death* and *Practice in Christianity*, Anti-Climacus fights a rearguard action against attempts to separate the concept of immortality from that of judgment. Heiberg had insisted that the contemporary age wanted quasi-mathematical proofs of the truth of Christianity.[17] In the discourse "There Will Be the Resurrection of the Dead, of the Righteous – and of the Unrighteous" Kierkegaard declares that desire for such proofs to be itself a sort of evasion of the truth of immortality: "Nothing is more certain than immortality; you are not to worry about, not to waste your time on, not to seek an escape by wanting to demonstrate it or wishing to have it demonstrated. Fear it, it is only all too certain; do not doubt whether you are immortal – tremble, because you are immortal" (CD, 203/SKS 10, 212).

To philosophical eyes, this is putting the normative cart before the metaphysical horse: Surely we must *first* determine whether and to what extent we survive death and what sort of judgment we might face there and *then* decide whether that's something to fear? But Anti-Climacus wants us to understand the notion of immortality, of eternity, as normative all the

(Slovakia: Kierkegaard Society in Slovakia and Kierkegaard Circle, University of Toronto, 2009), 132–149.

[15] Jon Stewart, *A History of Hegelianism in Golden Age Denmark, Tome I: The Heiberg Period: 1824–1836* (Copenhagen: C. A. Reitzel, 2007), 548.

[16] "Some envision eternity apocalyptically, pretend to be Dante, while Dante, no matter how much he conceded to the view of imagination, did not suspend the effect of ethical judgment" (CA, 153/SKS 4, 452).

[17] Marks, "Kierkegaard's 'New Argument' for Immortality," 152–153 n16.

way down. That applies too to the self that is the bearer of that soteriological judgment. Anti-Climacus does not want to construct an account of what selves are and *then* show us that this self is immortal and subject to final judgment. His self, *qua* spirit, is a subject of soteriological judgment in its very constitution.

In a somewhat Hegelian moment, Anti-Climacus presents us with the idea of the self as coming to a more adequate actualization of itself by engaging with fuller and fuller "criteria":

> And what infinite reality [*Realitet*] the self gains by being conscious of existing before God, by becoming a human self whose criterion is God! A cattleman who (if this were possible) is a self directly before his cattle is a very low self, and, similarly, a master who is a self directly before his slaves is actually no self – for in both cases a criterion is lacking. The child who previously has had only his parents as a criterion becomes a self as an adult by getting the state as a criterion, but what an infinite accent falls on the self by having God as the criterion! (SUD, 79/SKS 11, 193)

The allusion to Hegel's discussion of recognition and the master–slave dynamic in *The Phenomenology of Spirit* is quite blatant. For Hegel, self-consciousness must win itself in an encounter with another through a sort of mutual recognition, but the recognition offered by the slave, being merely compelled, is inadequate for the master's self-consciousness. Anti-Climacus's cattleman is in a much worse position: Before cattle, one can be no more than whatever a cow could recognize one to be. What is missing is a *higher* criterion against which one is both to recognize *and* *evaluate* oneself. Crucially, though, that evaluation is ethical: For the self, "that which is its qualitative criterion [*Maalestok*] is ethically its goal [*Maal*]" – and if one finds that one has *not* measured up to this criterion, "a person must himself have merited this disqualification" (SUD, 79–80/SKS 11, 193).

So becoming a self is already a moral matter. The self is not a morally neutral substrate that then bears moral predicates; rather *to be* a self is a moral imperative and a moral achievement. Every human being is "a psychical-physical synthesis [*sjelelig-legemlig Synthese*] intended to be spirit (SUD, 43/SKS 11, 158) and "primitively intended to be a self" (SUD, 33/SKS 11, 149); just to be a human being is to have a normative teleology of individual selfhood one can fulfill or fail. The self before cattle is not merely an undeveloped self (or rather, a human being who has not attained selfhood) but *culpably* undeveloped. Key to this account is that the very individuation of human beings is itself a normative category linked to the notion of soteriology – in a way that cuts against Hegelian visions of an afterlife of sublation into universal spirit.

For Anti-Climacus, the Hegelian position that sets "the generation over the individual" ends up melding all people together "in what Aristotle calls the animal category – the crowd" and ultimately amounts to a sort of blasphemous deification of the mob (SUD, 118/SKS 11, 229). Yet something like this is also unavoidable for speculative thought, just insofar as it must, by definition, deal with universals and can only comprehend individuals as tokens of those universal types. And "just as one individual person cannot be thought, neither can one individual sinner" (SUD, 119/SKS 11, 230).

What individuates us into specific persons is ultimately not our biology or our place in a family, society, or state, but *sin*. The sinner *is* the single individual, something that escapes comprehension through the categories of speculative, abstract thought (SUD, 119/SKS 11, 230). Each of us, for Anti-Climacus, is already a sinner, but it is only when we confront this that we encounter ourselves in a *fully* individuated way, rather than being at least partly taken up in these larger biological or social categories. Thinking of oneself as a sinner is a necessary condition for comprehending oneself as a single individual. While the concept "human" brings each individual human being under this species-concept, Anti-Climacus insists that even the doctrine of original sin "does not gather men together into a common idea, into an association, into a partnership" any more than the dead form a category or a society (SUD, 120/SKS 11, 231). Yet this has a whiff of paradox about it: How can each of us be sinners and yet sin not be a universal predicate under which every person falls?

The answer is that sin, for Kierkegaard, is ultimately linked to judgment. We might speak of collective guilt and may find ourselves in situations where it is practically impossible to punish all the guilty, but even in these cases the guilty must be judged individually if they are judged at all:

> The concept "judgment" corresponds to the single individual; judgment is not made *en masse*. People can be put to death *en masse*, can be sprayed *en masse*, can be flattered *en masse* – in short, in many ways they can be treated as cattle, but they cannot be judged as cattle, for cattle cannot come under judgment. No matter how many are judged, if the judging is to have any earnestness and truth, then each individual is judged. (SUD, 123/SKS 11, 234)

The callback to the image of cattle is clearly no accident. The undifferentiated nature of cattle (at least on Anti-Climacus's assessment, which is perhaps unfair to cows) means that just as they cannot provide a criterion against which to judge oneself *as* a self, so too they cannot be fit objects for judgment. To be judgeable is to be individuated, and to be individuated just is to be open to scrutiny before a judge. Before cattle, nobody is a self at all, but "before God they were and are continually single individuals; the person sitting in a showcase is not as embarrassed as every human being is in his transparency before God. This is the relationship of conscience" (SUD, 124/SUD 11, 235).

In other words, becoming judgeable is not something that happens to a self after it has been established; rather, it is constitutive *of* selfhood. To be a self is to be *finally* answerable.

The Temporality of Despair and Eternity

Once judgment gets into the picture though, we find ourselves in a curious temporal bind. A *final* judgment occurs at the end, not in the temporal flow of life but in eternity, "when the hourglass has run out, the hourglass of temporality" (SUD, 27/SKS 11, 143). Anti-Climacus dramatizes the point thus: "'Now I have spoken,' declares God in heaven; 'we shall discuss it again in eternity. In the meantime, you can do what you want to, but judgment is at hand'" (SUD, 122/SKS 11, 234). Judgment, it seems, is to happen in eternity, and eternity has not yet come for us but will do so in the future[18] – and yet, "judgment is at hand." Likewise, people are selves through judgment, and yet they are not *only* to become single individuals in eternity; "before God they were and are continually single individuals" (SUD, 124/SUD 11, 235).

This double temporality in fact runs throughout *The Sickness unto Death* – not just in the second part's overtly theological thematization of temporality.[19] As the Introduction makes explicit, the contrast between

---

[18] As Roe Fremstedal notes, for Kierkegaard, the Good and the Eternal are conceptually linked in a curiously Platonic way, and the eternal is "both unchangeable and the root of time itself, including the future (particularly the eschatological future)." See Roe Fremstedal, "Demonic Despair under the Guise of the Good? Kierkegaard and Anscombe vs. Velleman," *Inquiry* (2019): 1–21, at 15. On the relationship between eschatology and the direction of time in Kierkegaard, see Patrick Stokes, "Fearful Asymmetry: Kierkegaard's Search for the Direction of Time," *Continental Philosophy Review* 43, no. 4 (2010): 485–507.

[19] On the relationship between philosophy and theology in *The Sickness unto Death* see Amber Bowen, "Reviving the Dead: A Kierkegaardian Turn from the Self-Positing to the Theological Self," *Religions* 10, no. 633 (2019): 1–18. C. Stephen Evans claims that while our grounding relationship need not necessarily be toward God, the ontology of selfhood in the opening of *The Sickness unto Death* is nonetheless theologically grounded, while Alastair Hannay claims the book is in fact theological throughout: Despair is already a flight from God (that is, sin) from the outset. C. Stephen Evans, "Who Is the Other in *Sickness unto Death*? God and Human Relations in the

mortal time and eternity is set up in the very title of the book, taken from John 11:4. The resurrection of Lazarus is an event in a life, and so Jesus's declaration that "This sickness is not unto death" means, in one sense, that contrary to appearances Lazarus's life has not yet concluded. Yet in another sense there is something radically discontinuous between the Lazarus who enters the tomb and the Lazarus who leaves; a revived Lazarus who could still die is not yet truly saved from death. Foreshadowing Jesus's own resurrection, Lazarus now lives in a state in which he has *overcome* death soteriologically: "Of what good would it have been to Lazarus if He were not He who is the resurrection and the life for everyone who believes in Him!" (SUD, 7/SKS 11, 123–124). "Humanly speaking, death is the last of all" (SUD, 7/SKS 11, 124), whereas Christianity teaches that death is in fact *not* death but a passage to eternal life.

The thesis of the book is that despair (*fortvivlelse*, etymologically an intensification of *tvivl*, "doubt") is the titular sickness unto death. Yet this disease, unlike that which put Lazarus in his tomb, is temporally quite different from other forms of physical malady. If you recover from, say, cancer, you might get it again. Recovery from *fortvivlelse*, in contrast to other forms of illness or infirmity, has a once and for all character. To overcome this particular disease is to overcome the possibility of relapse: "Not to be in despair must signify the destroyed possibility of being able to be in despair; if a person is truly not to be in despair, he must at every moment destroy the possibility" (SUD, 15/SKS 11, 131). That claim, again, is temporally paradoxical: If we are not in despair we *have destroyed* the possibility of despair but also must *destroy* the possibility at every moment.

Moreover, once you have contracted a physical illness, the disease is already underway, on a trajectory from a past origin to a future resolution. We sometimes say we're "getting a cold," but what this really means is that we *have* a cold and the symptoms are yet to fully manifest. The disease already exists as an actuality. With despair, however, actuality and possibility are not temporally related in this way but collapsed into each other: "Every actual moment of despair is traceable to possibility; every moment he is in despair he *is bringing* it upon himself. It is always the present tense; in relation to the actuality there is no pastness of the past: in every actual moment of despair the person in despair bears all the past as a present in possibility" (SUD, 17/SKS 11, 132–123).

Despair is not something that a disease process does to us but something we are doing to *ourselves*. And just as the present-tense character of despair cancels out the temporal distance between the etiology of a disease and its existence as a disease (as if I already had the cold the moment I decided to visit my coughing, sneezing friend), so too despair cancels out the idea of a time *before* I became sick. If someone develops a fever now, "it can by no means be said that it is now apparent that he has had a fever all his life" (SUD, 24/SKS 11, 140). Yet with despair that is exactly how it is: When someone despairs, "it is immediately apparent that he has been in despair his whole life" (SUD, 24/SKS 11, 140).

Despair then is a disease where once you have it you have *always* had it, while you have it you're still giving it to yourself, and once you're cured of it you can never get it again – except that to despair is to fail to be a self, and according to Anti-Climacus you *can* indeed lose yourself, "the greatest hazard of all" (SUD, 33/SKS 11, 148). How are we to make sense of such a temporally self-contradictory pathology?

The answer is to be found in Anti-Climacus's reminder that we are dealing here not with a psychological complaint but with a disease of the spirit. While it may be true, as Merold Westphal tells us, that Kierkegaard is doing a kind of clinical psychology,[20] the asymptomatic despair that Anti-Climacus describes would be completely unintelligible to the contemporary clinical psychologist: How can someone be psychologically sick and yet perfectly comfortable and suffering no deficits of function?[21] Once we are talking about spirit [*aand*] – one level up from both body and *sjel* and the diseases that attend them – we enter a different kind of temporality: "Despair is a qualification of spirit and relates to the eternal in man" (SUD, 17/SKS 11, 133).

Kierkegaard's understanding of the eternal is neither univocal nor immutable, yet he is aware of the temporal duplexity of speaking of eternity as early as *Either/Or*, where Judge William tells us that one who marries "solves the great riddle, to live in eternity and yet to hear the cabinet clock strike in such a way that its striking does not shorten but lengthens his eternity, a contradiction that is just as profound as, but far

---

[20] Westphal, "Kierkegaard's Psychology and Unconscious Despair," 40.
[21] Equally, as Gordon Marino points out, Kierkegaard's claim that one is depressed but spiritually healthy also makes little sense to our contemporaries. Gordon Marino, *Kierkegaard in the Present Age* (Milwaukee, WI: Marquette University Press, 2001), 103.

more glorious than, the one in the familiar situation described in a story from the Middle Ages about a poor wretch who woke up in hell and shouted, 'What time is it?' – whereupon the devil answered, 'Eternity!'" (EO2, 108/SKS 3, 137). To "lengthen eternity" is an obvious contradiction, and yet like "infinity plus one" it is nonetheless thinkable for temporally emplaced beings like us. The condemned person waking up in hell seeks to orient themselves according to clock time, but they have in fact arrived at a "time" outside time. And yet despite this arresting image, eternity is absolutely *not* to be understood, as we're told in the discourse known as "Purity of Heart Is to Will One Thing," as "like a new world, so that the person who had lived in time according to the ways of time and busyness, when happy and well he had arrived in eternity, now could try his hand at adopting the customs and practices of eternity" (UDVS, 66/ SKS 8, 174). Likewise, the *Christian Discourses* tell us that "Immortality is not a continued life, a continued life as such in perpetuity," as if eternal life is *temporally* continuous with earthly life. Rather, "immortality is no continuation that results as a matter of course but a separation [between the righteous and the unrighteous] that results from the past" (CD, 205/ SKS 10, 214).

This curious dual temporality, of living in time *and* eternity, simultaneously within and without time, is instantly recognizable as Kierkegaard's concept of the moment (*Øjeblikket*, cognate with the German *augenblick*, "the glance of an eye"). The moment, as Vigilius Haufniensis puts it in *The Concept of Anxiety*, is "that ambiguity in which time and eternity touch each other, and with this the concept of temporality is posited, whereby time constantly intersects eternity and eternity constantly pervades time" (CA, 89/SKS 4, 392). This intersection is only possible insofar as eternity appears as a judgment of our lives in time. Once we posit the eternal, understood as final judgment, we are always living simultaneously in time and eternity, always both in the midst of our life and looking over the totality of it in concern for our soteriological fate. This has the effect, Kierkegaard tells us in "Purity of Heart," of turning each moment into "the eleventh hour," for judgment looms at every moment equally regardless of where we might be up to in the course of our biological lives. As Davenport puts it, we find ourselves both in the middle of our story and yet "already dead and our story finished, absolutely unchangeable."[22] Each moment is experienced, to borrow a phrase from Kierkegaard's discourse

---

[22] John J. Davenport, *Narrative Identity, Autonomy, and Morality: From Frankfurt and MacIntyre to Kierkegaard* (New York: Routledge, 2012), 161.

"At a Graveside," "as if it were the last and also the first in a long life" (TDIO, 96/SKS 5, 464) or at least as long as the actuaries will allow us. Each moment is just one more instant in your life and *also* the moment at which you stand accountable for the whole.

In *The Sickness unto Death*, this dual temporality expresses itself in the present-tense character of despair. The eternal, by definition, cannot be gotten rid of, and so if the self in despair tries to do so, "at any moment that he does not have it, he must have thrown it or is throwing it away – but it comes again, that is, every moment he is in despair he is bringing his despair upon himself" (SUD, 17/SKS 11, 133). Despair is a disease we are always coming down with and always giving ourselves. Anti-Climacus describes despair as "to die death" (*at døe Døden*) (SUD, 18/SKS 11, 134), which also has a curious temporality: "For to die signifies that it is all over, but to die death means to experience dying, and if this is experienced for one single moment, one thereby experiences it forever" (SUD, 18/SKS 11, 134). The reverse of this is that once despair has been eradicated, it is gone for good – even though, as we've seen, Kierkegaard thinks selfhood can indeed be lost, implying this disease *can* return.

The only way to make sense of this confusing, apparently self-contradictory picture is to realize that we are dealing with the temporality of *final* judgment as it appears *within* a life that is still underway. If despair were simply a psychological malady, like depression for example, it would make sense to ask questions like "Am I in despair again?" or to say things like "I have been in despair several times." But despair, on Anti-Climacus's telling, just won't let us say that, because despair is a matter of spirit and therefore the eternal. In the eternal, despair is a qualification of a whole life, one that stands outside of temporal extension:

> Eternity asks you and every individual in these millions and millions about only one thing: whether you have lived in despair or not ... And if so, if you have lived in despair, then, regardless of whatever else you won or lost, everything is lost for you, eternity does not acknowledge you, it never knew you – or, still more terrible, it knows you as you are known and it binds you to yourself in despair. (SUD, 27–28/SKS 11, 143)

Viewed as *menneske*, as human beings, we each live extended in time, our lives structured by biological limitations and social expectations. Viewed as *aand*, spirit, each of us lives in eternity. As such, each moment of our lives has eternal and soteriological significance. Each of us, whatever our age or health, is partway through a *totality* that will be judged in eternity – but as that judgment can come at any time, and as it will be outside of time, it is as true to say we *will be* judged in eternity as that we *already have been* judged. We answer for a life that is not yet complete, yet were we to be judged right now, there is *already* a fact of the matter about whether we are damned or saved. This double bind finds expression in one of Anti-Climacus's most striking images: "Essentially, everyone arrives in eternity bringing along with him and delivering his own absolutely accurate record of every least trifle he has committed or omitted. Thus a child could hold court in eternity; there is really nothing for a third party to do, everything down to the most insignificant word spoken is in order" (SUD, 124/SKS 11, 235).

When the account of our life is "held up to the light in eternity while eternity is auditing the consciences" (SUD, 124/SKS 11, 235), the action of the judge turns out to be superfluous: Even a child can do it, for it is simply a matter of reading off what one has done. (As Surah 17:30–31 in the Qur'an puts it, "And [for] every person We have fastened his fate upon his own neck, and We will produce for him on the Day of Resurrection a record which he will encounter spread open. [It will be said], 'Read your record. Sufficient is yourself against you this Day as accountant.'") When we die, our life simply is what it is. The facts are all there. And the clock is always striking eleven.

Express Train to Eternity

This brings us back, at last, to where we started: with the jarringly modern image of a murderer on a train pursued by telegram.

The two "great discoveries" of Kierkegaard's half-century, the railway and the telegraph, both have above all *temporal* implications for human life. Both radically transform the relationship between time and physical distance. (In the case of the railways, time itself becomes transformed into a relationship to timetables rather than the sun.) So it's fitting that the slightly mangled telegraph analogy in *The Sickness unto Death* is such a neat embodiment of the dialectical temporality of soteriology.

The central image in the analogy is not of the crime, or of the trial and execution, but of the murderer suspended at a moment between these two points. His crime lies behind him, his judgment ahead, and he is speeding forward uncontrollably into a future that contains a reckoning that, at this point, is still unknown to him. The future remains open, but progress toward it cannot be stopped. We are reminded here of a much earlier Kierkegaardian analogy of forward momentum, as offered by Judge William in *Either/Or*:

Imagine a captain of a ship the moment a shift of direction must be made; then he may be able to say: I can do either this or that. But if he is not a mediocre captain he will also be aware that during all this the ship is ploughing ahead with its ordinary velocity, and thus there is but a single moment when it is inconsequential whether he does this or does that. So also with a person – if he forgets to take into account the velocity – there eventually comes a moment where it is no longer a matter of an Either/Or, not because he has chosen, but because he has refrained from it, which also can be expressed by saying: Because others have chosen for him – or because he has lost himself. (EO 2, 163/SKS 3, 161)

Yet here, we might think, is where Anti-Climacus's analogy breaks down: The murderer has not in fact "personally brought his own denunciation along with him." A telegram is not like a letter that can only travel at the same speed as the person carrying it. In fact, this apparent infelicity is precisely the dialectical brilliance of the analogy: The telegram is not travelling at the same speed as the train coach but at the speed of light – in effect, instantaneous and hence no speed at all, meaning it is already at its destination at all moments of the train's journey. The murderer's fate was already sealed from the moment the train embarked. Yet this is not a statement of metaphysical determinism or fatalism, as if the causal openness of the future is just an illusion created by the epistemic limitations of being on the train (the murderer simply doesn't know that news of his guilt has already arrived at the destination and that his punishment is now inevitable). Rather, this is an illustration of the dual temporality of *øjeblikket*, the temporality of soteriology. The judgment is simultaneously travelling with the condemned and already, in a sense, always-already delivered. Whether the murderer knows it or not, he is simultaneously mid-journey and being judged for the totality.

There's one other respect in which the position of the murderer on the train is like ours, at least according to the soteriological worldview that Anti-Climacus – and Kierkegaard – inhabit. The murderer is stuck. There's no realistic prospect of escape from the moving train, even if he knows he carries his doom with him. He cannot save himself by his own efforts; he can only hope to be saved in some absurd and gratuitous way. He can do nothing but throw himself on the mercy of grace.

The murderer on the train is one of Kierkegaard's most startlingly up-to-the-minute analogies, so modern in fact that he clearly wasn't entirely in command of all the relevant details. Yet it is also here deployed as part of a very antimodern project: to insist, against the comforting assurances of the Hegelians, that each of us will answer for our sins individually in eternity.

In that, it stands as an emblem of the book as a whole. Anti-Climacus is someone who is both steeped in modern philosophical understandings of the self and yet determined to preserve a premodern theological view that those understandings threaten to undo. His book is not just a diagnostic manual but a warning to the reader: The train is always just about to reach the station.

CHAPTER 5

Kierkegaard's Metaphysics of the Self

Eleanor Helms

Introduction

Martin Heidegger opens *An Introduction to Metaphysics* with the timeless question inherited from the Greeks: "Why are there beings instead of just nothing?"[1] Kierkegaard approaches this question, as does Heidegger after him, by considering not only what *is* – that is, what exists in actuality – but also the possibilities that surround existence. Understanding "beings" requires illuminating what is not "there" or "present," as Heidegger will later put it, and in fact could never become present. When the existence of a human being is in question, the relevant empty possibilities are often conceptual. In addition to concrete activities like building a bird house, we humans lead lives that are rich in abstractions. We see an animal and identify it as an instance of a kind. We seek abstract goods like "justice" and "politeness." We engage in dialectical reframings of what appears to us. This means that our activities, or what we actually do as humans, include the work of conceptualizing, even if abstraction is always rooted in lived experience.

In *The Sickness unto Death*, the activity of abstraction helps answer the central question of what it means to be a self. Rather than the text motivating us in a practical sense to *do* more, *feel* more, or *commit* more decisively, I will argue that what we mainly find in *The Sickness unto Death* is an enumeration of conceptual distinctions that enable us to notice more, question more, and reason better that is, to engage in the kinds of activities normally associated with traditional philosophy. Good philosophy of course can and should lead to doing, feeling, and committing in

---

[1] "*Warum ist überhaupt Seiendes und nicht vielmehr Nichts?*" Martin Heidegger, *Einführung in die Metaphysik* [*Introduction to Metaphysics*] (Tübingen: Max Niemeyer Verlag, 1955), §1, my paraphrased translation.

new and better ways. As Aristotle observed, the conclusion of a syllogism is sometimes an action.[2]

This is not to say that Kierkegaard is a kind of pragmatist. Steven M. Emmanuel has argued that there is no rational way to choose between belief and unbelief but that the high stakes tip the scale toward faith for practical reasons.[3] More recently, Mark Wrathall has argued that Kierkegaard describes faith as a kind of "skillful concern" (a knowing-how rather than a knowing-that).[4] Pragmatist readings of Kierkegaard, like fideistic readings, treat the conceptual apparatus of faith as all neatly in place: All that's missing is an act of will (i.e., something other than understanding) to execute the program.[5] But what we actually find in Kierkegaard are new conceptual distinctions. In *Fear and Trembling*, for example, the variations on Abraham's journey to and from Mount Moriah in the "Exordium" are changes in how Abraham understands the situation and how it is experienced by Isaac (FT, 9–14/SKS 4, 105–111). Abraham's willingness to act remains the same, but his understanding of the meaning of his action changes. Similarly, in *The Concept of Anxiety*, Haufniensis offers a dialectical description of individuals as syntheses of the temporal and the eternal, which is at the same time a synthesis of body and soul (CA, 88/SKS 4, 392). Similarly, in *Works of Love*, Kierkegaard distinguishes between preferential love and neighbor love, even when these result in the same concrete actions.

But the standard view that Kierkegaard exhorts readers away from abstract reflection is too simplistic. Without a prominent place for

[2] On how a practical syllogism results in motion toward a goal for Aristotle, see especially Klaus Corcilius, "Two Jobs for Aristotle's Practical Syllogism?" in *Logical Analysis and History of Philosophy*, ed. Uwe Meixner and Albert Newen, Focus: The Practical Syllogism/*Schwerpunkt: der praktische Syllogismus*, vol. 11 (Paderborn: Mentis, 2008), 163–184.

[3] Steven M. Emmanuel. "Kierkegaard's Pragmatist Faith." *Philosophy and Phenomenological Research* 51, no. 2 (1991): 279–302.

[4] Wrathall argues that "Kierkegaard embraces the incoherence of Christian belief," concluding that faith offers an "existential stance for hearing and responding to the world" as opposed to propositional content. Faith is "adoxal" (without content) and "praxic" (performative): "We need to carefully distinguish between the doxastic and the existential – between what's relevant to the formation of opinions or beliefs on the one hand, and on the other what's relevant to the motivation of actions or to the creation of a coherent, distinct, style of living" (Mark Wrathall, "Coming to an Understanding with the Paradox," in *The Kierkegaardian Mind*, ed. Adam Buben, Eleanor Helms, and Patrick Stokes (New York: Routledge, 2019), 243).

[5] As an example of a fideistic reading with qualifications, see C. Stephen Evans, "Kierkegaard and the Limits of Reason: Can There Be a Responsible Fideism?" *Revista Portuguesa de Filosofia* 64, no. 2/4 (2008): 1021–1035. Robert Wyllie argues that Climacus is a "heavily qualified voluntarist," adding that an intuition of the beauty of the Incarnation might tip the scales without being decisive or evidential (Robert Wyllie, "Kierkegaard's Eyes of Faith: The Paradoxical Voluntarism of Climacus's *Philosophical Fragments*," *Res Philosophica* 90, no. 4 (October 2013), 562).

abstraction, Kierkegaard's richly varied modalities of existence would be reduced to just one: empirical actuality. Yet as Haufniensis observes in *The Concept of Anxiety*, it is often possibility more than actuality that defines us, as for the hypochondriac for whom "the significant actuality is after all not so terrible as the possibility he himself had fashioned" (CA, 162/SKS 4, 460). Sometimes Kierkegaard relies on parables, metaphors, and other literary tools to attune us to possibilities (as in the variations on Abraham in *Fear and Trembling*). For some texts in particular, however, the variations are modeled after dialectical progressions and changes in modality that originate in Kant (in his catalogue of the categories, see *Critique of Pure Reason*, 212 (A80/B106)) and are taken up by Hegel.[6]

The Sickness unto Death is one such work progressing not imagistically or poetically but through methodical variations at the level of abstraction. Through these variations, we gain an understanding of an underlying self that is not reducible to its situation. Patrick Stokes's account of a "naked" self that is distinct from its concrete situation and observable qualities is closest to the view I present here. He describes such a self as a bare first-personal perspective that is a precondition for attaining full selfhood.[7] However, Stokes *contrasts* the concrete (or what he calls "phenomenal") self with its "purely formal Kantian version," whereas I take the "naked self" in Kierkegaard to be merely formal or transcendental, arrived at through reflection, as it is for Kant.[8] I argue later that Kierkegaard's naked self is importantly a naked *abstract* self ("The Abstract Self").

Moreover, while Stokes focuses on personal identity, I think *The Sickness unto Death* also speaks to the broader metaphysical question of what makes any object the same over time. Like many traditional philosophers, Kierkegaard teaches the reader to look beyond appearances: Two presentations may look different (even contradictory) and yet be appearances of the same object. The basic Kantian distinction between appearances and things in themselves gets us started here: Since a thing itself is not found in its appearances, there will always be something we don't know. For Kant, the thing in itself is more than a reminder to be humble. It serves as a rational ground for our openness to objects appearing in ways that demand new language and new ways of making sense. The

---

[6] Immanuel Kant, *Critique of Pure Reason*, trans. Paul Guyer and Allen W. Wood (Cambridge: Cambridge University Press, 2009).
[7] Patrick Stokes, *The Naked Self: Kierkegaard and Personal Identity* (Oxford: Oxford University Press, 2015), 180–186.
[8] See Patrick Stokes, "Naked Subjectivity: Minimal vs. Narrative Selves," *Inquiry* 53, no. 4 (2010): 356–382, at 361.

importance of the reader acquiring new philosophical distinctions should not be overlooked in favor of pragmatic exhortations toward decision or humility.[9]

Identity and Appearances: Competing Senses of Phenomenology

In notes about the preface to *The Sickness unto Death*, Kierkegaard writes:

> To the closing passage, "But that the form is what it is," I have thought of adding: apart from the fact that it is also rooted in my being who I am. But this would be going too far in transforming a fictitious character into actuality; a fictitious character has no other possibility than the one he is; he cannot declare that he could also speak in another way and yet be the same; he has no identity that encompasses many possibilities. (SUD, 140/SKS 22, 135)[10]

The first thing to notice in this passage is that the actual individual is not defined by action but as the one who has many possibilities. The fictitious character, by contrast, has no enduring identity underlying different actualizations. This description cuts against a prima facie tendency to associate fiction with possibility and actuality with commitment: Here the fictional character is *merely* concrete – that is, a single concretion. Second, this passage is not an exhortation toward actuality but a descriptive, third-personal characterization. It does not require or guide practical belief. It instead invokes a fundamental question in metaphysics, namely the extent to which a being can undergo change and remain itself. It deals with actuality as a metaphysical modality rather than a goal for an individual to achieve.[11] Unfortunately, scholars tend to treat categories like "possibility" in Kierkegaard as referring to concrete possibilities that are real enough to exert an "unrelenting pull," as claimed for example by

---

[9] On humility as an antidote to the pride of reason, see Evans, "Kierkegaard and the Limits of Reason," 1033. On decision, see Merold Westphal, *Kierkegaard's Concept of Faith* (Grand Rapids, MI: Eerdmans, 2014), 198.

[10] In the preface, Anti-Climacus's point is that while the form of the treatise might be confusing (seeming overly rigorous to some and not rigorous enough to others (SUD, 5/SKS 11, 117)), its level of formality has been chosen for reasons related to its (internal) content. That is, the form is "psychologically correct" (SUD, 6/SKS 11, 118). In the journal entry, he rejects adding a further (external) reason, which is that the form is related to his being as its actual author as well.

[11] By contrast, most scholars treat actuality in Kierkegaard as concrete. For example, M. G. Piety writes that "choosing oneself is a process of self-actualization" (*Ways of Knowing: Kierkegaard's Pluralist Epistemology* (Waco, TX: Baylor University Press, 2010), 35) or a lived movement from potentiality to actuality. She is cited approvingly by Wyllie, "Kierkegaard's Eyes of Faith," 553.

Daniel Dahlstrom.[12] Dahlstrom reduces the meaningful sense of "possibility" to "concretely delimited possibilities of her history"[13] and specific choices "an individual alone is forced to make."[14] But the possibilities of identity in the passage quoted above aren't something one could choose or concretely become. Understood metaphysically, a self instead includes all its *logical* possibilities – even those that could not (even in principle) be concretely enacted. (I will elaborate this distinction as it relates to the forms of despair.) I propose instead that the kind of "lived experience" toward which Kierkegaard urges us requires a philosophically rich "life of the mind," including facility with abstract concepts. To be good readers of Kierkegaard, we need to do some good metaphysics. The possibilities Kierkegaard urges us to attend to are transcendental (achieved through the work of reflection) rather than empirical (achieved through action and commitment).

Kierkegaard's relation to metaphysics is particularly relevant for *The Sickness unto Death*. It is one of a handful of texts in which Kierkegaard, through Anti-Climacus, is likely to be treated as offering a "phenomenology," in this case of despair.[15] I think we do find a phenomenology of despair in *The Sickness unto Death* but one that progresses logically and dialectically rather than experientially or first-personally. First-personal description is the defining feature of phenomenology only in the popular sense, or what John Drummond calls the narrow sense, along the lines of Nagel's "What Is It Like to Be a Bat?"[16] The kind of

---

[12] Daniel Dahlstrom, "Freedom through Despair: Kierkegaard's Phenomenological Analysis," in *Kierkegaard as Phenomenologist: An Experiment*, ed. Jeffrey Hanson (Evanston, IL: Northwestern University Press, 2011), 74. See also Ralph Henry Johnson, *The Concept of Existence in the "Concluding Unscientific Postscript"* (The Hague: Martinus Nijhoff, 1972), 174, cited in Adam Welstead, "Kierkegaard's Movement Inward: Subjectivity as the Remedy for the Malaise of the Contemporary Age," *The Heythrop Journal* (2014): 814. Emphasizing the importance of one's immediate situation, Welstead cites the following from Johnson: "What is wanted is a communication which will prompt the recipient to take a close look at *his* situation, which will induce him to raise the pertinent questions *for himself*." In the same way, Dahlstrom takes Kierkegaard to be urging a specifically nonmetaphysical viewpoint but asks whether "Kierkegaard or anyone else" can take up such a viewpoint without being in "historical bad faith" (77 note 16), given our cultural immersion in existing metaphysical concepts. In any case, what I am arguing is that abandoning metaphysical abstractions is another kind of bad faith. Abstraction and the ability to abstract are essential to consciousness. They are unavoidable not because of historical precedent but because of their necessity.

[13] Dahlstrom, "Freedom through Despair," 64.   [14] Dahlstrom, "Freedom through Despair," 65.

[15] See for example Jon Stewart, "Kierkegaard's Phenomenology of Despair in *The Sickness unto Death*," *Kierkegaard Studies Year Book (1997)*, ed. Niels Jørgen Cappelørn and Hermann Deuser (Berlin: De Gruyter, 1997), 117–143.

[16] Thomas Nagel, "What Is It Like to Be a Bat?" *Philosophical Review* 83, no. 4 (October 1974): 435–450. John Drummond distinguishes this use from phenomenology as a philosophical method.

phenomenology Kierkegaard offers is more like what Drummond calls the broader sense that we find in Husserl and Hegel. The different uses of "phenomenological" create confusion, including for Kierkegaard studies: Dahlstrom, for example, proposes a purportedly phenomenological reading but concludes that *The Sickness unto Death* presents different despairs through which a person progresses *concretely*.[17] He insists that Kierkegaard's distinctions are not theoretical but relate to "living and practicing either one of two forms of despair: fatalism or autonomy."[18] Dahlstrom's interpretation fits in with other scholarly readings, where the forms of despair are not "formal,"[19] as we find in Husserl, but real states in which a person might live, say, for two years before transitioning to another for a different period of time.[20] Confusing these is the error of treating a formal or transcendental moment as a real object of possible experience (as happens for example when thinking falls into Kant's antinomies).[21] "Formal" in Kant's sense, as I use it here, means a universal structure that does not exist as an independent object.[22] Anti-Climacus is

---

See "Moral Phenomenology and Moral Intentionality," *Phenomenology and the Cognitive Sciences* 7, no. 1 (March 2008): 35–49.

[17] Dahlstrom, "Freedom through Despair," 58–64. He writes, for example, "despair is something that we do, the effects of which are painful" (59). Theoretical accounts miss "the agent's experience of existential possibilities as part of her life, concretely delimited parts of her history for which she nonetheless experiences herself as responsible" (64).

[18] Dahlstrom, "Freedom through Despair," 64.

[19] "Formal" and "transcendental" are not interchangeable in Kant or Husserl, but I use them both here to mean nonconcrete. Michelle Grier distinguishes, for example, between the logical (subjective) – probably most appropriately called formal – and the transcendental (objective) conditions of thought, though she argues these are "the same demand for systematic unity ... merely considered in two different ways" (Michelle Grier, "Kant on the Illusion of a Systematic Unity of Knowledge," *History of Philosophy Quarterly* 14, no. 1 (1997): 14). These both function as principles rather than objects of experience.

[20] For example, Ryan Kemp raises the problem of how transitions between stages come about in "Making Sense of the Ethical Stage: Revisiting Kierkegaard's Aesthetic-to-Ethical Transition," *Kierkegaard Studies Year Book* (2011): 323–340, in which he considers the stages to be things one can *be* (e.g., one becomes an ethicist).

[21] Dahlstrom's conclusion is that the forms of despair discussed in *The Sickness unto Death* – that is, both despair and freedom – are "hidden but operative" ("Freedom through Despair," 74).

[22] For example, a formal, a priori principle of the will is one from which "every material principle has been withdrawn" (Immanuel Kant, *Groundwork of the Metaphysics of Morals*, trans. Mary J. Gregor (Cambridge: Cambridge University Press, 1997), 13/Ak. 4:400). I take Davenport to be using "formal" in the same way when he writes, "A Kierkegaardian can still allow a *formal* distinction between the present operations of a person's consciousness and agency and their full practical identity, while holding that this is not a *real* distinction between entities" (John J. Davenport, *Narrative Identity, Autonomy, and Mortality: From Frankfurt and MacIntyre to Kierkegaard* (New York: Routledge, 2012), 154). We discover formal conditions and principles by reflecting on what necessarily belongs to consciousness or experience (e.g., time for Kant is a "formal condition of all perceptions" (*Critique of Pure Reason*, 310 (A199/B244))). Such conditions don't exist really or independently and aren't phenomena (i.e., they don't appear and aren't experienced).

clear that the forms of despair do not exist independently; if they did, there would be nothing to prevent them being described separately. Instead, he writes, "No form of despair can be defined directly (that is, undialectically), but only by reflecting upon its opposite" (SUD, 30/SKS 11, 146).[23]

Much as Kant solves such problems by recognizing that apparent "things" like space and time are merely formal, I suggest Kierkegaard's famous stages, as well as the variations of despair presented in *The Sickness unto Death*, are likewise formal. That is, they are idealized abstractions rather than temporally lived or developmental stages. We can fill these idealizations out fictionally, and at times Kierkegaard does this (as with the characters in *Either/Or* and *Stages on Life's Way*), with what he calls a "rhetorical" presentation (SUD, xiv; citing SKS 20, 365). We are missing the point of that rhetoric if we look around for actual aesthetes, ethicists, and humorists.[24]

In *The Sickness unto Death*, then, dialectical distinctions clarify freedom and despair as concepts (rather than performatively leading one out of despair, for example). Dialectic allows Anti-Climacus to present apparently contradictory conclusions as both true, such as that despair is a problem for freedom but also the cure (SUD, 6/SKS 11, 118).[25] Anti-Climacus, I suggest, is not here asking us to humbly accept ambiguity, nor is he proposing an act of commitment by choosing one or the other. Instead, he claims a healthy person can resolve the contradiction holistically, unlike a rheumatic, who is immediately at the mercy of the elements

---

[23] He does elsewhere suggest that it is possible to *be* in despair while also affirming that what he presents are mere abstractions. "Actual life is too complex merely to point out abstract contrasts such as that between a despair that is completely unaware of being so and a despair that is completely aware of being so" (SUD, 48/SKS 11, 163).

[24] We may still recognize features of these fictional categories in real life, since the abstractions show the foundations of selfhood that characterize all personality. Sometimes Kierkegaard fills in a logical category with a real character rather than inventing one, as when Petrus Minor is delighted to find Adler a "normal case of an illness" affecting the age (BA, 3/Pap. VIII² B 27 [not available in SKS]). In this spirit, Kierkegaard calls Socrates an ironist. However, since being an ironist is an abstract category rather than an image based on a concrete individual, Socrates can also be a pagan paradigm for the religious in *Philosophical Fragments*. How Kierkegaard classifies Socrates depends on which features (appearances) of Socrates are being considered. In the cases of Adler and Socrates, a real-life personality embodies the category (or in Socrates's case, multiple categories) so well there is no need to invent a fictional one. But just because something is conceptually distinct does not mean we can *always* find a historical example. This is one difference between Kierkegaard and Hegel, who readily transfers abstract categories onto historical events. In this sense, Kierkegaard is not less abstract than Hegel, as we might standardly think, but more. Concepts *can* be filled in for Kierkegaard, but often only fictionally, as a rhetorical aid.

[25] "Despair is indeed that dialectical. Thus, also in Christian terminology death is indeed the expression for the state of deepest spiritual wretchedness, and yet the cure is simply to die, to die to the world" (SUD, 6/SKS 11, 118).

(SUD, 31/SKS 11, 147). Anti-Climacus accuses the drafts from which the rheumatic suffers of being *undialectical*. He writes, "a draft is a contradiction, for a draft is disparately or undialectically cold and warm, but a good healthy body resolves this contradiction and does not notice the draft" (SUD, 40/SKS 11, 155). Physical health is a metaphor for conceptual health: An individual's mind robust with metaphysical distinctions does not immediately conclude opposite properties belong to separately existing things and commit to one in exclusion of the other. Instead, in encountering tensions and paradoxes, a metaphysically agile mind looks for ways in which differences might be synthesized as nonindependent elements of a surprisingly complex whole. What is needed, in other words, is something like the skill of Hegelian mediation. We miss the dialectical, unifying role of Kierkegaard's stages if we treat them as stand-alone states – that is, as something an individual is for some period of time.[26]

As abstracted aspects rather than lived attitudes, the "forms of despair" in *The Sickness unto Death* highlight different logical possibilities of consciousness rather than ways a person can live.[27] They are as idealized as any other abstractions: a perfect square, or the species giraffe. As concepts, these are not found immediately in reality; instead, conceptual work clarifies *aspects* of reality and provides a standard for comparing concrete things. This isn't to say no one can be in despair: Anti-Climacus distinguishes between "the abstract idea of despair [*den abstrakte Tanke Fortvivlelse*]" and "any thought of someone in despair [*at tænke nogen Fortvivlet*]" (SUD, 15/SKS 11, 130), with the implication that it's at least possible for someone to inhabit the forms described. But this is not the main reason he presents them. A medical or psychological textbook used for diagnosis would not have the logical progression and symmetry we find in *The Sickness unto Death* – that is, the unfolding of despair as a single "sickness" with various forms that occupy the positive and negative boxes of a logical table.

Yet scholars have often treated the forms of despair in *The Sickness unto Death* as lived attitudes, and moreover have moved fluidly between describing them as actual lived states and as abstract logical categories as if these interpretations hardly differ. Jon Stewart, for example, cites the draft of the introduction to "The Forms of This Sickness (Despair)" (Part

---

[26] Most recently, as already mentioned, Kemp treats stages this way in raising a question about transitions.

[27] In the same way, Kant's progressive description of first the form, then the content, and finally the synthesis of moral actions in *Groundwork of the Metaphysics of Morals*, for example, does not imply that anyone could *perform* an action that is merely formal or has content without form.

One, Section C) as "a psychological description of the forms of despair as these appear in actuality, in actual persons," in contrast with how they were treated abstractly in Section A. While he acknowledges this description is from a draft and goes on to quote the introduction in its published form, he nevertheless describes the drafted introduction as the way in which "Kierkegaard explains the relationship between these two parts of the section."[28] In the published introduction to Section C, Anti-Climacus states, "The forms of despair may be arrived at abstractly [*abstrakt*] by reflecting upon the constituents of which the self as a synthesis is composed" (SUD, 29/SKS 11, 145). Stewart does not seem to notice the contradiction in the two descriptions, between treating the forms abstractly and as applying to existing persons, which does not happen in *The Sickness unto Death* (and is presumably why Kierkegaard omitted this introductory comment). Stewart rightly then goes on to emphasize the dialectical movement between the various forms and clarifying their Hegelian roots.[29] But while for Hegel such dialectical motions take place in history, for Kierkegaard the applicability of concepts to actuality should not be taken for granted.

The Abstract Self

As Stewart has shown, a Hegelian dialectical structure guides *The Sickness unto Death*.[30] The well-known definition of the self as that which relates to itself is part of this description of the self as a dialectical synthesis (SUD, 13/SKS 11, 146). In Patrick Stokes's interpretation of Kierkegaardian selfhood, he describes the core self that grounds personal identity as an implicit background awareness that colors experiences as belonging to oneself. One key touchstone of Stokes's interpretation is the story in *The Sickness unto Death* of the peasant who fails to recognize his

---

[28] Stewart, "Kierkegaard's Phenomenology of Despair," 124, quoting SUD, 151, "Supplement," which is Pap. VIII² B 151 [not included in SKS].

[29] Jason Kido Lopez likewise argues that Kierkegaardian despair doesn't describe concrete states, but he draws this conclusion for the wrong reasons. He argues that Kierkegaardian despair is an internally contradictory state and is instead presented as a therapeutic way of overcoming despair. While this description fits with the dialectical progression of *The Sickness unto Death*, I disagree that different claims about awareness rule out its being experienced. Any kind of awareness is a matter of degree and is ambiguous enough for different statements to be true at the same time (e.g., "I know..." and "I do not know..."), as argued at length by Jean-Paul Sartre in *Being and Nothingness*, trans. Hazel E. Barnes (New York: Washington Square Press, 2012). See Jason Kido Lopez, "Kierkegaard's View of Despair: Paradoxical Psychology and Spiritual Therapy," *Res Philosophica* 90, no. 4 (Oct 2013): 589–607.

[30] Stewart, "Kierkegaard's Phenomenology of Despair," 124–133.

own legs in new stockings (SUD, 53/SKS 11, 169).[31] Stokes concludes
that implicit self-awareness is a kind of moral obligation that *ought* to be
part of all experience.[32]

This story occurs in Part B, as Anti-Climacus adds the role of consciousness in despair. The peasant suffers from passive despair and is
unwilling to be himself. It seems plausible this could be resolved by adding
a little more active commitment, getting us closer to an Aristotelian
Golden Mean (with a little more willingness to be oneself but not too
much). But as Stokes shows, that's not how dialectic works. What the
peasant lacks is not a comfortable half-way point between two extremes
but a self that is *nothing in particular* at all: what Anti-Climacus calls a
"naked abstract self" (SUD, 55/SKS 11,170).[33] As with a healthy body in a
draft, the naked abstract self survives changes and resolves conflicting
appearances in a unified synthesis. Anti-Climacus describes this capacity
as "consciousness of a self that is won by infinite abstraction from every
externality" (SUD, 55/SKS 11, 170). When passivity is the problem,
abstraction (oddly) is the solution. Rather than decisive action in concrete
actuality, as we might standardly expect from Kierkegaard, a mental act of
abstracting *from* concreteness is called for. The peasant's failing is not a
lack of resolute action or will. Instead, he commits single-mindedly to an
error about his own legs. (We can only hope the carriage driver doesn't
hold him to his choice.) Stokes is right here that what's missing is not some
kind of determination of the will; rather, the peasant's lack of self comes
from a failure to recognize the ways in which a self can change (in this case,
wear different stockings) and yet remain the same.

As put forward above, the core self that can take on different appearances is what Anti-Climacus calls the "naked abstract self." It has no
existence of its own, even a phenomenal one; rather, I argue, it names
the mental recognition of different elements as sharing an identity (which
is what fails to occur for the peasant). Selfhood is not an underlying reality
independent of the mind's constitutive work but instead requires the
recognitional contribution of a conscious mind. Because of its composition
through a cognitive act, and the impossibility of its existing as a concrete
object of experience, such a core self is rightly described as "abstract."[34]

---

[31] Patrick Stokes, *Kierkegaard's Mirrors* (London: Palgrave MacMillan, 2010), 99–103.
[32] Stokes, *Kierkegaard's Mirrors*, 102.
[33] See later in this chapter for my discussion of Stokes's use of this term.
[34] To say that the self is the work of a conscious mind does not entail that it is explicit. I think Stokes
is right that selfhood is implicit or prereflective (a Husserlian term I prefer to the Sartrean "pre-
thetic" adopted by Stokes). See Eleanor Helms, "Review of Patrick Stokes, *Kierkegaard's Mirrors:*

But Stokes describes this core self as just a "naked self," leaving out what I am arguing is the most important part. The difference is not just terminological: Stokes views the naked self as a specific power of acting that is so concrete it even has temporal existence. It takes up a real moment in time, though perhaps one too small to be noticed.[35] Stokes challenges John Davenport's view of a merely "imaginary abstract self,"[36] though he notes that Michelle Kosch also argues, like Davenport, that the moment of choice is not even *potentially* introspectable.[37] Stokes insists on a concrete, temporal (if perhaps extremely short) moment of transition, looking to Judge William's account in *Either/Or* for support.[38] But the Judge's description offers at least as much evidence for my interpretation, which is that the pure self is an abstraction produced by the mind and not a concrete entity. Williams writes, "in choosing myself, I separate myself from my relations to the whole world, until in this separation I end in *an abstract identity*" (EO 2, 240/SKS 3, 229, italics mine).[39] Stokes interprets this abstract self as an experienced moment of isolation that we have a duty to overcome quickly. If I am right instead that an abstract self is not something one *is*, then what worries Kierkegaard is the mistake of thinking I *can* be a naked self at all, rather than of being one too long. On my view, abstraction is a mental act (or the possibility of one) that is a permanent formal condition of any concrete choice. Only if I'm in some sense distinct from my temporal existence (as Kant might say, if I'm aware of my difference from nature) am I able to choose it with all the weight of eternity, though what I choose is always something concrete (EO 2, 247–248/SKS 11, 236–237). This realization happens in reflection (that is, in abstraction), and I disagree with Stokes that it matters much to Kierkegaard how long this work of reflection takes. On the other hand,

---

Interest, Self, and Moral Vision," *International Philosophical Quarterly* 50, no. 3 (September 2010): 355–357.

[35] "The locus of Judge William's discussion of selfhood is the self as a site of historical continuity, integrated through a conscious choice back into the factical context from which it momentarily distinguished itself" (Stokes, "Naked Subjectivity," 375). See also Stokes, "Naked Subjectivity," 366.

[36] Stokes, "Naked Subjectivity," 365. He is discussing John Davenport, "Towards an Existentialist Virtue Ethics: Kierkegaard and Macintyre," in *Kierkegaard after Macintyre: Essays on Freedom, Narrativity, and Virtue*, ed. John J. Davenport and Anthony Rudd (Chicago, IL: Open Court, 2001), 307.

[37] Stokes, "Naked Subjectivity," 366.

[38] Stokes is addressing fears that the self is a theoretical construct, as proposed for example by Daniel C. Dennett (Stokes, *The Naked Self*, 7; addressing Daniel C. Dennett, "The Self as a Centre of Narrative Gravity," in *Self and Consciousness: Multiple Perspectives*, ed. Frank S. Kessel, Pamela M. Cole, and Dale L. Johnson (Hillsdale, NJ: Erlbaum, 1992), 105.

[39] Cited by Stokes, "Naked Subjectivity," 366; Stokes, *The Naked Self*, 184.

any time spent being (or thinking one is) an abstract self is a misunderstanding.[40]

In contrast, Stokes is unwilling to let go of the abstract self as having some temporal duration, even if "infinitesimally small."[41] There is more-over, he thinks, an ethical responsibility to minimize it: "stalling there only compounds the subject's guilt."[42] I believe such warnings make the "naked abstract self" into the wrong kind of thing. If it can exist in places or times, even very small ones, it fails to be *everywhere* and *at all times* in the way Kierkegaard needs it to be, especially for contemporaneity.[43]

In rejecting the possibility that the "naked abstract self" is *merely* an abstraction lacking phenomenal (experiential) content (as I'm arguing here), Stokes appeals to Dan Zahavi for support.[44] Stokes's claim is that the minimal self is "a *phenomenal* datum rather than a metaphysical entity."[45] But Zahavi argues not that a minimal self has some phenomenal content (i.e., that it is experienced) but instead that it can be both abstract and *real*. Zahavi argues that an abstract self need not be a mere scientific construction with explanatory value (i.e., a theoretical self, as critiqued by Dennett) but something that *really does* ground the self and hold it together.[46] It will be arrived at, however, *through abstract reasoning*, not

---

[40] The Danish term *Moment* in *The Sickness unto Death* is translated by the Hongs (correctly, I think) as "constituents" [*Momenter*] (SUD, 29/SKS 11, 145) and "element" (SUD, 125/SKS 11, 236). These are "moments" in the phenomenological sense of component parts, as for example when Hegel distinguishes between essential and unessential moments in *Phenomenology of Spirit*, rather than increments of time.

[41] Stokes, "Naked Subjectivity," 366 and 375; Stokes, *The Naked Self*, 184.

[42] Stokes, "Naked Subjectivity," 366. Stokes adds in a footnote to *The Naked Self*, "Other pseudonyms make similar claims. Vigilius Haufniensis claims that even the time spent repenting of one's sins is itself a 'deficit of action' and therefore a new sin (CA, 117–118/SKS 4, 419); see also CUP, 1:526/SKS 7, 478 and SUD, 105/SKS 11, 217" (184 n84). Stokes argues that the time of abstraction should be minimized (in order to minimize the sin), but if lengthening the time is in fact a "new sin" (rather than more of the same sin), this new sin would *also* need to be repented of, *ad infinitum*. The only way out is if it is possible for an internal act, such as repentance and abstraction, to take no time, which is in fact possible if it is merely formal, as on my view.

[43] On contemporaneity, see Patrick Stokes, "'See for Your Self': Contemporaneity, Autopsy and Presence in Kierkegaard's Moral–Religious Psychology," *British Journal for the History of Philosophy* 18, no. 2 (April 2010): 297–319.

[44] Dan Zahavi, *Subjectivity and Selfhood: Investigating the First-Person Perspective* (Cambridge, MA: MIT Press, 2005), 130.

[45] Stokes, *The Naked Self*, 190. He insists further that the minimal self is "not simply something we discover reflectively" but is instead "a subjective dimension of experience rather than a feature of any metaphysical theory" (191). I take it that by "metaphysical entity" Stokes means the same thing as "a feature of any metaphysical theory." For Kant, by contrast, the categories (for example) are features of a metaphysical theory but not metaphysical entities (i.e., they are ideal and lack real existence).

[46] See Dennett, "The Self as Centre of Narrative Gravity," 105; cited in Stokes, *The Naked Self*, 7.

experience[47] – which is what Stokes denies.[48] Zahavi in fact distinguishes between two different minimal selves: (1) the phenomenal but implicit self, emphasized by Stokes, which is the prereflective awareness of experiences as "mine" and an implicit part of each and every particular experience, and (2) an abstract or transcendent self introduced by Husserl as a nonexperiential subjective pole of identity. The Husserlian abstract self holds different experiences together but is not "in" any of them, even implicitly. The minimal self Zahavi describes as abstract is distinguished from the one that appears phenomenally (rather than a different way of describing the same minimal self, as Stokes takes it).[49]

It is standard to think of Kierkegaard as urging readers to shift their attention from abstract reflection to first-personal experience and action. If this were the whole story, a Husserlian description of a self that is constituted through abstraction need not interest Kierkegaardians. And yet Zahavi's description of the abstract self is very Kierkegaardian. As it is not found in any single experience but composed by the mental work of comparison, Zahavi describes the abstract self as a "synthesis" by which we recognize what "retains its identity through changing experiences."[50] Abstracting what remains the same within a plurality allows the unity of selfhood to first emerge. As Zahavi puts it, "the self cannot be given as an act-transcendent identity in a *single* experience . . . It is only by comparing several experiences that we can encounter something that retains its identity through change."[51]

---

[47] A Kantian "thing in itself" plays the same role, and Zahavi correctly says the Kantian self is likewise abstract. "The notion of self at work here is obviously a formal and abstract one. Every experience is always lived through *by* a certain subject; it is always an experience *for* some subject. The self is, consequently, understood as the pure subject, or ego-pole, that any episode of experiencing necessarily refers back to. It is the subject of experience rather than the object of experience. Instead of being something that can itself be given as an object for experience, it is a necessary condition of the possibility for (coherent) experience. We can infer that it must exist, but it is not itself something that can be experienced. It is an elusive principle, a presupposition, rather than a datum or something that is itself given" (Zahavi, *Subjectivity and Selfhood*, 104).

[48] Stokes, *The Naked Self*, 191.

[49] Since the subject-pole is an abstraction *of the invariable "mine-ness" of experience*, Zahavi seems to take Husserl's view to differ on this point from Kant's. But I think it would be just as right to say that the transcendental unity of apperception in Kant is (as for Husserl) an abstraction from the basic unity of experience, while *also* being a condition for such unity occurring. I do not find Kant saying we must reason out the conditions of possible experience apart from the unity – we could call it "mine-ness" – that we actually live. Instead, we begin from the universal "mine-ness" of experience as that which requires explanation.

[50] Zahavi, *Subjectivity and Selfhood*, 131.

[51] Zahavi insists on the abstract self as "invariant" (*Subjectivity and Selfhood*, 131) but promptly fills this in by saying it is the "mine-ness" of experience that is invariant. He suggests it might be possible as well, in extreme cases, to experience the abstract self "in its purity" (130).

The implicit first-personal (and phenomenal) component of experience described so well by Stokes occurs as many times as anything is experienced at all. The work of thematically identifying the first-personal invariant of "mine-ness" *as* an invariant, however, occurs through abstraction. Zahavi's invariant self is not phenomenal or first-personal[52] and for that reason has no temporal duration.[53]

While it seems obvious that Kierkegaard urges us to ask first-personal, concrete questions rather than third-personal, metaphysical ones, I suggest that Kierkegaard's thinking on the relationship between existence and concreteness is not so direct. Recognizing the synthesis of temporal and eternal, or visible and invisible, in persons requires abstraction, including the conceptual ability to distinguish components of a self that always occur together in reality. As thinkers, we distinguish things mentally that never exist separately through the hard, sometimes tedious, work of dialectic.

I do not wish to underestimate the dangers of reflection and abstraction. Anti-Climacus writes:

> Christianly understood, every poet-existence (esthetics notwithstanding) is sin, the sin of poetizing instead of being, of relating to the good and the true through the imagination instead of being that – that is, existentially striving to be that. The poet-existence under consideration here is different from despair in that it does have a conception of God or is before God, but it is *exceedingly dialectical and is as if in an impenetrable dialectical labyrinth concerning the extent to which it is obscurely conscious of being sin.* (SUD, 77/SKS 11, 191, italics mine)

Dialectic of the wrong kind, or in the wrong context, can lead to serious problems, including ethical ones. Anti-Climacus describes the ethical as what "*does not abstract* from actuality but immerses itself in actuality" (SUD, 120/SKS 11, 231, italics mine). Even a useful abstraction can easily become hypostasized, or – as Anti-Climacus puts it – "it does not take long before this abstraction [*Abstraktum*] becomes God" (SUD, 118/SKS 11, 229). But none of this means Anti-Climacus is warning us away from abstraction altogether, any more than the extended passage above asks us

---

[52] The main reason it can't be "phenomenal" is that it has no new intuitive content other than the structures of the mind (i.e., content that is founded, as Husserl would say, on the original experience). It is of course first-personal in the sense that all mental activities, including third-person narration, must be performed by a subject.

[53] Zahavi briefly claims, vaguely, that it is not *merely* an abstraction since it is a real basis. Here Zahavi aims to avoid the conclusion that the minimal self is a theoretical construction. But formal elements in Kant and Husserl are abstracted "constituents" of real experience rather than theoretical productions.

to minimize poetry and imagination overall.[54] The abstraction in question is a particular one, namely "the crowd," or humanity treated as a type, where the species is proposed as a solution to the problems of individuals. Appealing to humanity as a species overcoming sin supposes quantity solves a qualitative problem. "By participating in *that* abstraction [*i hiint Abstraktum*]," Anti-Climacus writes, "the individual fancies that he has everything as a matter of course. Being a human being is not like being an animal, for which the specimen is always less than the species" (SUD, 120–121 n*/SKS 11, 231 n*, italics mine).[55] This particular error of confusing the individual with the species should not be taken as an indictment of abstraction in general. (In fact, traditional metaphysics often aims at *distinguishing* the individual from the universal, though Anti-Climacus claims it has little respect for the individual once the distinction is made).[56]

As already emphasized, Anti-Climacus claims that the forms of despair are abstractions (SUD, 29/SKS 11, 145), but their generality does not preclude describing the forms of despair *as if* they are experienced by individuals. He keeps these descriptions, however, in a poetic (or what he calls a "rhetorical") mode. They aren't what existing people do, think, feel, or say. Instead, a poet fills in the abstract form by creating a character to go along with a concept. Notably, the concept comes first, as a logical possibility. Next, Anti-Climacus explains, the form of despair "can be described directly, as the poet in fact does by giving him lines to speak" (SUD, 30/SKS 11, 146). (He obligingly provides some lines a little later

---

[54] On the positive role of imagination, see Anna Strelis, "The Intimacy between Reason and Emotion," *Res Philosophica* 90, no. 4 (2013): 461–480; Ryan Kemp, "The Role of Imagination in Kierkegaard's Account of Ethical Transformation," *Archiv für Geschichte der Philosophie* 100, no. 2 (2018): 202–231; Walter Wietzke, "Practical Reason and the Imagination," *Res Philosophica* 90, no. 4 (2013): 525–544.

[55] "Abstraction" in this case gives us a feature as it belongs to the human species. Anti-Climacus writes, "If only the abstract idea of despair is considered, without any thought of someone in despair, it must be regarded as a surpassing excellence. The possibility of this sickness is man's superiority over the animal, and this superiority distinguishes him in quite another way than does his erect walk, for it indicates infinite erectness or sublimity, that he is spirit" (SUD, 14–15/SKS 11, 131). This is not a description about abstraction that a person does – spending time speculating rather than doing, for example – but abstraction as the ability to give a generalized account (as Anti-Climacus does) of despair.

[56] Moreover, Anti-Climacus claims that dialectic is "inherent in the self as a synthesis" as "each constituent is its opposite" (SUD, 30/SKS 11, 146, and see also SUD, 35/SKS 11, 152). Kierkegaard views dialectic as formal (in contrast with rhetoric, which is more concrete). The relation of the human individual to the human race is of course taken up in *The Concept of Anxiety* with the question of original sin.

(SUD, 32/SKS 11, 148).[57]) These fictional concretions are a way of reasoning downward from dialectical concepts, which are an indispensable part of the process.

There are plenty of passages in *The Sickness unto Death* and other writings that raise concerns about abstraction. Nevertheless, an abstract self is a component of selfhood that is not available experientially. The "abstract self" is the self that depends on reflection: "The self is reflection and the imagination is reflection." It is not only true that "whatever of feeling, knowing, and willing a person has depends upon what imagination he has," but also that imagination is "how that person reflects himself" (SUD, 31/SKS 11, 148). Imagination and reflection are two ways in which a human individual, as a conscious being, exists in possibility.

---

[57] He prefaces them: "Such a fantasized religious person would say (to characterize him by means of some lines) ..." (SUD, 32/SKS 11, 149). Elsewhere Anti-Climacus distinguishes between what is plausible dialectically and what is plausible concretely. In describing the way in which a person of immediacy gains some reflection (i.e., "immediacy is dealt such a crushing blow that it cannot reproduce itself") and the person moves from immediacy into despair, Anti-Climacus adds: "Or – and although this is rarely seen in actuality, it is dialectically quite in order – this despair ... is occasioned by what the man of immediacy calls extraordinary good luck," as even something good – an excess – can bring about the small sliver of reflection that pushes one out of immediacy (SUD, 51/SKS 11, 167). Again, Anti-Climacus is not attempting to describe the conditions for how such a thing occurs in actuality but clarifying the formal components of reflection in contrast with those of immediacy. Anti-Climacus describes his presentation as a "formula," which is "a dialectical initial expression for the next form of despair" (SUD, 60/SKS 11, 175). Anti-Climacus does later describe what "frequently happens in actual life" (SUD, 52/SKS 11, 168), but not all his descriptions are of this kind.

CHAPTER 6

The Experience of Possibility (and of Its Absence)
The Metaphysics of Moods in Kierkegaard's Phenomenological Psychology

Rick Anthony Furtak

One thought succeeds another. No sooner is it thought and I want to write it down, than there is a new one: hold onto it, seize it, madness, insanity!
> – *Kierkegaard's Journals and Notebooks*, vol. 1, CC:21

Only a prosaic stupidity will think of it as a disorder.
> – *The Concept of Anxiety*, 52

On Being All Too Earthly

A fruitful line of inquiry in recent philosophical analyses of depression has focused upon the concept of possibility and has argued that possibilities are typically a feature of the world as it is experienced by human beings but that a depressed person has an altered phenomenology in which possibilities are felt to be severely impoverished or utterly absent.[1] I propose to draw on the resources of existential philosophy in order to develop this line of thought, showing how Søren Kierkegaard's writings provide resources for phenomenological psychology. In particular, I hope to shed light on the categories of depression and mania and how they are related to one another, especially through an interpretation of his pseudonymous work *The Sickness unto Death* from 1849. *The Sickness unto Death* is one of a few

For helpful feedback I am grateful to Antony Aumann, Iben Damgaard, Jeffrey Hanson, Eleanor Helms, Frances Maughan-Brown, Erin Plunkett, and especially Sharon Krishek. Conversations with Maria Alexandra Keller about this material, including while driving on the open road, played a crucial role in putting my ideas together.

[1] See, most notably, Matthew Ratcliffe, *Experiences of Depression: A Study in Phenomenology* (Oxford: Oxford University Press, 2015). See also Kevin Aho, "Depression and Embodiment," *Medicine, Health Care, and Philosophy* 16 (2013): 751–759; Gerben Meynen, "Depression, Possibilities, and Competence," *Theoretical Medicine and Bioethics* 32 (2011): 181–193.

Kierkegaardian texts designated specifically as "psychological,"[2] and in this chapter I will take that designation seriously by showing what the book, ascribed to Anti-Climacus, can contribute to our understanding of human psychology with respect to what may be called bipolar or cyclothymic moods.

Those who investigate this aspect of Kierkegaard's work, articulated in both signed and pseudonymous texts, often note that his is emphatically a "philosophical" or "phenomenological" psychology.[3] A shared motive for such statements is evidently to distance what Kierkegaard is doing from the varieties of "reductive" explanation that he himself would rightly abhor. It is with this aim that I propose to offer not only a *non*reductive but a specifically *anti*reductive account of how *The Sickness unto Death* can help us to appreciate the spiritual depth of these affective conditions that are eligible for being described in psychiatric terms. Such a project is urgent in our current intellectual climate, where even philosophical psychology is – in the name of being "naturalistic" – plagued by reductive portrayals of emotions. For example, some accounts describe emotions as being simplistically "caused" by nearby objects – a type of explanation that is better suited for capturing how fire causes a smoke alarm to beep than for doing justice to the affective experience of human beings.[4]

My aim in this chapter is to combine humanistic interpretation with psychiatric ideas in order to illuminate the affective psychology of *The Sickness unto Death*, following a hint offered almost half a century ago by Ernest Becker.[5] Developing further his brief yet highly suggestive remarks about how to explicate the sections in which Kierkegaard's pseudonym

---

[2] The other two works bearing *psychologisk* or *Psychologi* in their subtitles are *The Concept of Anxiety* and *Repetition*. Section titles in *Either/Or* and *Stages on Life's Way* also contain these descriptive terms.

[3] On Kierkegaard's "philosophical psychology" see, e.g., René Rosfort, "Kierkegaard's Conception of Psychology," in *A Companion to Kierkegaard*, ed. Jon Stewart (Malden, MA: Wiley Blackwell, 2015), 453–467, at 454; Vincent A. McCarthy, *Kierkegaard as Psychologist* (Evanston, IL: Northwestern University Press, 2015), 11. As for his "phenomenological psychology," see Patrick Stokes, *The Naked Self: Kierkegaard and Personal Identity* (New York: Oxford University Press, 2015), 66.

[4] See, e.g., Talia Morag, *Emotion, Imagination, and the Limits of Reason* (London: Routledge, 2016), 10–14; Jesse J. Prinz, *Gut Reactions: A Perceptual Theory of Emotion* (New York: Oxford University Press, 2004), 53–55. A contemporary phenomenologist writes, of Prinz's use of the "smoke alarm" analogy, that "any account that applies equally to human cognition and to smoke alarms will not cast light on the nature of emotional experience or of experience more generally," since it leaves material objects impacting other objects, with no subjectivity in sight. See Matthew Ratcliffe, *Feelings of Being: Phenomenology, Psychiatry, and the Sense of Reality* (Oxford: Oxford University Press, 2008), 29–30.

[5] For more about the underappreciated Becker, see Rick Anthony Furtak, "Ernest Becker: A Kierkegaardian Theorist of Death and Human Nature," in *Kierkegaard's Influence on the Social Sciences*, ed. Jon Stewart (Burlington, VT: Ashgate, 2011), 17–27.

Anti-Climacus deals with despair as characterized by infinitude and finitude or by possibility and necessity (SUD, 29–42/SKS 11, 145–157),
I follow a standard interpretation by taking "infinitude" and "possibility"
as parallel terms, which lie at one end of a continuum on which "finitude"
and "necessity" are at the opposite end. Both extremes of the spectrum are
aspects of human existence, because we are simultaneously both,[6]
stretched between the twin polarities of potentiality and actuality.

Here are two important passages about the form of despair that is
defined by a lack of possibility or infinitude:

> To lack infinitude is despairing ... narrowness ... [It] seems to permit itself
> to be tricked out of itself by "the others ..." Absorbed in all sorts of secular
> matters, more and more shrewd about the ways of the world – such a
> person forgets himself, forgets his name divinely understood, does not dare
> to believe in himself, finds it too hazardous to be himself and far easier and
> safer to be like the others, to become a copy, a number, a mass man ... Just
> by losing himself this way, such a man has gained an increasing capacity for
> going along superbly in business and social life, indeed, for making a great
> success in the world. (SUD, 33–34/SKS 11, 149–150)[7]

> Bereft of imagination, as the philistine-bourgeois always is, whether ale
> house keeper or prime minister, he lives within a certain trivial compen
> dium of experiences as to how things go, what is possible, what usually
> happens ... The philistine-bourgeois mentality reassures itself with the trite
> and obvious and is just as much in despair whether things go well or
> badly ... The philistine-bourgeois mentality thinks that it controls possi
> bility, that it has tricked this prodigious elasticity into the trap or madhouse
> of probability, thinks that it holds it prisoner; it leads possibility around
> imprisoned in the cage of probability, exhibits it, imagines itself to be the
> master, does not perceive that precisely thereby it has imprisoned itself
> in the thralldom of spiritlessness and is the most wretched of all.
> (SUD, 41–42/SKS 11, 156–157)

Depicted here is a life of possibilities foreclosed; however, what justifies the
pejorative tone? After all, finite existence must always unfold within limits.
Becker comments that Kierkegaard, that is, Anti-Climacus, offers these as
"portrait sketches of the styles of denying possibility" of "inauthentic"

---

[6] See Simone de Beauvoir, *The Ethics of Ambiguity*, trans. Bernard Frechtman (New York: Citadel
Press, 1948), 7: The human being "asserts himself as a pure internality against which no external
power can take hold, and he also experiences himself as a thing crushed by the dark weight of other
things."

[7] See also SUD, 35/SKS 11, 150: "So it is with finitude's despair. Because a man is in this kind of
despair, he can very well live on in temporality, indeed, actually all the better, can appear to be a
man, be publicly acclaimed, honored, and esteemed, be absorbed in all the temporal goals."

human beings. "They are 'inauthentic' in that they do not belong to themselves ... do not act from their own center, do not see reality on its terms."[8] This is, he adds, "a perfect description of the 'automatic cultural man,'" someone "confined by culture, a slave to it, who imagines that he has an identity if he pays his insurance premium" or "works his electric toothbrush." What is "philistinism?" Above all, "triviality, man lulled by the daily routines of his society, content with the satisfactions that it offers him: in today's world the car, the shopping center, the two-week summer vacation." The philistine is protected by the "limited alternatives his society offers him, and if he does not look up from his path he can live out his life with a certain dull security."[9]

This is not so much a criticism of our shallow cultural values as it is an indictment of people who take refuge in the shelter of conformism as a way of tranquillizing themselves from having to face the dizziness of possibility. Implied is a kind of subterfuge or self-deception that falls short of honestly acknowledging infinitude or the eternal. Accepting ready-made answers about what to think, to do, and to be, the philistine treats his existence as if it were a problem already solved. If his neighbors happen to be regular churchgoers, then he too goes to church; if they are contented atheists, then he follows this trend instead. Either way, he fails to become a self. His adversarial relation to possibility, as something merely to be restricted, indicates that the philistine does not conceive of himself as being singled out for any particular destiny. That, in the vocabulary of *The Sickness unto Death*, is the condition of "spiritlessness." However, what is disparaged as "the most wretched of all" states we could be in is only a mild form of something that can get much worse. In terms of the metaphysics of selfhood, possibility is tamed or cut down to size – placed in a cage, or in a trap – when we are *spiritless*. By heading further in this direction, we end up with the complete annihilation of possibility – which is compared by Anti-Climacus to suffocating because, as he explains, "without possibility a person seems unable to breathe" (SUD, 39/SKS 11, 154). It is one thing to live in such a way that everything has predictable meaning, but something else to find that "everything has become trivial" (SUD, 40/SKS

[8] Ernest Becker, *The Denial of Death* (New York: Free Press, 1973), 73.
[9] Becker, *The Denial of Death*, 74. See also Johannes Sløk, *Kierkegaards Univers: En Ny Guide til Geniet* (Viborg: Centrum, 1983), 27–30, where a similar characterization of the philistine can be found.

11, 155) – or, in other words, meaningless. Here we begin to see what might be plausible about Becker's provocative claim that to lack all possibility is to suffer from depression, in the contemporary sense of the term.[10] As one first-person account of depression describes, when one is experiencing such consummate spiritual desolation, "it's [literally] hard to breathe."[11]

The person who is "merely" spiritless would thus embody a subclinical depressive state: What enables him or her to function so capably in the everyday world is a lack of imagination as to how anything might be different than it is. He or she would never daydream, would not have racing thoughts, and would not be moved by aspirations of living differently.[12] Yet at its extreme this would no longer be a comfortable although bland life but would lead to "fatalism," in which alternative possibilities are so utterly absent that one loses a sense that anything could be in the slightest degree other than it is: "The fatalist has no God," as Anti-Climacus asserts, "or, what amounts to the same thing, his [or her] God is necessity" (SUD, 40/SKS 11, 155). The brute force of things impossible ever to change would stifle a person; as some depression narratives record, "what makes the condition intolerable is the foreknowledge that no remedy will come."[13] The world of someone who is depressed can be without a felt sense of the availability of anything besides the present, empty and desolate, state of things. With no attractive possibilities in sight, either now or in the future, a person seems deterministically incapable of acting freely, while the obligatory tasks of life appear overwhelmingly difficult. He goes about his business mechanically, without feeling the "affective pull of enticing possibilities" in the world that are typically available to him in nondepressive states.[14] It is no wonder that he is said to forget his name, "divinely understood." Passionate inspiration, and an awareness of one's highest potential, have gone missing.

---

[10] Becker, *The Denial of Death*, 78–80.

[11] Sally Brampton, *Shoot the Damn Dog: A Memoir of Depression* (New York: Norton, 2008), 34.

[12] See SUD, 59/SKS 11, 173–174: "Over the years, an individual may abandon the little bit of passion, feeling, imagination, the little bit of inwardness he had and embrace ... an understanding of life in terms of trivialities ... But he is in despair, devoid of spirit and in despair."

[13] William Styron, *Darkness Visible: A Memoir of Madness* (New York: Vintage Books, 1992), 62. See also Ratcliffe, *Experiences of Depression*, 65–71, 110–113, and 274–276.

[14] Edmund Husserl, *Analyses Concerning Passive and Active Synthesis*, trans. Anthony J. Steinbock (Dordrecht: Kluwer Academic Publishers, 2001), 98. On forgetting (or remembering) one's divine name, see Sharon Krishek, "Kierkegaard's Notion of a Divine Name and the Feasibility of Universal Love," *The Southern Journal of Philosophy* 57 (2019): 539–560, at 546–550.

Consequences of Depression

The experience of spiritual desolation is conveyed in Kierkegaard's writings, both from a knowledgeable observer's perspective and from within, from an experiential standpoint. We read in *Works of Love* about times "when despondency wants to make everything empty for you, to transform all life into a monotonous and meaningless repetition, then you do indeed see all of it, but with such indifference . . . [that] it seems to you as if [God] had withdrawn into himself, as if he were far off in heaven, infinitely far away from all this triviality that is scarcely worth living for" (WL, 300–301/SKS 9, 298–299), and in *Either/Or* we hear not only the Judge's ideas *about* depression but, more important, the attestations of "A" that give voice *to* a depressive state of mind. "My soul has lost possibility," he laments, "my life is utterly meaningless" (E/O 1, 41/SKS 2, 50 and 36/SKS 2, 45). Complaining of "the wretchedness of life," he writes: "The only thing I see is emptiness, the only thing I live on is emptiness, the only thing I move in is emptiness . . . If I were offered all the glories of the world or all the torments of the world, one would move me no more than the other" (E/O 1, 28/SKS 2, 37 and 37/SKS 2, 46).[15] "My soul is so heavy . . . over my inner being broods an oppressiveness . . . How empty and meaningless life is" (E/O 1, 29/SKS 2, 38).[16] Everything seems vacuous and insignificant, nothing affects him in one way or another, and as a result he feels debilitated. "I feel as a chessman must feel when the opponent says of it: That piece cannot be moved" (E/O 1, 22/SKS 2, 30). At these moments (although not when he is momentarily gripped by an enthusiasm that captivates his soul), it is appropriate to classify "A" as depressed.

Now, you might be thinking: Wait a minute. Although the young man in *Either/Or* speaks about his "depression," the word he actually uses is *Tungsind*, which is perhaps more accurately rendered in English as "melancholia" or "melancholy" – though this is not how it tends to appear

---

[15] In these fragments "A" also says that he doesn't feel like doing anything, and that his "depression" is his "intimate confidant," adding: "My sorrow is my baronial castle," in which he dwells "as one [who is] already dead." See E/O 1, 20/SKS 2, 28–29 and 42/SKS 2, 51.

[16] For a description of comparable experiences as characteristic of depression, see Peter C. Whybrow, *A Mood Apart: Depression, Mania, and Other Afflictions of the Self* (New York: Basic Books, 2015), 21. On how depression consists partially in an inability to find meaning in things, see also Ulrika Carlsson, "The Ethical Life of Aesthetes," in *The Kierkegaardian Mind*, ed. Adam Buben, Eleanor Helms, and Patrick Stokes (London: Routledge, 2019), 135–144.

in the Princeton edition of *Kierkegaard's Writings*.[17] Interestingly, one depression memoir that I cited earlier offers a comparable argument: "'Melancholia' would still appear to be a far more apt and evocative word for the blacker forms of the disorder, but it was usurped by a noun with a bland tonality," a "true wimp of a word for such a major illness,"[18] although it is only fair to observe that "depression" does convey a sense of being pressed down by a great weight, perhaps to the point of being driven into the ground. Within the context of Kierkegaard's work, there are further grounds for doubting the accuracy of translating *Tungsind* (or *Tungsindighed*) as "depression." Most germane is that, because psychology as an independent discipline had not yet been established when he was alive, Kierkegaard could not have had in mind most of the connotations that the term "depression" has acquired by now.

I concede that this is true. However, the question I'm concerned about here is whether *The Sickness unto Death* can illuminate what *we* call "depression," in colloquial speech and as a technical diagnostic term. And I believe that it can. In keeping with my antireductive approach, I want to maintain *not* that spiritual desolation or finitude's despair is *merely* depression but that depression at its worst can be more profoundly understood as a total spiritual desolation such as what the young man in *Repetition* discloses when he moans: "I am sickened by existence; it is insipid, without salt and meaning ... My mind is numb – or is it more correct to say that I am losing it?"(FT, 200/SKS 4, 68).[19] Without positing an identity between depression and despair, I think we can safely say that one form of despair tends toward depression or melancholy. According to analogies delineated in *The Sickness unto Death*, we need possibility in order to breathe, so the absence of possibility might asphyxiate us: It would be like attempting to speak words composed entirely of consonants, with no vowel sounds (SUD, 37/SKS 11, 153).[20] Expressing this in even stronger language, Kierkegaard claims that someone who lacks possibility

---

[17] See, e.g., McCarthy, *Kierkegaard as Psychologist*, 15–17. He suggests "brooding melancholy" as an alternative.

[18] Styron, *Darkness Visible*, 36–37. See also Whybrow, *A Mood Apart*, 84.

[19] Modified translation. Gordon Marino denies that certain forms of despair are linked with particular emotions, but I think *The Sickness unto Death* indicates that there is "something it's like" to suffer from despair of one sort or another. See Gordon Marino, *Kierkegaard in the Present Age* (Milwaukee, WI: Marquette University Press, 2001), 102.

[20] See also SUD, 40/SKS 11, 155: "Possibility is for the self what oxygen is for breathing"; SUD, 37/ SKS 11, 153: "If losing oneself in possibility may be compared with a child's utterance of vowel sounds, then lacking possibility would be the same as being dumb. The necessary is like pure consonants." In languages in which whole phrases can be written without vowels, it is difficult and may be impossible to utter them without introducing *some* vowel sounds.

is bereft of the divine. He states: "Possibility is a hint from God. One must follow it" (KJN 5, NB7:93/SKS 21, 126).[21] Depression could therefore be described as a state of being in which we have either missed the hint that possibility offers, failed to actualize it in our concrete surrounding world, or not been given it in the first place.

In spite of how frequently the notion is invoked, sufferers and expert analysts alike have remarked on how depression "remains a great mystery" about which "we have more questions than answers."[22] Kierkegaard's work can help to enhance our awareness of how depression is best understood both phenomenologically, in terms of *what it is like*, and metaphysically, in the sense of how it involves an asymmetric relation of the subject to the category of the possible. The physician of the soul "knows that just as there is merely imaginary sickness there is also merely imaginary health," as Anti-Climacus discerns; we have seen that one form of imaginary health, or "normotic illness," is a mode of stultifying bourgeois complacency in which someone has narrowed down their realm of possibility and simpli-fied the tasks of life in order to be sheltered inside a flat, unimaginative sanctuary (SUD, 23/SKS 11, 139).[23] When one's world of possibility is still more radically muted, one suffers from a smothering feeling of meaninglessness. The mild, low-level melancholy that hums in the back-ground of one's life when "a sense of security and tranquillity" signifies "being in despair" is on a continuum with deep and complete depression (SUD, 24/SKS 11, 140).[24] The ontological concept of the possible, which is typically an aspect of our experience, must be invoked if we are to make sense of how a person feels when significance has gone missing from his or her life. And what allows this to qualify as a pathological condition is that it closes us off to those "hints from the divine" that alone can give meaning to our finite lives. Someone who is lost in the possible is unaware of having *one* name divinely understood, unless that name is "legion," but the "fatalist" has completely lost touch with God as a source of possibility (SUD, 40/SKS 11, 155) and cannot even grasp what it means to say that for God all things are possible. The critical evaluation of the philistine by

---

[21] On hints from God, see SUD, 82/SKS 11, 195.

[22] I cite Styron, *Darkness Visible*, 11; then Jennifer Radden, *Moody Minds Distempered* (Oxford: Oxford University Press, 2009), 55.

[23] On "normotic illness" see Christopher Bollas, *The Christopher Bollas Reader* (New York: Routledge, 2011), 22–36. For the portrayal of philistinism as "spiritually sterile adult complacency," I am indebted to Alastair Hannay, *Kierkegaard* (New York: Routledge, 1991), 196.

[24] Regarding the slippery slope from "mild melancholy" to "deep depression" see S. Nassir Ghaemi, *On Depression: Drugs, Diagnosis, and Despair in the Modern World* (Baltimore, MD: Johns Hopkins University Press, 2013), 10–16.

Kierkegaard's pseudonym includes a telling image, that rather than allowing himself to have a distinct shape he lets himself be ground into the
neutral smoothness of a circulating coin (SUD, 33–34/SKS 11, 149),
indistinguishable from anyone else.

On Being All Too Ethereal

While one form of despair involves a stifling feeling of diminished or
absent possibility, another – infinitude's or possibility's despair – is defined
by an overabundance of meaningful possibilities, making it exactly
opposed to the first type. Rather than having mental processes slow down
to the point that one is plainly impaired, the person overflowing with
possibility has a quick mind, aswarm with many ideas. Yet there can be too
much of an inherently good thing, as Kierkegaard indicates in the journal
entry that served as my first epigraph. Citing *The Sickness unto Death* on
how the bourgeois philistine thinks he has "tricked" possibility "into a
madhouse," Becker interprets this to mean that "one of the great dangers
of life is *too much possibility*, and that the place where we find people who
have succumbed to this danger is the madhouse" (SUD, 41–42/SKS 11,
156–157).[25] Here is some further elucidation by Anti-Climacus of what it
is like to suffer from infinitude's despair, which lacks the finite:
"Infinitude's despair ... is the fantastic, the unlimited ... As a rule,
imagination is the medium for the process of infinitizing," which is why
it can be called the capacity *instar omnium* or capacity of all capacities: It is
sheer *being able* (SUD, 30–31/SKS 11, 146–147).[26] "The fantastic is
generally that which leads a person out into the infinite in such a way that
it only leads him away from himself and thereby prevents him from
coming back to himself," points out Anti-Climacus, even if "the intensity
of this medium is the possibility of the intensity of the self" (SUD, 31/SKS
11, 147). The possible may be the mode in which the eternal gets
expressed within time (WL, 249–253/SKS 9, 249–253), but if one's
infinitizing enthusiasm is not bound tightly to the finite realm then
this expansive factor continues to inflate, as in a feverish dream. "If
possibility outruns necessity so that the self runs away from itself in
possibility ... it flounders in possibility until exhausted but neither moves
from the place where it is nor arrives anywhere, for necessity is literally
that place; to become oneself is literally a movement in that place"

[25] Becker, *The Denial of Death*, 74–75.
[26] On "the anxious possibility of *being able*," see CA, 44/SKS 4, 350.

(SUD, 35–36/SKS 11, 151). What is needed is readily enough indicated: "to actualize *some* of what is possible" (SUD, 36/SKS 11, 152, emphasis mine). It is to become concrete, so that the self's volition once infinitized "comes back to itself in the most rigorous sense, so that when furthest away from itself . . . it is simultaneously and personally closest to carrying out the infinitely small part of the work that can be accomplished this very day, this very hour, this very moment" (SUD, 32/SKS 11, 148).[27] It is to keep eternity always in view *while* hearing the clock strike. This means "an infinite moving away from oneself in the infinitizing of the self, and an infinite coming back to itself in the finitizing process" (SUD, 30/SKS 11, 146),[28] yet "this infinitizing can so sweep a man off his feet that his state is simply an intoxication," a state in which a person becomes lost.

> Eventually everything seems possible, but this is exactly the point at which the abyss swallows up the self . . . Possibility becomes more and more intensive . . . the instant something appears to be possible, a new possibility appears, and finally these phantasmagoria follow one another in such rapid succession that it seems as if everything were possible, and this is exactly the final moment, the point at which the individual himself becomes a mirage. What the self now lacks is indeed actuality, and in ordinary language, too, we say that an individual has become unreal . . . What is missing is essentially the power to obey, to submit to the necessity in one's life, to what may be called one's limitations. (SUD, 36/SKS 11, 151–152)

As Becker comments, here "the self is unanchored, unlimited, not bound enough to everyday things." It "is abstract, ethereal, unreal; [it] billows out of the earthly categories of space and time," he remarks, adding that the words of Anti-Climacus at this point are "precisely clinical,"[29] in a sense to which I will return in just a moment. First, allow me to ask: What diagnostic label might fit the following description? "Legends and fairy tales tell of the knight who suddenly sees a rare bird and chases after it, because it seems at first to be very close; but it flies again, and when night comes, he finds himself separated from his companions and lost in the wilderness where he now is. So it is also with desire's possibility. Instead of taking the possibility back into necessity, he chases after possibility – and at last cannot find his way back to himself" (SUD, 37/SKS 11, 153). Ernest Becker's answer is: *schizophrenia*, an affliction in which it is indeed

---

[27] The image that follows is from E/O 2, 138/SKS 3, 137.   [28] Modified translation.
[29] Becker, *The Denial of Death*, 76.

true that significance appears everywhere in one's world.[30] However, another non-ordinary condition in which we feel dizzy from an over-abundance of meaning, and one that fits better with the diagnosis offered by Anti-Climacus, is *mania* – or so I want to suggest. Becker, working years in advance of even the DSM-III, may have had the cyclothymic or bipolar spectrum less in mind. Yet many currently accepted distinguishing features of manic and hypomanic episodes,[31] such as "flight of ideas," talkativeness, "excessive planning," distractibility, and "increase in goal directed-activity" (such as the pursuit of "multiple overlapping new projects," a constant theme in Kierkegaard's own life), could well be viewed as various ways in which a heightened awareness of enticing possibilities might manifest itself. Even some distinguished psychiatric diagnosticians, for instance Kay Redfield Jamison, admit that it is at least *understandable* why people who experience these so-called symptoms do not view them as in themselves undesirable[32] – at least, when not so excessive as to be completely incapacitating. Indeed, it would be cynical and narrow-minded to rule out a spiritually meaningful, as opposed to a reductively chemical, interpretation of these phenomena.

Infinitude and the Finite

It is striking that *The Sickness unto Death* puts forward a bipolar theory of being, or one that so readily lends itself to being interpreted in these terms. The manic quality of some forms of despair has been particularly little mentioned.[33] What I would like to suggest is that we can better appreciate why we tend toward the extremes of despair defined by a lack of either infinitude or finitude if we see the categories of depression and mania as one-sided ways of relating to factors that are endemically human. The interplay of these two polarities is relevant to each form of despair, as the

---

[30] Becker, *The Denial of Death*, 76–78. See also Frederic K. Goodwin and Kay Redfield Jamison, *Bipolar Disorders* (New York: Oxford University Press, 2007), 103–104, on how certain symptoms "can be similar in mania and schizophrenia."

[31] All of which, unless otherwise indicated, are from the DSM-5, or *Diagnostic and Statistical Manual of Mental Disorders, 5th edition* (Arlington, VA: American Psychiatric Association, 2013), 123–132.

[32] See, e.g., Kay Redfield Jamison, *An Unquiet Mind: A Memoir of Moods and Madness* (New York: Vintage Books, 1996), 5–7. See also Kay Redfield Jamison, *Touched with Fire: Manic-Depressive Illness and the Artistic Temperament* (New York: Free Press, 1994), 103: "Who would *not* want" an "illness" with some of these "symptoms?" she asks.

[33] The only reference of which I am aware to mania or hypomania as relevant to Kierkegaard's work is by McCarthy, *Kierkegaard as Psychologist*, 53 and 69, who mentions twice that "A" in *Either/Or* is not only melancholy but at other times "manic."

self "is composed of infinitude and finitude" (SUD, 29/SKS 11, 145).[34]
And, from the vantage point of seeking to understand what is going on in
moods that are susceptible to being described in psychiatric terms, invoking the ontological notion of possibility is, I think, a promising strategy. It
provides us with a conception of what is being experienced all across this
spectrum that does justice to its metaphysical depth. Presently, it is
infrequent at best to find "possibility" explicitly formulated in first- or
third-person explanations of the manic mode of existence,[35] yet as we can
see, there is reason to expect that the term will typically fit: Thus, the
category of the possible can serve to clarify varieties of experience that tend
to evade our grasp.

A frequent theme in memoirs of mania is the vast and fascinating range
of alternatives that seem to be available: "When you're manic, your mind is
running so fast that you can easily envision alternate endings to any given
moment."[36] Or: "I raced about like a crazed weasel, bubbling up with
plans and enthusiasms ... I felt that I could do anything, that no task was
too difficult."[37] One subject reports feeling surrounded by innovative
minds, visionaries "attempting to create utopia"; another narrative reports
that during mania one "believes all people are geniuses, if we can just
reignite the infant fires within us."[38] What makes it difficult simply to
pathologize this state of mind is that all of us *do* have great potential, which
we might access only when inspired or fired from within; one's friends
could alter the world somewhat to reflect their ideals, and so forth. Hence
there is a truth in mania, just as there is arguably a truth in depression,
since both states can provide a person with knowledge. "You have some

---

[34] See also SUD, 13/SKS 11, 129 and 35/SKS 11, 151.
[35] One source that makes ample use of the category of possibility in interpreting mania is Hannah
Mary Bowden, "A Phenomenological Study of Mania and Depression" (PhD diss., Durham
University, 2013), 17, 115–116, 184–189, 195, and 210. On the "manic mode of being-in-the-
world," see also Ludwig Binswanger, *Being-in-the-World*, trans. Jacob Needleman (New York: Basic
Books, 1963), 143–145. See also Ratcliffe, *Experiences of Depression*, 181: "The manic person thus
lives in an enticing present. It draws her in, but in a way that is unconstrained by longer-term
projects." See also Daniel Bird, "Phenomenological Psychopathology and an Embodied
Interpretation of Manic Bipolar Experience" (MA thesis, University of Copenhagen, 2015), 14,
37, 45–46, and 70; Jennifer Radden, "The Self and Its Moods in Depression and Mania," *Journal of
Consciousness Studies* 20.7–8 (2013): 80–102, at 84.
[36] Terri Cheney, *Manic: A Memoir* (New York: William Morrow, 2008), 95.
[37] Jamison, *An Unquiet Mind*, 36–37.
[38] I cite Charles Monroe-Kane, *Lithium Jesus: A Memoir of Mania* (Madison, WI: University of
Wisconsin Press, 2016), 95; then Michael Greenberg, *Hurry Down Sunshine: A Father's Story of
Love and Madness* (New York: Vintage Books, 2008), 18–20.

spiritual insights when manic; you experience enhanced empathy with the suffering of others when depressed," as one expert summarizes.[39]

A prominent feature of any Christian view is that there is an eternal significance to the life of the finite person; another is that we are nothing but dust and that to dust we shall return. Yet we cannot follow every "hint from God," nor can we live while remaining mired exclusively in a sense of our own nothingness. Kierkegaard views it as feasible, if rare, to feel "at one and the same time how great and how insignificant" one is (KJN 1, AA:6/ SKS 17, 14); more characteristically, these awarenesses would manifest themselves in succession, within different moods. Someone who is equally both infinite and finite at once, who is in touch with the possible and the necessary at the same time, may be ideally situated to feel simultaneously his or her own greatness *and* insignificance. This would represent a state of supreme spiritual well-being and existential self-awareness. Next best would be to achieve integration across the polarities, uniting the self over time throughout the fluctuations of having possibility either exceedingly present or else seemingly absent.

According to the affective psychology outlined in *The Sickness unto Death*, every human being must come to terms with the possible and the finite, since these metaphysical categories are constitutive elements of our being-in-the-world. In the nonordinary, arguably pathological states we have so far examined, we witness what it's like to experience a disorienting excess of either possibility or finitude. Because these categories or factors are always at issue in human existence, the extreme cases bring into sharp relief a challenge that each of us faces. Due to the very structure of the human psyche, we are burdened with the task of being both ethereal and mundane simultaneously. As possibility animates our concreteness, "the divine dwells within and finds itself in the finite."[40] The bipolar

---

[39] S. Nassir Ghaemi, "What Is Me? What Is Bipolar?" *Philosophy, Psychiatry, & Psychology* 20 (2013): 67–68, at 68. See also D. Jablow Hershman and Julian Lieb, *Manic Depression and Creativity* (Amherst, NY: Prometheus Books, 1998), 33: "Mild depression may foster empathy, sensitivity, and the discipline needed for work; mild hypomania can be conducive to both productivity and creativity." See also Jamison, *Touched with Fire*, 107–108 and 118–119.

[40] KJN 11, Part 1, Paper 264:1/SKS 27, 233. The emphasis on contingent finitude is analyzed well by Kresten Nordentoft, *Kierkegaard's Psychology*, trans. Bruce H. Kirmmse (Pittsburgh, PA: Duquesne University Press, 1978), 190–191 and 242–244. See also Rosfort, "Kierkegaard's Conception of Psychology," 462. It is also worth pointing out that "loss of the capacity to love" is cited as a distinguishing feature of melancholia or depression: see Sigmund Freud, "Mourning and Melancholia," in *General Psychological Theory* (New York: Touchstone, 1997), 164–179, at 165. On realizing one's "eternal validity" in the midst of one's contingent finitude, see also Clare Carlisle, *Philosopher of the Heart: The Restless Life of Søren Kierkegaard* (New York: Farrar, Straus and Giroux, 2020), 25.

temperament is thus an intensification of the distinctly human problem of bringing one's unlimited imagination into the context of one's facticity.[41]

Yet what unifies such traits as having racing thoughts or a flight of ideas, being talkative, making plans and pursuing ambitious projects, and having one's attention easily captured by an even more appealing object, is that all of these involve a keen sense of *possibility*. So bringing this term into the context of psychiatric theory and practice might aid our understanding of what otherwise presents itself as simply a list of miscellaneous symptoms. And since "possibility" is an axiological concept, making use of it also helps us in the pursuit of an antireductive explanation. The descriptions given in *The Sickness unto Death* of what it is like to experience an excess or a lack of possibility, and hence of the metaphysical aspect of moods, can enhance our understanding of conditions that are particularly difficult to describe, as others have noted.[42] As we have seen, Kierkegaard situates these states against the background of a thickened ontology of possibility – which is a real, nonnatural category that I have argued is essential for making sense of bipolar spectrum experience. We can follow in the spirit of his writings

---

[41] It should be unsurprising, then, to find that the historical Kierkegaard might fit on the cyclothymic spectrum: One biographer brings up the idea, only to dismiss it rather quickly; another observes that Kierkegaard was not so much a unipolar depressive, despite his famous melancholy or "depression," as a "mercurial" temperament, yet leaves it at that. See, respectively, Joakim Garff, *Søren Kierkegaard: A Biography*, trans. Bruce H. Kirmmse (Princeton, NJ: Princeton University Press, 2005), 438–439; Stephen Backhouse, *Kierkegaard: A Single Life* (Grand Rapids, MI: Zondervan, 2016), 82–83. Although he professes to be concerned with "Kierkegaard's psychology, not his psyche," another interpreter concedes that these are difficult to keep entirely separate, due to a "boundary area" in which the one blurs into the other. See Nordentoft, *Kierkegaard's Psychology*, xix and 314. I have deliberately refrained from stigmatizing manic and depressive tendencies as signs of a *disorder* or someone with these tendencies as a *patient* merely. The DSM-5 itself states on p. 136 that "heightened levels of creativity" are often evident in bipolar subjects. One might think here of Kierkegaard's claims that he feels well only when writing, that this activity is driven by an inner impetus that he cannot resist, and that he harbors an overflowing source of ideas that wash over him at times, ready to fill the pages of possible future works. See, for example, LD, 154/SKS 28, 149–153 (letter of May 25, 1843 to Emil Boesen); on the "half-manic" quality of some of the correspondence from Berlin, see Garff, *Søren Kierkegaard: A Biography*, 231. Rollo May remarks on the "heightened consciousness" that inspired Kierkegaard's writings, in *Love and Will* (New York: W. W. Norton and Company, 1969), 171–172. See also Edith Weigert, "Søren Kierkegaard's Mood Swings," *International Journal of Psycho-Analysis* 41 (1960): 521–525; H. J. Schou, *Religiøsitet og Sygelige Sindstilstande* (Copenhagen: Gads Forlag, 1924), 42–43. Other sources of educated conjecture include Johan Schioldann and Ib Søgaard, "Søren Kierkegaard (1813-1855): A Bicentennial Pathographical Review," *History of Psychiatry* 24.4 (2013): 387–398; Hjalmar Helweg, *Søren Kierkegaard: En Psykiastrisk-Psykologisk Studie* (Copenhagen: Hagerups Forlag, 1933).

[42] Bowden, for instance, notes that narratives of mania are "comparatively rare," with "less experiential detail than those of depression." See "A Phenomenological Study of Mania and Depression," 147.

and uphold a meaningful conception of what is at issue when a person's world seems to hold either a dizzying profusion or an appalling absence of captivating possibilities. In this manner, an existential psychology *could* do justice to the tension at the heart of human existence, that we are unbounded – inspired by the divine, as Kierkegaard might say – and yet, at the same time, entirely finite.

CHAPTER 7

Sin, Despair, and the Self

Roe Fremstedal

Introduction

The Sickness unto Death has been central to Kierkegaard scholarship for a long time.[1] This is particularly the case with the renewed interest in Kierkegaard since the 1990s, when the Søren Kierkegaard Research Centre, *Søren Kierkegaards Skrifter*, and *Kierkegaard Studies Year Book* and *Monograph Series* were established and *Kierkegaard's Writings* was finished. In this period, much of the scholarship was dominated by a discussion of despair in *The Sickness unto Death* in which Michael Theunissen, Arne Grøn, and Alastair Hannay participated.[2] More recently, *The Sickness unto Death* has been crucial to discussions of metaphysical, practical, and narrative identity, as well as ethics and hierarchical agency, in books by Anthony Rudd, John Davenport, and Patrick Stokes.[3] It has thus been important to discussions within Danish, German, and Anglophone philosophy. Particularly the contemporary focus on personal identity and psychopathology seems indebted to *The Sickness unto Death*.[4]

---

[1] This chapter draws upon and develops further Roe Fremstedal, *Kierkegaard and Kant on Radical Evil and the Highest Good: Virtue, Happiness, and the Kingdom of God* (Basingstoke: Palgrave Macmillan, 2014); Roe Fremstedal, "Kierkegaard's Post-Kantian Approach to Anthropology and Selfhood," in *The Kierkegaardian Mind*, ed. Adam Buben, Eleanor Helms, and Patrick Stokes (London: Routledge, 2019), 319–330; Roe Fremstedal, "Demonic Despair under the Guise of the Good? Kierkegaard and Anscombe vs. Velleman," *Inquiry: An Interdisciplinary Journal of Philosophy* (2019): 1–22, DOI: 10.1080/0020174X.2019.1610047; and Roe Fremstedal, "Kierkegaard on Hope as Essential to Selfhood," in *The Moral Psychology of Hope: An Introduction*, ed. Titus Stahl and Claudia Blöser (Lanham, MD: Rowman & Littlefield, 2020), 75–92.

[2] See Michael Theunissen, *Kierkegaard's Concept of Despair*, trans. Barbara Harshav and Helmut Illbruck (Princeton, NJ: Princeton University Press, 2005); Arne Grøn, *Subjektivitet og negativitet: Kierkegaard* (Copenhagen: Gyldendal, 1997).

[3] Anthony Rudd, *Self, Value, and Narrative: A Kierkegaardian Approach* (Oxford: Oxford University Press, 2012); John J. Davenport, *Narrative Identity, Autonomy, and Mortality: From Frankfurt and MacIntyre to Kierkegaard* (New York: Routledge, 2012); Patrick Stokes, *The Naked Self: Kierkegaard and Personal Identity* (Oxford: Oxford University Press, 2015).

[4] See Michael Theunissen, "Kierkegaard's Negativistic Method," in *Kierkegaard's Truth: The Disclosure of the Self*, ed. Joseph H. Smith (New Haven, CT: Yale University Press, 1981), 381–423.

This chapter proceeds by offering a brief overview of key concepts such as human nature, the self, despair, and wholeheartedness. It then discusses the relation between Part One and Part Two of *The Sickness unto Death*, offering a comparison of different types of despair. In this connection, it deals with the relations between faith and reason and philosophy and theology. Finally, it discusses how faith, hope, and charity can overcome despair. We will see that overcoming despair represents a moral task, which requires forming a wholehearted or coherent self.

Anticipating Heidegger and Sartre, *The Sickness unto Death* argues that human nature is constituted by both freedom and facticity (described as possibility and necessity, infinitude and finitude, respectively). However, these two poles represent opposites that stand in a *tense* relation to each other, since our freedom is always situated in a specific context or situation that limits it. Therefore, *The Sickness unto Death* argues that human agents tend to exaggerate either freedom or facticity. The former underrates the limitations of the situation, whereas the latter exaggerates them instead. But since both of these poles are constitutive of human nature, any attempt to identify with one at the expense of the other is self-defeating. Indeed, all such attempts imply *double-mindedness* split between freedom and facticity. Kierkegaard describes such double-mindedness as despair (UDVS, 30/SKS 8, 144). Indeed, the Danish word for despair, *Fortvivlelse*, is based on the numeral "two" (*tvi*), as is the German *Verzweiflung*.

Human nature has a latent *potential* for selfhood, but the actualized self differs from human nature and its different poles (SUD, 13/SKS 11, 129).[5] Specifically, the self is a reflexive self-relation that relates to human nature (as a whole) by forming higher-order volitions. Selfhood therefore requires not only self-consciousness but volitional identification with some lower-order motives and alienation from others.[6] Put in contemporary terms, it entails not only a personal identity but also *hierarchical* agency, in which higher-order motives reinforce and weaken lower-order motives.[7]

---

[5] Kierkegaard's account of human nature is either a form of broadly Aristotelian hylomorphism or a two-aspect account of body and mind (see John J. Davenport, "Selfhood and 'Spirit,'" in *The Oxford Handbook of Kierkegaard*, ed. John Lippitt and George Pattison (Oxford: Oxford University Press, 2013), 230–251, p. 234). Whereas human nature is temporally extended, the self only seems to exist in the present. See Stokes, *The Naked Self*, 213.

[6] Davenport, "Selfhood and 'Spirit,'" 235.

[7] However, such agency only seems rational or *autonomous* if the agent evaluates different motives based on whether or not they appear to involve normative *reasons* for action. It is only then that agency can avoid irrationality in the form of despair, akrasia, self-deception, wantonness, coercion, or incoherence. Indeed, such autonomous agency seems necessary for understanding the rationality and normativity of selfhood. See Davenport, *Narrative Identity, Autonomy, and Mortality*, 6. See also J. David Velleman, *The Possibility of Practical Reason*, 2nd ed. (Ann Arbor, MI: Maize Books, 2015),

However, the "imperfect" "actual self" differs from the "ideal self" (EO 2, 259/SKS 3, 247; see PC, 187/SKS 12, 186).[8] The former despairs consciously, while the latter overcomes despair actively at every instant. The latter is identified with spirit and represents the self we are supposed to become, something that represents a never-ending task that is highly demanding. It has an unreserved, wholehearted will to be itself before God in which "the self rests transparently in the power that established it" (SUD, 131/SKS 11, 242). As such, the ideal self is not self-estranged or unwilling to accept itself. But instead of accepting everything as it is, it hopes and strives for improvement, which reconciles ideals and reality (more on this later).

The imperfect self, by contrast, either "does not want to be the self it is" or it "desperately wants to be ... a self that he is not (for to will to be the self that he is in truth is the very opposite of despair)" (SUD, 20/SKS 11, 136). The former is estranged from its actual identity (e.g., by not accepting its own body), while the latter wants an identity it cannot realize. Neither accept themselves fully, since both identify with something they are not. Still, wholehearted selfhood (spirit) can only be reached by overcoming despair. We only become wholehearted selves by relating to ourselves, recognizing that we are in despair, and by forming higher-order motives that overcome despair. Put differently, a coherent personal identity is only possible by actively reconciling freedom and facticity.[9] On the one hand, such an identity prevents incompatible projects and roles. On the other, it avoids that form of selfhood that is fragmented into different projects and roles that are not integrated as parts of a single life.

The Relation between Part One and Part Two

Most of the existing scholarship focuses on Part One of *The Sickness unto Death*, while Part Two is often ignored (or at least not dealt with in much

25; Rudd, *Self, Value, and Narrative*, 91–112; Patrick Stokes, "Consciousness, Self, and Reflection," in *The Kierkegaardian Mind*, ed. Adam Buben, Eleanor Helms, and Patrick Stokes (London: Routledge, 2019), 269–280, at 278.
[8] This duality also shows up in recent debates on Kierkegaard and personal identity. Specifically, rich, narrative accounts of self seem to presuppose a minimal self (characterized by prereflexive mineness), just as higher levels of unity in consciousness presuppose basic levels of unity. The two latter seem constitutive of selfhood, whereas the two former seem normative. For a discussion, see Davenport, *Narrative Identity, Autonomy, and Mortality*, 46–49; Rudd, *Self, Value, and Narrative*, 196, 226; Stokes, *The Naked Self*, 104–116, 178–181.
[9] Rudd, *Self, Value, and Narrative*, 48–49. See also Theunissen, "Kierkegaard's Negativistic Method," 387–389; Grøn, *Subjektivitet og negativitet*.

detail).[10] Part One arguably gives a phenomenological description of despair reminiscent of the account given in Hegel's *Phenomenology of Spirit*[11] at the same time as it anticipates twentieth-century phenomenology.

Specifically, it describes, analyzes, and criticizes various forms of consciousness (or self-experience) on their own terms in a dialectical and teleological progression that can be seen as quasi-Hegelian. Allen Wood writes: "Kierkegaard follows the German idealist tradition in developing a concept systematically by beginning with the immediate, reflecting on it, and developing new determinations of it through each successive reflection, as Fichte proposes to do in his *Wissenschaftslehre*, Schelling in his *System of Transcendental Idealism*, or Hegel in his *Phenomenology of Spirit*."[12] *The Sickness unto Death* provides a systematic analysis of despair. Despair (and related phenomena) is described from the first-person perspective in a reflective, methodical, and systematic manner that partially anticipates twentieth-century hermeneutic phenomenology. Specifically, Kierkegaard emphasizes historicity and the relational nature of the self as Heidegger does.[13] Like Sartre and Heidegger, he views existence as always being mine, since immediate (pre-reflexive) self-referentiality (*Jemeinigkeit*, mineness) is built into our consciousness. Here Kierkegaard anticipates twentieth-century phenomenology, although he introduces an ethico-religious ideal for selfhood that deviates from the latter.[14]

The beginning of *The Sickness unto Death* anticipates the Christian ending of the work in its title, preface, and introduction.[15] Still, Part One mainly criticizes different forms of despair on their own terms, whereas Part Two criticizes them on Christian grounds.[16] Unlike Part

[10] As a result, the relation between the two parts and the entirety of the work remains somewhat unexplored. Worse still, the relations between faith and reason, and philosophy and theology, are hardly clear. See Arne Grøn, "The Relation between Part One and Part Two of *The Sickness unto Death*," *Kierkegaard Studies Year Book* (1997): 35–50, at 35; Kristen K. Deede, "The Infinite Qualitative Difference: Sin, the Self, and Revelation in the Thought of Søren Kierkegaard," *International Journal for Philosophy of Religion* 53 (2003): 25–48, at 37.
[11] See Jon Stewart, *Kierkegaard's Relations to Hegel Reconsidered* (Cambridge: Cambridge University Press, 2003), 550–595; Grøn, *Subjektivitet og negativitet*, 137–142.
[12] Allen Wood, "Evil in Classic German Philosophy: Selfhood, Deception and Despair," in *Evil: A History*, ed. Andrew Chignell (Oxford: Oxford University Press, 2019), 322–349, at 345.
[13] Claudia Welz, "Kierkegaard and Phenomenology," in *The Oxford Handbook of Kierkegaard*, ed. John Lippitt and George Pattison (Oxford: Oxford University Press, 2013), 440–463, at 447.
[14] Patrick Stokes, *Kierkegaard's Mirrors: Interest, Self, and Moral Vision* (Basingstoke: Palgrave Macmillan, 2010), 55–60.
[15] Deede, "The Infinite Qualitative Difference," 38; Grøn, *Subjektivitet og negativitet*, 299–300.
[16] Grøn, "The Relation between Part One and Part Two of *The Sickness unto Death*"; Deede, "The Infinite Qualitative Difference," 33–35.

One, Part Two is therefore written from an explicitly Christian standpoint, focusing on despair before God.[17] While Part Two speaks of the Christian God, Part One largely relies on an abstract and formal notion of "the other" as that which establishes the self. Part Two sees God as creator, whereas Part One mainly argues that the self does not constitute itself normatively. It is particularly defiance, the phenomenon of desperately wanting to be oneself, that supports the latter assumption (SUD, 14/SKS 11, 130), since the self is here confronted with constraints on selfhood that are external to its will (e.g., facticity or moral facts), which prevent it from creating itself autonomously (SUD, 68–69/SKS 11, 182–183). Any attempt to escape these constraints involves despair that is split between what it identifies with and what it fails to escape.

Part One diagnoses human despair and only briefly hints toward a Christian solution where the self rests "transparently in God," as "the power that established it" (SUD, 14, 30/SKS 11, 129, 146). Part Two, by contrast, not only suggests a solution, but it also *redescribes* the problem by relying on Christian standards. Specifically, the pre-Christian problem of despair is redescribed and reidentified in terms of *sin*, using specifically Christian language.[18] Therefore, Part Two is titled "Despair Is Sin." Doubleminded (incoherent) selfhood can then be described in terms of despair (without divine revelation) and in terms of sin (with divine revelation).

Clearly, the transition to Christianity here is motivated by the pre-Christian problem of despair. Still, this problem does not give a sufficient reason for becoming a Christian. Only sin-consciousness can provide a *decisive* motive for becoming a Christian (KJN 5, NB8:39/SKS 21, 163). So although there is a pre-Christian motive or reason for becoming a Christian, the decisive motive and reason is internal to Christian faith.[19] Thus, Part One provides an *aporia*, a problem we cannot get out of on our own, whereas revelation provides the real (positive) motive for becoming a Christian. Christianity fills a natural need, but it cannot be reduced to

---

[17] The book is attributed to the Christian pseudonym Anti-Climacus. Kierkegaard shares Anti-Climacus's views and ideals, but he does not claim to live up to them (see KJN 6, NB11:209/ SKS 22, 130). Therefore, these views and ideals may arguably be attributed to Kierkegaard, although not much depends on this here. See Theunissen, *Kierkegaard's Concept of Despair*, 122 n.

[18] See Poul Lübcke, "Kierkegaard's Concept of Revelation," in *Theologie zwischen Pragmatismus und Existenzdenken*, ed. Gesche Linde, Richard Purkarthofer, Heiko Schulz, and Peter Steinacker (Marburg: Elwert, 2006), 405–414, at 411–412.

[19] Kierkegaard does not distinguish between faith and belief, since the Danish "*Tro*" covers both, just as the German "*Glaube*" does.

human needs or natural theology since it relies on revelation, which has its own language and perspectives.

Part One describes selfhood in terms of "the human self," whereas Part Two describes it in terms of "the theological self":

> The previously considered graduation in the consciousness of the self [in Part One] is within the category of the human self, or the self whose criterion is man [*hvis Maalestok er Mennesket*]. But this self takes on a new quality and qualification by being a self directly before God. This self is no longer the merely human self but is what I ... would call the theological self, the self directly before God. (SUD, 79/SKS 11, 193)

Part One relies on natural, human standards for selfhood and despair, whereas Part Two relies on a supernaturally revealed, divine standard for selfhood and sin:[20]

> What infinite reality [*Realitet*] the self gains by being conscious of existing before God, by becoming a human self whose criterion [*Maalestok*] is God! A cattleman who (if this were possible) is a self directly before his cattle is a very low self, and similarly, a master who is a self directly before his slaves is actually no self – for in both cases a criterion is lacking ... but what an infinite accent falls on the self by having God as the criterion! The criterion for the self is always: that directly before which it is a self, but this in turn is the definition of "criterion." (SUD, 79/SKS 11, 193)

The criterion is then interpreted as the end and normative standard (*Maal og Maalestok*) for selfhood (SUD, 79–80/SKS 11, 193–194). Whereas the human self measures itself according to its own standards, the theological self measures itself with a divinely revealed standard (notably God's revelation in Christ as a paradigm for believers) (SUD, 79–80/SKS 11, 193–194). Kierkegaard makes essentially the same point elsewhere (SUD, 89, 95–96, 101/SKS 11, 202, 207, 209, 213), ascribing it to the Augsburg Confession:

> "Original sin" is yet another expression of the fact that Christianity uses God's standard of measure. God sees everything *in uno* [as one] ... The first consequence of this is that it recoils upon us to a degree that no human being would dream of or contemplate on his own. (Here is what is so masterful in the Augsburg Confession, etc.: that on his own, no human being has a true notion of how deep the corruption of sin is, that he must be enlightened about this through a revelation. And quite rightly, because having an inadequate notion of sin is precisely a part of what sin is; and furthermore because only God, the Holy One, has the true divine notion.) (KJN 7, NB16:6/SKS 23, 100; see also SUD, 83/SKS 11, 197)

---

[20] Grøn, "The Relation between Part One and Part Two of *The Sickness unto Death*," 40–41.

We are too sinful and too self-deceived to even understand that we are sinners, unless it is revealed to us by Christianity (CUP, 532–534/SKS 7, 483–485; SUD, 83–101/SKS 11, 197–213). More than anything, it is therefore the concept of sin that separates Christianity from paganism (SUD, 89/SKS 11, 202). Paganism lacks a proper concept of sin, but it has the related concepts of despair, guilt, and evil.[21] Indeed, we cannot be totally depraved, since we are perfectly capable of becoming aware of our despair, guilt, and evil without divine revelation. The Fall of man can then be described in terms of despair, guilt, and evil (without revelation) and in terms of sin (with revelation).[22] Sin-consciousness adopts God's revealed standard in order to recognize itself and its need for redemption. It relies on God's knowing hearts and minds (*Nyrer*, "reins") by seeing and assessing everything as a whole.[23] Therefore, Christianity has a truer idea of sin than paganism does, although pagan awareness of despair, guilt, and evil resembles and anticipates sin-consciousness.

Instead of rejecting natural human standards, Christianity dethrones these standards and changes our very self-conception. Sin-consciousness changes our identity, since it entails becoming reborn as a theological self (see CUP, 584/SKS 7, 531). By converting to Christianity, our self-conception is therefore broken and changed.[24] Pieter Vos explains:

> [Conversion] implies more than just the perfection or completion of nature, but less than the complete replacement of nature by grace. . . . Rather than by (natural) progress or a Thomistic completion of natural capacities, in this view virtue is marked by transformation that requires "inversion" and "conversion." In the end, this has to do with the radical nature of human fallibility and sin. . . . Human character is formed via a relation to God in Christ, who not only atones for human sin but also constitutes the qualitative criterion and ethical goal for human selfhood.[25]

---

[21] The Hongs comment that sin undermines our relation to God by involving disobedience against God. See JP 4, p. 657.

[22] Karen Carr makes a similar point, commenting on *Philosophical Fragments*: "Even on the Christian model, there is a sense in which the learner knows at least part of the truth of which he is ignorant; [the pseudonym Johannes] Climacus emphasizes that the ignorance is a product of an ongoing act of will on the learner's part, an act of will for which he is both responsible and culpable. We can only make sense of this act of will if, on some level, the individual knows the truth from which he is fleeing. That is, the individual, in order to flee the truth, must antecedently know what the truth is, otherwise he could not be said to be willing the flight" (Karen L. Carr, "Christian Epistemology and the Anthropology of Sin: Kierkegaard on Natural Theology and the Concept of 'Offense,'" in *The Kierkegaardian Mind*, ed. Adam Buben, Eleanor Helms, and Patrick Stokes (London: Routledge, 2019), 365–376, at 367).

[23] Grøn, *Subjektivitet og negativitet*, 355–356; Stokes, *The Naked Self*, 162.

[24] Grøn, "The Relation between Part One and Part Two of *The Sickness unto Death*," 41–42.

[25] Pieter H. Vos, "'A Human Being's Highest Perfection': The Grammar and Vocabulary of Virtue in Kierkegaard's Upbuilding Discourses," *Faith and Philosophy* 33, no. 3 (2016): 311–332, at 325.

Specifically, the sinner is *constituted* by his lapse or failing before God. He must therefore confess before God that he *is* a sinner and that he sins because it is his (second) nature.[26] By its very nature, sin entails a misrelation to oneself, God, and others.[27] Our self-relation is intertwined with our relations to God and others. Davenport therefore points out that "a discord in any" relation "prevents the others from taking their proper form."[28] Becoming oneself thus requires not only the right self-relation but also a proper relation to God and others. Claudia Welz comments: "If God is the yardstick for the self *coram Deo* – that is, the self living consciously 'before' or in the presence of God – the possibility of comparing oneself with others at the cost of others becomes less attractive, since one immediately becomes aware of one's own insufficiency."[29] However, the human self does not accept this, since it accepts neither sin-consciousness nor divine revelation. Still, it could concede that it has a flawed or corrupted character morally. But consciousness of guilt and despair does not involve a Christian conversion that changes the identity of the self, since it is still the same human self that despairs or is guilty (CUP, 583–584/SKS 7, 530–531).

Both within Part One and in the entire book there is an increased consciousness of the self and an *intensification* of despair. The lowest form of despair is the nonconscious (inauthentic) despair of Part One, while the highest form is open defiance before God in Part Two. Intensified despair involves not only increased consciousness of despair but a stronger will in the form of higher-order volitions and motives that fall short of whole-hearted self-acceptance (especially by being defiant). Particularly despair before God involves an intensification of despair, since it entails sin that does not want to be itself as created by God.[30] Presumably, it rebels against God instead of accepting that it is created in his image. Despite its awareness of God and personal sinfulness, it either wants to be a self it is not or it does not want to be the self it is. It either wants to create itself without proper restrictions, or it rejects facticity and the specific identity it already has. Both involve an unwillingness to be oneself before God that involves self-deception and intensified despair with increased will, self-consciousness, and higher-order motives that oppose God. The different forms of despair in *The Sickness unto Death* then form a dialectical

---

[26] See Merold Westphal, *Becoming a Self: A Reading of Kierkegaard's* Concluding Unscientific Postscript (West Lafayette, IN: Purdue University Press, 1996), 173.

[27] Claudia Welz, *Humanity in God's Image: An Interdisciplinary Exploration* (Oxford: Oxford University Press, 2016), 137.

[28] Davenport, "Selfhood and 'Spirit,'" 239 n.   [29] Welz, *Humanity in God's Image*, 128.

[30] See Davenport, "Selfhood and 'Spirit,'" 238–239.

progression that involves more and more volition, self-consciousness, and selfhood, ending with open defiance before God.[31]

The self is intertwined with self-consciousness and volition, so that intensified (higher-order) volition coincides with intensified self-consciousness and selfhood. Except for the ideal self, this intensification involves an intensification of despair that moves increasingly far from faith (SUD, 101/SKS 11, 213). *The Sickness unto Death* thus offers a taxonomy of despair that covers everything from nonconscious (inauthentic) despair to demonic despair that rejects Christianity. This taxonomy concerns not so much different acts as different characters, who all have character flaws by being double-minded.[32] Here Kierkegaard relies on a broad notion of moral evil as a type of character flaw, or even as a type of perverted or corrupted character similar to original sin and radical evil. Indeed, any character that falls short of wholeheartedness entails a moral flaw that can be described in terms of evil, guilt, and sin.[33]

The Theological Self in Part Two

Part Two claims that despair before God takes three forms:

(1)   The sin of despairing over one's sin;
(2)   the sin of despairing over the forgiveness of sin (offense);
(3)   the sin of dismissing Christianity.

The first gives up hope and courage because of its own sin. It is preoccupied with its own sin, something that involves an intensification of sin where higher-order motives focus on sin. Still, it does not repent or feel anguish. Rather, it remains in sin and does not think it can be overcome, since it cannot forgive itself. Instead of being open to the good or divine assistance, it demonically closes itself up within itself, trying to make itself impervious to the good (SUD, 109–112/SKS 11, 221–224). Like Luther, Kierkegaard takes sin to involve self-enclosure where the sinner ensnares himself by using his freedom to make himself unfree.[34] Thus, sin entails not only a misuse of freedom where creation rebels against its creator; it also entails freedom that undermines itself, something that cannot be undone by human powers.

---

[31]   Grøn, "The Relation between Part One and Part Two of *The Sickness unto Death*," 45–47.
[32]   Michelle Kosch, "Kierkegaard's Ethicist: Fichte's Role in Kierkegaard's Construction of the Ethical Standpoint," *Archiv für Geschichte der Philosophie* 88 (2006): 261–295, at 280.
[33]   Fremstedal, *Kierkegaard and Kant on Radical Evil and the Highest Good*, chapter 2; Fremstedal, "Demonic Despair under the Guise of the Good?"
[34]   Welz, *Humanity in God's Image*, 127.

The second form of despair, however, is concerned with the forgiveness of sins, rather than sin and goodness (SUD, 113–124/SKS 11, 225–236). It desperately wants to be – and remain – a sinner (so that there cannot be any forgiveness).[35] It therefore takes offense at the forgiveness of sins and the Incarnation, viewing both as impossible since neither can be understood. Although it is aware of itself as "a self directly before Christ" (SUD, 113, see also 124/SKS 11, 225, and 235), it is nevertheless provoked and scandalized by Christ. Presumably, it takes offense at a human being who is supposedly a divine savior, performing miracles, forgiving human sinners, and representing an ideal that all should follow (PC, 94–96/SKS 12, 103–105).[36]

The final form of despair openly rejects Christianity altogether (SUD, 125–131/SKS 11, 236–242).[37] It rebels against God by defiantly rejecting the Incarnation. It is further removed from faith than earlier forms of despair, since it breaks more explicitly and defiantly with Christianity (see SUD, 101/SKS 11, 213). It thus seems to represent a Christian radicalization of the *demonic* defiance that represents the end and peak of Part One (SUD, 71–74/SKS 11, 184–187). Otherwise, Christian defiance would not be more intense than non-Christian defiance. Both pagan and Christian defiance then seem to share the following features (although the account of the former is far more explicit than the account of the latter):

1. They strive to be themselves by creating themselves, something that they fail to do because of facticity.
2. Second, they are consciously aware of despairing over the realization of freedom, experiencing it as a serious loss.
3. They try but fail to ignore this despair.
4. Both therefore give up all hope, courage, and faith that despair can be overcome. Since they think it is too late to overcome despair, they reject all help to overcome it and take pride in despair and victimhood, by identifying with it (i.e., by letting higher-order motives reinforce and sustain despair and victimhood). They focus all their conscious attention on despair and are highly aware of it.

---

[35] Joachim Ringleben, "Zur Aufbaulogik der *Krankheit zum Tode*," *Kierkegaard Studies Year Book* (1997): 100–116, at 104.

[36] Like *Practice in Christianity*, Part Two here includes polemics against Christendom, since the latter removes the possibility of offense that is constitutive of genuine faith, although offense must be overcome by faith. See SUD, 113–124/SKS 11, 225–236.

[37] Two other variants of Christian defiance are less extreme. One is indifferent and lukewarm toward Christianity; another is concerned with Christianity but remains eternally undecided whether or not he should believe in it. See SUD, 129–131/SKS 11, 240–242.

Table 7.1 *Types of despair*

	Inauthentic – nonconscious despair	Authentic – conscious despair	
		Human self – Part One	Theological self – Part Two
Weakness or passivity	Despair of finitude; Despair of necessity	Despair in weakness; Despair over something earthly, the earthly, or oneself	Despairing over one's sin; Despairing over the forgiveness of sin (offense)
Defiance or activity	Despair of infinitude; Despair of possibility	Defiance – demonic despair	In despair to (defiantly) dismiss Christianity

5. Finally, both are uncommunicative and completely unwilling to share their problems with others. Demonic despair therefore involves *Indesluttethed*, uncommunicative self-enclosure (SUD, 71–73/SKS 11, 184–186).[38]

However, only one of these breaks explicitly with Christianity, by wanting to remain in despair before God. But neither of them has the power to escape the good (which Kierkegaard *identifies* with the divine):[39] "Despite all his defiance, [a person] does not have the power to tear himself away completely from the good, because it is the stronger, he also does not even have the power to will it completely" (UDVS, 33/SKS 8, 146). The demonic is even said to be close to salvation (see SUD, 71–72/SKS 11, 185–186).[40] Indeed, the intensification of despair makes the problem clear, which may eventually give rise to its undoing.

Types of Despair: A Comparison

Defiance involves some weakness, just as the despair of weakness involves some defiance. What separates them is only which element is dominant.

---

[38] This represents an extreme form of the self-enclosure that characterizes sin more generally. See Welz, *Humanity in God's Image*, 127.

[39] More on this later; see note 52.

[40] Commentators disagree over whether or not demonic despair pursues evil only because it is evil. This is not just an exegetical question but also a systematic question of whether (or not) despair and *acedia* represent counterexamples to the influential view that by acting intentionally we necessarily take acting to be good in some respect (i.e., the guise of the good thesis). Unlike Kosch, I argue that demonic despair presupposes the guise of the good thesis. See Fremstedal, "Demonic Despair under the Guise of the Good?"; Kosch, "Kierkegaard's Ethicist," 280.

Therefore, weakness and defiance (or passivity and activity) are both involved in all forms of despair (SUD, 20, 49/SKS 11, 135–136, 165). The "despair of weakness" does not want to be the self it is, whereas the defiant "desperately wants to be … a self that he is not (for the will to be the self that he is in truth is the very opposite of despair)" (SUD, 20/SKS 11, 136). Neither wholeheartedly wants to be himself as he is, since both identify with what they are not. And neither hopes against hope to overcome despair. Therefore, both find themselves stuck in intolerable situations (see SUD, 18, 37/SKS 11, 133–134, 153).

The non-Christian "despair in weakness" despairs over a loss or a misfortune ("something earthly") (SUD, 50–52/SKS 11, 165–167). If one does not overcome the loss or reconcile with it but instead sees it as fatal by attributing decisive importance, or infinite value, to it, this despair becomes despair over "the earthly" in general (SUD, 60/SKS 11, 175). Instead of despairing over one part of life (a specific misfortune), one then despairs over it in general. But the latter really implies despairing over oneself, as someone too weak to overcome or reconcile with the perceived loss. One then finds oneself stuck in a desperate situation in which one can neither cope with the loss nor with oneself (SUD, 60–62/SKS 11, 176–178). Still, the problem is not so much the initial loss or misfortune as the response to it, where one abandons all hope and courage.[41]

This despair over oneself resembles the nondefiant despair in Part Two.[42] Both give up hope and courage as a response to their situations. The pagan despairs over himself, viewing himself as too weak to deal with a loss and to realize himself. The Christian, by contrast, despairs because of his own sin, which he cannot overcome. The problem here is not a general despair over oneself but a much more specific despair over personal sin. Alternatively, the Christian may despair over divine forgiveness by taking offense at it. But this is still much more specific than a general despair over myself.

It therefore seems that the content of despair in Part Two *differs clearly* from that of Part One.[43] On the one hand, it is *more specific* and less general than the content of Part One. On the other hand, it excludes despair over something earthly and despair over the earthly (which are precursors of despair over oneself), while introducing some specifically

[41] Grøn, *Subjektivitet og negativitet*, 153; Fremstedal, "Kierkegaard's Post-Kantian Approach to Anthropology and Selfhood," 324.
[42] Ringleben, "Zur Aufbaulogik der *Krankheit zum Tode*," 112.
[43] *Pace* Ringleben, "Zur Aufbaulogik der *Krankheit zum Tode*," 112.

Christian content (the Incarnation notably). And there are no pagan counterparts to the moderate forms of Christian defiance, which are either indifferent to or undecided about Christianity (unless one assumes that pagan despair could be indifferent and undecided concerning morality, which perhaps seems possible).[44]

Still, defiance before God is a *Christian variant* of demonic despair, just as despairing over one's sin and despairing over the forgiveness of sin are Christian variants of despair over oneself. This has important implications for the relation between Part One and Two, and thereby also the relations between philosophy and theology as well as faith and reason. Specifically, it indicates that insofar as the internal critique of despair in Part One is valid, it holds for Part Two as well. Indeed, Part Two does not provide an independent analysis of despair but is largely based on Part One, which it *reiterates*.[45] Since the content clearly overlaps, the content of Part Two therefore seems supported by reasons holding independent of faith. Any valid critique of the pagan variants of despair would then also hold for the Christian variants.[46]

Wholeheartedness: How Morality and Christian Virtues Overcome Despair

Part Two takes the self to be established by God, so that any conflict in human nature (as a synthesis of opposites) reflects back on the God-relation. Despair is then contrasted with Christian faith, which involves an unreserved (higher-order will) to be oneself before God in which "the self rests transparently in the power that established it" (SUD, 131/SKS 11, 242). This transparency is interpreted as a moral conscience scrutinized by God, who knows hearts and reins (SUD, 124/SKS 11, 235).[47] As Merold Westphal argues, this appears to involve an openness to God and other human beings that is aware of the relational nature of the self, and which affirms it by being fully committed to Christian ethics, while recognizing our tendency toward sin, despair, and self-deception. In short, the believer

---

[44] See note 37.

[45] See Grøn, "The Relation between Part One and Part Two of *The Sickness unto Death*," 45.

[46] Ringleben denies that Part Two introduces any real new content compared to Part One. Presumably, the point is that it is the very same types (or structures) of despair that are found in both parts; the only real difference is that only the former is before God. Similarly, Grøn and Deede claim that Part Two *repeats* or reiterates Part One. See Deede, "The Infinite Qualitative Difference," 37–38; Grøn, "The Relation between Part One and Part Two of *The Sickness unto Death*," 45; Ringleben, "Zur Aufbaulogik der *Krankheit zum Tode*," 112.

[47] See Grøn, *Subjektivitet og negativitet*, 355.

humbly accepts himself as a sinner forgiven by God.[48] He rests transparently in God (SUD, 14, 49/SKS 11, 130, 164) by following God's will, loving his neighbor, and realizing his ideal self.[49] He thereby accepts himself wholeheartedly and is thus present to himself.[50]

Still, *The Sickness unto Death* merely suggests that Christian faith solves the problem of despair. It does not show it in any detail. But other writings add important material that helps us make sense of this claim. "Purity of Heart," Part One of *Upbuilding Discourses in Various Spirits*, contrasts despair not just with wholeheartedness but specifically with categorical moral commitment (UDVS, 25–27, 37–39, 50–52, 89–90/SKS 8, 139–141, 149–151, 161–162, 194–195). *Works of Love*, however, contrasts despair with hope and charity (WL, 248–260/SKS 9, 248–259), while *The Sickness unto Death* contrasts it with Christian faith (SUD, 81, 131/SKS 11, 195–196, 242).[51] Finally, *For Self-Examination* contrasts it with Christian hope (FSE, 77, 82–83/SKS 13, 99, 103–104).

Taken together, this suggests that wholeheartedness requires not just full moral commitment but also the Christian virtues of faith, hope, and charity. Indeed, it suggests that we only overcome despair or double-mindedness by having these virtues and being morally committed. Morality and Christian virtues must then work together to prevent despair, just as human activity and divine grace must work together in Christian existence. Clearly, morality and Christian virtues are interconnected here.

"Purity of Heart" is clear that it is impossible to choose between God and morality, since God *is* good and loving (UDVS, 268/SKS 8, 364). Like other writings, *Upbuilding Discourses in Various Spirits* then *identifies* the divine not only with charity but also with moral goodness more generally.[52] In addition, "Purity of Heart" argues that morality is

---

[48] Merold Westphal, *Kierkegaard's Concept of Faith* (Grand Rapids, MI: Eerdmans, 2014), chapter 12.

[49] Sharon Krishek, "Love for Humans: Morality as the Heart of Kierkegaard's Religious Philosophy," in *The Kierkegaardian Mind*, ed. Adam Buben, Eleanor Helms, and Patrick Stokes (London: Routledge, 2019), 122–132, at 129.

[50] Another perspective on "resting transparently" in God is found in *The Lily of the Field and the Bird of the Air*, a text that suggests that the joy that is presence to oneself rules out despair. See Anthony Rudd, "Kierkegaard on Nature and Natural Beauty," in *The Kierkegaardian Mind*, ed. Adam Buben, Eleanor Helms, and Patrick Stokes (London: Routledge, 2019), 145–155, at 146.

[51] *The Sickness unto Death* claims that "the opposite of sin is not virtue but faith" (SUD, 82/SKS 11, 196). Here, "virtue" refers to virtue independent of Christian faith, including pagan morality and prudence. The reference to faith, by contrast, could include not only the Christian virtue of faith but possibly also charity and hope.

[52] Here and elsewhere (WL, 252/SKS 9, 252) Kierkegaard *identifies* God with moral goodness in general and charity in particular. See Rudd, *Self, Value, and Narrative*, 45–46; C. Stephen Evans, *Kierkegaard's Ethics of Love: Divine Commands and Moral Obligations* (Oxford: Oxford University Press, 2006), 88, 105 n, 183.

inescapable, so that wholeheartedness requires valuing moral goodness over all competing goods. Anything else entails double-mindedness split between nonmoral and moral goods (UDVS, 24–25/SKS 8, 138–139). Ultimately, the reason for this is that nonmoral goods and evil are parasitic on morality. Both presuppose morality, since morality is inescapable. The relation between good and evil is therefore fundamentally asymmetric.[53]

However, morality, hope, and despair can all be approached from either non-Christian or Christian perspectives. The "first ethics" represents non-Christian ethics, whereas the "second ethics" represents specifically Christian ethics. Kierkegaard argues that the former is the natural default position, which collapses internally due to human despair and sin (CA, 16–18/SKS 4, 323–325). By failing to realize its own ideals, the self is split between ideals and reality, something that involves double-mindedness that prepares the conversion to Christianity. In contemporary terms, there is a moral gap between our moral obligations and our natural capabilities.[54] By relying on divine assistance and forgiveness of sins, Christian ethics closes this gap (CA, 16–18/SKS 4, 323–325).

In addition, Christianity involves hope that radically transcends ordinary hopes. Like St. Paul, Kierkegaard takes Christian hope to be "hope against hope," that is, to be hope in a humanly hopeless situation (FSE, 81–83/SKS 13, 102–104). Indeed, Christian hope is only possible as a response against human despair (JP 2, 1668/Pap. VI B 53:13). When everything collapses due to despair, God offers new hope as a divine gift that, if accepted, overcomes despair (FSE, 81–83/SKS 13, 102–104; see also EUD, 94–95/SKS 5, 100–101). Only He, for whom everything is possible, can guarantee that there is always hope (see SUD, 71/SKS 11, 185). Hope is an expectation of the possibility of good (WL, 249/SKS 9, 249), made possible by God, who makes good for all without distinction. Since God makes good for all, the believer expects that good is possible for all.[55]

Kierkegaard systematically distinguishes Christian hope from "natural hope" and "human hope" (UDVS, 112–114/SKS 8, 214–216; FSE, 77,

---

[53] Fremstedal, "Demonic Despair under the Guise of the Good?"

[54] John E. Hare, *The Moral Gap: Kantian Ethics, Human Limits, and God's Assistance* (Oxford: Clarendon Press, 2002); Evans, *Kierkegaard's Ethics of Love*, 49–50, 82–83; Philip L. Quinn, "Kierkegaard's Christian Ethics," in *The Cambridge Companion to Kierkegaard*, ed. Alastair Hannay and Gordon D. Marino (Cambridge: Cambridge University Press, 1998), 349–375; Robert Stern, *Understanding Moral Obligation: Kant, Hegel, Kierkegaard* (Cambridge: Cambridge University Press, 2012), 206, 246.

[55] David J. Gouwens, *Kierkegaard as a Religious Thinker* (Cambridge: Cambridge University Press, 1996), 157.

82–83/SKS 13, 99, 103–104; JP 2, 1668/Pap. VI B 53:13). He contends
that the latter collapses due to hopelessness or despair (see EUD, 94–95/
SKS 5, 100–101). On the one hand, misfortune, hardship, and distress
lead to hopelessness (CD, 106–113/SKS 10, 117–124). Presumably, the
agent gives up hope and courage by suffering a loss (or experiencing
normative conflict, which necessitates sacrifice). On the other hand,
Kierkegaard contends that we must despair or abandon hope, since we
fail to realize the infinite ethical requirement (WL, 252, 262/SKS 9, 252,
261). Presumably we should despair, due to our moral failure (represented
by the moral gap). But rather than presupposing immoral actions, this may
suggest that we fail by not unifying our personal identities. Indeed, it is
despair or double-mindedness itself that seems morally objectionable, since
it entails a character flaw for which we are responsible.[56] Becoming a
wholehearted self is thus seen as a moral and religious task.

In any case, Kierkegaard thinks we only become aware of Christian hope
when we despair over our whole situation. By despairing, we abandon
human hope and may procure Christian hope, which is hidden in our
innermost being (CD, 110–112/SKS 10, 121–123, see also UDVS,
112–114/SKS 8, 214–216). To procure it, we must both abandon human
hopes and accept the gift of divine assistance (which is given universally).

Unlike human hopes, Christian hope cannot be disappointed, since it is
based on eschatology, by patiently expecting what lies beyond all finite
schedules and probabilities.[57] Instead of being a specific hope for a
particular event (which can be disappointed), it therefore transcends all
calculations and time limits.[58] Thus, it may be realized in another form
and at another time than expected. But the assumption is still that it will
be realized somehow, sometime.[59]

However, Christian hope does require charity that expects good for
both oneself and one's neighbor alike. *Works of Love* therefore claims that
charity mediates between hope for oneself and hope for all others: "Love

---

[56] Fremstedal, "Kierkegaard on Hope as Essential to Selfhood," 83; see also Grøn, *Subjektivitet og negativitet*, 142–144.
[57] See Robert C. Roberts, "The Virtue of Hope in *Eighteen Upbuilding Discourses*," in *International Kierkegaard Commentary:* Eighteen Upbuilding Discourses, ed. Robert L. Perkins (Macon, GA: Mercer University Press, 2003), 181–203, at 192–194, 200–201. Kierkegaard shares St. Paul's view that someone who only hopes for this life is the most miserable of all. See UDVS, 228/SKS 8, 329; see also SKS 7, 355/CUP, 389.
[58] John Lippitt, "Learning to Hope: The Role of Hope in *Fear and Trembling*," in *Kierkegaard's* Fear and Trembling: A Critical Guide, ed. Daniel Conway (Cambridge: Cambridge University Press, 2015), 122–141, at 136–138.
[59] Fremstedal, "Kierkegaard on Hope as Essential to Selfhood," 84.

is ... the middle term: without love, no hope for oneself; with love, hope for all others – and to the same degree one hopes for oneself, to the same degree one hopes for others, since to the same degree one is loving" (WL, 260/SKS 9, 259). Justified hope requires neighbor-love, since there are moral restrictions on hope. Kierkegaard therefore holds that hope is nothing without charity (WL, 259/SKS 9, 258). But charity itself is "built up" (*opbygges*) and nourished by Christian hope (WL, 248/SKS 9, 248). Presumably, hope supports charity and prevents us from giving it up by despairing. Finally, the Christian believer expects that good is possible for himself and his neighbor alike, since God makes good for all. Thus, Christian hope requires faith and trust in God and vice versa.[60]

Taken together, this suggests that only faith, hope, and charity avoid despair (see UDVS, 100–101/SKS 8, 204–205; WL, 225–227, 248–250/ SKS 9, 227–229, 248–250; CD, 116–122/SKS 10, 127–132). Although he does not speak of the theological virtues,[61] Kierkegaard nevertheless follows St. Paul and much of the Christian tradition by assuming that faith, hope, and charity are interconnected. Gene Fendt comments:

> There is a unity of the theological virtues, but they are not the same thing. Insofar as faith believes God, believes in God, and believes that God makes good, it is distinct from hope which is an expectation of the good for both oneself and one's neighbor. But insofar as faith believes that God makes good it is inseparable from the hope which expects the good for both oneself and one's neighbor. If the first (faith) is given up, then the second (hope for both oneself and others) is *ipso facto* given up. If, on the other hand, one does not expect the good for both oneself and one's neighbor, then one lies if he says he has faith.[62]

To this, Mark Bernier responds, "(1) despair can be characterized as an unwillingness to hope in an authentic way; (2) authentic hope [hope for eternal happiness, the highest good] constitutes the primary task of the self; and (3) faith is a willingness to hope, wherein the self secures a ground for the possibility of hope."[63] However, it is not just hope but also faith and charity that constitute the primary task of the self. These three Christian virtues represent intrinsic, noninstrumental goods essential to coherent selfhood (see CD, 118/SKS 10, 129), just as categorical moral

---

[60] Gouwens, *Kierkegaard as a Religious Thinker*, 157; Fremstedal, "Kierkegaard on Hope as Essential to Selfhood," 84–86.

[61] See Vos, "'A Human Being's Highest Perfection,'" 326.

[62] Gene Fendt, *For What May I Hope? Thinking with Kant and Kierkegaard* (Bern: Peter Lang, 1990), 168.

[63] Mark Bernier, *The Task of Hope in Kierkegaard* (Oxford: Oxford University Press, 2015), 212.

commitment is (UDVS, 224–226/SKS 8, 138–140). Although faith is not identical to "a willingness to hope," the theological virtues are nevertheless *interconnected*.[64] These virtues represent character traits that must be actively maintained and renewed if we are to be wholehearted selves. Despair must therefore be constantly overcome by faith, hope, and charity as well as moral commitment. Indeed, Kierkegaard seems to view these virtues and morality as *constitutive* of coherent selfhood (spirit). A self without these is therefore double-minded or in despair (although an agent who is not even aware of his own despair has yet to realize his potential for selfhood).

Like faith and charity, Christian hope is not based on epistemic evidence or knowledge. Rather, it goes beyond the evidence (see WL, 227–229/SKS 9, 229–231).[65] Still, this does not amount to a blind leap of faith, since it is based on practical or pragmatic considerations. Specifically, religiousness fits a natural human need for coherent selfhood by overcoming despair. Instead of being justified epistemically, it therefore seems justified practically. Kierkegaard then seems to be a pragmatist (practical nonevidentialist) concerning religious belief and hope.[66] Again, Christianity fits a natural need, although it cannot be reduced to human needs or natural theology since it relies on revelation, which has its own language and perspectives.

---

[64] Fendt speaks of the unity of the virtues, while I only speak of their interconnectedness. The former is a stronger claim than the latter. Although the relation between the virtues has been discussed at length by eudaimonists and virtue ethicists, it has not been much discussed by Kierkegaard scholars. So far, it therefore seems unclear exactly what view Kierkegaard is committed to here. See Fendt, *For What May I Hope?*, 165–171; Fremstedal, "Kierkegaard on Hope as Essential to Selfhood," 78–86.

[65] What we hope for must be considered *possible* yet *uncertain* if there is to be room and need for hope (see CD, 106–113/SKS 10, 117–124; SUD, 38–39/SKS 11, 153–154). Moreover, it must be *difficult* to attain, since there is hardly any need for hope if the object of hope is easily attainable (CD, 106–113/SKS 10, 117–124).

[66] Fremstedal, *Kierkegaard and Kant on Radical Evil and the Highest God*, chapter 6; Fremstedal, "Kierkegaard on Hope as Essential to Selfhood," 84.

CHAPTER 8

Sin and Virtues

Robert C. Roberts

Introduction

Can sinners be virtuous? If so, what is implied concerning the nature of the virtues? And of sin? Kierkegaard's *oeuvre* is a mosaic of discussions of such spiritual excellences as faith, love, hope, patience, humility, compassion, courage, forgiveness, and gratitude. Besides these traditional Christian virtues, Kierkegaard identifies states of personal excellence such as earnestness, being a single individual, and bold confidence that are clearly traitlike and virtuous in his judgment.[1] Such personal traits seem to be the goal in his preoccupation with the edifying or upbuilding: To build the reader (and himself) "up" by way of reflection is to increase the reader's faith, humility, courage, earnestness, and so forth. But *The Sickness unto Death*, a "Christian Psychological Exposition for Upbuilding and Awakening" (title page), expounds an understanding of sin so stringent that not even the greatest success of the process of upbuilding will effect an escape. "No human being ever lived and no one lives outside of Christendom who has not despaired, and no one in Christendom if he is not a true Christian, and insofar as he is not wholly that, he still is to some extent in despair" (SUD, 22/SKS 11, 138). But despair turns out to be sin (SUD, 77/SKS 11, 191). This chapter explores the effect of the concept of sin on the concepts of the virtues.

The notion of a virtuous sinner makes sense in Kierkegaard's way of thinking because of some features of his Christian conception of virtues: (1) they depend on grace; (2) they are subject to an "inverse dialectic," the fact that the more aware you become of your failures to realize the ideal, the closer you come to the ideal; (3) several of the Christian virtues refer to

---

[1] In *Kierkegaard and Religion* (Cambridge: Cambridge University Press, 2018), Sylvia Walsh makes much of the relative infrequency with which Kierkegaard uses the word "virtue." I evaluate her arguments that Kierkegaard should not be regarded as a "virtue ethicist" in Robert C. Roberts, "Is Kierkegaard a 'Virtue Ethicist'?," *Faith and Philosophy* 36 (2019): 325–342.

sin in their conceptual structure; and (4) Christian virtues in this life are not states of perfection.

Sin

In *The Sickness unto Death*, sin is not fundamentally wrong*doing*. It is not acts of transgression against laws concerning specific kinds of actions but is the state of the sinner's attitude to herself before God (SUD, 81–82/SKS 11, 195). By "attitude" I mean the person's *understanding* of herself as infused with her *concern* for or willingness to be the person she understands herself to be. Wrongdoing is a symptom of sin rather than sin itself. If you are essentially a creature accountable to God (God being the good, the true, the source of the eternal law) but are uncomfortable with and resistant to being that, or even quite oblivious of the fact, you are likely to perform actions that express that discomfort or disrelation. You will be out of attunement to the good, and your actions will express that disharmony.

This lack of attunement is a split between what you are, both as a member of the human species and as the particular specimen with individual qualities and relations that you are, and what you are willing to be. As your consciousness of what you are grows deeper and more precise, the split shows up in awareness – the uncomfortable sense of the discrepancy between what you are (as you understand it) and what you are willing to be. The notion of what you are is here a normative or "qualitative" one. Put in modern ethical terms, it is what you "ought" to be; put in terms of virtue or character, it is what you would or will be if you actualize your essential nature, your "telos" both as an individual and as a member of the human species.

The discrepancy between what you are essentially and what you are willing to be is despair. Some people feel their despair, and some don't, despite being "in" despair. One of Anti-Climacus's favorite examples of despair that isn't felt is that of an adolescent girl whose life is going swimmingly: She's beautiful, popular, talented, and surrounded by approval, and her ideal for a human being (herself) is that of being beautiful, popular, talented, and appreciated for what one is. She is not attuned to what she is (which is "spirit"), even though what she *thinks* she is is perfectly attuned to what she wills to be. Maybe this picture itself is an idealization and such girls in real life have premonitions that this "happiness" won't last forever and even now is not quite real. However that may be, it is surely true that people can be pretty unaware of being out of sync with what they essentially are.

Anti-Climacus has a relational conception of what a self *is*, qualitatively; and also of what the self *takes itself to be*, qualitatively. The relation that every self is has the form of "before X."

> A cattleman who (if this were possible) is a self directly before his *cattle* is a very low self, and, similarly, a master who is a self directly before his *slaves* is actually no self – for in both cases a criterion is lacking. The child who previously has had only his *parents* as a criterion becomes a self as an adult by getting the *state* as a criterion, but what an infinite accent falls on the self by having *God* as the criterion! The criterion for the self is always: that directly before which it is a self. (SUD, 79/SKS 11, 193)

I have italicized the possible values for "X" in this quotation. Anti-Climacus seems to think of these possibilities as graded on a scale from ridiculously wrong to less wrong or even right. The "X" before which you think of yourself as a self – your true self, the self you essentially are – is a "criterion." That is, it is that by which you measure yourself, correctly or incorrectly. The Danish word is *Maalestok*, literally measuring stick. I think it helps our understanding of this idea to think of the "X," which in each case is a person or quasipersonal being, as a seat of approval or disapproval. The child wants approval from her parents and feels that she has let her*self* down if they disapprove of her; the herder who feels himself to be a success if his cattle approve of him has a rather low idea of personal success. The individual's concern for and conception of the criterion's approval is the relational leverage by which the criterion gets applied to the individual's self-concept. The grown-up whose criterion is the state is one who thinks his self is a success (that is, that he is a perfectly good person) if he obeys the laws of the state. The herder, the child, and the grown-up are ultimately mistaken about the qualitative or teleological identity of their selves. That before which every human self actually and truly exists is God, and so every person who isn't perfectly comfortable with existing before God is at odds with herself and thus in despair, whether she feels it or not. The more conscious the despairer becomes of her true identity, the greater her potential becomes for resolving her despair by willing to be the self that in truth she is, but also the deeper and more consciously she descends into despair if she does not resolve it.

A reader of *The Sickness unto Death* might hesitate a little about whether the person who thinks of himself as existing before God must be fully right. The notion of *God* in relation to whom every human self has its qualitative identity is ambiguous in *The Sickness unto Death*, as it is in Kierkegaard's writings generally. In a journal entry Kierkegaard remarks, "but just as no one has ever demonstrated [God's existence], so there has never been an atheist, even though there certainly have been many who have been unwilling to let what they knew (that the god exists) get control of their minds" (JP 3, 3606/Pap. V B 40:11). Socrates had a God-relationship: "Let us never forget that Socrates' ignorance was a kind of fear and worship of God, that his ignorance was the Greek version of the Jewish saying: the fear of the Lord is the beginning of wisdom" (SUD, 99/SKS 11, 211). But in another journal entry Kierkegaard says: "Socrates believed that he was divinely commissioned to show that all are ignorant – quite right, at that time divinity had not let itself be heard from" (JP 4, 4286/SKS 24, 372). The theological ambiguity in all these passages appears in *The Sickness unto Death* as a difference between Part One and Part Two.

In Part One Anti-Climacus writes of despair in relation to the infinite and the eternal and of the power that constituted the self and refers to the infinite and eternal creator as "God" (see SUD, 16, 26, 30, 32, 35, 38–42, 68–69, 71/SKS 11, 132, 143, 146, 148, 151, 153–156, 182, 185). In some of the kinds of despair treated in Part One the despairer knows he is a creature of God and must express that fact if he is to find himself. However, at the start of Part Two, titled "Despair Is Sin," Anti-Climacus writes as though he has not yet really mentioned God and says, "sin is: *before God or with the conception of God, in despair not to will to be oneself, or in despair to will to be oneself.* Thus, sin is the intensification of despair. The emphasis is on *before God*, or with the conception of God" (SUD, 77/SKS 11, 191; italics original). Then he says, "the point is that the previously considered gradation in the consciousness of the self is within the category of the human self, or the self whose criterion is man. But this self takes on a new quality and qualification by being a self directly before God. This self is no longer the merely human self but is what I, hoping not to be misunderstood, would call the theological self, the self directly before God" (SUD, 79/SKS 11, 193). Anti-Climacus also says, "the pagan and the natural man have the merely human self as their criterion ... paganism is 'to be without God in the world'" (SUD, 81/SKS 11, 195), and "only in Christ is it true that God is man's goal and criterion" (SUD, 114/SKS 11, 226).

So the contrast among Anti-Climacus's apparently conflicting statements about God resolves into the contrast between the "Socratic" religiousness that Johannes Climacus calls "Religiousness A" and the distinctively Christian religiousness that he calls "Religiousness B" (see CUP, 555–561/SKS 7, 505–510).

The former involves a kind of understanding of the divine that is accessible to human beings simply in virtue of their natural powers of moral sensitivity. This is why the criterion of the qualitative identity of the self afforded by the eternal and the infinite in the self, despite being the divine, is "the merely human self" (SUD, 81/SKS 11, 193). Human beings can be aware of the mystery of human existence, this existence in which, rising above mere vegetable and animal nature, we are conscious of the eternal law, of something infinite, of a demand for goodness and a sense of duty to it. To the infinite and the eternal in the human self[2] corresponds this "something" divine that is not merely the infinite and the eternal *in* the human self but something infinite and eternal in which the human self is *enveloped*;[3] it is that spiritual space in which the self lives and moves and has its being. Socrates is the paradigm individual for this kind of religiousness.

On the Socratic understanding of moral error, we err because and only because we do not fully understand what is required of us; the eternal in ourselves is not fully transparent to us. Were we completely clear about it, our souls would naturally conform to it and we would be morally perfect. We have a natural affinity to the good, so that only our ignorance stands between us and its realization in us. What we need, to be fully functioning human beings, is *enlightenment* or, as Kierkegaard sometimes puts it, "awakening." Within the Socratic understanding of ethics, God, and the human self, it is not impossible (perhaps just extremely unlikely) that a human being should exist who was so perfectly attuned to God and to herself that she was not in despair; such a human being would exemplify the virtue of faith as it is described at SUD, 50/SKS 11, 164: "in relating itself to itself and in willing to be itself, the self rests transparently in the power that established it." We might call this state "Socratic faith" to distinguish it from Christian faith – two different virtues.

Religiousness B, by contrast, results from an act in which God reveals himself to humankind. Here, God is no longer conceived as a Something infinite and eternal behind the universally accessible moral law. Instead, God reveals himself in a historical figure – Jesus of Nazareth, the Christ – who appears as the *Savior from sin*. The revelatory story is that of a

---

[2] The self is a conscious and self-conscious and choosing being that *is* a synthesis (integration) of the temporal and the eternal and can *actively synthesize* these aspects in itself (integrate them, accept itself as the synthesis – or refuse to do so, rejecting itself as such a synthesis).

[3] See Johannes Climacus's remark that "in immanence God is neither a something, but everything, and is infinitely everything, nor outside the individual, because the upbuilding consists in his being in the individual" (CUP, 561/SKS 7, 510).

sacrificial atonement for sin that God himself has accomplished on behalf of sinners. This is a story, not of an enlightenment but of a rescue, though a good portion of the morality that Jesus teaches overlaps with the universally accessible moral law. The predicament from which the Savior rescues the sinner is one from which the sinner cannot escape by his or her own powers. Unlike the Socratic knowledge of God, this rescue is not the sort of thing that can in principle be ascertained or predicted by careful and virtuous rational investigation. Even the prediction of such a thing must come by way of information that humans can access only if God, who is independent of the human self, elects to communicate it. The moral grievousness and inescapable depth of the sinner's predicament is so dire that nothing less than the interposition of God himself (in Christ) between the sinner and his sin can suffice as remedy. Thus the rescue from sin involves the historical presence of God in human flesh. "Before" God *so* conceived the sinner has his qualitative identity.

The beneficiary of the Christian revelation has a new concept of despair. Now despair is sin. Sin has some hitherto unconceived properties: It is not merely before the eternal disclosed immanently in humanity[4] but is before God conceived as the Father of Jesus Christ, conceived as the redeemer from sin. The new despair is built on the pagan one but has new depth and height in virtue of the new understanding of whom it is "before." Socrates, as a nearly miraculous exception among human beings, may be virtually without despair by pagan standards. But just as the feminine youthfulness can be in despair without having a clue about it, since she has no clue as to the criterion of her life (that she stands before the eternal as attested in her inner being), so Socrates can be in despair relative to the Christian revelation of what a human being is because he is ignorant of that revelation, that concept by which his self, like every human self, is measured. Just as the feminine youthfulness doesn't feel in despair by the human criterion, Socrates doesn't feel in despair by the Christian criterion.

---

[4] Socrates is Kierkegaard's paradigm for the immanent disclosure of the eternal in humanity. The eternal in humanity is a response or potential for response to a feature of extrahuman reality that can also be called the eternal: "The eternal touches the eternal in a human being" (WL, 258/SKS 9, 257). Socrates is unusually sensitive to the moral good and the need that it presents to choose in its favor in disregard of the temporal consequences. This is the eternal that touches the eternal in a human being. The eternal in the human being is the sensitivity to the eternal that touches it, or the fundamental human capacity for that sensitivity. Human beings vary in their sensitivity to the eternal, but all, presumably, have the fundamental human capacity, however oblivious of it they may have made themselves by spiritual slovenliness.

I have, I think inevitably, mentioned the atonement in connection with the concept of sin as it arises in *The Sickness unto Death*. Anti-Climacus raises a question about the order of the concepts of sin and atonement.

> It is specifically the concept of sin, the teaching about sin, that most decisively differentiates Christianity qualitatively from paganism, and this is also why Christianity very consistently assumes that neither paganism nor the natural man knows what sin is; in fact, it assumes that there has to be a revelation from God to show what sin is. The qualitative distinction between paganism and Christianity is not, as a superficial consideration assumes, the doctrine of the Atonement. No, the beginning must start far deeper, with sin, with the doctrine of sin – as Christianity in fact does. (SUD, 89/SKS 11, 202–203)

Anti-Climacus's claim seems to me to call for a distinction. The Christian revelation centers in the report of the atonement, conceived as the whole story of Jesus's advent, ministry, crucifixion, and resurrection. Since it is in the context of this event that we human beings come to conceive ourselves as in the desperate predicament that requires this sacrificial mediation of God in human affairs, it seems reasonable to think that the concept of the atonement is prior because the Christian concept of sin[5] derives from it. This is the *epistemic priority* of the atonement: We wouldn't know that we are sinners if we didn't know about the atonement for sin. But the atonement is a response to sin. This is the *ontological priority* of sin to the atonement: The atonement wouldn't have been required if we hadn't been sinners. We have to know about the atonement to know that we are sinners in the deep Christian sense, but what we come to know is that the reason for the atonement is the prior condition of sin.

Virtue and Selfhood

The concept of virtue gets little play in *The Sickness unto Death*, and in a notable mention of it Anti-Climacus says that faith, *not* virtue, is the "opposite" of sin. We'll address the implied opposition between virtue and faith in the next section, but here I'll connect a classical concept of virtue with the account of selfhood in *The Sickness unto Death*.

In the tradition that includes Socrates and Plato, virtues are dimensions of the maturity of the human soul. The idea is that the human soul, like other living things, has a "nature" – a way of being that determines what qualities the thing must acquire to be complete, mature, reaching its

---

[5] I write the qualifier "Christian" because, obviously, the Hebrew Bible has a concept of sin.

developmental *telos* or end. For example, just as a specimen of a rat species that hasn't yet learned to fear predators is not a "complete" rat, so a human specimen who isn't disposed to do justice to his fellow humans or show temperance in his sexual activity hasn't fully realized his natural end.

This tradition tends to exclude continence from the rank of the virtues because it is a kind of disunity or division within the soul. It assumes that the "parts" of the soul form a harmonious unity when the soul is complete. The continent person might have a good record of *behaving* temperately or justly but will not count as fully mature as long as, to behave properly, she must struggle against contrary inclinations. The cardinal virtues are wisdom, justice, temperance, and courage, and continent counterparts of these traits would be dispositions to action and emotion characteristic of the virtue (say, justice) but in internal combat with a counterdisposition that threatens to undermine it by motivating the soul contrary to justice (for example, impulses of avarice). In the mature, virtues will be unopposed by internal contrary desires. Furthermore, Aristotle makes clear that virtues are principles of choice. The just person reliably chooses just actions because she cares about justice and lacks contrary urges.

The Sickness unto Death presents a similarly structured picture of the self: It is potentially (that is, by nature) "spirit," and spirit is a relation of willing directed at oneself "before" God. To be actualized rather than merely potential spirit, an individual must be wholeheartedly willing to be the self he is before God. This classical distinction between the potential and actual self, the demand for wholeheartedness, and the connection of these to choice, are evident in the first paragraph: "A human being is a synthesis of the infinite and the finite, of the temporal and the eternal, of freedom and necessity, in short, a synthesis. A synthesis is a relation between two. Considered in this way, a human being is still not a self" (SUD, 13/SKS 11, 129). The human being is a natural synthesis, but this makes only for a potential self; to become an actual self, a person must choose to be that harmonious relation;[6] she must *actively* synthesize the temporal and the eternal in herself. To be spirit is to choose to be willing to be, before God, the self that one was created to be. The opposite of being spirit is despair, an unwillingness to be oneself before God. As such, despair is incompleteness as – indeed, resistance to being – a human being. The human self is completed as spirit by faith, the symmetrical opposite of

---

[6] Wholeheartedness is suggested by the notion of a synthesis, but it is extensively elaborated in "An Occasional Discourse," Part 1 of *Upbuilding Discourses in Various Spirits*. There it is contrasted with "double-mindedness."

despair: "that the self in being itself and willing to be itself rests transparently in God" (SUD, 82/SKS 11, 196). Thus faith is human maturity or psycho-ethical completeness, a state of the self analogous to the virtues in classical Greek ethics.

I began by pointing out that Kierkegaard's writings are a mosaic of explorations of such spiritual excellences as faith, love, hope, patience, compassion, forgiveness, being an individual, and bold confidence – explorations whose purpose is to build up the reader in exactly these spiritual qualities. Some of these virtue concepts come up in *The Sickness unto Death*, but faith is clearly central. So what is the relation between a self's being itself and willing to be itself while resting transparently in God and all the other spiritual qualities that Kierkegaard explores?

Aquinas distinguishes the "theological" virtues of faith, hope, and love from the "cardinal" virtues of wisdom, justice, temperance, and courage. The former three come from the New Testament, the latter four from the classical Greek tradition. But Aquinas thinks that when a Christian exhibits the cardinal virtues in a distinctively Christian way, these virtues too become "theological."[7] It is safe to say that, for Kierkegaard as for Aquinas, all the virtues that he promotes as an adherent of the Christian faith are "theological." Thus, all the virtues, each in its somewhat different way, involve their possessor in being him- or herself and willing to be him- or herself while resting transparently in God. This can be illustrated by the virtues that belong to neighbor-love. In the preceding paragraph, for example, a certain kind of hope,[8] compassion,[9] and forgiveness[10] are all subspecies of neighbor-love. But a general feature of neighbor-love is that God is the "middle term" between lover and neighbor.[11] So someone who loves his neighbor as himself will both will to be himself and do so as resting transparently in God. Insofar as neighbor-love is distinctively Christian, you will understand the God before whom you stand as the God who has atoned for your sins; and you'll will to be yourself as a

---

[7] Eleonore Stump sketches the complicated ways all the virtues are theological in "The Non-Aristotelian Character of Aquinas's Ethics: Aquinas on the Passions," *Faith and Philosophy* 28 (2011): 29–43. In a striking similarity to Kierkegaard, Aquinas makes the virtues a matter of passionate second-personal interactive relationship with God. However, Stump's thesis that Aquinas's ethics is therefore not Aristotelian has been challenged by Brandon Dahm in "The Acquired Virtues Are Real Virtues: A Response to Stump," *Faith and Philosophy* 32 (2015): 453–70.

[8] WL 2.III, "Love Hopes All Things – and Yet Is Never Put to Shame."

[9] WL 2.VII, "Mercifulness, a Work of Love Even If It Can Give Nothing and Is Able to Do Nothing."

[10] WL 2.V, "Love Hides a Multitude of Sins."

[11] WL 1.IIIA, "Love Is the Fulfilling of the Law." See especially 107/SKS 9, 110–111.

redeemed sinner. I think that an examination of any of the virtues that Kierkegaard explores in his works, both pseudonymous and non-pseudonymous, will yield a similar feature, with the variation that some of the virtues that Kierkegaard seeks to build up in his reader will be Religiousness-A virtues and others Religiousness-B virtues. Later I'll give brief examples of other cases.

If this is correct, then faith as treated in *The Sickness unto Death* has a special relation to the other Christian virtues and their Religiousness-A counterparts. Anti-Climacus says he will not enumerate particular sins; the discourse is "algebraic" (SUD, 82/SKS 11, 196). The definition of sin is abstract enough to encompass all possible sins. "Sin is: before God in despair not to will to be oneself, or before God in despair to will to be oneself" (SUD, 81/SKS 11, 195). And on the next page he gives a symmetrical definition of faith: "Faith is: that the self in being itself and willing to be itself rests transparently in God" (SUD, 82/SKS 11, 196). Thus faith is the diametrical opposite of sin. The definition of faith is exactly as "algebraic" as the definition of sin. If Anti-Climacus means the definition of sin to capture the essential sinfulness of all sins, it would seem that he means his definition of faith to capture the essential excellence of all the virtues. We might say that faith is the human excellence *par excellence*, the virtuous essence of all human virtues. It is that state of the human being in which people realize their telos; it is the completion of human nature; it is the state that Anti-Climacus earlier called "spirit." It is the essential form of what is realized in Christian traits such as love, hope, patience, gratitude, humility, bold confidence, and all the rest. All these virtues are particular manifestations of faith.

The Opposite of Sin Is Not Virtue but Faith

But in the paragraph following the one I have been expounding, Anti-Climacus seems to declare "Halt!" in response to my observations. "Very often . . . it is overlooked that the opposite of sin is by no means virtue. In part, this is a pagan view, which is satisfied with a merely human criterion and simply does not know what sin is, that all sin is before God. No, the opposite of sin is faith, as it says in Romans 14:23: "whatever does not proceed from faith is sin." And this is one of the most decisive definitions for all Christianity – that the opposite of sin is not virtue but faith" (SUD, 82/SKS 11, 196; see SUD, 124/SKS 11, 236).

Anti-Climacus's reading of Romans 14:23 is creative. Paul is discussing whether it is all right for Christians to eat food formerly declared "unclean" and he says, "I know and am persuaded in the Lord Jesus that nothing is unclean in itself; but it is unclean for anyone who thinks it is unclean." A few verses later he says, "But those who have doubts are condemned if they eat, because they do not act from faith; for whatever does not proceed from faith is sin" (New Revised Standard Version). My NRSV points out in a footnote that "faith" (*pistis*) in this context means "conviction," that is, conviction that the food is really clean. Clearly, *this* "faith" is not the opposite of sin in general. So our interpretation must use Anti-Climacus's definition of faith, not the one in the biblical text. But faith, as the symmetrical contrary ("opposite") of despair, is clearly an excellent attribute of the self, and that is what a virtue *is*. If despair is a deep state of dysfunction in the self, surely faith as its opposite is a deep state of well-being.

So why would Anti-Climacus say that the opposite of sin is *not* virtue *but* faith? A journal entry from the year Kierkegaard published *The Sickness unto Death* may hold a clue:

> Luther says, It is not good works that make a good man, but a good man who does good works, i.e., the man is what has become habitual, something more than all the individual actions. And, indeed, according to Luther, one becomes a good man through faith. Thus, first comes faith. It is not through a virtuous life, good works, and the like, that one attains faith. No, it is faith that causes one truly to do good works. (KJN 6, NB14:42/ SKS 22, 368)[12]

"The man ... has become habitual." In this rare Aristotelian sentiment of Luther, the man of faith has become a reliable source of good actions. His character has changed, and this change stems from faith. In this last mention, faith is not a virtue but an event in the man's life, a gift-event that explains the character change. It's the miracle about which we sing,

> 'Twas grace that taught my heart to fear,
> And grace my fears relieved;
> How precious did that grace appear
> The hour I first believed!
> Verse 2 of "Amazing Grace"

This event rearranged the man's fears, so that, having earlier feared death and the rejection of other human beings, he no longer fears them but now fears instead the callousness to his neighbor in which he formerly walked

---

[12] Quoted in Pieter Vos, "A Human Being's Highest Perfection: The Grammar and Vocabulary of Virtue in Kierkegaard's Upbuilding Discourses," *Faith and Philosophy* 33 (2016), 311–332, at 321.

and the threatening possibility of disloyalty to his God. No longer at odds with himself, he "rests" transparently in God and seeks to do his will. Here "faith" – this transforming moment of coming to believe and trust – is clearly not a virtue but instead the source of whatever virtues he has acquired – including the virtue of faith. Luther and Kierkegaard urge that our deliverance from sin is not to be assigned to anything we are or do – not to our virtues or our good works – but wholly to God's grace. Whatever good we are and do results from the rescue and not vice versa. The beginning of distinctively Christian virtue is not the performance of semivirtuous actions that habituate us, as Aristotle would have it, resulting eventually in full-fledged virtue but is the miracle of believing (faith) that God bestows on us. And the form of all those traits of character that we can trace to God's grace is the virtue of faith.

Peculiarities of Christian Virtues

Several peculiarities of Christian virtues turn on the Christian belief that all of us are sinners, helpless to become good specimens of humanity apart from God's grace. One of these is the etiological story that we have just noted. Another is the "inverse dialectic," the fact that moral and spiritual progress is marked by increasingly deep appreciation of the sin that remains in us, the apparent regress in virtue. A third peculiarity is what we might call the sin-reference of Christian virtues, and a fourth is the imperfection of Christian virtues in this life. Let us consider each of these.

Dependence on Grace

It may seem extreme to the point of inaccuracy to say that we are so mired in sin that we can't get started in the formation of virtues without an intervention of God in Christ. Surely many pagans have had virtues without such help! We all know unbelievers who are good people – sometimes better than we Christians. Kierkegaard's favorite pagan, Socrates, is a stellar example.

This objection doesn't take seriously enough the distinction between Religiousness A and Religiousness B. The distinction between God (SUD Part One) and God (SUD Part Two) seems to generate two sets of virtues – say, faith A (SUD, 49/SKS 11, 164) and faith B (SUD, 82/SKS 11, 196), patience A and patience B, gratitude A and gratitude B, etc. All these virtues exploit a relation to the divine, but the divine is understood differently in the A and B sets. And given the intimate involvement of the relationship to

God in the formation of the self, it stands to reason that the particular identity of God will be crucial to the character of the virtues that the self acquires in that relationship. To take one of the easier examples, the virtue of penitence or contrition will divide into two rather different character traits depending on whether the God-relationship is with the divine conceived Socratically or God conceived Christianly. Socratic penitence will be marked by the self-attribution *I have been insufficiently in touch with the divine in myself* and the self-exhortation/intention/motive *Let me attend more diligently to the divine in myself.* By contrast, Christian penitence will be marked by the self-attribution *I am dead and lost in my trespasses and sins* and the self-exhortation/intention/motive *Let me cast myself on the mercy of Christ.* The striving for moral improvement in Christian penitence will resemble in large ways the striving within Socratic penitence but will be engaged within the gracious parentheses of Christ's mercy.

In making this division in *The Sickness unto Death*, Anti-Climacus is consistent with the broad arc of Kierkegaard's writings. I have noted the parallel with the structure of *Postscript*. Other such divisions are that between indirect and direct communication and that broadly between the writings of Kierkegaard's first and second authorship. The notion of life "stages," along with the character traits that embody them, is a hallmark of Kierkegaard's thought. The stages are related to one another developmentally and analogically. Partly because of similarities, a lower stage prepares its adherent for the stage above it. The parallel formulations of faith (SUD Part One) and faith (SUD Part Two) indicate that the two virtues are formally similar. But if we read *The Sickness unto Death* in the light of the dialectical pathos passage in *Postscript*, which outlines the psycho-spiritual dynamic of actually trying on Religiousness A in all seriousness of its lonely striving, we will need to read the description of faith A (SUD Part One) as a static algebraic idealization that in the end isn't perfectly exemplified. The passage I quoted in the first paragraph of this chapter (SUD, 22/SKS 11, 138) supports this interpretation.

The objection that surely Socrates and many others who never heard of sin and the mercy of God in Christ have been virtuous people in approximation is correct about the A set of virtues. Anti-Climacus agrees with Johannes Climacus that the A virtues would be in themselves an enormous human achievement far beyond what most people in Christendom (or, indeed, in pagandom) represent. Furthermore, these virtues with their dialectic are sufficiently similar to the Christian virtues that they can function as a kind of primer for the latter.

Inverse Dialectic

This topic is the focus of the section in the *Concluding Unscientific Postscript* at Part Two, Section II, Chapter IV, Division 2A, where Johannes Climacus shepherds the reader through three stages of "existential pathos" that serve as an introduction to Christianity conceived as a way of living ("existing").

A pattern shows up frequently in Kierkegaard's writings. He starts with an idea that is generally available to the human mind, then develops it in a way that, still without presupposing anything not available to human thought, leads to the very cusp of an idea that cannot be known apart from revelation. In *The Sickness unto Death* Part One, Anti-Climacus develops the idea of despair in a way that allows him to expound sin as despair in Part Two, sin being a phenomenon that can be known only by revelation. But this pattern is especially characteristic of Johannes Climacus. *Philosophical Fragments* begins with the idea of a teacher as unlike Socrates as possible, and it turns out that Christ, as understood in the Christian tradition, fits it to a "T." In *Concluding Unscientific Postscript*, Climacus starts with the idea of a personal goal that he terms an eternal happiness, which properly subordinates every other possible human goal, and develops the idea of pursuing that goal as a life project in a way that yields a state of mind of the pursuer that is on the very border of the revealed idea of sin as the state of misery from which divine rescue is required. "An Occasional Discourse"[13] can also be read as conforming to this pattern: One is led through the dialectic of willing the good in truth (a "Socratic" exercise) as a preparation for the office of Christian confession, an action that culminates in casting oneself on the grace of God in Jesus Christ.

Climacus, in the section of *Postscript* that I mentioned earlier, designs the introductory tour through the stages of "existential pathos" to make becoming a Christian "repellently" as difficult as in fact it is. The purpose of this guidance, which is the most one person can do for another in this enterprise, is to "unsettle" the reader (CUP, 387/SKS 7, 351). He does this by starting with an idea that requires no revelation, that of the highest possible happiness. The person who takes this idea really to heart in application to his own existence will see that he must give it his all: "If it does not *absolutely* transform his existence for him, then he is not relating himself to an eternal happiness; if there is something he is not willing to give up for its sake, then he is not relating himself to an eternal happiness"

[13] UDVS Part 1.

(CUP, 393/SKS 7, 358; italics original). Thus the first stage (the "initial expression": this *orientation to the absolute*) of this development is for the individual to undertake to conform his will or passion to the idea of an eternal happiness by an absolute commitment to this absolute *telos* and thus no more than a relative commitment to all other ends.

Only the individual who takes seriously the task of the first stage, throwing himself wholeheartedly into the project, will experience the second stage (the "essential expression": *suffering*) – the frustration of the religious-ethical task by the individual's own immediacy, that is, his natural inclinations, his egoism, his competitiveness, his selfish desire for mastery, his sensuality, and the trivial joys that such passions yield when satisfied, and, to the extent that the effort to reorder his life succeeds, the pain of dying to these natural passions. The humiliating defeat at the hands of immediacy is a source of ongoing pain for the religiously serious person.

In the third stage (the "decisive expression": *guilt*) the suffering (frustration) takes on the more specifically spiritual character of guilt: I have taken on the task as an *agent*, as the one by whom the task is to be completed, but it is exactly as an agent that I fail. I fail by my own fault; I am guilty of failing at the most momentous task of my life. I cannot blame my immediacy or my weakness but must take responsibility for my failure. The deeper I go into the project of willing the good in truth – indeed, the more progress I make in realizing it – the more aware I become that I am simply not up to the task, morally. But this "inverse dialectic" of getting farther from the transformative goal the more seriously I undertake the task, is actually forward motion according to Climacus, or, as I would say, a growth in virtue. "The totality of guilt-consciousness [the fact that the consciousness of guilt encompasses the whole of my existence as a person] is the most upbuilding element in Religiousness A" (CUP, 560/ SKS 7, 509). In particular, through the awareness of this failure I become wiser, more deeply penitent, and humbler.

I am also readier to hear the good news that I am not just guilty but am a sinner and therefore a new creature.[14] The category *sin* doesn't strictly

---

[14] "The identity of the subject is such that the guilt does not make the subject into someone else, which is the expression for a break. But a break, in which the paradoxical accentuation of existence consists, cannot intervene in the relation between an existing person and the eternal, because the eternal embraces the existing person everywhere, and therefore the misrelation remains within immanence. If a break is to establish itself, the eternal itself must define itself as a temporality, as in time, as historical, whereby the existing person and the eternal in time have eternity between them" (CUP, 532/SKS 7, 484).

come into the picture as long as I am struggling, with only the resources of the eternal within me, to order (synthesize) the eternal and the temporal aspects of myself in a way that gives each its due and only its due. Any progress I make, and any guilt I incur, are strictly within my given personal identity. But once I come into a relationship with Christ, that relationship gives me a new identity: I the guilty am reborn as a sinner – as someone whose guilt cannot be overcome by action but only by redemption through the gift of the God in time.

But here looms a spiritual danger that Kierkegaard sees as emblematic of "Christendom," namely, that the earnestness with which I undertook the project will be undercut by my sense of relief at finding myself to be a sinner redeemed by Christ. The relief is right, but it remains right – and will rightly be felt as the relief that it is – only if I continue to take sin with the seriousness it merits. That is, it requires that sin-*consciousness* be maintained as pristine as possible. Anti-Climacus offers edifying guidance to this end in the introduction to Part Two, section B (SUD, 105–108/ SKS 11, 217–220) titled "The Continuance of Sin."

Sin is not to be identified with particular bad actions but is instead the general misorientation of the person from which bad actions spring. It is a "state" of the sinner. This state of the self is deplorable and so is to be repented of, to be regretted and disowned as far as honestly possible. To be complacent about your sin is further sin. Most people are so mired in this false orientation that it seems normal to them and not to be regretted. Remember that we are here in Part Two of *The Sickness unto Death*, the post-revelation part.

> The sinner, however, is so much in the power of sin that he has no idea of its wholly encompassing nature, that he is lost and on the way to destruction … Sin has become so natural to him, or sin has become so much his second nature, that he finds the daily everyday to be entirely in order, and he himself pauses only for a moment each time he perceives new impetus, so to speak, from new sin. (SUD, 105/SKS 11, 217)

The pagan in Christendom doesn't appreciate that he is a sinner but thinks himself a basically good person who from time to time gets off track and performs a bad action. But sin, like virtue, is a state of character. The sinner does not just perform bad actions now and then but is a bad character, a person whose orientation to himself, to others, and to God is perverse. This is the self-awareness of the truly penitent person, the person with the Christian *virtue* of penitence. It is the self-awareness that is made possible by the grace of God in Jesus Christ and stands side by side with the joy of redemption, the virtue of faith that consists in resting and having your life "in the consistency of the good" (SUD, 107/ SKS 11, 219), resting "transparently in the power that established" the self (SUD, 132/SKS 11, 242).

This teaching recalls the *simul iustus et peccator* of Luther, but with Kierkegaard's emphasis on character, it is even closer to the language and thought of the apostle Paul, who writes of the new or inner self (*anthrōpos*; Eph. 2:15, 4:24, Col. :3.10, Rom. 7:22, Eph. 3:16), which exists simultaneously with the flesh (Rom. 7:5, 18, 8:9, 13:14, Gal. 5:16–24), the body of sin (Rom. 6:6), the body of flesh (Col. 2:11), the old self (again *anthrōpos*; Rom. 6:6, Eph. 4:22, Col. 3:9). This self, Paul tells us, died with Christ on the cross (Rom. 6:6); it was buried with him by baptism (Rom. 6:4). The new self has Christian virtues, the old self a variety of vices. Kierkegaard's reflections about sin and faith in *The Sickness unto Death* and elsewhere can be profitably read against this Pauline background. The new self with her Christian virtues exists side by side with the sinner in her body of death.

Sin-Reference of Virtues

I began this chapter by noting the "edifying" purpose of Kierkegaard's writings, including *The Sickness unto Death*, and the frequent occurrence of such virtue concepts as faith, love, hope, gratitude, contrition (penitence), humility, patience, wisdom, purity of heart, compassion, bold confidence, earnestness, and (sense of) duty in his writings, both pseudonymous and signed. It seems plausible to the point of compelling that Kierkegaard thought his literary efforts might actually have the effect of "reintroducing Christianity to Christendom" in the sense of increasing these Christian traits in himself and some of those who read his writings. So it seems correspondingly implausible to suppose that he thought the pervasiveness and depth of sin ruled out all progress in the individual acquisition of these qualities.

Like Kierkegaard, Aristotle believed that virtues are acquired gradually. You don't "build up" character overnight. The *way* to virtue may be long and strenuous. But despite affirming that virtues are acquired gradually (by "habituation"), Aristotle seems to have believed that human virtues are perfections in the sense that a person cannot be said to have a virtue (say, justice) unless he possesses it to the maximum extent possible. This optimistic "perfectionism" shows up in at least two ways in Aristotle's thought. First, though he admits that continence (*enkrateia*: self-control) is a good trait (certainly better than either incontinence or outright vice), it is not a virtue because it presupposes that the agent has some dispositions (desires, urges, emotion dispositions) that are wayward enough to need to be managed.[15] And second, he says that the disposition to feel shame is not virtuous, even though it is vicious to be "shameless," because that disposition presupposes that the agent may have something to be ashamed of.[16] By contrast, Paul lists self-control (*enkrateia*) as a fruit of the Holy Spirit (Gal. 5:22). You might say that self-control is a virtue for sinners.

In fact, many of the virtues, as expounded within a Christian framework, presuppose sin, either in their possessor or others or both. Faith, to the extent that it is faith in the atonement of Christ, presupposes sin as what Christ atoned for. Love, insofar as it involves forgiveness, presupposes the guilt of the forgiven and may well be fostered by the forgiver's awareness that he himself is not without sin. Hope, to the extent that it is an expectation of a future state from which sin has been removed, presupposes sin in the present. The struggle to purify one's heart presupposes impurity of heart. And so forth. The Christian list of virtues is very different from the pagan lists, which do not presuppose sin or guilt as the Christian list does.

The church fathers called the virtues of the pagans (justice, wisdom, temperance, and courage) "glittering vices," notes Anti-Climacus, because they lacked the dimension of humble obedience to God, the ongoing awareness that their every thought and action was subject to God's scrutiny and approval or disapproval. They lacked the dimension of accountability to God. This failure made it possible for those who excelled their contemporaries in justice, courage, and so forth, to pride themselves on their comparative excellence. The autonomy they felt in the possession and exercise of these virtues also seemed to them to make their lives their own property, so to speak, which they could dispose of as they saw fit. This error, thinks Anti-Climacus, is the source of their deplorable approval of suicide (SUD, 46/SKS 11, 161). It seems unlikely that Anti-Climacus means to include the virtues of Socrates among the glittering vices – because Socrates does seem to exemplify accountability[17] to God (as he conceives God).

---

[15] *Nicomachean Ethics* VII.1. [16] *Nicomachean Ethics* IV.9.
[17] C. Stephen Evans has written a book arguing that the concept of accountability is fundamental to Kierkegaard's thought: *Kierkegaard and Spirituality: Accountability as the Meaning of Human Existence* (Grand Rapids, MI: Wm. B. Eerdmans, 2019).

Imperfection of Virtues in This Life

Kierkegaard does not think that anyone, himself included, possesses any of the Christian virtues flawlessly. All have sinned and fallen short of the glorious perfection that belongs alone to God. Everyone is to some extent in despair (SUD, 22/SKS 11, 138), and despair is the opposite of faith. No one *fully* rests *fully* transparently in the power that established him (see SUD, 132/SKS 11, 242). And yet Anti-Climacus can insist that *The Sickness unto Death* is, and must be, upbuilding if it is a truly Christian work (SUD, 5/SKS 11, 117–118). There is virtue even in being brought to recognize how little virtue there is in you. Because the Christian outlook presupposes sin, it is not perfectionist about the virtues in this life. A person may have the virtue of patience despite having the vice or sin of impatience. Kierkegaard may credit someone with having been built up in patience even though he is still somewhat impatient, or with faith despite his being somewhat weak in faith. Kierkegaard's writings are morally demanding; they hold the author and the reader to high spiritual standards. They have their eye on what Kierkegaard calls "ideality," and the virtue *concepts* exemplify this ideality. But the *virtues* are qualities that can be possessed in various approximations of perfection. If they could not be, virtue would not exist among human beings.

Conclusion

It is arguable that the idea of the deep sinfulness of humanity lies close to the heart of the Lutheran and Reformed discomfort with the idea of human virtues.[18] (Another, closely related idea located close to that center is the absolute sovereignty of God.) I have argued that theistic and Christian virtues, as understood in Kierkegaard's writings about faith, love, patience, bold confidence, earnestness, gratitude, hope, and other spiritual qualities, are compatible with being a sinner. My argument has turned on two features of Kierkegaard's thought. The first is that discussions of excellent spiritual traits pervade his writings, both signed and pseudonymous, and that in connection with these traits a fundamental goal of his reflections is what he calls "the upbuilding." A natural conclusion from this is that he aims to "build up" in himself and his reader exactly those spiritual traits or virtues. The second feature of Kierkegaard's

[18] See Jennifer Herdt, *Putting on Virtue* (Chicago, IL: University of Chicago Press, 2008), especially chapter 6.

thought is the difference between Christian virtues and secular ones, especially those posited by classical Greek philosophy. The distinctive features of Christian virtues are that they depend on grace, that they are subject to an "inverse dialectic," that the conceptual grammar of many of the virtues makes reference to sin and sinfulness and more broadly accountability to God, and that the Christian virtues are not, at least in this life, perfections.[19]

---

[19] Work on this chapter was supported by a grant from the Templeton Religion Trust by way of the Institute for the Study of Religion at Baylor University and the grant titled "Accountability as a Virtue." I am grateful to Sharon Krishek and Jeffrey Hanson for comments on an earlier draft. The opinions in the chapter are those of the author and not necessarily of the Templeton Religion Trust.

CHAPTER 9

Despair as Sin
The Christian and the Socratic
Merold Westphal

Elsewhere I have suggested that Kierkegaard is a four-dimensional thinker. He can be fruitfully read as an existentialist, a hermeneutical phenomenologist, a postmodernist, and an ideology critic. But he employs these genres as a Christian thinker, whether writing pseudonymously or not. So his existentialism differs decisively from that of Nietzsche or Sartre, his hermeneutic phenomenology from that of Gadamer or Ricoeur, his postmodernism from that of Derrida or Foucault, and his ideology critique from that of Marx or Habermas.[1]

But not always, or at least not in the first instance. When Kierkegaard writes as a Christian theologian, his models are thinkers such as St. Paul, St. Augustine, and Luther. But the Christian thinker is often in the background. He often writes, especially in the pseudonymous authorship, as a philosopher, and then his model is Socrates, whose appeal is not to some historically specific revelation but to the (in principle) universally human capacity for clear, hard thinking.[2] The "Socratic" claim that knowledge is recollection, throughout its many historical variations, is the claim that special revelation is not necessary since reason, our unaided intellect, is capable of discovering the truth about who we are and how we should live. Reason is also the norm by which any putative revelation should be interpreted and evaluated. As Kant will later put it, religion can and should be within the limits of reason alone, at least for the intellectually elite Schleiermacher will later call "cultured."[3]

---

[1] See Merold Westphal, "Kierkegaard as Four-Dimensional Thinker," in *Kierkegaard and Christian Faith*, ed. Paul Martens and C. Stephen Evans (Waco, TX: Baylor University Press, 2016), 13–23, 189–191. Ricoeur is also a Christian thinker, but he makes a sharper distinction between philosophy and theology than does Kierkegaard.

[2] The phrases "humanly speaking" (as distinct from "Christianly understood") and "the natural man" (SUD, 7–8/SKS 11, 124) are essentially synonymous with "the Socratic," as this latter phrase emerges in Part Two.

[3] In Friedrich Schleiermacher, *On Religion: Speeches to Its Cultured Despisers*, trans. John Oman (New York: Harper & Brothers, 1958), or, in other words, to the intellectual elite.

Kierkegaard highlights this contrast in "The Moral" with which he concludes *Philosophical Fragments*. Climacus does not claim truth for his presentation of Christian faith, only that it "goes beyond the Socratic," since "a new organ has been assumed here: faith; and a new presupposition: the consciousness of sin; and a new decision: the moment; and a new teacher: the god in time" (PF, 111/SKS 4, 306). The point is that the Socratic and the Christian are deeply different. The task for the reader is to choose between them without being seduced into thinking that some "Socratic" theology is a new and improved version of Christianity. The two are mutually incompatible rivals, decisively different. Either/Or.[4]

The Hongs suggest that "*The Sickness unto Death* presents the Socratic and Christianity in a correlation of complementary discontinuity" (SUD, xiv). My suggestion is that Part One is Socratic and only Part Two, "Despair Is Sin," is decisively Christian. One might better say "decisively biblical," for the concept of sin is as central to the Old Testament as to the New, and both belong to the Christian Bible (SUD, 101/SKS 11, 213). Kierkegaard is not reflecting on the differences between Judaism and Christianity but challenging those who take themselves to be Christians to recognize the difference between the Christian and the Socratic.

The "complementary discontinuity" of the two frameworks is almost Thomistic, at least in form. The Socratic is complementary to the Christian in that the latter does not need to disavow the former but can accept and presuppose it as a welcome product of "recollection," the work of human intellect unaided by any appeal to any special revelation (Scripture) as normative. In this respect Kierkegaard's phenomenology is formally like Aquinas's natural theology, even if the two are materially very dissimilar.

However, Christianity is discontinuous with the Socratic insofar as the former takes the latter to be inadequate by virtue of being incomplete. It is in need of completion with the help of presuppositions that contravene the Socratic assumption that as learners we already have the truth within ourselves and that any historically particular stimulus to reason's "discovery" of the truth is but the accidental occasion (Kant will say "vehicle") for "recollecting." Thus, in the *Meno* Socrates is the occasion for the slave boy's recollection of a certain geometrical truth to which Socrates is

[4] On the logic of this kind of argument in *Fear and Trembling* and *Philosophical Fragments*, see Merold Westphal, "Johannes and Johannes: Kierkegaard and Difference," in *International Kierkegaard Commentary:* Philosophical Fragments *and* Johannes Climacus, ed. Robert L. Perkins (Macon, GA: Mercer University Press, 1994), 13–32.

entirely external. The slave boy sees the truth for himself with Socrates's help but without relying on his authority. For Kierkegaard (as for Aquinas!) such reason needs to be supplemented and reinterpreted by historically specific revelation.[5]

Despair and Faith

In both parts of *The Sickness unto Death*, despair is the sickness in question. In German and Danish, despair is linguistically linked to doubt, not as an opposite but rather, perhaps, a curious cousin.[6] Often enough, the opposite of despair is hope. This is built into the French and Spanish languages.[7] But for Kierkegaard, with the help of no natural language, the opposite of despair is faith. He gives several versions of his formula for faith as the overcoming of despair. First in Part One:

> In relating itself to itself and in willing to be itself, the self rests transparently in the power that established it. (SUD, 14/SKS 11, 130)

> The self is healthy and free from despair only when, precisely by having despaired, it rests transparently in God. (SUD, 30/SKS 11, 146)

> The opposite of being in despair is to have faith ... the formula for faith: in relating itself to itself and in willing to be itself, the self rests transparently in the power that established it. (SUD, 49/SKS 11, 164)

Then in Part Two: "Faith is: that the self in being itself and in willing to be itself rests transparently in God" (SUD, 82/SKS 11, 196). Finally, the concluding lines of the book read:

> This contrast [sin/faith], however, has been advanced throughout this entire book ... the formula for the state in which there is no despair at all: in relating itself to itself and in willing to be itself, the self rests transparently in the power that established it. This formula in turn ... is the definition of faith. (SUD, 131/SKS 11, 242)

These definitions presuppose Kierkegaard's definition of the self: "a relation that relates itself to itself and in relating itself to itself relates itself to another" (SUD, 13–14/SKS 11, 130).

---

[5] Whether one gives a "Catholic" or a "Protestant" account of the relation of Scripture to tradition, neither is the product of "recollection," unaided, historically unsituated human reason.

[6] Thus *Verzweiflung/Zweifel* and *Fortvivlelse/tvivl.*

[7] Thus *désespoir/espérer* and *desesperación/esperanza.*

There are three elements to this crucial definition. First, the self is a relation insofar as it is "a synthesis of the infinite and the finite, of the temporal and the eternal, of freedom and necessity, in short, a synthesis" (SUD, 13/SKS 11, 129). To this list will be added the physical and the psychical (body and soul, SUD 13/SKS 11, 129) and consciousness and unconsciousness or ignorance (SUD, 42–74/SKS 11, 157–187).

The double use of "synthesis" here is unfortunate. Hegel almost never uses the language of thesis–antithesis–synthesis, and when others use it to summarize Hegelian thought a musical analogy is implicit: Antithesis is the unresolved chord that contains a dissonance, while synthesis is the resolution into consonance. The emergence of opposition (Hegel often says contradiction) cries out for peaceful coexistence, free of discord or variance. Or perhaps the analogy is chemical. When hydrogen and oxygen combine to form water, the two original elements have disappeared as such and are dissolved in a "synthesis."

But, for Kierkegaard, each "synthesis" would be better described as a dialectical duality. The opposition is not resolved into some kind of harmony, for the two moments remain in tension with each other. G. E. Moore quotes Bishop Butler on the title page of *Principia Ethica* as saying, "Each thing is what it is, and not another thing." Kierkegaard repudiates this pseudo-atomism and insists that for the self, at least, everything is always another thing. The self's infinity is infected with finitude, its finitude is always opened up to its infinity, and so on with the other "syntheses." In a circular rather than linear relation, each side is always already conditioned by the other and cannot be itself by itself. The two are united, to be sure, but only in their difference from and opposition to each other.

In fairness to Hegel it must be said that he sides with Kierkegaard over Moore. He distinguishes the dialectical moment of reason, not from the synthetic but from the speculative. Dialectical thought recognizes

> that one thing holds and the other does *also*. But a closer look shows that the finite is not restricted merely from the outside; rather it sublates itself [*sich aufhebt*] by virtue of its own nature, and passes over, of itself, into its opposite . . . the finite sublates itself because it contradicts itself inwardly . . . instead of being fixed and ultimate [*à la* Moore], everything finite is alterable and perishable . . . being implicitly the other of itself.[8]

---

[8] G. W. F. Hegel, *The Encyclopedia Logic [Lesser Logic]*, trans. T. F. Geraets, W. A. Suchting, and H. S. Harris (Indianapolis, IN: Hackett, 1991), 129–130 (§81). "Sublate" is not a happy translation of *aufheben*, since we only use it when translating Hegel. Alternatives such as "cancel and preserve" or "negate and affirm" are awkward. The meaning of any given *Aufhebung* is contextually understood.

The speculative moment of reason sees this as a positive result. It "apprehends the unity of the determinations *in their opposition* [emphasis added], the *affirmative* that is contained in their dissolution and their transition [into one another]."⁹ Nota bene: What is dissolved (resolved) is not the tension between the opposite moments but the moments themselves in their pseudo-atomic isolation as they evoke their opposites as essential to themselves. It is, in dialectic, "the grasping of the opposites in their unity, or of the positive in the negative, that speculative thought consists." What is grasped here is not a temporary tension to be overcome by reason; reason is rather the recognition of *"the necessity of the contradiction."*¹⁰ In other words, the dialectical duality that Kierkegaard finds the self to be has the dialectical-speculative structure Hegel finds in all finite things.

Second, the self is not just a relation, or better, a congeries of tensions; as such it also relates itself to itself. Both the cognitive and the volitional dimensions of this self-relation are dialectical. The self's consciousness is conditioned by unconsciousness or ignorance, but the reverse is also true, and the self is not entirely without a self-awareness that involves self-understanding and self-misunderstanding. Similarly, the self's freedom is conditioned by necessity, but the reverse is also true, and the self is not a stone. It is not entirely without self-choice, even if its autonomy is compromised by heteronomies of both nature and nurture.

Kierkegaard tells us that he wants his exposition to be both rigorously scientific and at the same time upbuilding. He is not willing to be a scholar at the expense of being "a physician … at the sickbed" (SUD, 5/SKS 11, 117).¹¹ So he will resist the temptation to make his goal a theoretical account of exactly how our consciousness is conditioned by unconsciousness or our freedom by necessity. His question will be whether our cognitive and volitional relations to ourselves are healthy, what might constitute that health, and how we might become healthier.¹²

Third, the self relates to an other. Notice where the "and" comes. It's not that the self relates to itself and relates to another. That bland "and"

⁹ Hegel, *The Encyclopedia Logic*, 131 (§82).
¹⁰ G. W. F. Hegel, *Hegel's Science of Logic*, trans. A. V. Miller (London: George Allen & Unwin, 1969), 56.
¹¹ Given his choice of the physician metaphor, "healing" might be preferred here to "upbuilding" (or "edifying" as in earlier translations). The medical doctor needs to be scientifically sound but in the service of healing.
¹² By "healthier" rather than simply healthy, I am suggesting we read *The Sickness unto Death* in the spirit of *Concluding Unscientific Postscript*, where the issue is "becoming" rather than simply "being" a Christian.

wouldn't be a dialectical relation. Rather, the self relates to itself *and* in relating to itself relates itself to another. The self's relation to itself and its relation to another do not sit side by side in mutual indifference. They are mutually implicative, mutually conditioning. The health of one depends on the health of the other.[13] Calvin puts the point in its cognitive aspect. He opens his *Institutes of the Christian Religion* (1, I, I) with the claim that "true and sound wisdom" has two parts: "the knowledge of God and of ourselves. But, while joined by many bonds, which one precedes and brings forth the other is not easy to discern." In this spirit, Kierkegaard writes, "Paganism [Socrates] required: Know yourself. Christianity declares: No, that is provisional – know yourself – and then look at yourself in the mirror of the Word in order to know yourself properly. No true self-knowledge without God-knowledge or [without standing] before God" (JP 4, 3902/SKS 24, 425).

There is an interesting progression to be noted. In the definition of the self the other is simply "another." But in the five definitions of faith that other is, more specifically "the power that established" the self (three times) and, still more specifically (perhaps) "God" (twice).

Why the "perhaps?" The reference to God occurs once in Part One and once in Part Two, and in the final definition of faith Kierkegaard tells us he has been discussing faith throughout the entire book (SUD, 131/SKS 11, 242). But Socratic "faith" is not Christian faith. I want to suggest the identification of the power that establishes the self with God is not the same in Part One and Part Two, and, moreover, that it is the concept of sin that marks the decisive difference. We can recall (see earlier) that sin was an essential ingredient in the distinction between the Socratic and the Christian in *Philosophical Fragments*. The same will be true in *The Sickness unto Death*, where, as we shall see, Socrates eliminates the concept of sin by equating it with ignorance (SUD, 87–100/SKS 11, 201–212).

Despair without Sin

Part Two, "Despair Is Sin," begins with an emphasis on the notion of the self "before God" as decisive. But this concept was already introduced in the Preface (SUD, 5/SKS 11, 117) and is repeated throughout Part One (SUD, 27/SKS 11, 143; SUD, 35/SKS 11, 151; SUD, 46/SKS 11, 161), where Kierkegaard also freely speaks about Christianity. But it does not

---

[13] This has important implications for the religiously oriented therapist. One cannot assume that the client's problems are simply psychological or simply spiritual, as G. E. Moore might assume.

follow that the identification of the power that established the self need be the Christian God so far as the analyses of Part One go. Kierkegaard signals where he is headed but not that he has necessarily arrived. (Similarly, in Aquinas the First Mover is not yet the God of the Bible, even if the God of the Bible is the First Mover. Or again, in Heidegger the "God" of ontotheology is not the God of Abraham, Isaac, and Jacob, even if that God has certain "ontotheological" characteristics such as First Cause.)

For broadly speaking there are at least three candidates for the ultimate other, the power that established the self: nature, society in human history, and the biblical God that Kierkegaard has in mind, the creator of heaven and earth, irreducible to the physical universe, and the lord of history, irreducible to any social/cultural, or political/economic order.

We need only to remember Spinoza and Hegel. For Spinoza it is nature as understood by the natural sciences that is the power that established the self, and he freely calls this nature God: *deus sive natura*. To be a self "before God" can only mean to be part of the order of matter in motion according to the laws science discovers. To rest transparently in this power is to practice a kind of stoic resignation that Spinoza strangely calls love of God. (At least he doesn't call it faith, though it is his analogue for what Kierkegaard calls faith!)

For Hegel, the power that established the self is human society as it unfolds throughout history on the stage of nature, and he freely calls this God, the spirit that becomes absolute in and as human history. To be a self "before God" means to be part of this process as an individual (subjective spirit) in dialectical duality with a historical society (objective spirit in its familial, economic, and political institutions) and to understand oneself as such in terms of that society's culture (art, religion, and most especially philosophy). To rest transparently in this power is to find this process the ultimate embodiment of Reason and thus to conform oneself to the laws of one's society and the values of one's culture.

Spinoza and Hegel are part of the "Socratic" rather than the "Christian" or biblical tradition. They know and use the language of the Bible and refer to it quite freely. But they revise and correct it in the light of what purports to be universal reason, the natural power of the unaided human intellect. The Bible is, like Socrates to the slave boy, the occasion for "recollecting" the truth, but not the ultimate source or norm for the truth. Scripture is subordinate to Reason. Scripture is the ultimate source or norm for truth only for those who cannot rise or have not risen with the intellectually elite to the level of (Spinoza's or Hegel's) philosophy.

I call the hermeneutical project of Spinoza and Hegel (and so many others), borrowing from Kant, the religion-within-the-limits-of-reason-alone project. I take Spinoza, Kant, and Hegel to be its most powerful practitioners in the seventeenth, eighteenth, and nineteenth centuries, respectively. The irony is that while each appeals to a reason that is supposed to be universal, free from conditioning by the contingent content of any particular society or cultural tradition, each is incompatible with both of the other two. Reason turns out to be as sectarian as the religions of revelation.[14] Its supposed privilege over them evaporates in a perspectival pluralism. So Kierkegaard sees the Scripture-based ontology he understands Christianity to be as having no need to subordinate itself to some denominational version of reason (even when it calls itself "Reason"). Such a theology is no more particular and contingent than such philosophies. It is this particularity and this contingency that give rise to the language of leap, risk, and objective uncertainty in *Concluding Unscientific Postscript*. It applies to Socratic philosophy just as much as to biblical theology.

Kierkegaard isn't often thinking about Spinoza, but he is very often thinking of Hegel. He regularly satirizes Hegel's account of what it means to be a Christian "before God" as merely the ideology of bourgeois society and culture. His critique brings to mind two phrases: Nietzsche's "wretched contentment" and Bonhoeffer's "cheap grace."[15] With Luther, Kierkegaard distinguishes civic virtue from Christian faith. He insists that the latter, properly understood, is the more demanding of the two and the proper judge of the former. But he does not claim that it represents "the view from nowhere."

My suggestion is that the analysis of the self in Part One fits just as well within Spinoza's naturalistic pantheism (scientific naturalism) or Hegel's socio-historical pantheism (secular humanism, with or without borrowed religious language) as it does within Christianity. In other words, it is too abstract to be necessarily biblical or even merely theistic. It's like that skeleton key that fits into many different kinds of lock, for Spinoza and Hegel have their own accounts of the ontological structures formed by the dialectical discord of the infinite and the finite, of the temporal and the eternal, of freedom and necessity along with the corresponding accounts of

---

[14] I have developed this analysis in detail in Merold Westphal, *In Praise of Heteronomy* (Bloomington, IN: Indiana University Press, 2017). For Hegel Reason is not ahistorical in the way it is for Spinoza and Kant, but in history's eschatological fulfillment it frees itself from what is historically contingent and particular and becomes universal (in Hegel's system).

[15] In *Thus Spoke Zarathustra* and *The Cost of Discipleship*, respectively.

the sickness or health of the self.[16] The therapist who is a scientific naturalist, the therapist who is a secular humanist, and the therapist who seeks to think biblically might each find Part One helpful in diagnosing their clients. But *if* Kierkegaard (like Aquinas) is right in thinking that human reason needs to be supplemented and corrected by divine revelation, the first two therapists will not have the conceptual tools they need to get to the innermost depths of the self, the presumed goal of "depth psychology."[17] This will be true *even if* they find Kierkegaard's account of the relation between consciousness and the unconscious at least as helpful as Freud's.[18]

What is especially important here is that the analyses of both Spinoza and Hegel effectively eliminate the notion of sin. Spinoza moves decisively "beyond good and evil" in his definitions. "It is clear that we neither strive for, nor will, neither want, nor desire anything because we judge it to be good; on the contrary, we judge something to be good because we strive for it, will it, want it, and desire it" (III, P 9, S).[19] Accordingly,

> By good here I understand every kind of joy [pleasure], and whatever leads to it, and especially what satisfies any kind of longing, whatever that may be. And by evil [I understand here] every kind of sadness [pain], and especially what frustrates longing. (III, P 39, S)

> *The knowledge of good and evil is nothing but an affect of joy or sadness, insofar as we are conscious of it.* (IV, P 8)

> By good I shall understand what we certainly know to be useful to us. By evil, however, I shall understand what we certainly know prevents us from being masters of some good. (IV, D 1–2)

In this context there can be no meaningful concept of sin, and it is not surprising that humility (III, Def. 26), repentance (III, P 30, S and

---

[16] Part One can also be seen as an analogue to Heidegger's account of onto-theology. It takes place within the horizons of abstract and impersonal terms that are too generic to evoke what Kierkegaard means by "before God."
[17] On the significance of this "if," see note 4.
[18] See my analysis in Merold Westphal, "Kierkegaard's Psychology of Unconscious Despair," in *International Kierkegaard Commentary: The Sickness unto Death*, ed. Robert L. Perkins (Macon, GA: Mercer University Press, 1987), 37–66.
[19] Quotations from Spinoza are from the *Ethics* (in Curley's translation). The Roman numeral indicates the Part. P indicates the Proposition. S indicates the Scholium. D indicates Definition. Def. indicates Definition of the Affects at the end of III.

Def. 27), and remorse (III, P 18, S 2 and III, Def. 17) are not in any way virtues.[20]

Nietzsche reflects with delight on this Spinoza,

> he who had banished good and evil to the realm of human imagination ... The world, for Spinoza, had returned to that state of innocence in which it had lain before the invention of the bad conscience: what then had become of the *morsus conscientiae*?[21] "The opposite of *gaudium* [joy, pleasure]" he finally said to himself – "a sadness accompanied by the recollection of a past event that flouted all of our expectations."[22]

In his demythologizing of "the myth of the Fall" in the familiar Genesis story, Hegel likewise eliminates sin from the horizons of his thought. It is all about knowing. Innocence is the immediate and natural life of those who have not risen above animal consciousness to the cognition (*Erkennen*) and thinking (*Denken*) that distinguishes Spirit from Nature. To say that humans are by nature evil is simply to say that they are not yet actually human, only potentially so. It is necessary that this prehuman immediacy be transcended by the emergence of Spirit in the form of cognition, thought, and knowledge, most especially philosophy. "Nature [animal consciousness] is, for man, only the starting point that he ought to transform ... Philosophy is cognition, and the original calling of man, to be an image of God, can be realized only through cognition."[23] The "Fall" is what ought to happen, for it is the upward movement from Nature to Spirit in which creation is completed and the potentially human animal becomes for the first time truly human. Of course, this may not occur as philosophy in the first instance but in those lesser and inadequate forms of thinking that Hegel labels Understanding rather than Reason.[24]

If one lives "before God" in some more or less Spinozistic or Hegelian pantheism from which sin has been systematically excluded, one is not talking about the God Kierkegaard tells us he has been talking about from

[20] See the discussion of remorse and repentance in Spinoza's *Short Treatise on God, Man, and His Well-Being*, in *Collected Works of Spinoza*, vol. 1, ed. Edwin Curley (New York: Random House, 1985), chapter X.
[21] Sting of conscience. In Spinoza sometimes translated as disappointment (his meaning) but more appropriately as remorse (the traditional sense).
[22] Friedrich Nietzsche, *Genealogy of Morals*, in *Basic Writings of Nietzsche*, ed. and trans. Walter Kaufmann (New York: Random House, 1958), II, 15. See the two passages in Spinoza cited above in relation to remorse.
[23] Hegel, *The Encyclopedia Logic*, §24, Addition 3 (60–63).
[24] Hegel, *The Encyclopedia Logic*, §25. This distinction maps quite nicely onto the distinction between *Vorstellung* (representation) and *Begriff* (concept) that Hegel regularly uses to express the superiority of philosophy to religion.

the beginning. Part One is a dazzling display of phenomenological insights into the self that does not live its dialectical dualities in healthy harmony – no, healthy tension. But the concept of God remains indeterminate. It is the task of Part Two to make this clear. It begins with a clear indication that we are about to learn what it means to live "before God" with the important qualification, "Christianly understood" (SUD, 77/SKS 11, 191).

One final note, however, on the structure of Kierkegaard's dialectic before turning to despair as sin. At one point (SUD, 46–47/SKS 11, 161–162) Kierkegaard speaks of "paganism in Christendom," and we are reminded that in this context Socrates is the philosophical paradigm of paganism. On three other occasions (SUD, 52/SKS 11, 168; SUD, 56–57/ SKS 11, 171–173; SUD, 63–64/SKS 11, 177–179) Kierkegaard stresses that being a Christian in Christendom is no guarantee that one is not more pagan than Christian.

This means either (a) that the pagan (Socratic) dimensions of the self have corrupted the truly Christian dimensions or (b) that the "Christian" dimensions of the self are themselves the root source of the self's paganism. The quotation marks around "Christian" here signify the misunderstanding of Christianity that Kierkegaard refers to as Christendom.[25] There is a place for Christendom in the truly Christian life, but as with Luther's critique of civic virtue and the prophets' critique of the ancient people of the covenant, it must not be allowed autonomy or even hegemony. Its contribution must always be subject to reinterpretation and correction by a revelation to which Christendom is subordinate.

Despair as Sin

Against this background there are several things to note about the thesis that defines Part Two that despair is sin.

Despair Is Not Depression

Kierkegaard is not telling us that it is a sin to be sad. As the metaphor of sickness suggests, despair is objective more than subjective. That is to say it is more like an organism that is malfunctioning than it is like a mood or an

---

[25] On this theme in *Christian Discourses*, see Merold Westphal, "Paganism in Christendom," in *International Kierkegaard Commentary:* Christian Discourses *and* The Crisis and a Crisis in the Life of an Actress, ed. Robert L. Perkins (Macon, GA: Mercer University Press, 2007), 13–33. See note 16.

emotion.[26] If we are tempted to simply identify despair with depression (as most Kierkegaard scholars are careful not to do), we need to pay closer attention to the text. We mustn't assume that Kierkegaard's usage is the same as ours. After the Fall, for him the opposite of despair is not hope but faith, which is neither an emotion nor a mood.

Kierkegaard seems to hold a view of the self as three-dimensional. It has cognitive, volitional, and affective capacities. Moreover, he has a good deal to say about such affective states as melancholy and anxiety. But if, as could happen, we add despair to this list, we must not assimilate it too closely with the other two, at least so far as *The Sickness unto Death* is concerned.[27]

In the first place, it has its own distinctive way of relating to the structures of the self that make up what I've been calling its dialectical dualities, thus the point just made about the objectivity of despair. It is a way of (mis)relating to oneself. To switch metaphors, we can say that despair is a machine in need of repair, not the funny noises it makes that tell us of this need. It is more nearly ontological than psychological.

Moreover, it is primarily related to the volitional dimension rather than the affective dimension of the self. That is clear from the fact that its opposite, faith, is regularly described as a kind of willing. Faith is also described as a resting, but this resting is more nearly an action like trust than a feeling. Kierkegaard's analyses of melancholy, an affective state (with ontological roots, to be sure),[28] comes closer than despair to what we call depression.

It does not follow that despair (and thus sin) has nothing to do with depression, for the latter can be a symptom of the former. I think it is

---

[26] Robert C. Roberts distinguishes emotions from moods in terms of being intentional or nonintentional. I am angry *at* someone or afraid *of* something. Such emotions are construals and have a propositional content, for example, "X is dangerous." But a mood, such as elation or melancholy, need not be *of* or *about* anything, though it can be, in which case, for Roberts, it is an emotion. Robert C. Roberts, *Emotions: An Essay in Aid of Moral Psychology* (Cambridge: Cambridge University Press, 2003), 112. Moods are not the only (possibly) nonintentional aspects of our affective life. There are also what used to be called "raw feels" such as nausea or itches. Thus we can and should distinguish "meaningless sensations and meaningful perceptions." Rick Anthony Furtak, *Wisdom in Love: Kierkegaard and the Ancient Quest for Emotional Integrity* (South Bend, IN: University of Notre Dame Press, 2005), 13.

[27] Judge William (the pseudonymous author of *Either/Or, Part II*) equates depression with despair and calls the former a sin (EO 2, 188–189, 204–205/SKS 3, 183–184, 197–198). The author of *The Sickness unto Death* (pseudonymous or actual) makes despair a sin but without this equation.

[28] Perhaps this is why Simon Podmore can emphasize the objectivity of melancholy and treat it as virtually synonymous with despair. He sees it as "an integral and irrevocable element within the self's relation to God." *Kierkegaard and the Self before God: Anatomy of the Abyss* (Bloomington: Indiana University Press, 2011), 68. But see note 31.

misleading to say that despair in *The Sickness unto Death* is a "stronger version" of depression[29] or to say that depression is a "subset" of Kierkegaard's despair.[30] Depression can be a symptom of despair, but then so can narcissistic bullying and egomaniacal boasting. Just as a cough is qualitatively and ontologically different from the serious lung disease of which it may be a symptom, so depression is not a special case of despair. But as a symptom it may be a "presentiment of despair."[31]

In *The Sickness unto Death*, then, despair is sin but is not to be identified with depression. It does not follow that depression has nothing to do with sin except as a symptom. Kierkegaard is not only a good Lutheran but, I think, a good Calvinist as well on at least one relevant point. Calvin teaches a doctrine of total depravity.[32] Careful Calvinists always point out that this does not mean that we are as completely sinful as possible or that there is no goodness in us. It means rather that there is no dimension of human life in which the goodness of creation has not been contaminated by sin, damaged but not destroyed. In particular, against Scholastic teaching, not only the will but also the intellect has been distorted, so that sin is an epistemological and not only a moral category. In cognitive terms, blindness or distorted vision can arise from fault. Paul speaks of those "who by their wickedness suppress the truth" (Rom. 1:18).

Similarly, in terms of our affective life, total depravity thus means that our joys and our sorrows, our delights and our depressions are scarred by our sinfulness. If we are not purely evil, we are not purely good either. But this does not mean that depression simply is sin any more than it means that parental love is a sin, though parental love can be sinful. The mystery writer tells us, "Divorce does more than split things apart. It taints things, all things, especially the good ones."[33] If he had been a Calvinist theologian, he would have spoken more generally: "Sin taints all things, especially the good ones."

---

[29] Roberts, *Emotions*, 242.

[30] In spite of this language, Mark Tietjen emphasizes the medical analogy and is clear that despair "cannot simply be identified with depression. "Many people psychologists would consider in good mental health are in despair according to Kierkegaard." See his *Kierkegaard: A Christian Missionary to Christians* (Downers Grove, IL: IVP Academic, 2016), 97–98. For a more sustained discussion of the distinction between despair and depression in Kierkegaard, see Gordon Marino, *Kierkegaard in the Present Age* (Milwaukee, WI: Marquette University Press, 2001), 99–111

[31] Podmore, *Kierkegaard and the Self before God*, 61. But see note 28.

[32] This is the (in)famous T in the TULIP summary of his teaching as presented in the Canons of the Synod of Dort.

[33] Reed Farrel Coleman, *Empty Ever After* (Madison, WI: Bleak House Books, 2008), 146.

Sin Is Not Ignorance

In *Fragments* and *Postscript*, Johannes Climacus distinguishes the Socratic from the Christian by distinguishing Reason from Revelation. Reason is understood in terms of recollection, and the difference is between the assumption that the Truth is already deep within us and needs but to be brought to the surface and the assumption that this is not the case and that we are separated, by fault (as well as by finitude), from the essential Truth that tells us who we are and how we should live. Philosophic wisdom cannot save us (as Spinoza and Hegel assume).

This polemic is misread as an argument that recollection is always simply false. The logic of the argument is that Revelation is irreducibly different from Reason and that Christianity is dramatically distorted if made to rest on Reason as recollection. It rather presupposes that the knowledge ingredient in saving faith must be received from outside as a gift of grace.[34]

A sneaky, Socratic way around this argument, implicit at least in the gnosticisms of Spinoza and Hegel, is that sin is ignorance and that Reason in some philosophic version of the recollection thesis is the overcoming of ignorance. Philosophical Reason thus takes the place of atonement and forgiveness and brings about reconciliation between God and human beings, individual and social. Kierkegaard's argument is that such a god is not God, "Christianly understood." So in *The Sickness unto Death* Anti-Climacus offers a sustained polemic against the Socratic assimilation of sin to ignorance (SUD, 87–96/SKS 11, 201–208) and insists that in a biblical frame of reference sin is understood as disobedience (SUD, 81–82/SKS 11, 195–196), self-willfulness (SUD, 81–82/SKS 11, 195–196), and defiance (SUD, 90, 93/SKS 11, 203, 205–206). It resides in the will, as does faith, its remedy (SUD, 88, 94–95/SKS 11, 201–202, 207–208).

The references earlier to Spinoza and Hegel are supported when Kierkegaard identifies the Socratic account of sin with pantheism (SUD, 96, 117–118/SKS 11, 209, 229–230).[35] In *Postscript*, recollection is regularly identified with "immanence," signifying a loss of transcendence in the relation between God and human persons and societies, building on the argument in *Fragments* that sin is the "absolute difference" between the human and the divine (PF, 44–47/SKS 4, 249–252). So, in *The Sickness*

---

[34] See the essay cited in note 4.
[35] Kierkegaard seems to have Hegelian pantheism in mind more than Spinoza's, for he talks about the way in which the "crowd" crowds God out of the picture and "becomes God."

unto Death, once Kierkegaard has argued that sin is not ignorance, he explicates the Christian idea of what it means to be "before God" as sinners in terms of the "infinite qualitative difference" between God and humans (SUD, 99, 117, 121–122, 127, 129/SKS 11, 211, 229, 233, 238–239, 239–240).[36] Nota bene: All these references come in Kierkegaard's discussion of despair as sin. As in *Philosophical Fragments*, it is sin and not some impersonal, metaphysical (ontotheological) relationship such as finite and infinite that is the "absolute difference."

Podmore tells us that he began with the assumption that sin is the "infinite, qualitative difference" but that "mercifully" he eventually concluded that "the true meaning of the abyss between God and humanity is expressed through *forgiveness*."[37] Such a view is expressed in the collect for the Sunday closest to September 28: "O God, you declare your almighty power chiefly in showing mercy and pity."[38]

It is true that in his discussion of despair as sin, Kierkegaard speaks of grace (SUD, 109–110/SKS 11, 222), atonement (SUD, 89, 100, 159/SKS 11, 203, 212/Pap. X⁵ B 18), and especially of the forgiveness of sins (SUD, 111–125/SKS 11, 221–236). Throughout his writings Kierkegaard often suggests that we do not believe in authentic Christianity, not because of mere doubt but because we find it offensive. Here the offense is "the sin of despairing of the forgiveness of sins," which leads to the command, "Thou shalt believe in the forgiveness of sins" (SUD, 113, 115/SKS 11, 225, 226–227). This is related to the absolute difference. "As sinner, man is separated from God by the most chasmal qualitative abyss. In turn, of course, God is separated from man by the same chasmal qualitative abyss when he forgives sins ... there is one way in which man could never in all

[36] I cite this version of the phrase because of its twentieth-century importance in Karl Barth's *Epistle to the Romans* and the discussion of Rudolf Otto's *The Idea of the Holy*, where God is "wholly other." The phrase occurs in various forms in several Kierkegaard texts. They include one or more of the following adjectives: infinite, qualitative, chasmal, absolute, and eternal, and sometimes "difference" is replaced with "abyss." See, for example, SUD, 89, 99, 117, 121–122, 127, 129/SKS 11, 202, 211, 229, 233, 238–239, 239–240; PF, 44–47/SKS 4, 249–252; CUP, 217, 220, 223, 227, 412–413, 557–558, 566/SKS 7, 198–199, 201–202, 203–204, 207–208, 376, 506–507, 513–514; JP 1, 236/KJN 5, NB10:57/SKS 21, 286; JP 1, 693/KJN 5, NB10:54/SKS 21, 284–285; JP 2, 1383/KJN 5, NB9:59/SKS 21, 235; JP 3, 3087/Pap. VII² B 235; JP 3, 3645/KJN 6, NB14:118/SKS 22, 413; JP 3, 3646/KJN 7, NB17:92/SKS 23, 236–237; JP 3, 3647/KJN 8, NB24:18/SKS 24, 329; JP 3, 3648/KJN 9, NB28:57/SKS 25, 265–266; JP 3, 3649/KJN 9, NB29:18/SKS 25, 309; JP 3, 3650/KJN 10, NB31:159/SKS 26, 113–114; WA, 100/SKS 11, 104; UDVS, 287/SKS 8, 382; PC, 28–32, 63, 128, 131, 140/SKS 12, 42–46, 75, 132–133, 135, 143.
[37] Podmore, *Kierkegaard and the Self before God*, xi. See also xvi, xviii, xxi, 1, 7. This is his central thesis about Kierkegaard's "anatomy of the abyss."
[38] *The Book of Common Prayer*, 234.

eternity come to be like God: in forgiving sins" (SUD 122/SKS 11, 233).[39]

This passage gives some support to Podmore's change of mind. But insofar as it does, it seems to me that both he and Kierkegaard are wrong. We are sometimes able to forgive others for wrongs done against us, and in doing so we are like God. Of course, we need some doctrine of analogy to remind us that in this, as in every other way in which, as created in the image and likeness of God, we are like God, we are also unlike God. But as sinners, we are not a pale and imperfect likeness of God but enemies of God.[40] We are not like the less skilled players who warm the bench while the stars and superstars battle the opponent; we are on the other team, using whatever skill we may have against the victory of truth and righteousness. This is why Kierkegaard writes, "The qualitative distinction between paganism and Christianity is not, as a superficial consideration assumes, the doctrine of the Atonement. No, the beginning must start far deeper, with sin, with the doctrine of sin – as Christianity in fact does" (SUD, 89/SKS 11, 202–203).

Actually, I think that at least from the claim in *Fragments* that sin is the "absolute difference," Podmore's first impression is truer to the spirit of Kierkegaard's texts than the view he "mercifully" came to hold. To be sure, Kierkegaard's narrative is one of sin and salvation, fault and forgiveness. But I think he (rightly) sees the good news of divine "mercy and pity" as bridging the abyss, not deepening it. Since it is an infinite gulf, only God can bridge it in acts of incarnation, atonement, evoked repentance, and forgiveness. But that does not mean that there are not finite gaps that we can bridge. That's an important part of what *imitatio Christi* is about. As reconciled with Christ we are called to be reconciled with one another.

Sin Is Not Sins

Kierkegaard defines sin as follows: "Sin is, before God in despair not to will to be oneself or before God in despair to will to be oneself." He then asks why there is no mention here of "murder, stealing, fornication, etc.? ... Are they not also self-willfulness against God, a disobedience that defies his commandments?" Then he answers his own objection: "If in considering sin we mention only such sins, we so easily forget that, humanly speaking, all such things may be quite in order up to a point, and yet one's whole life may be sin" (SUD, 81–82/SKS 11, 195).

[39] See SUD, 127–128/SKS 11, 238–239, where Kierkegaard links this to the Incarnation.
[40] See Luke 19:27, Rom. 5:10, Phil. 3:18, and James 4:4.

Kierkegaard expands on this point in a section entitled "The Continuance of Sin." "The cursory observation that merely looks at the new sin and skips what lies between ... the two particular sins, is just as superficial as supposing that a train moves only when the locomotive puffs ... the particular sins are not the continuance of sin but the expression for the continuance of sin; in the specific new sin the impetus of sin merely becomes more perceptible to the eye" (SUD, 106/SKS 11, 218).

In distinguishing particular sins from the "continuance" of sin or the "impetus" of sin, Kierkegaard is, as so often, a good Lutheran. In his commentary on Psalm 51, Luther writes, "We must not concentrate on those external sins, but go further and look at the whole nature, source, and origin of sin. The psalm talks about the whole of sin, about the root of sin, not merely about the outward work, which springs like fruit from the root and tree of sin."[41]

Accordingly he argues that "we are not sinners because we commit this or that sin, but we commit them because we are sinners first. That is, a bad tree and bad seed also bring forth bad fruit, and from a bad root only a bad tree can grow."[42]

Going back to Kierkegaard's unexpected definition of sin (just given), we see that this "continuance," this "impetus" (Luther's "bad root" that is the "nature, source, and origin of sin") is an ongoing unwillingness to be oneself, the self that one is called to be "before God." It comes in two forms.

Sins Are Rooted in Sin as Weakness and/or Defiance

In Part One Kierkegaard distinguishes two modes of despair: weakness and defiance, a distinction he will carry over into Part Two, where despair is sin. Several things to notice. First, this distinction comes right after we are given a definition of faith as the opposite of despair: "In relating to itself and in willing to be itself, the self rests transparently in the power that established it" (SUD, 49/SKS 11, 164). The opening of Part Two thus reads as follows: "Sin is: *before God or with the conception of God, in despair not to will to be oneself, or in despair to will to be oneself.* Thus sin is intensified weakness or intensified defiance" (SUD 77/SKS 11, 191). But

---

[41] "Psalm 51," *Luther's Works* 12, ed. Jaroslav Pelikan (Saint Louis, MO: Concordia Publishing House, 1955), 305–306.
[42] "Psalm 51," 348. See also 304, 307–308, 319, 337, 339, and 350.

"the opposites are relative. No despair is entirely free of defiance; indeed, the very phrase 'not to will to be' implies defiance. On the other hand, even despair's most extreme defiance is never really free of some weakness. So the distinction is only relative" (SUD, 49/SKS 11, 164).

Second, although Kierkegaard insists that the opposite of sin is not virtue but faith (SUD, 82/SKS 11, 196), he also seems to suggest that faith is *the* virtue, the *sine qua non* of all true virtue. In this connection he develops a mini unity-of-the-virtues thesis. In both Parts One and Two he insists that overcoming despair involves humility and courage, or, as these seem to require one another, faith is a matter of "humble courage" (SUD, 85/SKS 11, 198; see also SUD, 8–9, 61–62, 65, 71, 78, 86, 95, 112/SKS 11, 125, 176–177, 179–180, 185, 191–192, 199, 207, 223–224).

Third, drawing on stereotypes less challenged in his day than in ours, Kierkegaard calls the two types of despair "feminine" and "masculine" with the qualifiers "so to speak" (SUD, 49/SKS 11, 164), "could be called" (SUD, 67/SKS 11, 181).[43] Both forms of despair represent an unwillingness to be the selves we are called to be before the God before whom we are sinners. If I find this task too hard or too dangerous, it is because in weakness I lack the courage to undertake it. If I find it too demeaning or offensive it is because in defiance I lack the humility to submit to it. But remember, "the distinction is only relative" (SUD, 49/SKS 11, 164).

Sin as "Before God": The Relational Self

We have seen that the self in relating to itself relates to an other and that this other is specified as the power that has established the self or as God. But there are other others in relation to whom the self may define itself. "A cattleman who (if this were possible) is a self directly before his cattle is a very low self, and similarly a master who is a self directly before his slaves is actually no self – for in both cases a criterion is lacking. The child who previously has had only his parents as a criterion becomes a self as an adult by getting the state [better: society] as a criterion, but what an infinite accent falls on the self by having God as a criterion!" (SUD, 79/SKS 11, 193).

The cartoonist might have been reading Kierkegaard when he had Jon say to Garfield, "I am not pathetic!" and then, two frames later, ask "Am

---

[43] For helpful discussion, see Sylvia I. Walsh, "On 'Feminine' and 'Masculine' Forms of Despair," in *International Kierkegaard Commentary: The Sickness unto Death*, ed. Robert L. Perkins (Macon, GA: Mercer University Press, 1987), 121–134.

I?" Garfield's response: "Jon, you're asking a cat's opinion." In Kierkegaard's intersubjective view of subjectivity, the quality of selfhood depends upon but is not fully determined by the quality of the other self before whom one is a self. That is why bullying dehumanizes the bully, who treats the victim as less than fully human.

So, in order to distinguish "Christianly understood" from pagan (Socratic) understandings, he asks what it means to be "before God" when the God in question is the biblical God. As we have seen, this involves incarnation, atonement, reconciliation, and forgiveness. Incarnation cannot mean the embeddedness of the self in Nature (Spinoza) or in Society and History (Hegel). It has to mean "the God in time" as in the offensive paradox of *Philosophical Fragments*. Atonement cannot mean the way in which we ourselves pay the price for our violations of the moral law (Kant). Reconciliation cannot mean insight into the necessity of the dialectical tension between impersonal, metaphysical parameters such as infinite and finite (Spinoza, Hegel). If one is to speak Christianly, these terms must be understood in terms of forgiveness, the overcoming of a broken, interpersonal relation in which one party owes the other respect, faithfulness, and obedience, has violated that relation, but is restored to friendship and fellowship by the gracious act of the one violated. In short, "before God," Christianly understood, means that one is always already a sinner in need of a forgiveness that is always already offered. An infinite abyss is bridged by an infinite act of mercy.

CHAPTER 10

Fastening the End and Knotting the Thread
Beginning Where Paganism Ends by Means of Paradox
Sylvia Walsh

According to Anti-Climacus, Part Two of *The Sickness unto Death* takes "a new direction" in dialectical contrast to the preceding part, which focuses on the gradations in the consciousness of despair and selfhood within the category of the human self in paganism, whose criterion is the human being (*Mennesket*) or what it means to be a human being as determined by a merely human understanding of selfhood (SUD, 79/SKS 11, 193).[1] Now the self is viewed in terms of a Christian understanding of despair and the self, whose criterion is God, not one's parents, state, or nation, and despair is defined more precisely as sin, not merely as a sickness of the self with respect to the consciousness of having a self and not willing to become or be that self. Moreover, Christianity is viewed as beginning precisely where paganism ends, namely with the concept of sin, which is what decisively differentiates it from paganism.[2] What distinguishes Christianity from paganism most of all is the fact that the Christian concept of sin is rooted scripturally in disobedience, self-willfulness, or defiance of God in not willing or doing what is right rather than not knowing or understanding what one should do, as is the case in paganism (SUD, 81–82, 88–89, 92–93/SKS 11, 195–196, 201–202, 205–206). Christianity "fastens the end" and "knots the thread" of this concept, Anti-Climacus observes, with

---

[1] The English translation of "Menneske" is amended here and throughout this essay to reflect its gender-neutral meaning in distinction from "Mand," the Danish word for a man or person of male gender.

[2] On the opposition of Christianity to paganism in Kierkegaard's authorship, see also CD, Part One, on "The Cares of the Pagans," and CA, 93–98/SKS 4, 397–401. Paganism is briefly addressed in a number of Kierkegaard's other works as well. On his concept of sin see Jason A. Mahn, "Sin: Leaping and Sliding and Mysteries Pointing to Mysteries," in *T & T Clark Companion to the Theology of Kierkegaard*, ed. Aaron P. Edwards and David J. Gouwens (London: T & T Clark Bloomsbury, 2020), 261–277; Jason A. Mahn, *Fortunate Fallibility: Kierkegaard and the Power of Sin* (Oxford: Oxford University Press, 2011). See also Sylvia Walsh, "Søren Kierkegaard," in *T & T Clark Companion to the Doctrine of Sin*, ed. Keith L. Johnson and David Lauber (London: T & T Clark Bloomsbury, 2016), 267–283; Sylvia Walsh, *Kierkegaard: Thinking Christianly in an Existential Mode* (Oxford: Oxford University Press, 2009), 80–110.

the doctrine of hereditary sin and the paradox that sin is not a negation such as weakness, sensuousness, finitude, or ignorance but a position before God that cannot be comprehended and must be believed through a revelation from and relation to God, thereby creating the possibility of offense (SUD, 96–100/SKS 11, 209–212).[3]

Despair as Spiritlessness in Paganism

Part One is nevertheless preparatory for this turn inasmuch as it defines a human being and the self as spirit or a synthesis of the temporal and the eternal, the finite and the infinite, freedom and necessity that relates itself to itself and is established in that relation by virtue of a relation to another reality, namely God, who is defined here in terms of the concept of possibility: "the being of God means that everything is possible, or that everything is possible means the being of God" (SUD, 40/SKS 11, 156).[4]

---

[3] The images of fastening the end and knotting the thread appear in several of Kierkegaard's journals and writings: JP 3, 3540/KJN 11.2, Pap:451/SKS 27, 555–557; JP 3, 3689/KJN 8, NB23:184/SKS 24, 293–294; JP 6, 6760/KJN 8, NB24:40/SKS 24, 340; JP 6, 6803/KJN 9, NB26:11/SKS 25, 20; CI, 34n/SKS 1, 96n; PV, 20/SKS 13, 26; MLW, 126/SKS 13, 168. In JP 3, 3540 he cites Till Eulenspiegel telling the tailors "that they must not forget to tie a knot in the thread, for otherwise they would lose the first stitch," but Kierkegaard does not entirely agree that only the first stitch will be lost, stating that "he also loses the next, and so on and on, and the whole thing gets to be a mess." Christianity, for example, goes about "without tying a knot in the thread" by the way it is understood and practiced by the so-called Christians of his day as a matter of quantity, which is not Christianity. "No," he says, "if in the Christian sense the end is to be tied, in order to keep the whole thing from becoming nonsense, we must either have [persons] of character again who actually renounce the world, or we must at least make admissions, and above all we must come out from behind the mask" of quantity. In JP3, 3689 he notes that Vinet, the French-Swiss literary critic and theologian, lectures on individuality but "is not in character" because he does not existentially tie the knot himself as an individual. In JP 6, 6760 Kierkegaard accuses Bishop Mynster of being afraid to tie the knot tightly "despite the fact that it is so loose that it cannot hold without being tied more securely." In JP 6, 6803 he indicates that the end must be tied or else one remains in reflection, for "to tie the end, a life, an existence, is required." In CI, 34 n, the first reference to Till Eulenspiegel's advice to the tailors appears. In "On My Work as an Author" in PV, 20 he claims that in 1848 the "threads of sagacity broke," with the result that "Even the greatest events and the most strenuous lives are nevertheless a vortex or like sewing without fastening the end – until the end is once again fastened by the application of the unconditional, or by the single individual's relating [him/herself] to an unconditional," which Kierkegaard claims to do to the best of his ability in fighting against "the tyranny of the numerical." Finally, in MLW, 126 he characterizes "God in heaven" as being "a poor wretch of the old school, so simple as actually to think that when one wants to sew one must knot the thread."

[4] On the concept of spirit in Kierkegaard's thought see C. Stephen Evans, *Kierkegaard and Spirituality: Accountability as the Meaning of Existence* (Grand Rapids, MI: Eerdmans, 2019), 1–17; John J. Davenport, "Selfhood and 'Spirit,'" in *The Oxford Handbook of Kierkegaard*, ed. John Lippitt and George Pattison (Oxford: Oxford University Press, 2013), 230–251.

Spiritlessness or the ignorance of being in despair, identified by Anti-Climacus as the most common form of despair, is also identified with paganism, both in its historical form and within Christendom, although the former is seen as being qualified in the direction of spirit whereas "paganism in Christendom lacks spirit in a departure from spirit or a falling away and therefore is spiritlessness in the strictest sense" (SUD, 45, 47/SKS 11, 160, 161–162).[5] As Anti-Climacus sees it, paganism, like the natural human being and secular or philistine-bourgeois mentality in general, did not recognize the true God but worshipped an idol instead (SUD, 8, 35, 41, 45–47/SKS 11, 125, 150–151, 156, 160–162). It thus lacked/lacks a spiritual definition of the self as well as a consciousness of existing before God as spirit. It was for this reason, he explains, that the ancient church fathers, especially St. Augustine, branded the heart of paganism as despair and its virtues as "glittering vices" (SUD, 46 and 49n/SKS 11, 161). Part One points out the universality of despair and tracks the progression and intensity of despair in terms of the degree of consciousness of being a self or spirit and the state of the self as being one of despair. It thus tracks the movement of unconscious despair to conscious forms of despair in the despair of weakness or "feminine despair" in not willing to be oneself and the despair of defiance or "masculine despair" in willing to be the self one wants to be rather than the self one is intended to become by virtue of a relation to God (SUD, 49/SKS 11, 164).[6] The opposite of despair, or the formula for the state of the self when all despair has been rooted out, is further identified as faith (SUD, 49/SKS 11, 164). For that to happen, however, a metamorphosis in the form of a radical upheaval (*Omvælting*) or "about-face" (*Omvendelse*) that allows a consciousness of the eternal or God as the power that establishes the self to break through in order to put one on the right path to faith (SUD, 20–21, 26–27, 60, 61n, 65/SKS 11, 135–136, 142–143, 174, 175n, 179).

---

[5] On paganism in Christendom, see also Merold Westphal, "Paganism in Christendom: On Kierkegaard's Critique of Religion," in *International Kierkegaard Commentary 17: Christian Discourses and The Crisis and a Crisis in the Life of an Actress*, ed. Robert L. Perkins (Macon, GA: Mercer University Press, 2007), 13–33; Merold Westphal, "Kierkegaard, Theology and Post-Christendom," in *T & T Clark Companion to the Theology of Kierkegaard*, ed. Aaron P. Edwards and David J. Gouwens (London: T & T Clark, 2020), 604–607.

[6] See also Sylvia Walsh, "On 'Feminine' and 'Masculine' Forms of Despair," in *International Kierkegaard Commentary: The Sickness unto Death*, ed. Robert L. Perkins (Macon, GA: Mercer University Press, 1987), 121–134, reprinted in *Feminist Interpretations of Søren Kierkegaard*, ed. Céline Léon and Sylvia Walsh (University Park: Pennsylvania State University Press, 1997), 203–215.

Despair as Sin in Christianity

Building on his initial analysis of despair in paganism in Part One, Anti-Climacus begins Part Two with a further delineation of the concept of despair as sin in Christianity, where the believer is conscious of existing directly "before God" or with the conception of God as the qualitative criterion (*Maalestok*) and ethical goal (*Maal*) for what it means to be a human being in the form of a "theological self" in contrast to paganism, the natural man, the secular or philistine-bourgeois mentality, modern philosophy, speculation, speculative dogmatics, and the system (SUD, 8, 35, 41, 45, 81, 83, 87, 93, 97, 116, 119/SKS 11, 125, 150–151, 156, 160, 194–195, 197, 200, 206, 209, 228, 230). Anti-Climacus proceeds to show how the Christian concept of sin differs from the perception of sin as human guilt in paganism, defining the sin of paganism essentially as a "despairing ignorance of God" and paganism itself as existing "without God in the world," with the ironic result that, strictly speaking, sin did/does not exist in paganism since it lacked/lacks a sense of existing directly before God, which is "what really makes human guilt into sin" for Anti-Climacus (SUD, 80, 81/SKS 11, 194–195). From his standpoint, "every sin is before God," including "every imaginable and every actual form of sin" (SUD, 80, 82/SKS 11, 194, 196). The opposite of sin for him, therefore, is not virtue, as in paganism, but faith in God.[7] In his view, this antithesis constitutes "one of the most decisive definitions for all Christianity" inasmuch as it "Christianly reshapes all ethical concepts and gives them one additional range" in viewing the human self as existing directly or consciously before God as the power that establishes it, thereby introducing the "crucial criterion" of "*the absurd, the paradox, the possibility of offense*" (SUD, 82, 83/SKS 11, 196).

The possibility of offense is seen as "Christianity's weapon against all speculation," which for Anti-Climacus is identical to "the old paganism" inasmuch as it lacks a sense of the individual before God, universalizing "individual human beings fantastically into the race" instead of viewing them as standing directly before God as individuals (SUD, 83, 85/SKS 11, 197, 198). The "real reason" why people are offended by Christianity, Anti-Climacus contends, is not because it is "dark," "gloomy," or "so

---

[7] On the relation of Christianity to virtue in Kierkegaard's thought, see Sylvia Walsh, *Kierkegaard and Religion: Personality, Character, and Virtue* (Cambridge: Cambridge University Press, 2018); Mark Tietjen, *Kierkegaard, Communication, and Virtue: Authorship as Edification* (Bloomington: Indiana University Press, 2013).

rigorous" as "much talk" claims, but because it is "too high," requiring "something so extraordinary" of human beings that they "cannot grasp the thought" (SUD, 83, 85/SKS 11, 197, 199). Like the pagan or natural human being, they plead the Aristotelian "golden mean" of "nothing too much" (*ne quid nimis*), claiming that Christianity "makes too much of being human" (SUD, 83, 85, 86–87/SKS 11, 197, 199, 200–201). In opposition to such worldly wisdom, Christianity takes "an enormous giant stride" into the realm of the absurd and the possibility of offense, which in Anti-Climacus's estimation is "very appropriately present in the Christian definition of sin" inasmuch as it places the individual directly before God, thereby establishing an "infinite qualitative difference" between them (SUD, 87, 121–122, 125, 127/SKS 11, 200, 236, 238). As Anti-Climacus sees it, "the possibility of offense is the dialectical element in everything essentially Christian. If this is taken away, then Christianity is not only paganism but also something so fanciful that paganism would have to call it nonsense" (SUD, 125/SKS 11, 236).

The Socratic Definition of Sin

Anti-Climacus continues to draw a contrast between Christianity and paganism by engaging in a close examination of the Socratic definition of sin as ignorance, which in his view is "so genuinely Greek" that it can be regarded as representative of paganism in general, although he does make an important distinction between Socrates and the "Greek mind" as reflected in modern philosophy concerning the transition from understanding something to acting in accordance with it, which is seen as taking place by necessity in modern speculative thought (SUD, 88, 90, 93/SKS 11, 201, 203, 206). The defect in the Socratic definition of sin, as Anti-Climacus sees it, is its ambiguity concerning the origin of this ignorance, namely whether it is an original ignorance or one acquired at a later time, in which case it would be due to an effort on the part of the individual to obscure his or her original knowledge of the good and therefore a matter of not willing the good rather than not knowing what the good is. Moreover, from Anti-Climacus's perspective, Socrates did not actually arrive at the category of sin, for if sin is ignorance it does not exist; that is, there is no such thing as "knowing what is right and doing wrong, or knowing that something is wrong and going ahead and doing wrong" (SUD, 89/SKS 11, 202). Whereas Socrates assumed that if one does not do the good it is because one has not understood what the good is, Christianity views sin as a matter of consciousness, not of ignorance, and sees it as residing in the will, not in the understanding. Anticipating the Kantian notion that "ought implies can," the Socratic definition of sin lacks the constituent of will or defiance (SUD, 90/SKS 11, 203). Consequently, when a person claims to understand what is right and says what is right yet does the wrong, Anti-Climacus finds this to be "exceedingly comic" as well as ironic, indicating that the Socratic definition of sin "lacks a dialectical determinant appropriate to the transition from having understood something to doing it," namely the concept of will, which establishes a distinction between understanding and understanding, that is, between not being able to understand something and not being willing to understand it (SUD, 91–93, 95/SKS 11, 203–204, 205). Whereas Socrates assumed that if a person does the wrong it is because he or she has not understood what is right, Christianity roots sin squarely in the will, which governs the lower nature of human beings, often leading them to obscure their knowledge and understanding of what is right by identifying and corrupting it with what the will wants, thus doing the wrong even though they know what is right. From a Christian standpoint, therefore, "neither paganism nor the natural human being [*Menneske*] knows what sin is," which requires a revelation from God to know inasmuch as no person of and by him/herself can declare what sin is, precisely because she or he is in sin (SUD, 89, 95/SKS 11, 202–203, 207).

The Christian Doctrine of Hereditary Sin

For Anti-Climacus, then, what most decisively distinguishes Christianity from paganism is the doctrine of sin, to which Christianity adds the doctrine of hereditary sin (*Arvesynd*) "to fasten the end" (SUD, 93/SKS 11, 206). He does not indicate how or in what way hereditary sin fastens the end in Christianity, but this concept is discussed at length by another pseudonym, Vigilius Haufniensis, in an earlier psychological examination of the concept of sin in *The Concept of Anxiety*, which focuses on the question of how sin comes into the world, namely, through the first sin of Adam and that of every subsequent individual out of anxiety over the possibility of freedom both prior to and as a consequence of sin (CA, 25–80/SKS 4, 332–384). The Christian doctrine of hereditary sin thus places responsibility for sin squarely on the individual, who enters into the state of sinfulness through a qualitative leap, not on the basis of a quantitative determination via participation in the race. According to Vigilius Haufniensis, "the whole of paganism and its repetition within Christianity lie in a merely quantitative determination from which the qualitative leap of sin does not break forth" (CA, 93/SKS 4, 396). Identifying modern philosophy as "neither more nor less than paganism" in its non-Socratic Greek form (Socrates being too much of an ethicist to confuse speculation with Christianity as modern philosophy does), Anti-Climacus applies this quantitative understanding of paganism to the so-called "secret in comprehending" sin on the part of modern speculative philosophy, which in his view goes on sewing and sewing "without fastening the end and without knotting the thread" (SUD, 93/SKS 11, 206). As an example of this ongoing reflective practice he cites Descartes's claim that "to think is to be" as standing in direct contrast to Christianity's claim that "to believe is to be" (SUD, 93/SKS 11, 206). As he sees it, Christianity cannot be comprehended by thought but must be believed: "To comprehend is the range of [a human being's] relation to the human, but to believe is a [human being's] relation to the divine" (SUD, 95/SKS 11, 208).[8] Belief is made possible by a revelation from God, thereby establishing the possibility of offense and along with it the ironic result that "sin is indeed ignorance" – ignorance of what sin is from a merely human point of view (SUD, 96/SKS 11, 208). The previous definition of sin as ignorance is thus amended by the following reformulation: "sin is – after being taught by a revelation from God what sin is – before God in despair not to will to be oneself or in despair to will to be oneself" (SUD, 96/SKS 11, 208).

Sin as a Position and Paradox

Another aspect of the definition of sin for which "the end must be fastened very firmly," as Anti-Climacus sees it, is the Christian contention that sin is a position, not a negation in the form of "weakness, sensuousness, finitude, ignorance, etc." as claimed in pantheistic definitions of sin by "pagan wisdom" (SUD, 96–97/SKS 11, 209). With regard to this distinction he observes that "orthodoxy has perceived very correctly that the battle must be fought here" (SUD, 96/SKS 11, 209). The enemy against which Anti-Climacus proposes to do battle on this issue is the speculative dogmatics of his time, namely, that of H. L. Martensen, Kierkegaard's former tutor at Copenhagen University, and the German Hegelian scholar Philipp Marheineke, whose lectures Kierkegaard attended in Berlin in

---

[8] Translation of *Menneske* amended.

1841.[9] Speculative thought is accused of ironically affirming the definition of sin as a negation by claiming to comprehend the qualification that sin is a position, thereby nullifying the latter. Over against this speculative viewpoint, Anti-Climacus steadfastly maintains that sin cannot be explained or comprehended by human reason but is a paradox that must be believed and ethically repented. Appealing to Socrates as an ally rather than a foil on this issue, he suggests that what is needed in his time is precisely a little "Socratic, God-fearing ignorance" by which to safeguard faith against speculation and to maintain the gulf of infinite qualitative difference between God and human beings instead of merging them as one in and through the system (SUD, 99/SKS 11, 211). A further implication and paradoxical consequence of the qualification of sin as a position, according to Anti-Climacus, is that Christianity "seems to be working against itself by establishing sin so securely as a position that now it seems to be utterly impossible to eliminate it again" yet proceeds to eliminate sin so completely by means of the doctrine of the Atonement that it is "as if it were drowned in the sea" (SUD 100/SKS 11, 212).

The ironic moral that results from the foregoing portrayal of sin, as Anti-Climacus sees it, is the "strange" outcome and conclusion that sin is a "great rarity" inasmuch as it "is not to be found at all in paganism but only in Judaism and Christendom, and there again very seldom," since the great majority of human beings "live a life so far from the good (faith) that it is almost too spiritless to be called sin" (SUD, 100, 101/SKS 11, 212, 213). Moreover, the kind of Christianity that is preached in Christendom, he contends, is "a shabby edition of the essentially Christian" as well as "a misuse," "profanation," and "prostitution" of true Christianity, thereby making it "utterly inconsequential" for the majority of human beings,

---

[9] On Marheineke see Heiko Schulz, "Marheineke: The Volatilization of Christian Doctrine," in *Kierkegaard and His German Contemporaries: Tome II: Theology*, ed. Jon Stewart (Aldershot: Ashgate, 2007), 117–142. On Martensen, see Jon Stewart, ed. *Hans Lassen Martensen: Theologian, Philosopher and Social Critic* (Copenhagen: Museum Tusculanum, 2012); Niels Thulstrup, "Martensen's *Dogmatics* and Its Reception," in *Kierkegaard and His Contemporaries: The Culture of Golden Age Denmark*, ed. Jon Stewart (Berlin: Walter de Gruyter, 2003), 181–202; Curtis L. Thompson, "H. L. Martensen's Theological Anthropology," in *Kierkegaard and His Contemporaries: The Culture of Golden Age Denmark*, ed. Jon Stewart (Berlin: Walter de Gruyter, 2003), 164–180; Curtis L. Thompson, "Hans Lassen Martensen: A Speculative Theologian Determining the Agenda of the Day," in *Kierkegaard and His Danish Contemporaries, Tome II: Theology*, ed. Jon Stewart (Aldershot: Ashgate, 2009), 229–266. See also George Pattison, "Kierkegaard the Theology Student," in *T & T Clark Companion to the Theology of Kierkegaard*, ed. Aaron P. Edwards and David J. Gouwens (London: T & T Clark, 2020), 89–109. On the relation of Kierkegaard to German Idealism in general, see Lore Hühn and Philipp Schwab, "Kierkegaard and German Idealism," in *The Oxford Handbook of Kierkegaard*, ed. John Lippitt and George Pattison (Oxford: Oxford University Press, 2013), 62–93.

whose lives "are far too spiritless to be called sin in the strictly Christian sense" (SUD, 102, 104/SKS 11, 214).

The Continuance and Intensification of Sin in the State of Sin

Anti-Climacus proceeds to take up the continuance of sin in the state of sin, which constitutes a new sin insofar as one's previous sin is unrepented and continues anew, giving sin an ongoing consistency in evil. In his view, it is the state of sin, not particular sins, that constitutes the continuance of sin inasmuch as the state of sin is "a worse sin than the particular sins," which are "merely the expression for the continuance of sin" in the state of sin (SUD, 106, 108/SKS 11, 218, 220). The continuance of sin in the state of sin in turn "becomes the internal intensification of sin" in the form of "a conscious remaining in the state of sin," thereby resulting in a "greater and greater intensity of consciousness" (SUD, 108–109/SKS 11, 220). Anti-Climacus identifies three forms the intensification of the state of sin takes, namely: (1) the sin of despairing over one's sin or over that which binds one in despair; (2) the sin of despairing of the forgiveness of sins or of that which releases one from despair, namely, the forgiveness of sin by Christ, and (3) the sin of positively dismissing Christianity by declaring it to be untruth (SUD, 60n and 61n/SKS 11, 175; SUD 113n/SKS, 225n).

The Sin of Despairing over One's Sin

The first form of the intensification of sin as despair over one's sin or over that which binds one in despair secures the internal consistency of sin through a further severance of the sinner from the good so as to become inaccessible to it by declaring "everything called repentance and grace" to be "empty" and "meaningless" as well as an "enemy" against which one must defend oneself by demonically enclosing oneself within oneself in the refusal to hear anything about them (SUD, 109/SKS 11, 221). As a result of this severance, all relation to oneself and grace is lost, although one may give this form of sin and despair the "appearance of being something good" by proudly declaring that one will never forgive oneself or by blasphemously claiming that God can never forgive one for relapsing into sin after having "successfully resisted temptation for such a long time" rather than humbly thanking God for helping one to resist temptation for so long (SUD, 111, 112/SKS 11, 222, 223).

The Sin of Despairing of the Forgiveness of Sin

The second form of intensification of sin as despair of the forgiveness of sin or of that which releases one from despair has to do with a person's relation to Jesus Christ, which establishes another major difference between Christianity and paganism as well as between paganism and Christendom with respect to their conceptions of God.[10] From a Christian standpoint, Jesus Christ is the very incarnation of God, who "allowed himself to be born, become [a human being], suffer, and die" for the sake of humankind (SUD, 113/SKS 11, 225). The knowledge of Christ thus places the self directly before God in the person of Jesus Christ as the criterion for what it means to be a self as well as a sinner. This has the effect of reversing sin as despair in the forms of weakness and defiance as laid out in Part One so that each becomes the other; that is, the despair of weakness becomes defiance in not willing to be oneself as a sinner, and the despair of defiance becomes weakness in willing to be oneself as a sinner in such a way as to despair of the forgiveness of sins by denying the possibility of forgiveness, thereby distancing oneself from God. Ironically, however, from Anti-Climacus's (and Kierkegaard's) perspective, this is precisely what must happen if one is to come close to God in an appropriate manner inasmuch as "in order to be able to be forward toward God, one has to go far away from him" (SUD, 114/SKS 11, 226). Here we have another instance of the "inverse dialectic" that characterizes Kierkegaard's thought in general and despair of the forgiveness of sins in particular, which in Anti-Climacus's view is generally conceived erroneously as "a sign of a deep nature" or genius in Christendom, "where Christian conceptions float unchristianly in the air" and are misused in a "shameless manner" that is worse than in classical paganism (SUD, 114, 115/SKS 11, 226, 227).[11] Whereas cursing the name of God was not customary in classical paganism, which "as a rule named the name of God with tremendous solemnity," Anti-Climacus observes that "it is right at home in Christendom," where "God's name is the word that most frequently appears in daily speech and is clearly the word that is given the

---

[10] See also Abrahim H. Khan, "Sin before Christ in *The Sickness unto Death*," in *Kierkegaard and Christianity*, Acta Kierkegaardiana 3, ed. Roman Králik, Abrahim H. Khan, Peter Šajda, Jamie Turnbull, and Andrew J. Burgess (Šal'a, Slovakia, 2008), 197–217; Walsh, "Søren Kierkegaard," 267–283.

[11] On "inverse dialectic" in Kierkegaard's thought, see Sylvia Walsh, *Living Christianly: Kierkegaard's Dialectic of Christian Existence* (University Park: The Pennsylvania State University Press, 2005), 7–16.

least thought and used most carelessly" (SUD, 115/SKS 11, 227). Moreover, the sin of despairing of the forgiveness of sin by Christ constitutes offense, which "takes a singularly high degree of spiritlessness ... as ordinarily found in Christendom," whereas "this sin could not be found" in classical paganism since it lacked a true conception of sin as well as God and therefore "could not have gone any further" than despair over sin (SUD, 116/SKS 11, 227–228). For that, Anti-Climacus claims, "the pagan must be eulogized," inasmuch as despair over sin may be understood dialectically as "pointing toward faith" as well as being "the first element in faith" in the form of offense as an "annulled possibility" (SUD, 116/SKS 11, 228). In contrast to classical paganism, despair of the forgiveness of sins characterizes "the situation of Christendom" to such a degree that "even the consciousness of sin is not reached, and the only kinds of sins recognized are those that paganism also recognized" (SUD, 117/SKS 11, 228–229). It thus reflects a "pagan peace of mind" that goes beyond classical paganism by identifying peace of mind with consciousness of the forgiveness of sin, as congregations were encouraged to do by the clergy of the time (SUD, 117/SKS 11, 229).

As Anti-Climacus sees it, however, the "basic trouble" (*Grund-Ulykke*) of Christendom is the Christian teaching about the God-man or God-human being (*Gud-Menneske*),[12] which in his view is "pantheistically abolished" first of all in a "highbrow" (*fornemt*) way through speculation and then in a "lowbrow" (*pøbelagtigt*) way "in the highways and byways" so that God and humankind are merged into one (SUD, 117/SKS 11, 229).[13] Foremost among the first group that Anti-Climacus may have in mind is D. F. Strauss (1808–1874), whose demythologizing Christology in *The Life of Jesus Critically Examined* (1835) was a major perspective with which Kierkegaard became acquainted as a theological student.[14] What particularly bothers Anti-Climacus concerning the Christian doctrine about the God-man or God-human being in Christendom is the way in which it has "brazenly" turned that teaching around so as to foist kinship of human

---

[12] As noted above, the Danish word "Menneske" usually refers to a human being in a gender-neutral manner, whereas the word for a man or person of male gender is "Mand." Jesus was of course a man, but he was a model for all human beings, not just males.

[13] The accompanying Danish commentary for this SKS volume identifies the first group with "Hegelian philosophy," especially the Right Hegelian theologians of Denmark, and the second with the Left Hegelian materialistic anthropology of Ludwig Feuerbach, according to which God is a projection of humankind's desires and wishes (SKS 11, 229 comment).

[14] On Kierkegaard's knowledge of Strauss, see George Pattison, "Kierkegaard and Radical Demythologization," in *Kierkegaard and His German Contemporaries, Tome II: Theology*, ed. Jon Stewart (Aldershot: Ashgate, 2007), 233–253.

beings upon God, thereby compromising the infinite qualitative difference
between God and humankind (SUD, 118/SKS 11, 230). As he sees it,
Christianity protects itself against such human identification with the
divine precisely with its teaching about sin, which corresponds to the
category of individuality and therefore cannot be thought. The concept
of humanity can be thought but not an individual human being. Likewise,
the concept of sin can be thought but not sin itself, which falls under the
category of earnestness and therefore of ethical and individual striving.
Speculation, by contrast, favors the generation over the individual and
"does not take into consideration that with respect to sin the ethical is
involved" (SUD, 120/SKS 11, 231). As Anti-Climacus sees it, the ethical
"points in the opposite direction to that of speculation" and takes "the very
opposite steps" from speculation inasmuch as it "does not abstract from
actuality but immerses itself in actuality and operates with that specula-
tively disregarded and scorned category: individuality" (SUD, 120/SKS 11,
231). Although sin is common to all human beings, it "does not gather
[human beings] together in a common idea, into an association, into a
partnership" (SUD, 120n/SKS 11, 231n).[15] On the contrary, the category
of sin is a category of individuality, not the "animal category" of the crowd
or mob (SUD, 118, 119/SKS 11, 229). Moreover, "in no way is a [human
being] so different from God as this, that he [or she], and that means every
[human being], is a sinner, and is that 'before God'" (SUD, 121/SKS 11,
233).[16] Indeed, as Anti-Climacus sees it, sin "is the one and only predication about a human being that in no way, either *via negationis* [by denial]
or *via eminentiæ* [by idealization], can be stated of God" (SUD, 122/SKS
11, 233). Just as a human being, as sinner, "is separated from God by the
most chasmal qualitative abyss," God "is separated from [a human being]
by the same chasmal qualitative abyss in the forgiveness of sins," for "there
is one way in which [a human being] could never in all eternity come to be
like God: in forgiving sins" (SUD, 122/SKS 11, 233).[17] For this reason,
Anti-Climacus explains, Christianity begins with the possibility of offense,
which is "the most decisive qualification of subjectivity, of the single
individual, that is possible" and therefore constitutes the intensification
of sin, although in his view people usually "give this scarcely a thought"
and do not "identify offense with sin," only "sins," and even less with the
intensification of sin (SUD, 122, 124/SKS 11, 233, 235).

---

[15] Translation of *Mennesker* amended.   [16] Translation of *Menneske* amended.
[17] Translation of *Menneske* amended.

The Sin and Possibility of Offense in Dismissing Christianity as Untruth

The third form of intensification of sin is the sin of dismissing Christianity "modo ponendo [positively]" by "declaring it to be untruth" (SUD, 125/ SKS 11, 236). At this level of the intensification of sin the self experiences "the highest intensity of despair," which is directed against the Holy Spirit (SUD, 125/SKS 11, 236). Here the intensification of sin changes tactics, moving from a defensive posture to an offensive one by declaring war against Christianity and totally renouncing it as untruth. Once again, the Christian doctrine of kinship between God and human beings is the main question at issue, but the focus this time is on the difference between paganism and Christianity with regard to the concept of God. Although the Christian teaching about the God-man or God-human being establishes a kinship between God and a human being in and through the man Jesus Christ, who is the model for what it means to be a human being in likeness to God, Christianity protects itself from human beings coming too close to an identification with God through the possibility of offense, without which it would be "only paganism" or something worse, namely "something so fanciful that paganism would have to call it nonsense" and others would call "the invention of a mad god" (SUD, 125–126/SKS 11, 236, 237). Whereas classical paganism conceived god as a human being ("the man-god" or "the human being-God"), Christianity maintains that the divine makes itself a human being ("the God-man" or "God-human being") out of its infinite love and merciful grace (SUD, 126/SKS 11, 237).[18] Yet the possibility of offense established by the infinite qualitative difference between God and humanity cannot be removed, which has the effect of reversing God's act of love so as to become "the most extreme misery" for the person who takes offense at Christ and continues in it (SUD, 126/SKS 11, 237). As Anti-Climacus sees it, "this is the case practically everywhere in Christendom," where "the experience of thousands upon thousands confirms that one can have faith in Christ without having noticed the slightest possibility of offense" (SUD, 128n/SKS 11, 239n). He identifies three forms of offense that characterize this level, all of which are primarily related to the paradox of Christ and thus arise with "every determination of the essentially Christian" (SUD, 129/SKS 11, 240). The first and lowest form of offense is "to leave the whole issue of Christ undecided" by remaining neutral about him and thus implicitly denying his divinity, whereas the "earnestness of existence" requires that

[18] Translation of *Menneske* amended.

"everyone *shall* have an opinion" about him (SUD, 129, 130/SKS 11, 240, 241). The second form of offense does not ignore Christ but cannot believe the paradox of God's incarnation in him and thus remains "constantly preoccupied with this decision" within the self (SUD, 131/SKS 11, 241–242). The third form of offense either docetically or rationalistically denies Christ outright as the paradox and along with it "all that is essentially Christian," namely, sin and the forgiveness of sins, with the result that Christ either "does not become an individual human being but only appears to be one or else he becomes only an individual human being," thus either a fiction or "an actuality who makes no claim to be divine." Anti-Climacus labels this form of offense as "sin against the Holy Spirit" inasmuch as it "makes Christ an invention of the devil" (SUD, 131/SKS 11, 242).

Fastening the End and Tying the Knot

Having drawn a contrast between sin and faith throughout Part Two of *The Sickness unto Death*, Anti-Climacus fastens the end and knots the thread of his "Christian psychological exposition for upbuilding and awakening" with a restatement of "the formula for the state in which there is no despair at all," namely, that "in relating itself to itself and in willing to be itself, the self rests transparently in the power that established it," which, as he again points out, "is the definition of faith" (SUD, iii, 131/ SKS 11, 115, 242). To fasten the end and tie the knot of the present analysis as well, let us review the main points made and emphasized in this work. The primary goal of *The Sickness unto Death* in Part Two is to present an analysis of the concepts of despair, selfhood, spirit, sin, offense, faith, paradox, and God from the standpoint of a Christian understanding of these concepts in contrast to a pagan or a merely human understanding of them as laid out in Part One. In the process of carrying out this goal, Anti-Climacus draws a dialectical contrast between Christianity and classical paganism, on the one hand, and between Christianity and Christendom, on the other, with respect to these concepts. Further contrasts as well as some important similarities are noted between the Socratic and/or Greek forms of classical paganism, the paganism of Christendom in general, and the paganism of modern speculative philosophy in particular, in relation to which some Socratic ignorance is seen as being needed in order to guard faith against speculation. A second major goal of Part Two is to emphasize the infinite qualitative difference between God and humankind, which in Anti-Climacus's view has been compromised by the tendency of modern speculative thought to favor the race over the individual and to identify the former with the divine. At the same time, however, he views the incarnation of God in Jesus Christ as the exemplar for what it means to be a human being in the form of a theological self or a self in relation and likeness to God. Anti-Climacus thus seeks to point out the infinite difference between God and human beings as well as the potential similarity of the latter to the divine. In the process of drawing these correlations, he also makes a number of important distinctions between understanding and understanding (not being able to understand versus not being willing to understand), understanding and doing, knowing and willing, believing and comprehending, being and thinking, offense and faith, all of which must be taken into account in an analysis of the concept of sin. These goals and distinctions establish this work as one of the most important writings in the Kierkegaardian corpus with respect to the delineation of the concept of sin, the relation of Christianity to classical paganism and its corresponding forms in Christendom and modern speculation, and the similarity as well as the difference between humankind and the divine, all of which must be taken into account for a proper understanding of the relation of human beings to God.

CHAPTER 11

Despair the Disease and Faith the Therapeutic Cure

Jeffrey Hanson

One of the nagging uncertainties that besets the interpretation of *The Sickness unto Death* is the vagueness that attaches to the promised cure for the disease of despair – faith. Presented in capsule form (SUD, 82/SKS 11, 196) at the beginning, middle, and end of the book (SUD 14, 49, 131/ SKS 11, 130, 164, 242), it is otherwise left without much expatiation. "The formula that describes the state of the self when despair is completely rooted out is this: in relating to itself and in willing to be itself, the self rests transparently in the power that posited it" (SUD, 14/SKS 11, 130).[1] While despair is analyzed in exquisite detail, the presumably important topic of faith is hardly elaborated; if despair is indeed a universal affliction, and faith is its only cure, it would seem that the acquisition of faith is a crucial concern of the text, though one that is not treated at length by it. Yet Anti-Climacus's brief treatment of faith is consistent with others of Kierkegaard's pseudonymous writings, wherein faith is spoken of only indirectly, though it is undeniably important.

My aim in what follows is to reconstruct from the text what we might be able to claim confidently about faith as the cure for despair according to Anti-Climacus. I pursue that aim in three steps. In order to come to a deeper appreciation of faith's effective resolution of the problem of despair we have to first understand the precise nature of the disease at stake. This is the task of the chapter's first section: "The Nature of the Disease." There I argue that despair is diagnosed by Anti-Climacus as a condition rather than merely a feeling. This means that the development of despair is governed by a limited repertoire of available "moves" that are designed

---

[1] Translation modified. There is no need to translate a reflexive verb formulation like *forholde sig til* into a reflexive form in English. Also with respect to the translation of the Danish verb *sætte* I would argue that "establish" carries a stronger implication than Anti-Climacus relies upon. In this respect I am following Rasmus Rosenberg Larsen in his "The Posited Self: The Non-Theistic Foundation in Kierkegaard's Writings," *Kierkegaard Studies Year Book* (2015): 31–54. I do not, however, follow him in the conclusions he draws from this preferred choice of term.

to force the despairing person into a conceptual bottleneck that can be escaped only by faith.

I then turn in the second and third sections to an analysis of faith, which I argue has a twofold structure. According to Anti-Climacus's version of Christianity, "there is infinitely much more hope in death than there is in life – not only when in the merely human sense there is life but this life in consummate health and vitality" (SUD, 8/SKS 11, 124). The reason that there is more hope for the believer in death than in life is that the faithful person has been taught what is "truly horrifying" (SUD, 8/SKS 11, 125) – "a miserable condition that man as such does not know exists. This miserable condition is the sickness unto death" (SUD, 8/SKS 11, 124). Faith then warns the believer off the most menacing threat to the self: despair, the only sickness unto spiritual death, a fate worse than physical death. This is the first aspect of faith, which I exposit in the section below entitled "Relating to God."

In the third section, "Willing to Be Yourself," I explain the second lesson faith has to teach, which is that there is no threat to the self from "earthly and worldly matters, death included," in short, "everything that men usually call misfortune or the worst of evils" (SUD, 8/SKS 11, 124). Faith thus weans the believer from reliance on external events that we readily interpret as putatively "good" or "bad" fortune, events upon which we are tempted to rely as the basis for the self's integrity. For the faithful person, "need, illness, misery, hardship, adversities, torments, mental sufferings, cares, grief" all fail to have a determinative effect on the self. Despite their apparent threat, the faithful person debunks these misfortunes as "not horrifying" and thus not worth shrinking from. By the same token, all prosperity and peace, everything that travels under the name of a superficial "happiness," is equally incapable of delivering the self from the only real and "truly horrifying" danger. Thus I contend that faith has a therapeutic function: It is meant to extirpate from the self the only genuine danger, which is persistence in unforgiven sin, while maturing the self to cope with the ordinary hazards of human life and to avoid its false consolations.

This twofold function of faith – positively warning the self against its only real threat and negatively clearing away false consolations and imagined dangers – is grounded, I argue, in the definition of faith Anti-Climacus supplies. Recall that according to the first formulation cited earlier, the self is said to be "relating to itself and in willing to be itself, the self rests transparently in the power that posited it" (SUD, 14/SKS 11, 130). I would simply point out here that faith involves two distinct elements: willing to be itself and resting transparently in God. The same observation pertains to the later, slightly different, version of the definition of faith provided in the middle of the book: "Faith is: that the self in being itself and in willing to be itself rests transparently in God" (SUD, 82/SKS 11, 196). Here again it would seem that faith involves both willing to be one's self and resting transparently in relation to God. Obviously these are two aspects of one phenomenon, but the critical literature often contents itself with a fairly brisk account of the correlation between these two aspects. What I intend to explore further here is the precise sense in which the faithful self relates to God and the therapeutic benefits that come from the faithful person's ability to genuinely will to be themselves. To appreciate these two related aspects with a bit more depth and precision we need to take exact account of the nature of the disease faith is meant to cure.

The Nature of the Disease

Despair as Anti-Climacus analyzes it is a condition, not merely a feeling.[2] A feeling is subject to bidirectional modulation along a continuum; one can feel more or less angry, more or less excited, and can do so by quantitative gradation from no anger or excitement at all to maximal anger or excitement and back again. If one is too angry or overexcited then the "solution" is simply to "dial down," as it were, one's feelings to an acceptably moderate level. By contrast, a condition affords only certain "moves" that lie along a unidirectional axis of intensification. A condition only worsens, and to "dial down" a condition would inevitably court a kind of bad faith, a denial of the state in which one finds oneself. The "solution" to a condition is not simply to have less of it but to be rid of it altogether. In the case of despair, the moves that signpost the condition's progression – if allowed to culminate in their ultimate stage – strand the self in a bottleneck. The logic of despair's progression conforms to what Anti-Climacus calls "the law of intensification" (SUD, 18/SKS 11, 134).

This law serves as a kind of internal principle of organization that governs the moves internal to despair's typical progression, which does not operate on the less–more spectrum. Moreover, breaking out of despair cannot be a matter of simply reaching a kind of putative equilibrium, either between the constitutive poles of the human being that underpin

---

[2] The contrast is inspired by Robert C. Roberts, "The Grammar of Sin and the Conceptual Unity of *The Sickness unto Death*," in *International Kierkegaard Commentary: The Sickness unto Death*, ed. Robert L. Perkins (Macon, GA: Mercer University Press, 1987), 135–160.

the four forms of unconscious despair (infinitude/finitude, possibility/ necessity) or between the co-implicated valences of conscious despair (weakness and defiance). The cure cannot take the form of some kind of "balance."[3] Particularly when Anti-Climacus is emphatic that if a despairing person "with all his power seeks to break the despair by himself and by himself alone – he is still in despair and with all his presumed effort only works himself all the deeper into deeper despair" (SUD, 14/SKS 11, 130), we have to acknowledge that there is no obvious exit from despair, at least not in Part One's diagnostic.

Intensification is aggravating, but it is important to be clear about what is being aggravated as the itinerary of despair develops over the course of Part One's analysis. One either is or is not in despair, not more or less despairing, strictly speaking. One can undergo different forms of the one condition that is despair, which are organized by modulations in awareness, not necessarily modulations in feeling. Numerous passages identify in fact two valences along which consciousness can progress, both of which can vary independently of one another: consciousness of what despair is and consciousness of being in despair (SUD, 48, 49, 50–51, 62, 67/SKS 11, 163, 164, 165, 176, 181). Anti-Climacus is at best, though, noncommittal as to whether it helps to be conscious of one's state as despair and conscious of what despair is. "Purely philosophically, it could be a subtle question," he demurs, "whether it is possible for one to be in despair and be fully aware of that *of* which one despairs" (SUD, 61n/SKS 11, 175n). He punts again, framing two seeming imperatives that can't really co-exist: On the one hand, he wants to say conscious despair requires holding a true conception of despair, while on the other hand we must have clarity about ourselves. "To what extent perfect clarity about oneself as being in despair can be combined with being in despair, that is, whether this clarity of knowledge and of self-knowledge might not simply wrench a person out of despair, make him so afraid of himself that he would stop being in despair, we will not determine here" (SUD, 47/SKS 11, 162). It is fair, I think, to conclude on the basis of this reluctance that Anti-Climacus considers the development of despair by itself incapable of delivering the conscious

---

[3] Anti-Climacus writes that "no form of despair can be defined directly (that is, undialectically), but only by reflecting upon its opposite" (SUD, 30/SKS 11, 146). This point further implies that all forms of despair involve co-implicated polarities (not just the four unconscious forms), no one member of which can afford a cure for despair since each is bound to its dialectical pair. Here I owe a debt to Robert Stern and Daniel Watts, "Valuing Humanity: Kierkegaardian Worries about Korsgaardian Transcendental Arguments," *International Journal of Philosophy and Theology* 80, no. 4–5 (2019): 424–442.

despairer from their despair. This is why the only way out of the condition is to work through it.

Anti-Climacus suggests as much again on several occasions in the text. Keeping in view his caution that to actually be in despair is "the worst misfortune and misery – no, it is ruination" (SUD, 15/SKS 11, 131), there are nevertheless various points at which he indicates that despair is also a condition for faith. Indeed, he says that the "infinite benefaction" of knowing one's self and knowing one's self as existing before God "is never gained except through despair" (SUD, 27/SKS 11, 143). Sometimes Anti-Climacus is even more emphatic, as when he asserts that the self becomes itself "precisely by having despaired" (SUD, 30/SKS 11, 146). Even more emphatic still: "if repentance is to arise, there must first be effective despair, radical despair, so that the life of the spirit can break through from the ground upward" (SUD, 59/SKS 11, 174). Nevertheless, all these passages prove is that despair must be lived through at least to some extent in order to make faith possible. That would seem to leave the door open for the possibility that free agents can embrace faith at any point, a claim that plausibly can be attributed to Kierkegaard.

However, Anti-Climacus provides a memorable image that implies that one must pursue despair to its end in order to break its spell, if not in actuality then at least conceptually. "However, to reach the truth, one must go through every negativity, for the old legend about breaking a certain magic spell is true; the piece has to be played through backwards or the spell is not broken" (SUD, 44/SKS 11, 159). This striking image recalls a point made by Vigilius Haufniensis in regard to anxiety as saving through faith. He refers to the Carpocratian heretics, who held the view that one had to sin in order to receive grace, such that salvation only came by means of damnable behavior. Haufniensis's point is that while it is blasphemy to affirm this heresy in the concrete, the abstract truth in this view is that one must indeed be aware of the enticing nature of manifold sins, but precisely in order to avoid committing them (CA, 103/SKS 4, 405–406). In this case, the practice of vigilance amounts to a kind of spiritual exercise in self-awareness (so as to be on guard against what I find particularly alluring) and in guilt-consciousness (so as to meticulously avoid sinning before the God who judges such sin). I suggest that Anti-Climacus is making a comparable point about despair: Like anxiety, despair can be an ally to faith when it promotes self-awareness, putting me on guard against my failings, and foregrounds sin-consciousness, placing me before a rather particular, not a generic, God, one who judges me for those failings.

The explicit introduction in Part Two of the "before God" criterion, and its companion doctrine of sin-consciousness, marks a qualitative breach in the development of the condition of despair. The full meaning of the self's being before God is only realized when we appreciate that "God" here is the God who can serve as "criterion" and "goal" (SUD, 79/ SKS 11, 194) of the self, not just any God but the one of whom Anti-Climacus affirms "only in Christ is it true that God is man's goal and criterion" (SUD, 114/SKS 11, 226). This reading has direct support from Kierkegaard himself, who wrote in his journal:

> With respect to despair it is not a matter merely of equilibrium between the two, or, more accurately, *the human being as spirit simply cannot have equilibrium in himself.* He is, as the composite (the synthesis), a relation, but a relation which relates itself to itself. Yet he has not established himself as a relation; the relation which he is, even though a relation for itself, is established by another. Only by the relation to this other can he be in equilibrium. (JP 1, 749/Pap. VIII² B 168, emphasis mine)

The only resolution then is to embrace a proper diagnostic of the true nature of the problem, which is that despair is not a disease that can be cured without outside intervention. As we have seen, despair of its own internal structure propels one who despairs toward a crisis point at which this realization – that outside intervention is required – becomes at least graspable from within the condition of despair. We must recall that with despair everything is dialectical, such that the deepest immersion within it is also the nearest exit from it.[4]

Relating to God

The facet of faith's work having to do with the self's capacity to rest transparently in the power that established it is the more conspicuous in the text and the one that has attracted more attention from commentators than the facet of faith having to do with willing to be oneself. However, even then there has been a lack of precision about what exactly it means to relate to the God whom Anti-Climacus identifies expressly with the Holy Trinity at the end of the book. Obviously the relation to this God is

---

[4] If I am correct that there is a parallel between despair as Anti-Climacus describes it and Haufniensis's argument about anxiety as saving through faith, it may be possible to claim that despair in a way makes one ready for faith. Like anxiety, despair does not lead automatically to faith, but it can bring the sufferer to its verge. For more on this possibility see Jeffrey Hanson, "Holy Hypochondria: Narrative and Self-Awareness in *The Concept of Anxiety,*" *Kierkegaard Studies Year Book* (2011): 239–261.

connected to the relation the self in faith bears toward itself. The self can only be itself fully in relation to the divine. Recall though that in the Introduction Anti-Climacus showed that faith debunks the threat of the external, teaching the believer that suffering is not the true threat to the self's integrity, and instead makes the believer aware of the one truly horrifying threat to the self, which is despair. I argue that this threat really only comes into full view with despair understood as sin, the theme of Part Two. In Part One certain defective views of the relation to "God" have already been studied and found wanting; this suggests that the real danger is not just despair before a generic God but persisting in sin before the God who both judges sin and stands ready to forgive it.

To take just two illustrative examples of inadequate relations to the divine, both the person in necessity's despair and in infinitude's despair have a sort of relation to "God." For the person in necessity's despair, "his God is necessity" (SUD, 40/SKS 11, 155). This person relates to a "God" who is the god of fate. The fatalist knows only that all that happens must happen. "God" is not a criterion and goal, not a providential giver of good gifts, but is rather the name given to what must be. Such a person cannot pray, for they are spiritually suffocated by the weight of their own self, which they cannot envision being other than it is (SUD, 38–39/SKS 11, 153–155). For the fatalist, God is not that everything is possible, which is the conviction of the believer (SUD, 38/SKS 11, 153). For the believer, then, possibility, radical possibility, is always available. The fatalist can see impossibility all too easily, and the "philistine-bourgeois mentality" imagines it can manage possibility as an exercise in risk management, life by actuarial tables (SUD, 41/SKS 11, 156).

To believe, however, is stronger than this; it is to accept that "humanly speaking, his collapse is altogether certain" (SUD, 39/SKS 11, 154). The believer thus is not heedless but is convinced that, humanly speaking, "in what has happened to him, or in what he has ventured" (SUD, 39/SKS 11, 154) his downfall is certain. Yet the believer, while accepting his downfall, also does not credit it. The faithful person cannot know how she will be helped in the face of what is humanly impossible, but she believes that with God all things are possible. "To understand that humanly it is his downfall and nevertheless to believe in possibility is to believe. So God helps him also – perhaps by allowing him to avoid the horror, perhaps through the horror itself – and here, unexpectedly, miraculously, divinely, help does come" (SUD, 39/SKS 11, 154–155). The deliverance of the self through faith comes regardless of external circumstances. Salvation does not necessarily come as a result of avoiding the worst-case scenario; it may come precisely *through* the worst-case scenario. The fatalist cannot grasp how this is possible with the God for whom all things are possible because this is not the God to whom they are related.

The person in infinitude's despair also has a deficient relation to "God." Anti-Climacus describes how such a person is carried away by the fantastical, a distancing of the self from its own factical situation that can manifest itself with respect to the self's feeling, knowing, or willing (SUD, 31–32/SKS 11, 147–148). When it comes to the religious, this person is no less fantastical, which results in alienation from reality and the supplanting of real lived relationships with airy abstractions.

> The God-relationship is an infinitizing, but in fantasy this infinitizing can so sweep a man off his feet that his state is simply an intoxication. To exist before God may seem unendurable to a man because he cannot come back to himself, become himself. Such a fantasized religious person would say (to characterize him by means of some lines): "That a sparrow can live is comprehensible; it does not know that it exists before God. But to know that one exists before God, and then not instantly go mad or sink into nothingness!" (SUD, 32/SKS, 148)

For a person in this form of despair, "God" is again not a criterion and goal for the self, not a loving father who knows each sparrow that falls[5] but a remote and intimidating presence before whom one cannot be a self at all. This "God" is annihilating, wondrous perhaps, but making no contact with the actual lived situation of the self, caring nothing for its needs or cares.

So faith involves a relation with not just any God, it would seem, but with a God before whom it is possible to know and be myself. This is why Anti-Climacus is emphatic that the God before whom one is conscious of oneself in faith is the God who is a "qualitative criterion" and "ethically its goal." A criterion is a standard of evaluation, in the absence of which one cannot be fully oneself, and an ethical goal is an ideal one should strive to attain. Taken together, "the criterion and goal are what define something, what it is" (SUD, 79/SKS 11, 193–194). So the self can only be defined as what it is by reference to its criterion and goal. To be a criterion is to be an evaluative standard. To be a self before God in the fullest sense is to be a self before a God before whom I can *fail*, hence the lengthy discussion of sin in Part Two. The fatalist and the person carried away by the intoxication of infinitude cannot fail before their "Gods." That is because they are

---

[5] The choice of a sparrow seems to intentionally recall the words of Jesus in Matthew 10:29: "Are not two sparrows sold for a farthing? And one of them shall not fall on the ground without your Father."

not evaluated by their "Gods," which idolatrously only reconfirm their own respective forms of misrelation, reflecting back to the dysfunctional self nothing but its own species of dysfunction. Furthermore, the God before whom I am fully myself is the God to whose likeness I should be aspiring, hence this God is the self's goal.

We know what something is by its criterion and goal, but Anti-Climacus qualifies this rule for defining a thing's nature by indicating that in the sphere of freedom, "where by not qualitatively being that which is his goal and his criterion a person must himself have merited this disqualification" (SUD, 80/SKS 11, 193). So in the realm of freedom, a self is defined precisely by its contrast to its criterion and goal, a shortfall for which the self is responsible. It is here, as he says of all despair, that we must understand phenomena "inversely" (SUD, 78/SKS 11, 192). The self is known by what it is *not*. Being free, it is responsible for its own failure to be what it ought to be in accord with its criterion and goal (SUD, 80/SKS 11, 194–195).

It is not for some time that Anti-Climacus specifies the one and only respect in which the self cannot be likened to God and thus is inversely known as what it is: "Sin is the one and only predication about a human being that in no way, either *via negationis* or *via eminentiæ*, can be stated of God" (SUD, 122/SKS 11, 233). That God is the criterion and goal is thus nowhere more apparent than in the (non)correspondence between God and the human being with respect to sin. So drastic is the "chasmic qualitative abyss" that separates God and humanity in this respect that even the denial that God is a sinner would be "blasphemy," presumably because even the denial of such a predication itself would presume to attribute this quality to the divinity – even by way of negation. Conversely, "there is one way in which man could never in all eternity come to be like God: in forgiving sins" (SUD, 122/SKS 11, 233).

My argument throughout this chapter is that faith performs the negative task of clearing away from the believer all non-horrifying delusions about the source of the self's despair and the positive task of warning the believer off from what is truly horrifying. The truly horrifying is, I would argue, sin, which is a result of will, unlike tragedy, adversities, and the torments of human life. More specifically, we confront sin at its most horrifying here at the end of the text, when we reach the "most extreme concentration of offense, and this has been found necessary by the very doctrine that has taught the likeness between God and man" (SUD, 122/SKS 11, 233). It is Christian faith that teaches what is truly horrifying, and with this doctrine of offense, Anti-Climacus flatly asserts, "Christianity begins" (SUD, 122/ SKS 11, 233).

Offense is a well-known concept for readers of Kierkegaard; certainly much can be learned from *The Sickness unto Death* on this subject, but I will concentrate on the highest pitches of offense, since these are the threats to integrity of the self that are to be avoided at all costs.[6] Interestingly, we can discern in the final three stages of offense an exact parallelism with the forms of despair having to do with consciousness traced out in Part One. According to that exposition, despair develops along a unidirectional axis of intensification through various forms of consciousness, from despair over something earthly or despair over the earthly itself, through despair of the eternal (and these are forms of weakness), to the despair of defiance. A precisely parallel escalation of sinful despairing over sin itself takes place, again in three stages that are isomorphic with those of Part One section C – despair over the earthly, despair of the eternal, and defiance. Consequently, the condition itself fundamentally changes, and the self living in the condition of sin submits to a wholesale redescription of this condition and its intensification.

In the first state the sinful person retrenches themselves in their own sin, cutting themselves off from the good within a self-enclosed carapace (SUD, 109/SKS 11, 221). It goes without saying, though Anti-Climacus says it more than once on this page, that this is yet another intensification. "To describe the intensification in the relation between sin and despair over sin, the first may be termed the break with the good and the second with repentance" (SUD, 109/SKS 11, 221). This is sin against God the Father. Like the despair over the earthly, the person in this stage of sin despairs over the possibility of help being furnished by any external situation. Intriguingly, such a person is in a sense correct: The external cannot save. Here we find a direct parallelism between the first and second functions of faith. Faith disabuses the believer from placing any hope in earthly affairs for the deliverance of the self; the aggravated sin is to then also despairingly disbelieve that any help can come from God, to despair over not just the earthly but over the prospect of help from the eternal.

The second form is once more an advance in consciousness, one that Anti-Climacus calls the "continuance of sin," which is not the

---

[6] The dialectically opposite state, of total ignorance about being in despair, has its own sort of menace, so much so that it can be "the most dangerous form of despair." Yet Anti-Climacus says this is a purely dialectical observation, holding only in the abstract, and he reiterates that it is the highly conscious despairer who is in real ethical danger (SUD, 44/SKS 11, 159).

multiplication of particular new sins but rather the sedimentation of pluriform sins into a settled state. This state again results from "the law of motion in intensification, [which] here as everywhere else, is inward, in greater and greater intensity of consciousness" (SUD, 108–109/SKS 11, 220). Here one despairs over one's own sin, which is itself a new sin. This is a more active, willful form of sin, corresponding to the increased activity and consciousness of despair over the earthly. This sinner *wants* to remain a sinner. This nefarious condition can convincingly cloak itself as bearing "the mark of a deep nature" (SUD, 111/SKS 11, 223). One sometimes hears persons lament "'I will never forgive myself.' This is supposed to show how much good there is in him, what a deep nature he has. It is a subterfuge" (SUD, 111/SKS 11, 223). The reason this is a subterfuge is that if forgiveness is available, that is, if God in Christ is willing and ready to forgive, then one must accept that forgiveness rather than reject it. The apparent high-mindedness of the sentiment is a disguise for a prideful refusal to accept forgiveness where it is possible (SUD, 111–112/SKS 11, 223).

This vignette provides a clue to the next form of sin, which despairs not over one's own sin only but of the forgiveness of sins specifically. This stage of sin is not merely before God but before Christ in particular. This is the sin against the Son, and it is analogous to the second form of conscious despair, the despair over the eternal. To sin against the Son is to intimate that forgiveness of sin is available, that help can come from the eternal, and yet to reject it. Anti-Climacus also calls this reaction offense, since a sinner of this sort is actively scandalized by the claim of Christ to forgive sins: The offended sinner does not just reject the possibility of forgiveness; she recoils at it.

Anti-Climacus's argument here is that Christianity begins with the teaching of sin. He has said this before, but here again it comes up, because now he makes a strong association between the revelation of what sin is with the capacity to be the single individual, that highly conscious ideal self to whom Kierkegaard dedicated his authorship. While sin is common to all, sin-consciousness is individuating (SUD, 120n/SKS 11, 231). Once again, this is a highly dialectical pivot, for it is obviously bad to be a sinner, but to have the capacity to recognize oneself as such is an advantage over the animals and a precondition for becoming the true and genuine single individual.

Offense is the highest mark of subjectivity. Like sin itself it is only ever actual, resulting when an actual single individual is offended (SUD, 122/SKS 11, 233). When realized in this manner, offense is yet another intensification (SUD, 124/SKS 11, 235–236). Offense is a scandalized reaction against the prospect of accepting forgiveness and thus having faith in Christ's ability and willingness to forgive sins. A yet higher form of intensification still awaits, however: "This is sin against the Holy Spirit. Here the self is at the highest intensity of despair; it not only discards Christianity totally but also makes it out to be a lie and untruth" (SUD, 125/SKS 11, 236). The sin against the Holy Spirit is probably Anti-Climacus's terminology for what the Gospels call "blasphemy against the Holy Ghost." In Matthew 12:31–32, Jesus teaches the following:

> Wherefore I say unto you, All manner of sin and blasphemy shall be forgiven unto men: but the blasphemy against the Holy Ghost shall not be forgiven unto men. And whosoever speaketh a word against the Son of man, it shall be forgiven him: but whosoever speaketh against the Holy Ghost, it shall not be forgiven him, neither in this world, neither in the world to come.

Commonly referred to as the "unforgiveable sin," this passage seems to teach that while all sins can be forgiven, even those against Jesus Christ himself, the one sin that cannot be forgiven is the direct, reflexive repudiation of the forgiveness of sin, the availability of which (even in the absence of the bodily presence on earth of the incarnate Son) is constantly present thanks to the ongoing ministry of the Holy Spirit in the church.

Anti-Climacus here likens this qualitative intensification to a change in battle tactics. The war is still between God and the human being, but now we give up the defensive posture and go on the offensive. In this way, "sin against the Holy Spirit is the positive form of being offended" (SUD, 125/SKS 11, 236). It is almost as if in this form of sin the sinner is preemptively offended. In a final analogy to the last form of conscious despair from Part One, which is wholly active and highly self-conscious demonic defiance, here too sin is on an active footing against God, and the sinful self insists on its own outraged rectitude. Like demonic despair, the sin against the Holy Spirit is not reactive to an external situation or occasion but wholly self-willed from within and thus at the highest pitch of consciousness and will (SUD, 67/SKS 11, 181).

Offense, then, is yet one final inner intensification of the already intensified condition of being in sin. Consciousness and will again combine in an escalating progression, exit from which is possible in only one way. Like the demoniac, the person who sins against the Holy Spirit is perversely obsessed with God. The demoniac "must above all take care to adhere to what it denounces" (SUD, 73/SKS 11, 187), in this case the God who appears in the disguise of an author who has introduced an error into his writing. Not long before Anti-Climacus reaches this famous conclusion to Part One, though, he already anticipates the solution that will only become clear in Part Two. When it comes to the prospect of being helped by the divine out of defiant despair, the demonic person cannot endure the "humiliation" of accepting aid, is loath to become "a nothing in the hand of the 'Helper' for whom all things are possible" (SUD, 71/SKS 11, 185).

What Anti-Climacus is here forecasting is the advent of not just God as author of existence but the God who offers deliverance from sin. "The 'Helper' in particular is another biblical name for the Holy Spirit,[7] against whom the most intensive form of sin is committed, again in parallel with the demonic defiance that is the most intensive form of despair. God is here presented as the one for whom all things are possible, even the forgiveness of sin, even for a maximally defiant sinner. The aspect of faith then that involves relating to God is specifically about accepting forgiveness of sins from that God, even when it means the humiliation of the self's pride. At the same time, the faithful person is acutely conscious of themselves as sinner, and this sin-consciousness is entirely compatible with the acceptance of forgiveness. The believing person is as intensely conscious of their own sinfulness as the defiant sinner is intensely conscious of their unwillingness to be forgiven. That sin-consciousness ultimately individualizes in the same way faith does means that the two are compatible in the end, another indication of how thoroughgoingly dialectical despair really is. What the highest pitches of offense demonstrate is that awareness alone is insufficient for faith. The person who retrenches themselves in their own sin, despairs of its forgiveness, or rejects the very possibility of that forgiveness is aware of themselves as sinful but refuses to relate to God in such a way as to relinquish this self-conception, while knowing precisely what would be entailed by doing so. Consequently, such a person can never genuinely will to be themselves, can never be at peace with who they are, though they see what this would mean to an extent that persons not as fully conscious of their own despair cannot see. In this sense they are the exact inverse of – and yet so very close to – the faithful person, who in relating to God constructively is also able to be herself, and indeed herself at rest.

---

[7] Although it must be admitted here that Kierkegaard's choice of word, *Hjælperens*, is not the term used to translate the name for the Holy Spirit given by Jesus himself in the Gospel of John chapter 14, which in the Bible of Kierkegaard's day was rendered by the term *Talsmand*.

Willing to Be Yourself

This aspect of faith – its capacity to make the believer simultaneously conscious of their own sin and its forgiveness – makes it possible not only for the self to relate to God but also to will to be itself. In faith the self is posited by itself, but the self that stands "before God" not only is posited by itself but also by God. It is not a question of choosing but of harmonizing. Faith will resolve despair by riveting the self to itself as well as to the God who not only posits the self but forgives it. In this respect the faithful person enjoys a high degree of self-awareness; she knows who she is and accepts herself as forgiven, which allows her to accept herself in full.

As we have seen, it would seem to be all but impossible to really break with the constitutive relationship with God. The person in defiance Anti-Climacus asserts is mired in an attempt at "severing the self from any relation to a power that has established it, or severing it from the idea that there is such a power" (SUD, 68/SKS 11, 182). Consistent with a strong reading of the degree to which the relation of the self to God is constitutive of selfhood itself, this characterization suggests that at best the self can sever itself effectively only from the consciousness of its presence before God.[8] Likewise we cannot escape being ourselves. Faith then conjoins the spiritual reality of being a self and being a self before God. This bivalence implies that the phenomenon of faith will confirm the self as a self and a self before God. The judgment of eternity referred to by Anti-Climacus is one that rivets the self to itself. The question of this judgment is not whether you will be the self you are or not; it is whether you will be yourself in despair or in faith. Eternity thus "knows you as you are known" (SUD, 28/SKS 11, 144).[9] Eternity thus ratifies the self as what it is, as that complex of what it has repudiated within itself (sin) and accepted as an ineliminable part of itself (suffering).

The only question then is how faith makes the self one that the self can genuinely will to be in peace, a question all the more urgent since despair is compatible with any number of external circumstances that would on the face of it and in the eyes of worldly judgment amount to success and even "happiness." Because despair affects the spirit "both health and sickness are

---

[8] This would seem to be implied by Anti-Climacus's brief but punchy declaration that "God is not some externality in the sense that a policeman is" (SUD, 80/SKS 11, 194). The God-relation is instead constitutive of the self, and any disturbance in this relation reverberates throughout the self.
[9] The reference is to St. Paul's vision of the eschaton from 1 Corinthians 13:12: "For now we see through a glass, darkly; but then face to face: now I know in part; but then shall I know even as also I am known."

critical; there is no immediate health of the spirit" (SUD, 25/SKS 11, 141). Consequently, any apparent success in life must be subjected to critical scrutiny, and even an apparent failure to live well may also be unrelated to genuine spiritual health. The only thing that matters is whether the self gains an understanding of itself before God and thus evades the pernicious lure of both "life's joys" and "its sorrows" (SUD, 26/ SKS 11, 142–143).

Thus the therapeutic of faith does part of its effective work by clearing away illusory ideals and, hand-in-hand with this, it teaches the believer that apparent sources of unhappiness are also not to be feared, not even death itself (SUD, 8/SKS 11, 124). So the believer learns through faith to weather the adversities of the world. Simultaneously, the faithful person learns that all these putative sources of unhappiness are as nothing in contrast to the one real source of worry in human life: the sickness unto death that is nothing other than despair (SUD, 8–9/SKS 11, 124–125). The "natural man" spoken of by St. Paul[10] is like a child who shudders at what is not really fearful, while the believer or spiritual person is like an adult who has been tutored by faith to regard only spiritual death, despair, or sin as truly horrifying and to overcome the lesser threats to peace and contentment.

At various points in the text, to which we will turn shortly, Anti-Climacus argues that part of what is required to break out of despair is the ability to accept parts of one's self that one might be tempted to disavow. To use Anti-Climacus's technical vocabulary, we need to distinguish between what the self despairs *over* and what the self despairs *of*. "We despair *over* [*over*] that which binds us in despair – over a misfortune, over the earthly, over a capital loss, etc. – but we despair *of* [*om*] that which, rightly understood, releases us from despair: of the eternal, of salvation, of our own strength, etc. ... And the haziness, particularly in all the lower forms of despair and in almost every person in despair, is that he so passionately and clearly sees and knows *over* what he despairs, but *of* what he despairs evades him" (SUD, 60–61n/SKS 11, 175n).

To use a pair of classic examples, Anti-Climacus depicts a woman who is jilted by her lover (SUD, 20/SKS 11, 135) and the case of Cesare Borgia, who fails to attain his life goal of becoming Caesar (SUD, 19/SKS 11, 134–135). In both instances the person in despair thinks they despair "over *something*," but this is merely a momentary illusion (SUD, 19/SKS

---

[10] See 1 Corinthians 2:14: "But the natural man receiveth not the things of the Spirit of God: for they are foolishness unto him: neither can he know them, because they are spiritually discerned."

11, 134). These people imagine they are in despair over a particular occasion: a setback that amounts to what Anti-Climacus called a perceived source of "misery, hardship, adversities." The jilted lover says she is in despair, and this is true, but she thinks she is in despair because she has been jilted, but this is not the reason for her despair. Cesare Borgia says he is in despair and this is true, but he thinks he is in despair because he has failed to become Caesar, but this failure is not the cause of his despair. Both see what they are in despair *over*, but neither sees what they despair *of.* The truth of the condition that is despair, though, is that the despairing persons only despair of themselves. This fundamental dis-ease with oneself is the real basis of the despairing person's condition, which means that the exact opposite outcome could have just as easily revealed the despairing persons' true condition to themselves: If the jilted lover did get her husband, if Cesare Borgia did get to be Caesar, they *still* would have been in despair (SUD, 19, 20/SKS 11, 134, 135) because what they despair *over* is just the occasion for realizing that they are in despair about themselves, not about any external circumstance.

We can think about the difference with a grammatical distinction (one that admittedly is not discernible in Danish). To despair *over* in Anti-Climacus's terminology can be thought of as an accusative: The despairing person thinks they are in despair over some definite object. The truth is, though, that despair takes the dative case: The despairing person in fact despairs *of*[11] themselves, which is to say, of the self that is the indirect object of the occasion, the object over which they imagine they despair. This is why Anti-Climacus says the self is doubly dialectical and thus over the self alone do we both despair *over* and *of.* To complete a passage cited in part earlier: "With respect to the self, we say both: to despair *over* and *of* oneself, because the self is doubly dialectical" (SUD, 61n/SKS 11, 175n). Because the self is the ground of both the disease and the cure, we despair *over* it inasmuch as it is the self that is the real indirect object of our despair. It is that self over which we despair anterior to any specific putative direct object of despair like a misfortune or tragedy. We despair *of* it inasmuch as in despair we cannot see how this self can be redeemed, how it is also the cure to despair if we can learn to live with it. Faith thus

---

[11] This sounds somewhat awkward in English, but in Danish *om* principally means "about" or, better in my judgment, "concerning." This captures a double sense explained later, in which the person despairs about themselves in the sense that it is her own self that is the *concern* to her and that it is *concerning* her self that she really despairs.

resolves this double bind by forgiving the sin of the self while also clearing it of the misconception that its suffering is damning.

What this means is that the person in despair must come to accept themselves, quite apart from and, so to speak, prior to what befalls them. There are a handful of underappreciated passages where Anti-Climacus counsels that faith will involve a kind of reconciliation of the self with undesirable parts of itself or unfortunate events that befall it. Speaking of a source of specific suffering, he writes, "although suffering under it, the self will still not make the admission that it is part of the self [*det hører med til Selvet*], that is, the self will not in faith humble itself under it" (SUD, 70–71n/SKS 11, 184n). Part of what faith can effectuate for the believer then is their humble acceptance of suffering as part of the self itself, a part that cannot be evaded.

The Sickness unto Death therefore presents faith as a kind of self-acceptance without limit or qualification. Anti-Climacus makes this point with respect to the peculiar anguish of the poet inclined to the religious memorably described at the opening of Part Two: "He became unhappy in the religious life, dimly understands that he is required to give up this anguish – that is, in faith to humble himself under and take it upon himself as a part of the self [*hørende med til Selvet*]" (SUD, 78/SKS 11, 192). Finally, at the stunning conclusion of Part One, when Anti-Climacus describes the person in defiant despair, he analogizes his condition to that of a scribal error that has become conscious of itself as an error and refuses to be corrected in order to stand as an outraged witness to the second-rate status of the author who is responsible for the error's existence. Yet it is possible, Anti-Climacus writes, that the error was "not a mistake but an essential part of the whole production [*væsentligt Medhenhørende i hele Fremstillingen*]" (SUD, 73/SKS 11, 187). Here again, it seems reasonable to suppose, given the similarity of language and imagery, that the defiant person can be healed only if he or she accepts this perceived "error" as not a mistake at all but as a "part" of the self that cannot be wished away but only humbly accepted in faith.

These passages give the reader a more fulsome sense of how faith might operate in the sense we have been describing: by dispelling the shades of what is not truly horrifying to the believer, those torments and adversities that Anti-Climacus refers to in his Introduction. If faith is to do its saving work, it will deliver the self from subjection to the vicissitudes of human life, exposing them as being sufficient neither to save nor condemn the self. These external circumstances cannot be the *cause* of despair or of its overcoming; they are at most occasions. The jilted lover cannot be the self she wants; Cesare Borgia cannot be the self he wants. Nor can these selves be delivered from despair if the opposite state of affairs were to come about, since it is still possible for the married bride and the regnant Borgia to remain in despair. Faith does not promise a different outcome; it allows each to humbly accept themselves in and amidst the situation in which the self finds itself. In one of his starker formulations, Anti-Climacus summarizes this aspect of faith by echoing the paradoxical words of Jesus:[12] "The despair that is the thoroughfare to faith comes also through the aid of the eternal; through the aid of the eternal the self has the courage to lose itself in order to win itself" (SUD, 67/SKS 11, 181). Equilibrium is not possible on the self's own power, but in relation to the God who forgives, equilibrium is possible. It is faith that attains the equilibrium that allows the self to accept itself as it is, while relating to God in the only way that secures that self-acceptance.

While faith then is not explicitly fleshed out in *The Sickness unto Death*, it elusively looms over the whole text. What I have tried to show is that its presence is indirectly detectable along two parallel vectors: the dispelling of false threats to the self in the name of total self-acceptance and the caution against the extremity of offense and rejection of the forgiveness of sins offered by the triune God. The faithful self is one that accepts itself completely, not editorializing away the unpleasant or unfortunate aspects of its self or what befalls it, having learned that these things are ineradicable parts of a self that in faith I will to be unreservedly. To achieve this therapeutic peace with one's self though, one must be aware of the true threat to selfhood, the despair that would prevent acceptance of the cure for what really does ail the self and is thus truly the sickness to be avoided. If we are to be at peace with the selves we are, we have to be rid of that which obstructs that prospect and accept forgiveness from the God who offers it unreservedly. The conception of the divine then, of which the self is conscious of itself as being posited, is of utmost importance and always has been. The final question of the text – "What do you think of Christ?" – which Anti-Climacus calls "the most crucial of all questions" (SUD, 131/ SKS 11, 241), is actually tacitly present from the beginning. The question of how this most crucial of all questions will be answered by the self is therefore the question of the self itself – and has been all along.[13]

---

[12] Matthew 16:25: "For whosoever will save his life shall lose it: and whosoever will lose his life for my sake shall find it."

[13] I would like to thank Michael R. Kelly and Wojciech T. Kaftański for their extensive assistance with this chapter.

CHAPTER 12

The Long Journey to Oneself
The Existential Import of *The Sickness unto Death*

Sharon Krishek[1]

Every human being is primitively intended to be a self, destined to become himself.

– The Sickness unto Death, 33

The Sickness unto Death, arguably one of Kierkegaard's most important books, explores the meaning of being a "self" or, more accurately, an *intended* self. Kierkegaard demonstrates this conception by means of an analysis of despair. Rather than a psychological state, despair, in Kierkegaard's understanding, is an ontological state: It is the state of *failure* to be one's intended self.[2] In what follows I illustrate how the idea of selfhood as an *individual essence*, a conception that I present and defend here, helps to clarify Kierkegaard's complex analysis of despair. Such a reading of the text, I suggest, establishes that *The Sickness unto Death*, despite its religious premises and framework, is primarily an existential treatise, focused on one's way of living *in the world*.

A Metaphysical Sickness

As soon as man ceases to be regarded as defined by spirit ... but only as psychical-physical synthesis ... mental or physical sickness is the only dialectical qualification. But to be unaware of being defined as spirit is precisely what despair is.

(SUD, 25/SKS 11, 141)

A human being, according to Kierkegaard, is unique in having not only a physical and mental aspect, but also a spiritual one – with the latter indicating one's connection to God. This connection is ontological: It is

---

[1] The writing of this article was supported by the Israel Science Foundation (grant no. 111/16).
[2] I use the term "ontological" to emphasize that despair, for Kierkegaard, is independent of the despairer's understanding or acknowledgment of her state. This is the way she *is*, regardless of what she thinks or feels about herself.

determined by being created by God and in His image (and hence is independent of one's awareness of being thus connected). Becoming oneself, Kierkegaard posits, must involve an adherence to the *spiritual* aspect of being human. God intends one to be a *specific* self (what this means will be explained shortly), and the failure to become that self *is* despair.

Despair is thus the failure to understand that one is (ontologically) connected to God. In other words, it is the state of failing to adhere to one's essence as God-created. Hence, despair is a sickness that pertains not to a malfunction in our body or psyche: It pertains to a malfunction in our way of being, our way of existence. This makes despair a difficult sickness to trace.

Despair, Kierkegaard clarifies, cannot be diagnosed by relying on one's mental state. What is usually understood by despair – a state of "unrest, inner strife, anxiety" (SUD, 22/SKS 11, 138) – is only a symptom, not the sickness itself. And symptoms may come and go, while the sickness remains: A person may feel happy while she is in fact in despair. Symptoms are important because they are indicative of something being wrong, but in this case this wrongness cannot be diagnosed by either a physician of the body or by a psychologist but, to use Kierkegaard's words, by "the physician of the soul" (SUD, 23/SKS 11, 139). In other words, this sickness is the object of philosophy, and its proper diagnosis requires an understanding of what it means to be a human being and, more concretely, what it means to be a self.

To Be Angular

> Every human being is primitively intended to be a self . . . and as such every self certainly is angular, [which] means that it is to be ground into shape.
>
> (SUD, 33/SKS 11, 149)

To be a self is to be a human being who is an individual, while to be an individual is to be identical to oneself, and distinct – numerically and qualitatively – from others. In this sense, a human being is not "smooth," which for Kierkegaard designates being like everybody else, but rather "angular." To say that every human being is *created* angular, then, is equivalent to saying that every human is created unique and distinct, an individual.

Now, "being a self," an individual, can be signified by the conception of having a name.[3] "Anna Karenina" (for example) does not stand for a person in general but rather for a specific person with a distinct identity. By "identity" I am referring to the particular combination of qualities that makes Anna the distinct person that she is. This, please note, is not akin to personal identity: While, following Locke, the criterion for personal identity is one's psychological continuity, this is not the case here. One's self-identity – let us call it name-identity, i.e., that which individuates and singles one out – is determined, I suggest, by one's *individual essence*.[4]

What is "individual essence?" To conceive humans as created in God's image – a biblical idea that Kierkegaard endorses – is to understand humans as possessing a universal quality that determines them as persons (rather than, say, cats or tables). In this sense, the idea of being created in a certain way – namely, in God's image – is akin to the idea of having an essence: Every person, by virtue of being created in a certain way, essentially possesses "God's image." Let us call the universal quality that determines that one is a person (as opposed, say, to a cat), "personhood." Personhood may simply amount to rationality (as Kantians would have it), but understood as reflective of God's image, it may arguably amount to a combination of qualities that are traditionally attributed to God (wisdom, imagination, free will, caring, and so on). Continuing with the idea of humans possessing the universal quality of personhood/God's image, to claim possession of an *individual* essence is to claim that every person possesses a *specific version* of God's image, unique to him or her. This means (I suggest) that every person possesses a combination of particular essential qualities that express, in the best way relative to that person, the image of God.[5] My claim is that to possess an individual essence is what Kierkegaard means by being a self.

"Eternity . . . will nail him to himself so that . . . he cannot rid himself of his self . . . Eternity is obliged to do this, because to have a self, to be a self, is the greatest concession . . . given to man, but it is also eternity's claim upon him" (SUD, 21/SKS 11, 136–137). Assuming (as is reasonable) that

---

[3] And indeed, Kierkegaard uses the conception of "divine name." See later. See also Sharon Krishek, "Kierkegaard's Notion of a Divine Name and the Feasibility of Universal Love," *Southern Journal of Philosophy* 57 (2019): 539–560.

[4] For an elaboration of the conception of *self*-identity see Sharon Krishek, *Lovers in Essence: A Kierkegaardian Defense of Romantic Love* (New York: Oxford University Press, 2022), chapter 1. Segments of the present chapter parallel ideas discussed in chapters 1 and 6 of this book.

[5] The criterion for the essentiality of a particular quality is its efficiency in expressing a universal essential quality (so that in the case of X a talent in philosophy is an essential particular quality because it best expresses X's rationality, while in the case of Y it is wit that fills this function).

"eternity" in this context is a synonym for God, the claim is that we are created in such a way that we cannot *but* be who we were created to be. Namely, we have an *essence* that necessitates that we be who we are: We are "nailed" to ourselves so that we cannot become someone else. In the same way that being created a human being, one cannot become a cat, so to be created a *self* means that being created Anna, one cannot become Kitty.[6]

However, the fact that despite being thus created we can nevertheless *fail* in being ourselves – after all, "not to be [oneself] is precisely despair" (SUD, 30/SKS 11, 146) – indicates that our individual essence is bestowed upon us in a state of potential. To be "primitively intended" (SUD, 33/ SKS 11, 149) to be Anna – just like the need to grind her "Anna-hood" into shape – means that Anna's selfhood, her individual essence, is given to her in a state of *potential*, which she needs to actualize. In this sense Anna *becomes* herself: One becomes who one is by actualizing one's potential.

As with all potentials, there can be different degrees of actualization, but unlike other types, with potential *selfhood* there is always *some* degree of actualization. Every person actualizes her selfhood simply by virtue of existing. Thus, every person is a self – but it is "rare, very rare" (SUD, 23/SKS 11, 139) that one becomes the self that one is *intended* to be. Hence, it is equally very rare "that one is in truth not in despair" (SUD, 23/SKS 11, 139).

Returning to the simile of "being angular," we can say that it signifies not only being unique but also being *initial*. "Primitively" one's selfhood is angular: Like an unpolished diamond it is rough and needs to be "ground into shape." Such a shaping, the *actualization* of the potential, takes place over the course of a person's lifetime and as such is contingent on external circumstances as well as on the person's choices and will. Hence, the conception of actualizing one's (initially-given-as-a-potential) individual essence and becoming the self that one is intended to be, involves both contingency and essence, limitations and transcendence, the necessities of reality and the freedom of one's will. This picture of what "being a self" amounts to is presented, even if in different terms, in the notoriously condensed paragraph that opens Kierkegaard's discussion of despair.[7]

---

[6] The more common view holds that when Kierkegaard speaks of being a self he refers to being *a* particular person (be it Anna, Kitty, or Jane), while I claim that he refers to being a *specific* person (Anna). For an elaboration on this debate, see Krishek, "Kierkegaard's Notion of a Divine Name and the Feasibility of Universal Love."

[7] See SUD, 13/SKS 11, 130.

In this paragraph, Kierkegaard distinguishes *conceptually* between a human being and a self. Every self is a human being and vice versa,[8] but it takes something beyond the definition of a human being in order to capture the nature of a self. And what is a human being? Kierkegaard uses three sets of opposing existential categories to describe the nature of human beings: They are both finite and infinite, temporal and eternal, subject to necessity and free.

Using these categories expresses the idea that humans are simultaneously limited in their abilities and capable of transcending their limitations. While being necessitated by finite facts such as one's place and time of birth, the body and talents one is born with, and the family and society one is born into (for example), one is capable – by human powers of rationality, imagination, and will – of transcending these limitations and acting differently from what these facts prescribe.

In addition to describing this twofold state of limitedness and transcendence, the category set of temporal/eternal also describes a further idea: A human being is at once "temporal" – living in time and immersed in worldly existence – as well as "eternal." And she is "eternal" by virtue of being, as elaborated earlier, ontologically connected to God, namely, created by God and in a specific version of His image. Thus we see that the first two category sets (finitude/necessity and infinitude/freedom) describe the human being as a psycho-physical entity, but in order to describe the human being as a *spiritual* entity, we need the third set (temporal/eternal) as well.

The three sets of categories are sufficient to describe what being a *human being* is. However, to describe what a *self* is takes, as we said, something further. As Kierkegaard puts it, "the self is not the relation" – that is, it is not only the syntheses (finite/infinite etc.) – "but is the relation relating . . . to itself" (SUD, 13/SKS 11, 129). That is, to be a self is to relate to your being both finite and infinite, subject to necessity and free, temporal and eternal. It is to acknowledge (to different degrees) your limitedness and your capacity to transcend this limitedness, and, more implicitly, it is to acknowledge your origin: to acknowledge your being created by God. To be a self, then, is to be an entity that shapes its own identity as an

[8] There are commentators who claim that Kierkegaard uses the term "self" to denote only the accomplished state. Given my understanding of the term "self" – i.e., a person with a distinct identity, a person with a name – it is clear that every person is a self (although, of course, not as yet the self she is intended to be). In my understanding this is also Kierkegaard's view, and I defend this interpretation elsewhere (See Krishek, *Lovers in Essence*, chapter 1).

individual, with this shaping being understood as putting the relevant existential categories in a relation.

In continuation with this, I suggest that the third set (being temporal and eternal) describes the idea that being a self is a function of both possessing an individual essence in a potential state and the actualization of this potential over the course of one's life. Let us call one's individual essence in its potential state "the kernel of individuality" and one's individual essence in its actualized state the "individual persona." Anna's individual persona in her youth and Anna's individual persona in her adulthood are two different actualizations of the same kernel of individuality. In the same vein, we can imagine a version of Anna who does not marry Karenin, or live happily with Vronsky, but who is nevertheless "Anna."[9]

It is therefore correct to describe the potential (the "kernel") as eternal, not only because it is a version of God's image but because it is independent of temporal and contingent circumstances.[10] At the same time, it is significant that the Anna we know is a nineteenth-century Russian woman who decided to commit suicide. This is because to be Anna is no less a function of the actualization than of the potential. This accentuates the importance of the other two sets of categories (finitude/necessity-infinitude/freedom). *These* describe how one exists in the world – the world being the arena, as it were, for the actualization – given both one's limitedness and one's capacity for transcendence.[11]

Hence, to be a self is a mutual endeavor of God as creator and the human being, His creation. God bestows upon each one the potential to be a specific self – He creates one angular. But this is only half the story, as this is only the "eternal" side of the synthesis. The other half is the "temporal" side: the task of actualizing the potential, grinding into shape one's angularity, and becoming the self that one is intended to be. Thus, the actualization, which depends on one's worldly existence, has an equally

---

[9] See Krishek, *Lovers in Essence*, chapter 1, for a more detailed discussion of the qualitative content of the potential and its relation to the actualization.

[10] Hence, I suggest that when Kierkegaard speaks of "the eternal in man" (see, for example, SUD, 17/ SKS 11, 133) we should understand him quite literally as referring to what I term the kernel of individuality. This is one's individual essence in its potential state, which expresses one's ontological connection to God.

[11] For a thorough discussion of how crucial the interplay between one's limitedness and one's transcendence is for the development of one's selfhood, see Anthony Rudd's *Self, Value, and Narrative: A Kierkegaardian Approach* (Oxford: Oxford University Press, 2012), in particular 11–16, 38–48.

significant role in one's becoming, and being, a self. This significance is evident when it comes to the analysis of the forms of despair.

The Sickness: The Failure to Become One's Intended Self

> [The] task is to become itself, which can be done only through the relationship to God ... But if the self does not become itself, it is in despair.
>
> (SUD, 29–30/SKS 11, 146)

Every human being shapes her "name-identity" (that is, her identity as an individual, in the sense explained earlier) by virtue of existing. Every human being actualizes her potential by virtue of encountering, in the face of reality and in the context of interacting with other people, both her limits and her capacity to transcend these limits. Thus, every human being is a self. But only a few are the self they are intended to be; only a few succeed in properly actualizing their potential. Any partial or failed actualization of the potential is a state of despair.

In analyzing the forms of despair, Kierkegaard uses the same existential categories that he uses to define human nature: finitude/infinitude, necessity/freedom, and, more implicitly, the temporal and the eternal.[12] Despair is the failure to adhere to one's nature as a spiritual entity that is both limited and capable of transcending its limitations. Accordingly, despair is a state of disharmony between the relevant categories, namely, when one understands oneself in terms of only one category (say, as essentially only finite/subject to necessity/temporal). In failing to adhere to one's nature, one in fact fails to be the self that God intends one to be. This, plainly, is the idea at the basis of Kierkegaard's analysis of despair.

Now, while the analysis is basically of one phenomenon – the failure to be the self that God intends one to be – Kierkegaard examines this failure from different perspectives (discussed in the following three subsections). He begins by presenting an understanding of the sickness as if from the point of view of the doctor. Then he examines the patient's understanding of her sickness. And, finally, he examines the patient's refusal to be cured.

---

[12] Kierkegaard presents finitude's despair, infinitude's despair, necessity's despair, and possibility's despair. He does not use this formula with regard to the temporal/eternal set, but, as I demonstrate below, such forms of despair are implicit in his analysis of conscious despair.

Two Versions of Being Sick: Confinement and Detachment

When considered from the "outside" (i.e., from the point of view of the "doctor"), there are four patterns of despair that share the same kind of misconception. In each, the despairer understands herself as belonging to only one side of each set, that is, as only finite or only infinite; as essentially determined by necessities or as essentially free – so that "everything is possible" for her. Finitude's despair and necessity's despair (as Kierkegaard calls them) express a state that can be described as a confinement to the world; infinitude's despair and possibility's despair express a state that can be described as a detachment from the world. To clarify the meaning of these two basic versions of despair, let us examine finitude's despair as an example of confinement and possibility's despair as an example of detachment.

When Kierkegaard claims that humans are infinite (just as they are finite) he does not mean that we are somehow immortal, capable of transcending the limitedness imposed on us by death. Rather, given that Kierkegaard connects infinitude primarily with imagination (SUD, 30–31/ SKS 11, 147), and since what imagination transcends is the facts of reality (such as where we live, our inborn qualities, choices that we have made, and so on), I suggest that by "finitude" Kierkegaard refers to this kind of facts. Facts are "finite" in the sense that they are nonnegotiable. For example, while I can change my nationality by moving to a different country, I cannot change the fact that I was born in the country that I leave behind. I can regret leaving my homeland and return, but I cannot undo the fact of my past leaving and its consequences.

Finitude's despair, then, is the despair of a person who submits himself to the facts of his life, taking them to be the determining force of his existence. Kierkegaard describes such a person as someone who gets along "in business and social life." Being a conformist – conforming to the facts in his life – his will is compatible with the will of others: his family, friends, milieu, and so on. In this sense "he is as smooth as a rolling stone, as passable as a circulating coin" (SUD, 34/SKS 11, 150). In other words, he lives his life with no resistance: Conforming his will to external facts secures this "smooth" living. The price, however, is that he "forgets himself, forgets his name divinely understood" (SUD, 33–34/SKS 11, 149).

Keeping in mind that despair is an "ontological" sickness, it is clear why Kierkegaard defines the state of disregarding one's divine name – one's individual essence – as despair. After all, this is a failure to adhere to one's nature, which is precisely what Kierkegaard takes to be despair. The Kierkegaardian framework, then, allows us to substantiate what is accepted as a truism in other existential and philosophical thinking (as well as in folk wisdom): To be "like everybody else," to disregard one's individuality, is not a desirable state.

Despair of confinement, then, is the submission of oneself to the limitations imposed on one by reality. Despair of detachment, on the other hand, is the other extreme, as exemplified by possibility's despair: "The mirror of possibility is no ordinary mirror ... That a self appears to be such and such in the possibility of itself is only a half-truth, for in the possibility of itself the self is still far from or is only half of itself" (SUD, 37/SKS 11, 152). Possibility is that which transcends the actual and the necessary. Looking in the mirror of possibility, a failed actor (for example) can see himself, by means of his imagination, desires, and fantasies, as a celebrated film star. Now, it is a mirror, and so it does reflect *him*: *his* desires, inclinations, and will (he does not see, say, a successful football player). However, it does so in a twisted way. This is because it reflects, as Kierkegaard says, only half the truth. The other half, needed for sober reflection, is the necessity in his life.

There are two kinds of necessity. One is akin to the category of the finite, namely the necessity imposed on one by the facts of one's reality. For example, the failed actor from earlier cannot be a film star because (let us say) he lacks the relevant skills, is the wrong age, in the wrong milieu, and has made too many wrong decisions.[13] This failed actor could have made better decisions, known other people, improved his skills earlier in his career – in other words, he could have been a different version of himself, could have actualized his potential differently. These facts make up one kind of necessity; let us call it contingent necessity. The other kind of necessity, however, is essential. This is the necessity entailed in the *potential*: "Possibility is like a child's invitation to a party; the child is willing at once, but the question now is whether the parents will give permission – and as it is with the parents, so it is with necessity" (SUD, 37/SKS 11, 152).

Likening necessity to a child's parents is telling. Parents are not like contingent finite facts that one can ignore when reflecting in a mirror.

---

[13] Decisions can be understood as belonging to necessity in the sense that one's decisions determine (among other facts) the actualization of one's potential. At any given moment, one's individual persona is a specific actualization of one's kernel of individuality; the necessity in one's life includes also facts of *this* sort.

Parents are a loving authority who sustain an intimate relation to their child; they know, and are interested in, what is best for him or her. In this connection, then, necessity seems to pertain to something deeper than contingent facts: It seems to pertain to the necessity entailed in possessing an individual *essence* or a "divine name." In other words, this is the necessity of being created as an intended self. The despairer, however, fails to understand this: "The tragedy is that he did not become aware of himself, aware that the self he is is a very definite something and thus the necessary" (SUD, 36/SKS 11, 152).

One's selfhood is "definite" (and hence a necessity) in the sense that it is determined by God: This is one's individual essence. At the same time, recall, each person possesses her individual essence in a state of *potential*. Hence, Anna's kernel of individuality (her selfhood in its potential state) is not a finite fact in the same sense that her being Russian or beautiful are finite facts. The actualization of her selfhood is a lifetime task. Accordingly, it is indeed necessary that she be Anna. As we said, being created Anna, she cannot become Kitty, no less than being created a person she cannot become a cat: This is *essential* necessity. However, having her Anna-hood possessed primarily in a state of potential allows her to constantly transcend her partial actualizations, the latter being *contingent* necessity. As Kierkegaard puts it: "Insofar as it is itself, it is the necessary, and insofar it has the task of becoming itself, it is a possibility" (SUD, 35/SKS 11, 151).

One's selfhood, then, is both determined (in its potential state) and changeable (in its being constantly in the process of actualization); both fixed and unfixed; both a necessity and a possibility. But the despairer of possibility, the despairer of detachment, fails to understand this. His detachment is from necessity in both senses. As the actualization is *of* the potential, the latter is detectable in the former. Hence, by disregarding the necessity imposed on him by his partial actualization (contingent necessity) he in fact disregards the deeper necessity of his potential (essential necessity).

Thus, just as the parents' role is to help their child navigate her way between manifold possibilities, so necessity's role is to help the person navigate his way so that he does not lose himself in the mirror of possibilities. If he doesn't let necessity help him in this way, he is in despair. While the despairer of confinement forgets his divine name, the despairer of detachment flees from his name. This, of course, is doomed to fail: He cannot escape his name; he cannot avoid his essence. This failure is precisely despair.

The Consciousness of Being Sick: Weakness and Defiance

Having characterized the sickness regardless of the understanding of the sick person, Kierkegaard then turns to examine despair by analyzing the approach of the sick person to her sickness. One crucial question asked in this regard is whether the despairer correctly understands the object of her despair and correctly identifies what it is that she is despairing about.

Inasmuch as the despairer fails to understand the nature of her sickness and judges her state only by the symptoms, she also fails to recognize the real reason for her despair. Hence, she takes herself to despair "over the earthly or over something earthly" (SUD, 56/SKS 11, 172). She believes that her despair is rooted outside herself, and that if only things were different – if she were not deprived of that which she desires in the world – she would not be in despair. However, "despair over the earthly or over something earthly is in reality also despair of the eternal and over oneself, insofar as it is despair, for this is indeed the formula for all despair" (SUD, 60/SKS 11, 175). What does this mean?

According to Kierkegaard, as we said, despair is an ontological (as opposed to psychological) state. It is the failure to be the self, the specific individual, that one is created and intended to be; it is the failure to live up to one's divine name and fulfill one's individual essence to its maximum. As such, one is in despair independently of one's understanding of one's state. According to Kierkegaard, a person begins to understand her state – namely, becomes conscious of her despair – when she begins to acquire a sense of selfhood, a sense of being a person with a distinct identity, an individual. Hence, even if one does not characterize it as such, or characterizes it wrongly as a despair over the earthly, the real object of one's despair is oneself. And – given that to be a self is rooted in one's connection to God, the eternal – to despair over oneself is *eo ipso* to despair of the eternal.[14]

"The progression is as follows. First comes the consciousness of the self . . . that there is something eternal in it . . . If a person is to despair over himself, he must be aware of having a self; and yet it is over this that he despairs, not over the earthly or something earthly, but over himself" (SUD, 62/SKS 11, 176). Kierkegaard's analysis of the consciousness of

---

[14] It is to despair of the possibility of changing and becoming a better version of herself; it is to be unable to see that – despite all of the adversities facing her – being a self is rooted in goodness, the goodness of her connection to God, with all the implications that this bears regarding her existence in the world. As Kierkegaard puts it, "despair of the eternal [is] an unwillingness to be comforted by and healed by the eternal" (SUD, 70/SKS 11, 184).

despair is in fact an analysis of the understanding of oneself as a "self." And, given that this state is of despair, the analysis is thereby of the *failure* to understand the true nature of one's selfhood, namely, one's failure to understand that it is rooted in God. Thus, one's reflection upon one's selfhood – upon one's identity as an individual, upon one's being who one is – is *eo ipso* a reflection, even if yet unacknowledged as such, on one's connection to God. Accordingly, the analysis of one's consciousness of despair – of one's approach to being a self – is the context for using the category of the eternal. And as we shall shortly see, the synthesis temporal/ eternal – absent from the analysis of despair from the "outside" – is fitting to characterize the kind of despair that Kierkegaard terms "defiant." What is "defiance" in this connection?

When a person is conscious of herself as a "self" (namely, in my reading, conscious of herself as a person with a distinct identity) but is still not the self that she is intended to be (namely, in despair), she has two basic ways to regard herself. She either wills to be herself, which Kierkegaard terms defiance, or she does *not* will to be herself, which he terms "weak" despair.

Now, the self that one does, or does not, will to be is one's actualized self – what I termed one's individual persona – which is, given that one is in despair, necessarily only a partial actualization. Each of the two versions of despair – confinement and detachment – can appear in either a weak form or a defiant one. The *defiant* form of each of these versions (that is, defiant confinement and defiant detachment) is best described in terms of the temporal/eternal synthesis. But before turning to these defiant forms (which I call, further to the former forms of despair, "temporality's despair" and "eternity's despair"), let us say a few words on weak despair.

Kierkegaard characterizes the weak despairer as follows:

> He has no consciousness of a self that is won by infinite abstraction from every externality, this naked abstract self, which, compared with immediacy's fully dressed self, is the first form of the infinite self and the advancing impetus in the whole process by which a self infinitely becomes responsible for its actual self with all its difficulties and advantages. (SUD, 55/SKS 11, 170)

I suggest that the "naked abstract self" stands for what I termed one's kernel of individuality (namely, one's selfhood in its potential state), while "immediacy's fully dressed self" stands for what I termed one's individual persona (namely, one's selfhood in its actualized state). The potential is discernible in any instance of actualization, but such uncovering requires an effort of the imagination. That is, one needs to create distance from one's individual persona in order for the potential – of which the "fully dressed self" is an actualization – to be revealed.

The distancing of oneself from one's individual persona is, in my understanding, what Kierkegaard means by "infinite abstraction," and it is this kind of distancing that gives rise to one's "infinite self" – namely, the infinite possibilities of being oneself, the infinite versions that one can imagine oneself to be. Having one's selfhood primarily in a state of a potential, then, is "the advancing impetus" at the root of the process of becoming oneself.

However, the weak despairer lacks this understanding. He is conscious enough to understand that he *is* a self (that is, a person with a distinct identity), but he fails to understand his responsibility for himself and the role that he has in his own shaping. In this sense, his relation to himself is passive (and hence "weak"): He does not do anything to change himself. He regards his actualized self as fixed and settled. In my terms, failing to understand that his individual persona is only a possible, and partial, actualization – he rather regards it as the *only* actualization. And his attitude to his individual persona is negative: He does *not* want to be this self.

Now, his unwillingness to be himself can take either the form of detachment or confinement. After all, there are various ways not to will to be oneself, to evade or run away from oneself. One such way is by detaching oneself from reality, in the manner that Kierkegaard's aesthete[15] does. Another is by immersing oneself in the minutiae of one's life, as a way of distraction from the need to change[16] – say, in the way the bourgeois philistine[17] does.

While weak despair is the state of *not* willing to be oneself, the attitude to oneself in defiance is of a different kind. Defiance "is really despair through the aid of the eternal, the despairing misuse of the eternal within the self to will in despair to be oneself" (SUD, 67/SKS 11, 181). In defiance, the despairer places himself in the position of God: He takes himself to be his own master, his own creator; in his view, it is for him to decide how, and who, he will be. He does so either by denying the

---

[15] From writings such as *Either/Or*, for example.

[16] Take, for example, someone like Tolstoy's Ivan Ilyich, who, whenever he felt unhappy about himself, found a new preoccupation to distract himself from himself: getting promoted at work, refurbishing his house, and so on. In Kierkegaard's words: "He may try to keep himself in the dark about his state through diversions and in other ways, for example, through work and busyness as diversionary means" (SUD, 48/SKS 11, 163).

[17] From *The Sickness unto Death* as well as other writings.

existence of a different creator (detachment) or by rebelling against this idea (confinement). The former, whom Kierkegaard terms an "*acting self*" (SUD, 68/SKS 11, 182), exemplifies, I suggest, eternity's despair; the latter, whom Kierkegaard terms a self "*acted upon*" (SUD, 70/SKS 11, 183), exemplifies, I suggest, temporality's despair. Let us examine each.

The defiant despairer of detachment severs "the self from any relation to a power that has established it, or [severs] it from the idea that there is such a power ... [He] wants to be master of itself or to create itself, to make his self into the self he wants to be" (SUD, 68/SKS 11, 182). This despairer makes a "misuse of the eternal." He is conscious enough to understand that he has the capacity to *become* an individual, to shape his own identity, but he denies the divine origin of this capacity. Being "an acting self," he "constantly relates ... to [himself] only by way of imaginary constructions ... [He] recognizes no power over [himself]" (SUD, 68/ SKS 11, 182). Accordingly, given that the shaping of his identity is subject to his changeable (and hence unsettled) will, this kind of despairer lacks any stable grounding: "At any time [he] can quite arbitrarily start all over again" (SUD, 69/SKS 11, 183). In this sense: "This absolute ruler is a king without a country, actually ruling over nothing; his position, his sovereignty, is subordinate to the dialectic that rebellion is legitimate at any moment. Ultimately, this is arbitrarily based upon the self itself" (SUD, 69/SKS 11, 183).

Denying that he has an essence bestowed on him (in a state of potential) by a power external to him (God), this despairer lacks a criterion for the shaping of his self: "In the very moment when it seems that the self is closest to having the building completed, it can arbitrarily dissolve the whole thing into nothing" (SUD, 69–70/SKS 11, 183). By this attitude, the despairer anticipates Sartre's conception of "radical freedom," which amounts to rejecting any idea of one's possessing an essence that precedes one's existence.[18] In Sartre's view, any fact in one's reality, any necessity, can be transcended by the power of negation (that is, of refusing to identify oneself with that fact). The Kierkegaardian despairer, likewise, uses his powers of will and imagination to transcend his reality. In this sense, as we said, he assumes the position of God: He takes nothing external to bind him, to determine him, to help him.

It is therefore fitting to see this "Sartrean" type as exemplifying eternity's despair. Having his essence in a state of potential gives him the freedom to

---

[18] For more on this point see Evans's and Rudd's references to Sartre in their respective chapters in this collection.

shape himself. However, he misuses this freedom, conceiving himself as having no potential at all or, rather, as the self-creator of constantly changing "potentials," i.e., his imaginary constructions regarding what he envisions himself to be. Defiance, however, can also take the form of confinement, which is temporality's despair.

When the "Sartrean" despairer – being conscious of being a "self" and taking himself to be the sole authority of his own shaping – "encounters some difficulty or other . . . something the Christian would call a cross, a basic defect, whatever it may be" that he cannot in any way transcend, his powers of creation take the opposite direction. As he feels "nailed to this servitude" – and, in this sense, "a self acted upon" (SUD, 70/SKS 11, 184) – he now invests all his powers in willing to be this "defective" self.

Hence, acknowledging the fault and willing to be defined by this fault, this despairer is the darkest of all the types. He may well be described as "demonic" as he willfully affirms what he takes to be bad, and defiantly rejects the possibility of goodness. "He has convinced himself that this thorn in the flesh gnaws so deeply that he cannot abstract himself from it" (SUD, 70/SKS 11, 184), and so he "takes it along, almost flouting his agony . . . Rather than to seek help, he prefers, if necessary, to be himself with all the agonies of hell" (SUD, 71/SKS 11, 185). It is therefore fitting to characterize his state as "temporality's despair." Rejecting any prospect for change and willfully adhering to the limits of his actual, faulty self, he is as confined to the world as can be.[19]

In sum, the "map" of despair is as follows. There is one phenomenon – despair – which is the state, conscious or not, of failing to be the self that God intends one to be. This phenomenon has two basic forms. Given that despair is a distorted way of relating to being the self that one is, one can either *not* will to be the (present) self that one is or *will* to be that self. The former is weak despair, the latter defiance. Both weak despair and defiance can appear in a confined or detached version. Hence, we may say that there are four basic prototypes of despairers. The detached version of weak

---

[19] Hence, further to the forms that are defined by the other two sets of syntheses, the forms of despair that are defined by the temporal/eternal synthesis are also detected. These "discovered" forms, please note, comply with the principle that A's despair is to lack the opposite of A (as in "infinitude's despair is to lack finitude," etc.). In my interpretation, as demonstrated above, "the eternal" stands for one's divine name in its potential state, and "the temporal" stands for the actualization. Accordingly, eternity's despair is to lack temporality in the sense that the despairer gives too much weight to the potential, disregarding the importance of *actualizing* it and *becoming* the self that God intends her to be. And on the other hand, temporality's despair is to lack eternity in the sense that the despairer gives too much weight to her partially actualized selfhood, disregarding her *potential* to become the self that God intends her to be.

despair (in Kierkegaard's terms: infinitude's despair and possibility's despair) is exemplified by the Kierkegaardian aesthete. The confined version of weak despair (in Kierkegaard's terms: finitude's despair and necessity's despair) is exemplified by the bourgeois philistine. The detached version of defiance (in my terms, further to Kierkegaard's formulation: eternity's despair) is exemplified by the Sartrean type (in Kierkegaard's terms: an acting self), and the confined version of defiance (in my terms: temporality's despair) by the demonic type (in Kierkegaard's terms: a self acted upon).

Now, the self that one in weakness does not will to be, and in defiance wills to be, is one's present self, namely, one's individual persona. This is the necessarily partial actualization of one's potential. Hence, on the one hand, not to will to be one's actualized self is *eo ipso* to reject the potential, of which one's present self is an actualization. On the other hand, to will to be one's only partially actualized self is to reject the need to actualize the potential properly and become the self that God intends one to be. Ultimately, then, all the forms of despair converge into the same formula: Despair is the failure to become the self that God intends one to be.

Sin: The Refusal to Be Cured

Kierkegaard identifies despair with sin: Despair *is* sin, as the second part of *The Sickness unto Death* is titled. The analysis presented in the first part of the book is therefore as informative as the second part with regard to the understanding of sin. The different types of despairers from the first part are (obviously) also sinners, and the tools for understanding both their state as sinners and what is required for them to be cured is presented already in the first part.[20] What does the second part add, then?

> Sin is: *before God, or with the conception of God, in despair not to will to be oneself, or in despair to will be oneself.* Thus sin is intensified weakness or intensified defiance: sin is the intensification of despair. The emphasis is on *before God* or with a conception of God; it is the conception of God that makes sin ... "aggravated" despair. (SUD, 77/SKS 11, 191, emphasis in the original)

---

[20] By claiming that the first part presents the tools required for the cured state, I express an opinion that diverts from the more common interpretation that takes the first part to be incomplete in this regard. See, for example, the chapters by Evans (13), Fremstedal (7), Hanson (11), Roberts (8), Walsh (10), and Westphal (9) in this collection.

As with despair, there is a need to distinguish between an account of one's state from the "outside" and an account of it when one's consciousness of one's state is taken into consideration. From the outside, every state of failing to be the self that God intends one to be is sin, regardless of whether or not, or to what extent, the sinner is conscious of her state. However, in a stricter or more severe sense of the word, the spiritually sick person is best described as a sinner when she understands her sickness and refuses to be cured. In such a case she understands that she fails to be the self God intends her to be and rejects her potential by way of weakness (that is, not willing to be herself) or defiance (willing to be her failed self).

Hence, the second part presents a further intensification of one's consciousness of being a self, and, accordingly, the refusal (either in weakness or defiance) to be one's intended self is a more extreme rejection and thus also a more culpable one. At the same time, given that the second part presents a direct refusal – "before God," as Kierkegaard puts it – to be the self that God wills one to be, one's relationship with God, although twisted and incorrect, is acknowledged and explicit. Accordingly, the second part is more theological in nature. It elaborates on the framework for sustaining the correct relationship with God, which, for Kierkegaard, is a decisively Christian one.

However, my claim is that in spite of this, the main message of *The Sickness unto Death* is not Christian but existential (and hence religiously universal) in nature. As I now turn to argue, the main message of this pivotal Kierkegaardian work is that living one's earthly life correctly is a necessary and sufficient condition for fulfilling the highest relationship with God. In other words, one's relationship with God depends on one's relationship with the world. This is the fundamental formula, and it remains the same regardless of the exact nature (Christian or otherwise) that one's relationship with God assumes.[21]

The Healing from Despair: Becoming One's Intended Self by Means of Living Correctly

To despair is a qualification of spirit and relates to the eternal in man.
(SUD, 17/SKS 11, 133)

According to my interpretation, outlined earlier, "the eternal in man" is one's selfhood in its potential state, which I termed one's "kernel of

---

[21] For the character of the relationship with God, Christianly understood, and in particular on the significance of the forgiveness of sins for becoming a self, see Hanson's chapter (11).

individuality." It is "eternal" both in the sense that it originates in God and manifests (a particular version of) His image and in the sense of being independent of time and circumstances (that is, of worldly existence). However, the only way to *actualize* this potential is within worldly existence. Hence, becoming the self that God intends one to be depends, equally, on both one's (temporal) worldly existence and one's (eternal) potential.

In this sense "the eternal" reflects one's connection with God and "the temporal" one's engrossment in the world. The two other sets of synthesis – the finite and the infinite, necessity and possibility – depict the states of either being confined to the world or detached from it. The healing from despair is the (rare) state when equilibrium is achieved. In this state, the person lives in accordance with the understanding that she is both limited and capable of transcending her limitation, and that her self – her individuality – is a function of both (divine) potential and (worldly) actualization. This twofoldness – the double relationship with God and the world – is the key to healing from despair. "The formula that describes the state of the self when despair is completely rooted out is this: in relating ... to itself and in willing to be itself, the self rests transparently in the power that established it" (SUD, 14, 49/SKS 11, 130, 164).

To rest transparently in God is to fully fulfill the will of God and become the self that God intends one to be (namely, the best possible self that one can be). This is achieved by relating to oneself properly. This proper self-relating is the actualization of one's potential, by virtue of living in the world in a way that balances the polarities and conflicting forces in one's nature as well as in one's reality. The point, then, is simple but crucial. The closest possible relationship with God ("resting transparently" in Him) is achieved by becoming the self that He intends us to be. Becoming this intended self depends on a proper actualization of the potential that He has bestowed on us in our creation. Such an actualization is a function of living correctly in the world given the human condition of constantly encountering limitations and loss.[22] Hence, inasmuch as living correctly in the world in the face of the human predicament is the subject matter of existential thinking, *The Sickness unto Death* is an existential treatise no less than a religious one.

---

[22] The model for living correctly in the face of adversity is (arguably) the subject of *Fear and Trembling*. In this sense, the two works support and complete each other. See also the following note.

To conclude, *The Sickness unto Death* can be read as depicting the long journey of a person to herself, which is the way of a person to her creator. This journey, significantly, takes place in the world: It is located in space and time and, importantly, is permeated by the presence of other people. Earthly life, then, is not a competitor for one's relationship with God but rather an ally. When lived correctly, worldly existence does not *distract* one's attention from relating properly to God but, rather, *makes it possible* for this relationship to reach its highest level. Resting transparently in God, as *The Sickness unto Death* teaches us, is achieved by working in the world.[23]

---

[23] This work is, crucially, a work of love. The connection between loving correctly and living correctly is analyzed in Kierkegaard's *Works of Love*. Hence, and further to my previous note, for a complete picture of the good life – one that portrays the indissoluble ties between faith, worldly existence, loving another person, and fulfilling the will of God (by becoming the self that He intends us to be), we have to read *The Sickness unto Death* alongside *Fear and Trembling* and *Works of Love*. For this kind of project, see my *Lovers in Essence*, chapter 7. Now, the question as to whether, according to Kierkegaard, one can work one's way to faith is one that goes beyond the scope of this chapter, and all I can say is that the thesis that I present here is entirely consistent with the conception of needing divine help in order to achieve the desirable state of transparent resting in God. That is, while I claim that human responsibility for living correctly is a necessary condition for transparent resting, I do not claim that it is a *sufficient* condition. I'm grateful to the anonymous reader for Cambridge University Press for suggesting that I clarify this point.

CHAPTER 13

Accountability to God in The Sickness unto Death
Kierkegaard's Relational Understanding of the Human Self
C. Stephen Evans[1]

Kierkegaard is popularly known as "an individualist." It is of course true that Kierkegaard wrote a great deal about what it means to be "that individual" (*hiin Enkelte*) and also true that many of his works were dedicated to "that individual." It is true to say that Kierkegaard saw human existence as a task in which we are all called to become authentic individuals. However, this emphasis on the individual has sometimes been misunderstood. There is a sense of "individualism" that sees individuals as in some way prior to relationships with other individuals. One might think here of John Locke's contractual view of the state, in which persons who already exist as individuals in a "state of nature" come together and establish the state through a contractual agreement, whose purpose is to secure their own good and rights. Of course Locke knew that human selves are raised in families and are causally dependent on others as children. Still, in some sense Locke sees individual identity as logically prior to communal identity, unlike Hegel, who thought that genuine individual identity requires participation in a community that recognizes that individuality.

This chapter argues that Kierkegaard's ontology of the self is closer to Hegel's than to Locke's. That is, Kierkegaard sees human selves as fundamentally relational. He does not believe that human selves exist as atomic individuals that come together to form social relationships. Rather, they are formed in and through social relationships, and their identity as selves continues to be grounded in such relationships. Individuality is for Kierkegaard an aspirational goal, not a property of atomic selves. Furthermore, we shall see that even authentic individuality is still achieved through a relationship.

[1] This essay was made possible by support from a grant provided by the Templeton Religion Trust. The opinions it contains are those of the author and not necessarily those of the Templeton Religion Trust.

I shall explore and defend this view that Kierkegaard has a relational ontology of the self by a close examination of *The Sickness unto Death*. On the view I defend, the self is essentially social and has an identity that is grounded in social relations, and this most decidedly includes human social relations. However, there are many different forms of human identity, depending on the nature of the relationships that form the self. Kierkegaard affirms that the intended identity of human selves is one in which the self is formed by a relation to God that transcends relations to other humans. This intended identity is one that allows humans to achieve genuine spiritual health and a kind of authentic individuality, while identities that are grounded solely in human social relations are to some degree always pathological. Humans were intended to "live before God," and thus the specific form of the social relationship that grounds a healthy human self is the relation in which persons see themselves as *accountable* to God.[2]

The Relational View of the Self in *The Sickness unto Death*

This social view of the self is present in much of Kierkegaard's authorship but is particularly prominent and explicit in *The Sickness unto Death*. In the opening pages of the book the pseudonymous author Anti-Climacus[3] affirms that a human being is "spirit" and tells us what it means to be spirit: "The self is a relation that relates itself to itself or is the relation's relating itself to itself in the relation" (SUD, 13/SKS 11, 129). Furthermore, the relationality of the human self is not simply intra-psychic in character but is grounded in a relation to "another" that is external to the self. Interestingly, Anti-Climacus does not see this social character as a *logical* requirement for selfhood. Rather, he says that there are two possible ways of being a self: "Such a relation that relates itself to itself must either have established itself or have been established by another" (SUD, 13/SKS 11, 129). In other words, one can conceive of a self that would be, like God, dependent on nothing other than itself for its

---

[2] For a more extended investigation of this theme see C. Stephen Evans, *Kierkegaard and Spirituality: Accountability as the Meaning of Human Existence* (Grand Rapids, MI: Wm. B. Eerdmans, 2019).

[3] Although I shall follow Kierkegaard's request to cite the pseudonymous author, I have no hesitation in accepting the views of Anti-Climacus as Kierkegaard's own. I here follow the view of many authors that the Anti-Climacus pseudonym was adopted by Kierkegaard because he believed that he was not personally entitled to express the strictly Christian ideals of Anti-Climacus and thus put these words in the mouth of a pseudonym so that he could see the words as addressed to himself. However, this distancing does not imply that Kierkegaard disagrees with those ideals in any way but that he saw himself as unable to realize them in his own life.

identity. Such a self would be absolutely autonomous. Humans are not such godlike creatures, however. A human self is not completely autonomous but is "a derived, established relation, a relation that relates itself to itself and in relating itself to itself relates itself to another" (SUD, 13–14/ SKS 11, 130).

Given this clear proclamation that the human self is relational, how is it that Kierkegaard is sometimes read as someone with an individualist ontology? I believe this reading is grounded in the following line of thought: When Kierkegaard says that a human self is grounded in a relationship to an "other," he is thinking of God as the "other." However, so the line of thought goes, God is not a genuine person with whom one might have a social relationship that could ground one's identity. By focusing solely on God, Kierkegaard ignores the way actual human selves are formed by relations to other humans, and he thereby fails to recognize the way relations to other humans help constitute our identity.

I believe this line of thinking is doubly mistaken. First, as I shall try to show, Kierkegaard does not think that God is the only "other" that can be the basis of a human person's identity. To the contrary, Kierkegaard thinks we are initially all formed through such human relations and that it is very difficult indeed to transcend such relations. Identities grounded solely in human relations are ubiquitous, even if they are also to some degree pathological.

There is one important qualification to this point. When I say that a human self's identity can be grounded in relations to other humans, I am using "identity" in a psychological sense. However, philosophers often use the term "identity" in a metaphysical sense, to refer to what grounds the fact that a human person is the same person over time. Thus, Locke held that the basis of identity in this metaphysical sense was psychological continuity through memory. Descartes believed that the identity of a human person was grounded in the soul, while many contemporary materialists hold that metaphysical identity is grounded in physical continuity. In the metaphysical sense, I think Kierkegaard did hold that human selves have their ground in God, who continuously holds them in being as their creator. When I speak of psychological identity I mean something like what people have in mind when they say such things as: "I don't know why I did that; I just wasn't myself" or "I would never do something like that; it's just not who I am." Here identity is connected to my sense of who I really am. In this psychological sense, Kierkegaard sees identity as a temporal achievement. Here the self is not a metaphysical entity but is a condition to strive for. In this psychological sense, a person's identity can indeed be formed through relations to other human persons.

Second, I shall argue that Kierkegaard understands God as personal in character, a being with whom one can indeed have a genuine social relation. To be sure, it is a relation with a unique character. The social relation to God that is possible for humans is one in which humans recognize God as one who has authority over the whole of one's life. Although Kierkegaard does not deny that there is such a thing as a common human nature, he believes God has created human persons as individuals. Furthermore, God wills that each person become the unique person he or she was created to be. The person who achieves a God-relationship has an identity that is grounded in a sense that he or she is accountable to God for how a person lives the whole of life.

How Are the Two Parts of *The Sickness unto Death* Related?

I believe the role God plays in *The Sickness unto Death* is often misunderstood, and one source of the misunderstanding concerns the relationship between Part One and Part Two of the book. I have taught the book many times, and I have found that frequently students find it difficult, at least initially, to figure out how the two parts are related to each other. Part One has the title "The Sickness unto Death Is Despair" while Part Two has the title "Despair Is Sin." Both parts describe various forms of human despair, of different types and intensity, and there are clear parallels between them. In both parts of the book, despair is understood not simply as an emotion but as a condition of the self. But how are these two accounts of despair different from each other?

I believe what is confusing to students is that Anti-Climacus tells us, very early in Part Two, that in Part One the "previously considered gradation in the consciousness of the self is within the category of the human self, or the self whose criterion is man" (SUD, 79/SKS 11, 193). In Part Two, however, Anti-Climacus says that the self he is going to examine "takes on a new quality and qualification by being a self directly before God" (SUD, 79/SKS 11, 193). He goes on to say that the account given of the self in Part Two will be different. In Part Two, he does not describe "the merely human self" but "what I, hoping not to be misinterpreted, would call the theological self, the self directly before God" (SUD, 79/SKS 11, 193). It is as if Anti-Climacus is saying that God has been left out of the picture in Part One but now will become part of the story in Part Two.

However, it is simply not the case that God first makes an appearance in Part Two, and so it is somewhat natural to find Anti-Climacus's statement at the beginning of Part Two puzzling. References to God abound in Part One. For example, in Part One Anti-Climacus describes "necessity's despair," the kind of despair that "lacks possibility" (SUD, 37/SKS 11, 153). The person in this form of despair is a kind of determinist or fatalist who sees no possibility for becoming the self he or she wants to become. Anti-Climacus makes it plain that the antidote to this form of despair (which is of course one form of "the sickness unto death") is faith in God "because for God everything is possible at every moment" (SUD, 39–40/ SKS 11, 155).

Interestingly, Anti-Climacus seems at least to suggest that the cure for the opposite form of despair, the despair of possibility that lacks necessity, also requires a God-relationship. The person who is in the despair of possibility gets lost in fantasy and imagination and cannot acknowledge the necessary elements of the self, which leads to a loss of touch with actuality. Such a person has lost the sense of finitude and lacks "the power to obey" (SUD, 36/SKS 11, 152). Obey whom? God is the most obvious candidate. It is natural to see this as a suggestion that the person who suffers from this kind of despair is rebelling against the creaturely limits that stem from being a created being.

Yet another example can be found in the section on finitude's despair, the despair that "lack[s] infinitude" (SUD, 33/SKS 11, 149). This despairing figure is a person who "divinely understood, does not dare to believe in himself, finds it too hazardous to be himself and far easier and safer to be like the others, to become a copy, a number, a mass man" (SUD, 34/SKS 11, 149). This kind of despair is a kind of "secular mentality" that is "nothing more or less than the attribution of infinite worth to the indifferent" (SUD, 33/SKS 11, 149). The cure for this "narrow-minded-ness" requires a person to believe in the self he was intended to become, and those who cannot do this "have no self, no self for whose sake they could venture everything, no self before God" (SUD, 35/SKS 11, 151). Once more it seems that a form of despair is being defined by a lack of a relationship to God.

So why does Anti-Climacus say that it is only in Part Two that he will describe the self in theological terms? I think the answer is that it is only in Part Two that Anti-Climacus brings in distinctively Christian categories such as sin, offense, and faith. Actually, to be precise, Christianity is explicitly brought into the picture in the Preface and the Introduction to *The Sickness unto Death*, however I take it that these are not included in

Part One but are rather introductory material for the book as a whole. Also, faith is briefly mentioned near the conclusion of Part One (SUD, 65, 71n/SKS 11, 179, 184n), as more intense forms of despair are discussed, but it makes sense to see this material as part of the transition to Part Two, where the most intense forms of despair are considered.

Even if Christianity is in the background of Part One, it is not made the center of attention. This can be seen by noting that sin is not really discussed in Part One. Kierkegaard consistently holds that human sinfulness (as distinguished from guilt) is something that unaided human reason does not really understand. We only come to understand our sinfulness when this is revealed to us by God in a special revelation, and Kierkegaard believes this revelation comes from Christianity.[4] Anti-Climacus emphasizes this point repeatedly. "This is why Christianity begins in another way: man has to learn what sin is by a revelation from God" (SUD, 95/SKS 11, 207).

So Part Two looks at despair in a new way by understanding it as sin. The way I would put the difference between Part One and Part Two is this: The descriptions given in Part One of despair are not incorrect, but they do not provide the clarity and depth that is made possible when humans are seen through the lens of the Christian revelation. Part Two and Part One both provide descriptions of despair. The same territory is traversed in both sections, but in Part Two we are provided with a deeper, sharper picture of that territory.

One might think this would mean that God would not appear in Part One, but this does not follow. Part One gives us a picture of the human self that does not presuppose the Christian revelation; however, this does not mean that Anti-Climacus thinks one can give an accurate picture of the human self that ignores God. Kierkegaard himself does not think that Christian spirituality is the only kind of spirituality or that apart from the Christian revelation humans would have no knowledge of God whatsoever. A person who is not a Christian can and should know God and strive for a relation with God. Kierkegaard provides in his writings an extensive account of what is called in *Concluding Unscientific Postscript* "Religiousness A," a kind of religiousness that does not rest on the Christian revelation. This kind of religiousness can be present within

---

[4] When I speak of Kierkegaard's view of the "Christian revelation" I mean to include the Hebrew Bible, understood as Kierkegaard did, as the Old Testament, an essential part of the Christian revelation. It is evident from Kierkegaard's *Fear and Trembling*, as well as his use of such Old Testament figures as Job, how important the Old Testament is to him.

Christendom among people who think of themselves as Christians, as well as in a genuine pagan such as Socrates.[5] So it is not incoherent for Anti-Climacus to bring God into the picture in Part One and yet maintain that a genuinely Christian theological perspective does not appear until Part Two.

There is a widespread myth, visible in such writers as Camus, that Kierkegaard thinks that belief in God is irrational and requires a "leap of faith."[6] However, this is simply false. Kierkegaard certainly claims that the Christian belief that God became incarnate as a human being is "the absolute paradox" that poses the "possibility of offense." Belief in Christ as God requires a leap. However, Kierkegaard never claims that mere belief in God is an offense to reason or is contrary to reason. It is true that Kierkegaard does not think that God's existence can be proven by rational arguments, but he also believes just as strongly that rational proofs are not necessary in order to believe in God, and he never characterizes such a belief as unreasonable.[7]

There is no doubt that Anti-Climacus presumes in Part One that human selves are created by God and that they are intended to have a relation with God that is central to their identity. Without such a relationship, humans to some degree will fail to become the selves God intended them to be. However, this perspective does not really depend upon any specifically Christian beliefs, such as the claim that Jesus was a divine person who became incarnate to bring salvation to the human race. The closest Anti-Climacus comes to making a specifically Christian claim in Part One is in the section "The Universality of This Sickness (Despair)." Here Anti-Climacus might be thought to be enunciating the Christian doctrine of original or universal sin because he claims that despair is a universal human condition: "Anyone who really knows mankind might say that there is not one single living human being who does not despair a little, who does not secretly harbor an unrest, an inner strife, a disharmony,

---

[5] In *Kierkegaard and Spirituality* I explore this kind of spirituality at some length, particularly in chapters 3, 4, and 5, which discuss the idea of a natural knowledge of God that comes through conscience, the treatment of Religiousness A in *Concluding Unscientific Postscript*, and the *Upbuilding Discourses*, which present a kind of spiritual life that does not presuppose what Kierkegaard calls "the distinctive Christian categories." These discourses, for example, do not treat the idea of atonement.

[6] See Albert Camus, *The Myth of Sisyphus and Other Essays*, trans. Justin O'Brien (New York: Penguin, 1979), 39–40.

[7] For an elaboration and defense of this claim see C. Stephen Evans, "Kierkegaard, Natural Theology, and the Existence of God," in *Kierkegaard and Christian Faith*, ed. Paul Martens and C. Stephen Evans (Waco, TX: Baylor University Press, 2016), 25–38.

an anxiety about an unknown something or a something he does not even dare to try to know" (SUD, 22/SKS 11, 138). However, Anti-Climacus does not here claim that this universal human despair is *sin* but leaves that to Part Two.

There is no real appeal to Christian doctrine here. The key is to recognize that Anti-Climacus is simply appealing to psychological knowledge that anyone "who really knows mankind" might have. The Kierkegaardian claim that sin is a distinctively Christian concept that must be provided through a special revelation certainly does not mean that a wise human being cannot recognize that there is something seriously flawed in the human condition. Socratic spirituality, or Religiousness A, may not see human beings as sinful in the Christian sense, but it certainly understands guilt as a central feature of the human condition.

Structural and Normative Descriptions of the Self in *The Sickness unto Death*

The key to understanding Part One of *The Sickness unto Death* is to distinguish the descriptions Anti-Climacus gives of the *structure* of the human self from the normative diagnoses he provides about various forms of selfhood in his capacity as a kind of "physician of the soul." There is no doubt that Anti-Climacus knows that humans were created by God and intended for a relation with God, and he believes that without such a relation humans cannot fully be what they were intended to be. However, diagnoses of health and its lack presuppose an understanding of the nature of the organism being diagnosed, and Anti-Climacus must provide an account of the structure of human existence itself as a foundation in order to present his diagnoses. This structure is the nature a human self necessarily possesses, regardless of whether that self is healthy or diseased.

At the beginning of Part One, the structure is defined. The key passage has already been quoted, but I will reiterate it here to emphasize the abstract, formal quality of the description: "The human self is such a derived, established relation, a relation that relates itself to itself and in relating itself to itself relates itself to *another*" (SUD, 13–14/SKS 11, 130, emphasis mine). The language here is intentionally abstract, and there is nothing specifically Christian in it. Anti-Climacus uses Christian language precisely, and he knows when that language is necessary. Anti-Climacus is telling us in this passage that human selves are never totally autonomous; they do not create an identity out of nothing but always define themselves in relation to some "other." It is true that immediately after providing this description of the self, he makes normative claims about the self. Despair is a condition in which the self fails to relate properly to itself. It is a "misrelation" of the self to itself. Anti-Climacus clearly thinks this condition is due to a failure to relate properly to the "power" that ontologically established the self. Since we are derivative, socially constituted selves, when we fail to relate properly to ourselves it is because we fail to relate properly to the power that constituted the self.

Isn't this power God? Well, yes and no. Ontologically or metaphysically, God is indeed the power that established the self, and God intends the self to become itself by relating to God. However, when God creates humans as selves, he gives them the gift of freedom. "God, who constituted man a relation, releases it from his hand, as it were – that is, inasmuch as the relation relates itself to itself" (SUD, 16/SKS 11, 132). God does not ontologically release the self; he only releases humans "as it were." God created humans, and humans are created by God as creatures who have becoming a self psychologically as their task. Without God's creative, sustaining power, human beings, who are intended to be selves, would not exist at all, a point I made earlier in distinguishing metaphysical from psychological identity. However, *psychologically* God does release the self and allows the self to define itself by relating itself to various "others," various "powers" that can in some ways serve as a basis for the self's identity. Thus, the abstract language Anti-Climacus uses in Part One is not accidental.

Even the description of a healthy self has to incorporate this abstract character: "The formula that describes the state of the self when despair is completely rooted out is this: in relating itself to itself and in willing to be itself, the self rests transparently in the power that established it" (SUD, 14/SKS 11, 129). There is no doubt that Anti-Climacus believes the power that established the self is God and that selves that attempt to ground their identity in other "powers" will be unable to "rest transparently." But this failure is one that he attempts to *show* through his descriptions of the various forms of despair, making it clear that when humans try to base their identity on something other than God, they will fail to carry out the task of selfhood successfully. Anti-Climacus is not saying that actual selves necessarily ground themselves in a relation to God. He is saying just the opposite. Despair is universal just because humans naturally attempt to fashion a self out of something other than God. The descriptions given of selfhood must then be abstract to reflect the possibility of doing this.

If this is not completely clear to the reader in Part One, Anti-Climacus makes it perfectly clear at the beginning of Part Two. He says that in Part

One he has been describing the condition of humans in which "the consciousness of the self is within the category of the human self, or the self whose criterion is man" (SUD, 79/SKS 11, 193). Things change when the self becomes a "self directly before God" and thereby acquires an "infinite reality" (SUD, 79/SKS 11, 193). However, Anti-Climacus makes it clear that this consciousness is an achievement and that there are selves of a sort who never accomplish it:

> A cattleman who (if this were possible) is a self directly before his cattle is a very low self, and similarly a master who is a self directly before his slaves is actually no self − for in both cases a criterion is lacking. The child who previously had only his parents as a criterion becomes a self as an adult by getting the state as a criterion, but what an infinite accent falls on the self by having God as the criterion! (SUD, 79/SKS 11, 193)

The cattleman is only a sort of self, because his "criterion" (that he is superior to cows!) is too low. An identity fashioned out of a conscious relation to cattle does not really make someone a self. The slaveowner fails in a similar way. This passage (which probably echoes Hegel's famous description of the master–slave relationship in *The Phenomenology of Spirit*) says that the slaveowner's criterion of selfhood is also too low. A slaveowner who only "exists before his slaves" is not fully a self. The issue is not that the slaves are not persons but that the master does not regard them as persons. They are only seen as property, subject to the master's control, so their recognition of him does not make him a self. Nor does his sense of superiority to them give him a genuine identity. If the master's identity is grounded only in his ability to control beings who are regarded as property he owns, then the status the master hopes to achieve through this domination will be illusory.

Things are however different for other selves. The child who only has his or her parents as a "criterion" is still not fully a self, probably because the child has no choice in the matter but simply absorbs this parental criterion immediately. However, Anti-Climacus says that when the child becomes an adult, matters change. The child who acquires "the state" as a criterion really does become a self. I believe the idea here is that the person who becomes an adult now can appropriate for himself or herself the conception (or conceptions) of selfhood put forward by society. Such a person now has an ideal self (a "criterion") by which to measure himself or herself, and such a person really can relate itself to itself by relating to "another," even though this other is provided by the social system the person is participating in. The person now has a criterion, and that criterion is provided by the person's character as a social being in a particular society.

There is, I believe, no reason to think that there can only be a single ideal of selfhood approved by a society and offered to human beings. Human beings have a strong tendency to define themselves in terms of some socially approved ideal that involves a comparison with some lesser group, but there are many ways this can be done. The male sexist has a consciousness of self that is rooted in a conviction that he is a superior self because he is not a woman. The racist has a consciousness of self that is rooted in a conviction that he or she is superior to others because of race. The social elitist has a sense of identity grounded in a presumption of class superiority, and so on down the line.

Human identities are always defined by some ideal, and those ideals are given to us through relations to others. It is obviously not the case that humans ground their selves only in God. They root their selves in socially given ideals that often take the form of "isms." Nationalism, racism, sexism, classism are names for movements composed of people whose identities are grounded in various "powers." Structurally, humans always define themselves by an "other," but there many "others" that seem, at least for a time, to offer a secure identity. Anti-Climacus recognizes these alternative ways of becoming a self. He specifically says that anyone who fails to rest transparently in God but "rests in and merges in some abstract universality (state, nation, etc.)" is in despair even if they seem to accomplish a great deal from a world-historical point of view (SUD, 46/SKS 11, SKS 11, 161). One of the advantages of defining oneself by a relation to God is that one is freed from the temptation to see one's value in terms of superiority to any other humans or human group. Anti-Climacus is trying to show us that such identities always fail at some point, but even in our failings we humans reflect our spirituality: We are beings who "relate ourselves to ourselves by relating ourselves to another." We are truly social beings; even our individual identities reflect relations to others by which we come to define ourselves.

Living before God: Identity as Grounded in Accountability to God

Kierkegaard sees human beings as ontologically relational beings. However, as already noted, he holds up an ideal of individuality. We are not born as completed individuals but are created as individuals with possibilities that must be actualized. Nor do we accomplish the task of becoming authentic selves simply by growing up and becoming socialized in a particular culture. Rather, becoming an individual is a task – and a difficult one. However, since the structure of the human self is relational, even this task is not one we can carry out by ourselves, apart from any relationship to another.

Anti-Climacus recognizes the possibility that a human self might attempt to become an individual autonomously, making use of what he calls "the negative form of the self" (SUD, 69/SKS 11, 183). It is true that by becoming conscious of some socially given identity I can distance myself from that identity. Much later than Kierkegaard, Sartre in *Being and Nothingness* famously describes human consciousness as the power of the self to step back from any given identity. The waiter who becomes conscious of being a waiter is no longer simply a waiter, since in being conscious of being a waiter he distances himself from the role he is playing.[8] However, Anti-Climacus argues that this negative power cannot achieve an enduring identity: "The negative form of the self exercises a loosening power as well as a binding power; at any time it can quite arbitrarily start all over again" (SUD, 69/SKS 11, 183). As a result, the "absolute self" that seeks complete autonomy turns out to be "a king without a country, actually ruling over nothing" (SUD, 69/SKS 11, 183). The conscious self through its negativity can distance itself from a chosen identity, but it cannot create a new, positive identity that is stable.

To avoid this arbitrariness, the identity of the self that is to be achieved must in some way be *given*. My task is not to create myself out of nothing but to choose to become the self I already am. Of course the self that is given must be given as a possibility to be chosen, but the self must somehow be able to recognize this possibility as one that has a claim on the self. The successful choice of the self must be a choice of a possibility I recognize as binding on me in some way.

It is clear that for Anti-Climacus this possibility of authentic selfhood is a gift from the creator. The task of becoming an authentic self is possible for humans precisely because of the following conditions: God has created every human as a unique being, and God intends every human person to become the authentic individual God created that self to be. It is difficult to say just what that uniqueness consists in. I do not think Kierkegaard's idea is simply that one must strive to be different from everyone else, for such a project would still mean that the self is being shaped by "others" or "the crowd." Rather, I think the idea is that a person should strive to be the

---

[8] Jean-Paul Sartre, *Being and Nothingness*, trans. Hazel E. Barnes (New York: Washington Square, 1992), 56–86.

individual that God intends the person to become, without worrying about how similar to or different from others the self is. It does seem plausible that the total set of properties (including possibilities) a self possesses will be different from the set of properties of other individuals, but what is important is not being different but being faithful to one's calling or vocation. (Understood not necessarily as a calling to a profession or occupation but a calling to become a person of character.) However, God grants to every human person the freedom to choose to be that self or not to be that self. Becoming a self turns out to be a task that is assigned to each one of us. The task is one that is meaningful because it stems from God. One might think that to have one's identity as an assigned task would be demeaning or degrading, but that is not so. It turns out that to have such an assigned task is not demeaning or degrading, because the task itself is meaningful and worthwhile and because we are given the relative autonomy of choosing or not choosing to carry out the task.

That God creates human persons as unique individuals is already clear in Part One of *The Sickness unto Death*, where Anti-Climacus describes the kind of despair that afflicts the person who lacks what the Hongs call "primitiveness" (*Primitivitet*). This is a difficult term to translate, but I don't think "primitiveness" conveys the right idea. The Danish term might be better translated as "authenticity" or "genuineness." The idea is perhaps that there are unique potentialities (or, perhaps better, a unique constellation of potentialities) in each person that God has put into that person and that God wills that the person develop and express. But what can this be? It is obvious that almost everything a human being can do is something others can do. Whether I am a philosopher or a plumber, there will be other philosophers and plumbers. Perhaps the idea is that whatever I do, whatever roles I play in life, I should strive to do what I do and play the roles I play in a way that reflects my own individual constellation of qualities, including those qualities acquired through one's history. There are other philosophers, and they may be better philosophers than I, but I have the task of bringing what is genuine and authentic in my self to the task of philosophizing. (And also to the tasks of being a husband, a father, a citizen, etc.) The idea is not to strive to be different but to strive to be the self one senses one is called to be.

> Every human being is primitively intended to be a self, destined to become himself, and as such certainly is angular, but that only means that it is to be ground into shape, not that it is to be ground down smooth, not that it is utterly to abandon being itself out of fear of men, or even simply out of fear of men not dare to be itself in its more essential contingency. (SUD, 33/ SKS 11, 149)

The phrase "essential contingency" here is striking. It suggests something like the view held by Duns Scotus that human persons possess, in addition to a common human nature, a *haecceity*, an individual essence that defines them. Perhaps the idea is just that our individuality, though certainly composed of contingent and not necessary facts about us, is something that is essential to ourselves. We are not just a placeholder that is occupied by universals, but we have a kind of reality as individuals. A *haecceity* may be something like what contemporary philosophers call a trope, something like a property but that cannot be shared as universal properties can be shared.

Further light is shed on this by Anti-Climacus later in the book when he contrasts God's knowledge of humans with human knowledge of humans. We humans can only keep a few individuals in our consciousness at one time. To describe a multitude of people we must make use of universal concepts. We classify humans by race, or sex, or nationality, or by other characteristics, and make generalizations using such concepts. Anti-Climacus says that God has no need of such concepts: "God does not avail himself of an abridgment; he comprehends actuality itself, all its particulars; for him the single individual does not lie beneath the concept" (SUD, 121/SKS 11, 233).

Since humans are spiritual creatures, God does not just create them as members of a species but as individuals. Anti-Climacus affirms that one form that despair takes is that a person "forgets himself, forgets his name, divinely understood" (SUD, 33–34/SKS 11, 149). The idea, I think, is that though many people may have the same human name, God has a unique name for every person. This Kierkegaardian image of a divine name may echo the biblical passage from Revelation 2:17, in which it is promised to those righteous ones "who overcome" that they will all receive "a white stone with a new name written on it, known only to him who receives it."

The idea that humans have an ideal self that is particular to each individual is thus rooted in God's creation. That is why this concept is already present in Part One of *The Sickness unto Death*. However, when humans are viewed through the lens of Christianity, this ideal of individuality is accentuated. Hence, in Part Two this individual call or vocation is even more prominent. From the Christian point of view, humans do not simply live before God but before Christ, and the meaningfulness and significance of every individual human life is greatly magnified: "A self directly before Christ is a self intensified by the inordinate concession from God, intensified by the inordinate accent that falls upon it because God allowed himself to be born, become man, suffer, and also die for the sake of this self" (SUD, 113/SKS 11, 225). Humans now should recognize that the task of becoming oneself is one that should not only be motivated by the fact that God has created the self out of nothing, but also by the enormously greater debt that is grounded in Christ's sacrifice, made for every human individual.

When human life is viewed through the lens of Christ's atonement, the task of becoming a self is both intensified and transformed. In one sense the task is no longer seen as one that a person can accomplish, for the story begins with the claim that humans are sinful and that this means it is not possible for anyone to become his or her true self simply by willing. Here Anti-Climacus fleshes out the obscure hint he provides early on that despair is not only the disease, the sickness unto death, but also the cure (SUD, 6/SKS 11, 118). The cure requires that one accept that one's own attempt to become the self one is intended to become is bankrupt. Rather, the path to selfhood lies through faith in Christ, who offers the forgiveness of sins, something one is commanded to believe in (SUD, 115/SKS 11, 226–227). When one has been given new life through this offer, then the debt of gratitude owed to God is transformed. Now Christ himself becomes "the criterion," for "only in Christ is it true that God is man's goal and criterion" (SUD, 114/SKS 11, 226).

The debt of gratitude means that one is accountable to God in a new way as well. A person who has accepted Christ's offer is thus one "foolish enough to make his own life concerned and accountable in fear and trembling" (SUD, 123/SKS 11, 234). Even Socratic spirituality has a kind of analogue to this fear and trembling. Anti-Climacus says that Socratic ignorance "was the Greek version of the Jewish saying: The fear of the Lord is the beginning of wisdom" (SUD, 99/SKS 11, 211). However, the fear and trembling that comes with being a follower of Christ is profoundly different. The fact that one is accountable to Christ means that ultimately one will face judgment, since accountability and judgment go hand in hand. To refuse to believe in the forgiveness of sins is to be offended, and offense is damnation, loss of selfhood.[9] Anti-Climacus puts

---

[9] What this loss of selfhood might mean depends on one's eschatological view of divine judgment and how one views the doctrine of hell. If one is an annihilationist, one might hold that the self literally ceases to exist. If one believes in eternal punishment, then God might metaphysically preserve the self while allowing it to continue in its psychological misery. If God's grace and mercy are infinite, perhaps damnation is never final, and there might always be a chance for the self to become itself. On such a view, it is sometimes said that the "gates of hell are locked from the inside." It is unclear what Kierkegaard thinks about this, but I think it is certain he does not believe that divine

the following words in the mouth of God: "Now I have spoken. We shall discuss it again in eternity. In the meantime, you can do what you want to, but judgment is at hand" (SUD, 122/SKS 11, 234).

At this point Anti-Climacus's proclamation begins to look less appealing, and that is no accident, for it is an essential part of his attack on Christendom, which, in an attempt to make Christianity appealing, has falsified it. Even before reading Part Two of *The Sickness unto Death*, one can easily imagine that many secular thinkers in the contemporary world would find it repugnant to think that becoming an authentic self requires accepting the idea that one's true self is given to one as a task. Now, however, the task is one that leads to judgment. Is this not a return to a kind of "fire and brimstone" Christianity? Is the Christian God a wrathful avenger who punishes those who spurn his offer of forgiveness?

I think the answer is "not really." It is true that Anti-Climacus insists that the "possibility of offense" is an essential part of the Christian message. However, he insists just as strongly that it is divine love that lies behind the possibility of offense. God's love is universal and unconditional; he offers forgiveness to those totally lacking in merit, and he desires only the salvation of everyone. God is not a vengeful person who wants to "get even" with those who have spurned him. Anti-Climacus believes it is only by suffering for us and with us that Christ can save us.[10] If he is right, then the God who wants to save us can only do so by allowing us the possibility of rejecting him. He comes to us "incognito," as the suffering servant, not as someone who is obviously almighty. To accept his help one must follow him in his humility. To save us he cannot overawe us with power or seduce us with offers of worldly pleasures. He must come as the God who is a humble servant and who thereby reveals the true nature of the God who seeks a love relation with us: "Precisely this is Christ's grief, that 'he cannot do otherwise'; he can debase himself, take a servant's form, suffer, die for men, invite all to come to him, offer up every day of his life, every hour of the day, and offer up his life – but he cannot remove the possibility of offense" (SUD, 126/SKS 11, 237).

punishment is retributive in character but rather that God always "chastens" out of love and a desire to help the individual.

[10] What one might want at this point is some kind of theological account of the atonement and how it is supposed to work. However, I do not think Kierkegaard offers us this. Rather, he seems to believe Christianity proclaims that atonement is made possible through Christ's life, death, and resurrection, and we can believe this is so without having anything that resembles a *theory* of atonement. For us to benefit from that atonement we must be joined to Christ, and that requires a willingness to suffer as he suffered.

So Anti-Climacus insists that the possibility of offense is an essential part of the message of Christianity. However, this does not mean that God is cruel or vindictive, and it does not mean that the offer of forgiveness is not ultimately attractive to the person humble enough to accept his own helplessness. In fact, offense is indirect testimony to the attractiveness of the offer. Anti-Climacus compares offense to the skepticism of a day-laborer who is invited to become the son-in-law of a mighty emperor (SUD, 84/SKS 11, 197–198). The day-laborer might have been grateful if the king had merely given him the favor of allowing the laborer to meet him, but he cannot get it into his head that the emperor would desire such a relationship with him. If he cannot find it within himself to trust the emperor and believe him, he will be offended, sure that the emperor is actually making fun of him. However, the imaginary emperor's offer pales in comparison with God's offer in Christ:

> Christianity teaches that this individual human being – and thus every single individual human being, no matter whether man, woman, servant girl, cabinet minister, merchant, barber, student, or whatever – this individual human being exists *before God*, this individual human being who perhaps would be proud of having spoken with the king once in his life . . . this human being exists before God, may speak with God any time he wants to, assured of being heard by him – in short, this person is invited to live on the most intimate terms with God! (SUD, 85/SKS 11, 198–199)

The amazing character of the offer is carried further by the fact that this God "comes to the world, allows himself to be born, to suffer to die, and this suffering God – he almost implores and beseeches this person to accept the help that is offered to him" (SUD, 85/SKS 11, 199).

The person who is "lacking the humble courage to dare to believe this" will be offended, not because the God who makes the offer is unloving or wrathful but because "it is too high for him, because his mind cannot grasp it" (SUD, 85/SKS 11, 199). Anti-Climacus claims that offense is "unhappy admiration," something related to envy (SUD, 86/SKS 11, 199). The possibility of offense arises not because God is wrathful or vengeful but because his love does not make sense to a prideful, self-sufficient person.

Actually Kierkegaard himself rejects the view that God's "punishment" is an expression of anger or wrath. God is love through and through, and even his "punishments" are actually "chastisements" that are given for the sake of the good of the one who receives the "medicine." A person who really understood his own good would actually welcome God's chastening and not fear it (UDVS, 52/SKS 8, 161–163). We should welcome being accountable to such a God, who only desires our own good and loves us unselfishly, as no human does or can.

Kierkegaard is indeed a kind of individualist, who thinks that every human person has a call to become the "individual" that God created the person to be and for whom Christ died. However, paradoxical as it may seem, he believes that one becomes such an individual through a relationship to God. Human selfhood is relational through and through, and even our individuality is a gift made possible by a relationship to God.

Bibliography

Aho, Kevin. "Depression and Embodiment," *Medicine, Health Care, and Philosophy* 16 (2013): 751–759.

Aristotle. *Nicomachean Ethics*. Translated with an Introduction by David Ross, revised by J. L. Ackrill and J. O. Urmson. Oxford: Oxford University Press, 1980.

Augustine. *Confessions*. Translated by Henry Chadwick. Oxford: Oxford University Press, 1991.

Backhouse, Stephen. *Kierkegaard: A Single Life*. Grand Rapids, MI: Zondervan, 2016.

Baker, Lynne Rudder. *Naturalism and the First-Personal Perspective*. Oxford: Oxford University Press, 2013.

Barrett, Lee C. *Eros and Self-Emptying: The Intersections of Augustine and Kierkegaard*. Grand Rapids, MI: William Eerdmans, 2013.

"Johannes Climacus: Humorist, Dialectician and Gadfly." In *Kierkegaard's Pseudonyms, Kierkegaard Research: Sources, Reception and Resources*, vol. 17. Edited by Jon Stewart and Katalin Nun, 141–166. Farnham: Ashgate, 2015.

Beabout, Gregory. *Freedom and Its Misuses: Kierkegaard on Anxiety and Despair*. Milwaukee, WI: Marquette University Press, 1996.

Becker, Ernest. *The Denial of Death*. New York: Free Press, 1973.

Bernier, Mark. *The Task of Hope in Kierkegaard*. Oxford: Oxford University Press, 2015.

Binswanger, Ludwig. *Being-in-the-World*. Translated by Jacob Needleman. New York: Basic Books, 1963.

Bird, Daniel. *"Phenomenological Psychopathology and an Embodied Interpretation of Manic Bipolar Experience."* MA diss., University of Copenhagen, 2015.

Bollas, Christopher. *The Christopher Bollas Reader*. New York: Routledge, 2011.

Bowden, Hannah Mary. *"A Phenomenological Study of Mania and Depression."* PhD diss., Durham University, 2013.

Bowen, Amber. "Reviving the Dead: A Kierkegaardian Turn from the Self-Positing to the Theological Self." *Religions* 10, no. 633 (2019): 1–18.

Brampton, Sally. *Shoot the Damn Dog: A Memoir of Depression*. New York: Norton, 2008.

Camus, Albert. *The Myth of Sisyphus and Other Essays*. Translated by Justin O'Brien. New York: Penguin, 1979.

237

Carlisle, Clare. "How to Be a Human Being in the World: Kierkegaard's Question of Existence." In *Kierkegaard's Existential Approach.* Edited by Arne Grøn, René Rosfort, and K. Brian Söderquist, 113–130. Berlin: DeGruyter, 2017.

    Philosopher of the Heart: The Restless Life of Søren Kierkegaard. London: Allen Lane, 2019.

    Philosopher of the Heart: The Restless Life of Søren Kierkegaard. New York: Farrar, Straus and Giroux, 2020.

Carlsson, Ulrika. "The Ethical Life of Aesthetes." In *The Kierkegaardian Mind.* Edited by Adam Buben, Eleanor Helms, and Patrick Stokes, 135–144. London: Routledge, 2019.

Carr, Karen L. "Christian Epistemology and the Anthropology of Sin: Kierkegaard on Natural Theology and the Concept of 'Offense.'" In *The Kierkegaardian Mind.* Edited by Adam Buben, Eleanor Helms, and Patrick Stokes, 365–376. London: Routledge, 2019.

Cheney, Terri. *Manic: A Memoir.* New York: William Morrow, 2008.

Churchland, Patricia. *Neurophilosophy.* Cambridge, MA: MIT Press, 1988.

Churchland, Paul. *Scientific Realism and the Plasticity of Mind.* Cambridge: Cambridge University Press, 1979.

Coleman, Reed Farrel. *Empty Ever After.* Madison, WI: Bleak House Books, 2008.

Corcilius, Klaus. "Two Jobs for Aristotle's Practical Syllogism?" In *Logical Analysis and History of Philosophy.* Edited by Uwe Meixner and Albert Newen, 163–184. Focus: The Practical Syllogism/*Schwerpunkt: der praktische Syllogismus*, vol. XI. Paderborn: Mentis, 2008.

Dahlstrom, Daniel. "Freedom through Despair: Kierkegaard's Phenomenological Analysis." In *Kierkegaard as Phenomenologist: An Experiment.* Edited by Jeffrey Hanson, 57–78. Evanston, IL: Northwestern University Press, 2010.

Dahm, Brandon. "The Acquired Virtues Are Real Virtues: A Response to Stump." *Faith and Philosophy* 32 (2015): 453–470.

Davenport, John J. *Narrative Identity, Autonomy, and Morality: From Frankfurt and MacIntyre to Kierkegaard.* New York: Routledge, 2012.

    "Selfhood and 'Spirit.'" In *The Oxford Handbook of Kierkegaard.* Edited by John Lippitt and George Pattison, 230–251. Oxford: Oxford University Press, 2013.

    "Towards an Existential Virtue Ethics: Kierkegaard and Macintyre." In *Kierkegaard after Macintyre: Essays on Freedom, Narrativity, and Virtue.* Edited by John J. Davenport and Anthony Rudd, 265–323. Chicago: Open Court, 2001.

De Beauvoir, Simone. *The Ethics of Ambiguity.* Translated by Bernard Frechtman. New York: Citadel Press, 1948.

De Caro, Mario and Macarthur, David, eds. *Naturalism in Question.* Cambridge, MA: Harvard University Press, 2008.

Deede, Kristen K. "The Infinite Qualitative Difference: Sin, the Self, and Revelation in the Thought of Søren Kierkegaard." *International Journal for Philosophy of Religion* 53 (2003): 25–48.

Dennett, Daniel C. *Consciousness Explained*. Harmondsworth: Penguin, 1991.
"The Self as a Centre of Narrative Gravity." In *Self and Consciousness: Multiple Perspectives*. Edited by Frank S. Kessel, Pamela M. Cole, and Dale L. Johnson, 103–115. Hillsdale, NJ: Erlbaum, 1992.
Descartes, René. *Meditations on First Philosophy*. In *Selected Philosophical Writings*. Translated by John Cottingham, Robert Stoothoff, and Dugald Murdoch. Cambridge: Cambridge University Press, 1988.
Dreyfus, Hubert L. "Kierkegaard on the Self." In *Ethics, Love, and Faith in Kierkegaard: Philosophical Engagements*. Edited by Edward F. Mooney, 11–23. Bloomington: Indiana University Press, 2008.
Drummond, John J. "Moral Phenomenology and Moral Intentionality." *Phenomenology and the Cognitive Sciences* 7, no. 1 (March 2008): 35–49.
Ellis, Fiona. *God, Value, and Nature*. Oxford: Oxford University Press, 2017.
Elrod, John. *Kierkegaard and Christendom*. Princeton, NJ: Princeton University Press, 1981.
Emmanuel, Steven M. "Kierkegaard's Pragmatist Faith." *Philosophy and Phenomenological Research* 51, no. 2 (1991): 279–302.
Evans, C. Stephen. "Kierkegaard and the Limits of Reason: Can There Be a Responsible Fideism?" *Revista Portuguesa de Filosofia* 64, no. 2/4 (2008): 1021–1035.
"Kierkegaard, Natural Theology, and the Existence of God." In *Kierkegaard and Christian Faith*. Edited by Paul Martens and C. Stephen Evans, 25–38. Waco, TX: Baylor University Press, 2016.
Kierkegaard and Spirituality: Accountability as the Meaning of Human Existence. Grand Rapids, MI: William P. Eerdmans, 2019.
Kierkegaard's Ethics of Love: Divine Commands and Moral Obligations. Oxford: Oxford University Press, 2006.
"Who Is the Other in Sickness unto Death? God and Human Relations in the Constitution of the Self." In *Kierkegaard Studies Year Book*, 1–15. Berlin: De Gruyter, 1997.
Fendt, Gene. *For What May I Hope? Thinking with Kant and Kierkegaard*. Bern: Peter Lang, 1990.
Ferreira, M. Jamie. *Kierkegaard*. Chichester: Wiley-Blackwell, 2009.
Fichte, J. G. *The Science of Knowledge*. Translated by Peter Heath and John Lachs. Cambridge: Cambridge University Press, 1982.
Frankfurt, Harry. "The Faintest Passion." In *Necessity, Volition and Love*, 95–107. Cambridge: Cambridge University Press, 1999.
"Freedom of the Will and the Concept of a Person." In *The Importance of What We Care About*, 11–25. Cambridge: Cambridge University Press, 1988.
"Identification and Wholeheartedness." In *The Importance of What We Care About*, 159–176. Cambridge: Cambridge University Press, 1988.
The Reasons of Love. Princeton, NJ: Princeton University Press, 2004.
Fremstedal, Roe. "Demonic Despair under the Guise of the Good? Kierkegaard and Anscombe vs. Velleman." *Inquiry: An Interdisciplinary Journal of Philosophy* (2019): 1–21.

Kierkegaard and Kant on Radical Evil and the Highest Good: Virtue, Happiness, and the Kingdom of God. Basingstoke: Palgrave Macmillan, 2014.

"Kierkegaard on Hope as Essential to Selfhood." In *The Moral Psychology of Hope: An Introduction*. Edited by Titus Stahl and Claudia Blöser, 75–92. Lanham, MD: Rowman & Littlefield International, 2020.

"Kierkegaard's Post-Kantian Approach to Anthropology and Selfhood." In *The Kierkegaardian Mind*. Edited by Adam Buben, Eleanor Helms, and Patrick Stokes, 319–330. London: Routledge, 2019.

Freud, Sigmund. "Mourning and Melancholia." In *General Psychological Theory*, 164–179. New York: Touchstone, 1997.

Furtak, Rick Anthony. "Ernest Becker: A Kierkegaardian Theorist of Death and Human Nature." In *Kierkegaard's Influence on the Social Sciences*. Edited by Jon Stewart, 17–27. Burlington, VT: Ashgate, 2011.

Wisdom in Love: Kierkegaard and the Ancient Quest for Emotional Integrity. South Bend, IN: University of Notre Dame Press, 2005.

Garff, Joakim. *Søren Kierkegaard: A Biography*. Translated by Bruce H. Kirmmse. Princeton, NJ: Princeton University Press, 2005.

Ghaemi, S. Nassir. *On Depression: Drugs, Diagnosis, and Despair in the Modern World*. Baltimore: Johns Hopkins University Press, 2013.

"What Is Me? What Is Bipolar?" *Philosophy, Psychiatry, & Psychology* 20 (2013): 67–68.

Glenn, John D. Jr. "The Definition of the Self." In *International Kierkegaard Commentary*, vol. 19: *The Sickness unto Death*. Edited by Robert L. Perkins, 5–22. Macon, GA: Mercer University Press, 1987.

Goodwin, Frederic K. and Jamison, Kay Redfield. *Bipolar Disorders*. New York: Oxford University Press, 2007.

Gouwens, David J. *Kierkegaard as a Religious Thinker*. Cambridge: Cambridge University Press, 1996.

Greenberg, Michael. *Hurry Down Sunshine: A Father's Story of Love and Madness*. New York: Vintage Books, 2008.

Grier, Michelle. "Kant on the Illusion of a Systematic Unity of Knowledge." *History of Philosophy Quarterly* 14, no. 1 (1997): 1–28.

Grøn, Arne. "Der Begriff Verzweiflung." *Kierkegaardiana* 17 (1994): 25–41.

"Kierkegaards Phänomenologie?" In *Kierkegaard Studies Year Book 1996*. Edited by Niels Jørgen Cappelørn and Hermann Deuser, 91–116. Berlin: De Gruyter, 1996.

"The Relation between Part One and Part Two of *The Sickness unto Death*." *Kierkegaard Studies Year Book* (1997): 35–50.

Subjektivitet og Negativitet: Kierkegaard. Copenhagen: Gyldendal, 1997.

Habermas, Jürgen. *The Future of Human Nature*. Translated by Hella Beister and William Rehg. Cambridge: Polity Press/Blackwell, 2003.

Hannay, Alastair. "Basic Despair in *The Sickness unto Death*." *Kierkegaardiana* 17 (1994): 6–24.

Kierkegaard. New York: Routledge, 1991.

Kierkegaard: A Biography. Cambridge: Cambridge University Press, 2001.

"Kierkegaard and the Variety of Despair." In *The Cambridge Companion to Kierkegaard*. Edited by Alastair Hannay and Gordon D. Marino, 329–348. New York: Cambridge University Press, 1998.

"Spirit and the Idea of the Self as a Reflexive Relation." In *International Kierkegaard Commentary: The Sickness unto Death*. Edited by Robert L. Perkins, 23–38. Macon, GA: Mercer University Press, 1987.

Hanson, Jeffrey. "Holy Hypochondria: Narrative and Self-Awareness in *The Concept of Anxiety*," *Kierkegaard Studies Year Book* (2011): 239–261.

Hanson, Jeffrey, Editor. *Kierkegaard as Phenomenologist: An Experiment.* Evanston, IL: Northwestern University Press, 2010.

Hare, John E. *The Moral Gap: Kantian Ethics, Human Limits, and God's Assistance*. Oxford: Clarendon Press, 2002.

Hegel, G. W. F. *The Encyclopedia Logic [Lesser Logic]*. Translated by T. F. Geraets, W. A. Suchting, and H. S. Harris. Indianapolis: Hackett, 1991.

Hegel's Science of Logic. Translated by A. V. Miller. London: George Allen & Unwin, 1969.

Phenomenology of Spirit. Translated by A. V. Miller. Oxford: Oxford University Press, 1977.

Heidegger, Martin. *Being and Time*. Translated by John Macquarrie and Edward Robinson. Oxford: Blackwell, 1962.

Einführung in die Metaphysik. Tübingen: Max Niemeyer Verlag, 1955.

Helms, Eleanor. "Review of Patrick Stokes, *Kierkegaard's Mirrors: Interest, Self, and Moral Vision*." *International Philosophical Quarterly* 50, no. 3 (September 2010): 355–357.

Helweg, Hjalmar. *Søren Kierkegaard: En Psykiastrisk-Psykologisk Studie*. Copenhagen: Hagerups Forlag, 1933.

Herdt, Jennifer. *Putting on Virtue: The Legacy of the Splendid Vices*. Chicago: University of Chicago Press, 2008.

Hershman, D. Jablow and Lieb, Julian. *Manic Depression and Creativity*. Amherst, NY: Prometheus Books, 1998.

Hirsch, Emmanuel. *Kierkegaard Studien* 2. Gütersloh: Bertelsmann, 1933.

Horn, Robert Leslie. *Positivity and Dialectic: A Study of the Theological Method of Hans Lassen Martensen*. Copenhagen: C. A. Reitzel, 2007.

Hühn, Lore and Schab, Philipp. "Kierkegaard and German Idealism." In *The Oxford Handbook of Kierkegaard*. Edited by John Lippitt and George Pattison, 62–93. Oxford: Oxford University Press, 2013.

Husserl, Edmund. *Analyses Concerning Passive and Active Synthesis*. Translated by Anthony J. Steinbock. Dordrecht: Kluwer Academic Publishers, 2001.

Jamison, Kay Redfield. *Touched with Fire: Manic-Depressive Illness and the Artistic Temperament*. New York: Free Press, 1994.

An Unquiet Mind: A Memoir of Moods and Madness. New York: Vintage Books, 1996.

Johnson, Ralph Henry. *The Concept of Existence in the "Concluding Unscientific Postscript."* The Hague: Martinus Nijhoff, 1972.

Kant, Immanuel. *Critique of Pure Reason*. Translated by Paul Guyer and Allen W. Wood. Cambridge: Cambridge University Press, 2009.

Groundwork of the Metaphysics of Morals. Translated by Mary J. Gregor. Cambridge: Cambridge University Press, 1997.

Kemp, Ryan S. "Making Sense of the Ethical Stage: Revisiting Kierkegaard's Aesthetic-to-Ethical Transition." *Kierkegaard Studies Year Book* (2011): 323–340.

"The Role of Imagination in Kierkegaard's Account of Ethical Transformation." *Archiv für Geschichte der Philosophie* 100, no. 2 (2018): 202–231.

Khan, Abrahim H. "Sin before Christ in *The Sickness unto Death*." In *Kierkegaard and Christianity, Acta Kierkegaardiana* 3. Edited by Roman Králik, Abrahim H. Khan, Peter Šajda, Jamie Turnbull, and Andrew J. Burgess, 197–217. Šal'a, Slovakia: Kierkegaard Society in Slovakia and Kierkegaard Circle, 2008.

Kido Lopez, Jason. "Kierkegaard's View of Despair: Paradoxical Psychology and Spiritual Therapy." *Res Philosophica* 90, no. 4 (October 2013): 589–607.

Kierkegaard, Søren. *The Sickness unto Death*. Translated by Alastair Hannay. London: Penguin Books, 1989.

Kirkpatrick, Kate. *Sartre on Sin: Between Being and Nothingness*. Oxford: Oxford University Press, 2017.

Kirmmse, Bruce H. *Encounters with Kierkegaard: A Life as Seen by His Contemporaries*. Edited by Bruce H. Kirmmse. Translated by Bruce H. Kirmmse and Virginia R. Laursen. Princeton, NJ: Princeton University Press, 1996.

Korsgaard, Christine. *Self-Constitution: Agency, Identity, and Integrity*. Oxford: Oxford University Press, 2009.

The Sources of Normativity. Cambridge: Cambridge University Press, 1996.

Kosch, Michelle. "Kierkegaard's Ethicist: Fichte's Role in Kierkegaard's Construction of the Ethical Standpoint." *Archiv für Geschichte der Philosophie* 88 (2006): 261–295.

Krishek, Sharon. "Kierkegaard's Notion of a Divine Name and the Feasibility of Universal Love." *Southern Journal of Philosophy* 57 (2019): 539–560.

"Love for Humans: Morality as the Heart of Kierkegaard's Religious Philosophy." In *The Kierkegaardian Mind*. Edited by Adam Buben, Eleanor Helms, and Patrick Stokes, 122–132. London: Routledge, 2019.

Lovers in Essence: A Kierkegaardian Defense of Romantic Love. New York: Oxford University Press, 2022.

Lappano, David. *Kierkegaard's Theology of Encounter: An Edifying and Polemical Life*. Oxford: Oxford University Press, 2017.

Larsen, Rasmus Rosenberg. "The Posited Self: The Non-theistic Foundation in Kierkegaard's Writings." In *Kierkegaard Studies Year Book*, 31–54. Berlin: DeGruyter, 2015.

Lear, Jonathan. *A Case for Irony*. Cambridge, MA: Harvard University Press, 2011.

Therapeutic Action: An Earnest Plea for Irony. Abingdon: Routledge, 2018.

Lippitt, John. "Learning to Hope: The Role of Hope in *Fear and Trembling*." In *Kierkegaard's Fear and Trembling: A Critical Guide*. Edited by Daniel Conway, 122–141. Cambridge: Cambridge University Press, 2015.

Locke, John. *An Essay Concerning Human Understanding*. Edited by Peter H. Nidditch. Oxford: Clarendon Press, 1975.

An Essay Concerning Human Understanding. Edited by John Yolton. London: Everyman Books, 1993.

Lübcke, Poul. "Kierkegaard's Concept of Revelation." In *Theologie zwischen Pragmatismus und Existenzdenken*. Edited by Gesche Linde, Richard Purkarthofer, Heiko Schulz, and Peter Steinacker, 405–414. Marburg: Elwert, 2006.

Luther, Martin. "Psalm 51." In *Luther's Works 12*. Edited by Jaroslav Pelikan, 301–410. Saint Louis: Concordia Publishing House, 1955.

Works XXI. Edited by Jaroslav Pelikan and Hilton C. Oswald. St Louis, MO: Concordia House, 1956.

Mackintosh, Hugh Ross. *The Christian Experience of Forgiveness*. London: Fontana, [1927] 1962.

Types of Modern Theology: Schleiermacher to Barth. London: Nisbet & Co., 1937.

Mahn, Jason A. *Fortunate Fallibility: Kierkegaard and the Power of Sin*. Oxford and New York: Oxford University Press, 2011.

"Sin: Leaping and Sliding and Mysteries Pointing to Mysteries." In *T & T Clark Companion to The Theology of Kierkegaard*. Edited by Aaron P. Edwards and David J. Gouwens, 261–277. London: T & T Clark Bloomsbury, 2020.

Marek, Jakub. "Anti-Climacus: Kierkegaard's 'Servant of the Word.'" In *Kierkegaard's Pseudonyms. Kierkegaard Research: Sources, Reception and Resources 17*. Edited by Jon Stewart and Katalin Nun, 39–51. Farnham: Ashgate, 2015.

Marino, Gordon. *Kierkegaard in the Present Age*. Milwaukee, WI: Marquette University Press, 2001.

Marks, Tamara Monet. "Kierkegaard's 'New Argument' for Immortality." *Journal of Religious Ethics* 31, no. 1 (2010): 143–186.

Martin, Raymond and Barresi, John. *Naturalization of the Soul: Self and Personal Identity in the Eighteenth Century*. London: Routledge, 2000.

The Rise and Fall of Soul and Self. New York: Columbia University Press, 2006.

May, Rollo. *Love and Will*. New York: W. W. Norton and Company, 1969.

McCarthy, Vincent A. *Kierkegaard as Psychologist*. Evanston, IL: Northwestern University Press, 2015.

Merleau-Ponty, Maurice. *Phenomenology of Perception*. Translated by Donald A. Landes. Abingdon: Routledge, 2013.

Meynen, Gerben. "Depression, Possibilities, and Competence." *Theoretical Medicine and Bioethics* 32 (2011): 181–193.

Monroe-Kane, Charles. *Lithium Jesus: A Memoir of Mania*. Madison, WI: University of Wisconsin Press, 2016.

Morag, Talia. *Emotion, Imagination, and the Limits of Reason*. London: Routledge, 2016.

Nagel, Thomas. "What Is It Like to Be a Bat?" *The Philosophical Review* 83, no. 4 (October 1974): 435–450.

Nicholson, Graeme. "The Intense Communication of Kierkegaard's Discourses." In *International Kierkegaard Commentary: Upbuilding Discourses in Various Spirits*. Edited by Robert L. Perkins, 349–369. Macon, GA: Mercer University Press, 2005.

Nietzsche, Friedrich. *On the Genealogy of Morals and Ecce Homo*. Edited and translated by Walter Kaufmann. New York: Vintage, 1989.

Nordentoft, Kresten. *Kierkegaard's Psychology*. Translated by Bruce H. Kirmmse. Pittsburgh, PA: Duquesne University Press, 1978.

Parfit, Derek. *Reasons and Persons*. Oxford: Oxford University Press, 1984.

Pattison, George. "Kierkegaard and Radical Demythologization." In *Kierkegaard and His German Contemporaries, Tome II: Theology*. Edited by Jon Stewart, 233–253. Aldershot: Ashgate, 2007.

Kierkegaard and the Theology of the Nineteenth Century. Cambridge: Cambridge University Press, 2012.

"Kierkegaard the Theology Student." In *T & T Clark Companion to the Theology of Kierkegaard*. Edited by Aaron P. Edwards and David J. Gouwens, 89–109. London: T & T Clark, 2020.

Kierkegaard's Upbuilding Discourses: Philosophy, Literature, Theology. London: Routledge, 2002.

Pattison, George and Shakespeare, Steven, Editors. *Kierkegaard: The Self in Society*. Basingstoke: Macmillan Press, 1998.

Piety, M. G. "Alone for Dinner: Kierkegaard's Sombre Outlook." *Times Literary Supplement*, October 10, 2019.

Ways of Knowing: Kierkegaard's Pluralist Epistemology. Waco, TX: Baylor University Press, 2010.

Podmore, Simon. *Kierkegaard and the Self before God: Anatomy of the Abyss*. Bloomington: Indiana University Press, 2011.

Prinz, Jesse J. *Gut Reactions: A Perceptual Theory of Emotion*. New York: Oxford University Press, 2004.

Quinn, Philip L. "Kierkegaard's Christian Ethics." In *The Cambridge Companion to Kierkegaard*. Edited by Alastair Hannay and Gordon D. Marino, 349–375. Cambridge: Cambridge University Press, 1998.

Radden, Jennifer. *Moody Minds Distempered*. Oxford: Oxford University Press, 2009.

"The Self and Its Moods in Depression and Mania." *Journal of Consciousness Studies* 20, no. 7–8 (2013): 80–102.

Ratcliffe, Matthew. *Experiences of Depression: A Study in Phenomenology*. Oxford: Oxford University Press, 2015.

Feelings of Being: Phenomenology, Psychiatry, and the Sense of Reality. Oxford: Oxford University Press, 2008.

Ringleben, Joachim. "Zur Aufbaulogik der *Krankheit zum Tode*." *Kierkegaard Studies Year Book* (1997): 100–116.

Roberts, Robert C. *Emotions: An Essay in Aid of Moral Psychology*. Cambridge: Cambridge University Press, 2003.

"The Grammar of Sin and the Conceptual Unity of *The Sickness unto Death*." In *International Kierkegaard Commentary: The Sickness unto Death*. Edited by Robert L. Perkins, 135–160. Macon, GA: Mercer University Press, 1987.

"Is Kierkegaard a 'Virtue Ethicist'?," *Faith and Philosophy 36* (2019): 325–342.

"The Virtue of Hope in *Eighteen Upbuilding Discourses*." In *International Kierkegaard Commentary: Eighteen Upbuilding Discourses*, edited by Robert L. Perkins, 181–203. Macon, GA: Mercer University Press, 2003.

Rosfort, René. "Kierkegaard's Conception of Psychology." In *A Companion to Kierkegaard*. Edited by Jon Stewart, 453–467. Malden, MA: Wiley Blackwell, 2015.

Rudd, Anthony. "Kierkegaard and the Critique of Political Theology." In *Kierkegaard and Political Theology*. Edited by Roberto Sirvent and Silas Morgan, 17–29. Peabody, MA: Pickwick Publications, 2018.

"Kierkegaard on Nature and Natural Beauty." In *The Kierkegaardian Mind*. Edited by Adam Buben, Eleanor Helms, and Patrick Stokes, 145–155. London: Routledge, 2019.

"Narrative, Expression, and Mental Substance." *Inquiry* 48, no. 5 (2007): 413–435.

Self, Value, and Narrative: A Kierkegaardian Approach. Oxford: Oxford University Press, 2012.

Rudd, Anthony and Davenport, John J., Editors. *Love, Reason, and Will*. London: Bloomsbury, 2015.

Sands, Justin. *Reasoning from Faith: Fundamental Theology in Merold Westphal's Philosophy of Religion*. Bloomington: Indiana University Press, 2018.

Sartre, Jean-Paul. *Being and Nothingness*. Translated by Hazel Barnes. New York: The Philosophical Library, 1956.

Being and Nothingness. Translated by Hazel E. Barnes. New York: Washington Square, 1992.

Being and Nothingness: An Essay on Phenomenological Ontology. Translated by Hazel E. Barnes. New York: Washington Square Press, 2012.

Existentialism and Humanism. Translated by Philip Mairet. London: Methuen, 1948.

Schechtman, Marya. *The Constitution of Selves*. Ithaca, NY: Cornell University Press, 1996.

Schioldann, Johan and Søgaard, Ib. "Søren Kierkegaard (1813–1855): A Bicentennial Pathographical Review." *History of Psychiatry* 24, no. 4 (2013): 387–398.

Schleiermacher, Friedrich. *On Religion: Speeches to Its Cultured Despisers*. Translated by John Oman. New York: Harper & Brothers, 1958.

Schou, H. J. *Religiøsitet og Sygelige Sindstilstande*. Copenhagen: Gads Forlag, 1924.

Schulz, Heiko. "Marheineke: The Volatilization of Christian Doctrine." In *Kierkegaard and His German Contemporaries: Tome II: Theology*. Edited by Jon Stewart, 117–142. Aldershot: Ashgate, 2007.

Sløk, Johannes. *Kierkegaards Univers: En Ny Guide til Geniet*. Viborg: Centrum, 1983.

Spinoza, Benedict de. *Ethics*. In *A Spinoza Reader: The* Ethics *and Other Works*. Edited by Edwin Curley, 85–265. Princeton, NJ: Princeton University Press, 1994.

Short Treatise on God, Man, and His Well-Being. In *Collected Works of Spinoza*. Vol. 1. Edited by Edwin Curley. New York: Random House, 1985,

Stern, Robert. *Understanding Moral Obligation: Kant, Hegel, Kierkegaard*. Cambridge: Cambridge University Press, 2012.

Stern, Robert and Watts, Daniel. "Valuing Humanity: Kierkegaardian Worries about Korsgaardian Transcendental Arguments." *International Journal of Philosophy and Theology* 80, no. 4–5 (2019): 424–442.

Stewart, Jon, Editor. *Hans Lassen Martensen: Theologian, Philosopher and Social Critic*. Copenhagen: Museum Tusculanum, 2012.

Stewart, Jon. *A History of Hegelianism in Golden Age Denmark, Tome I: The Heiberg Period: 1824–1836*. Copenhagen: C. A. Reitzel, 2007.

"Kierkegaard's Phenomenology of Despair in *The Sickness unto Death*." In *Kierkegaard Studies Year Book*, 117–143. Berlin: DeGruyter, 1997.

Kierkegaard's Relations to Hegel Reconsidered. Cambridge: Cambridge University Press, 2003.

Stokes, Patrick. "Consciousness, Self, and Reflection." In *The Kierkegaardian Mind*. Edited by Adam Buben, Eleanor Helms, and Patrick Stokes, 269–280. London: Routledge, 2019.

"Fearful Asymmetry: Kierkegaard's Search for the Direction of Time," *Continental Philosophy Review* 43, no. 4 (2010): 485–507.

"Kierkegaard's Critique of the Internet." In *Kierkegaard and Contemporary Ethics*. Edited by Mélissa Fox-Muraton, 125–145. Berlin: De Gruyter, 2020.

Kierkegaard's Mirrors: Interest, Self, and Moral Vision. London: Palgrave Macmillan, 2010.

The Naked Self: Kierkegaard and Personal Identity. Oxford: Oxford University Press, 2015.

"Naked Subjectivity: Minimal vs. Narrative Selves." *Inquiry* 53, no. 4 (2010): 356–382.

"The Science of the Dead: Proto-Spiritualism in Kierkegaard's Copenhagen." In *Kierkegaard and the Religious Crisis of the 19th Century*. Acta Kierkegaardiana IV. Edited by Roman Králik, Peter Šajda, and Jamie Turnbull, 132–149. Šal'a, Slovakia: Kierkegaard Society in Slovakia and Kierkegaard Circle, University of Toronto, 2009.

"'See for Your Self': Contemporaneity, Autopsy and Presence in Kierkegaard's Moral-Religious Psychology." *British Journal for the History of Philosophy* 18, no. 2 (April 2010): 297–319.

Bibliography 247

Strawson, Galen. *Locke on Personal Identity: Consciousness and Concernment.* Princeton, NJ: Princeton University Press, 2011.

Strawson, P. F. *Individuals: An Essay in Descriptive Metaphysics.* London: Methuen, 1959.

Strelis, Anna. "The Intimacy between Reason and Emotion." *Res Philosophica* 90, no. 4 (2013): 461–480.

Stump, Eleonore. "The Non-Aristotelian Character of Aquinas's Ethics: Aquinas on the Passions," *Faith and Philosophy* 28 (2011): 29–43.

Styron, William. *Darkness Visible: A Memoir of Madness.* New York: Vintage Books, 1992.

Taliaferro, Charles. "The Promise and Sensibility of Integrative Dualism." In *Contemporary Dualism: A Defense.* Edited by Andrea Lavazza and Howard M. Robinson, 199–211. London: Routledge, 2014.

Taylor, Charles. "Responsibility for Self." In *The Identities of Persons.* Edited by Amélie Rorty, 281–300. Berkeley, CA: University of California Press, 1976.

Theil, Udo. *The Early Modern Subject: Self-Consciousness and Personal Identity from Descartes to Hume.* Oxford: Oxford University Press, 2011.

Theunissen, Michael. *Der Begriff Verzweiflung: Korrekturen an Kierkegaard.* Frankfurt am Main: Suhrkamp, 1993.

  Kierkegaard's Concept of Despair. Translated by Barbara Harshav and Helmut Illbruck. Princeton, NJ: Princeton University Press, 2005.

  "Kierkegaard's Negativistic Method." In *Kierkegaard's Truth: The Disclosure of the Self.* Edited by Joseph H. Smith, 381–423. New Haven, CT: Yale University Press, 1981.

Thompson, Curtis L. "Hans Lassen Martensen: A Speculative Theologian Determining the Agenda of the Day." In *Kierkegaard and His Danish Contemporaries, Tome II: Theology.* Edited by Jon Stewart, 229–266. Aldershot: Ashgate, 2009.

  "H. L. Martensen's Theological Anthropology." In *Kierkegaard and His Contemporaries: The Culture of Golden Age Denmark.* Edited by Jon Stewart, 164–180. Berlin: Walter de Gruyter, 2003.

Thulstrup, Niels. "Martensen's *Dogmatics* and Its Reception." In *Kierkegaard and His Contemporaries: The Culture of Golden Age Denmark.* Edited by Jon Stewart, 181–202. Berlin: Water de Gruyter, 2003.

Thust, Martin. "Das Marionettentheater Sören Kierkegaards." *Zeitwende* 1 (1925): 18–38.

Tietjen, Mark. *Kierkegaard: A Christian Missionary to Christians.* Downers Grove, IL: IVP Academic, 2016.

  Kierkegaard, Communication, and Virtue: Authorship as Edification. Bloomington: Indiana University Press, 2013.

Tillich, Paul. *Mysticism and Guilt-Consciousness in Schelling's Philosophical Development.* Lewisburg, PA: Bucknell University Press, 1974.

Velleman, J. David. *The Possibility of Practical Reason.* 2nd. ed. Ann Arbor, MI: Maize Books, 2015.

Vogel, Lawrence. *The Fragile "We": Ethical Implications of Heidegger's Being and Time.* Evanston, IL: Northwestern University Press, 1994.

Vos, Pieter. "A Human Being's Highest Perfection: The Grammar and Vocabulary of Virtue in Kierkegaard's Upbuilding Discourses." *Faith and Philosophy* 33 (2016): 311–332.

Walsh, Sylvia. *Kierkegaard and Religion: Personality, Character, and Virtue.* Cambridge: Cambridge University Press, 2018.

Kierkegaard: Thinking Christianly in an Existential Mode. Oxford: Oxford University Press, 2009.

Living Christianly: Kierkegaard's Dialectic of Christian Existence. University Park: Pennsylvania State University Press, 2005.

"On 'Feminine' and 'Masculine' Forms of Despair." In *International Kierkegaard Commentary: The Sickness unto Death.* Edited by Robert L. Perkins, 121–134. Macon, GA: Mercer University Press, 1987. Reprinted in *Feminist Interpretations of Søren Kierkegaard.* Edited by Céline Léon and Sylvia Walsh, 203–215. University Park: Pennsylvania State University Press, 1997.

"Søren Kierkegaard." In *T & T Clark Companion to the Doctrine of Sin.* Edited by Keith L. Johnson and David Lauber, 267–283. London: Bloomsbury T & T Clark, 2016.

Watkin, Julia. *The A to Z of Kierkegaard's Philosophy.* Plymouth: Scarecrow Press, 2001.

Watson, Gary. "Free Agency." In *Free Will.* 2nd ed. Oxford: Oxford University Press, 2003.

Weigert, Edith. "Søren Kierkegaard's Mood Swings." *International Journal of Psycho-Analysis* 41 (1960): 521–525.

Weir, Todd. "The Secular Beyond: Free Religious Dissent and Debates over the Afterlife in Nineteenth-Century Germany." *Church History* 77, no. 3 (2008): 629–658.

Welstead, Adam. "Kierkegaard's Movement Inward: Subjectivity as the Remedy for the Malaise of the Contemporary Age." *The Heythrop Journal* 55 (2014): 809–816.

Welz, Claudia. *Humanity in God's Image: An Interdisciplinary Exploration.* Oxford: Oxford University Press, 2016.

"Kierkegaard and Phenomenology." In *The Oxford Handbook of Kierkegaard.* Edited by John Lippitt and George Pattison, 440–463. Oxford: Oxford University Press, 2013.

Westphal, Merold. *Becoming a Self: A Reading of Kierkegaard's Concluding Unscientific Postscript.* West Lafayette, IN: Purdue University Press, 1996.

In Praise of Heteronomy. Bloomington: Indiana University Press, 2017.

"Johannes and Johannes: Kierkegaard and Difference." In *International Kierkegaard Commentary: Philosophical Fragments and Johannes Climacus,* edited by Robert L. Perkins, 13–32. Macon, GA: Mercer University Press, 1994.

"Kierkegaard as Four-Dimensional Thinker." In *Kierkegaard and Christian Faith*, edited by Paul Martens and C. Stephen Evans, 13–23. Waco, TX: Baylor University Press, 2016.

"Kierkegaard, Theology and Post-Christendom." In *T & T Clark Companion to the Theology of Kierkegaard*. Edited by Aaron P. Edwards and David J. Gouwens, 604–607. London: T & T Clark, 2020.

Kierkegaard's Concept of Faith. Grand Rapids, MI: Eerdmans, 2014.

"Kierkegaard's Psychology and Unconscious Despair." In *International Kierkegaard Commentary: The Sickness unto Death*. Edited by Robert L. Perkins, 39–66. Macon, GA: Mercer University Press, 1987.

"Paganism in Christendom: On Kierkegaard's Critique of Religion." In *International Kierkegaard Commentary 17: Christian Discourses and The Crisis and a Crisis in the Life of an Actress*. Edited by Robert L. Perkins, 13–33. Macon, GA: Mercer University Press, 2007.

Whybrow, Peter C. *A Mood Apart: Depression, Mania, and Other Afflictions of the Self.* New York: Basic Books, 2015.

Wietzke, Walter. "Practical Reason and the Imagination." *Res Philosophica* 90, no. 4 (2013): 525–544.

Wolf, Susan. "Sanity and the Metaphysics of Responsibility." In *Free Will*. 2nd ed. Edited by Gary Watson, 227–244. Oxford: Oxford University Press, 2003.

"The True, the Good, and the Lovable: Frankfurt's Avoidance of Objectivity." In *Contours of Agency: Essays on Themes by Harry Frankfurt*. Edited by Sarah Buss and Lee Overton, 322–349. Cambridge, MA: Bradford Books/MIT Press, 2002.

Wood, Allen. "Evil in Classical German Philosophy: Selfhood, Deception and Despair." In *Evil: A History*. Edited by Andrew Chignell, 322–349. Oxford: Oxford University Press, 2019.

Wrathall, Mark. "Coming to an Understanding with the Paradox." In *The Kierkegaardian Mind*. Edited by Adam Buben, Eleanor Helms, and Patrick Stokes, 239–253. New York: Routledge, 2019.

Wyllie, Robert. "Kierkegaard's Eyes of Faith: The Paradoxical Voluntarism of Climacus's *Philosophical Fragments*." *Res Philosophica* 90, no. 4 (October 2013): 545–564.

Zahavi, Dan. *Subjectivity and Selfhood: Investigating the First-Person Perspective*. Cambridge, MA: MIT Press, 2005.

Zuidema, S. U. *Kierkegaard*. Philadelphia: Presbyterian and Reformed Publishing Co., 1960.

Index

Milton Keynes UK
Ingram Content Group UK Ltd.
UKHW021847080424
440407UK00017B/173

9 781108 793308